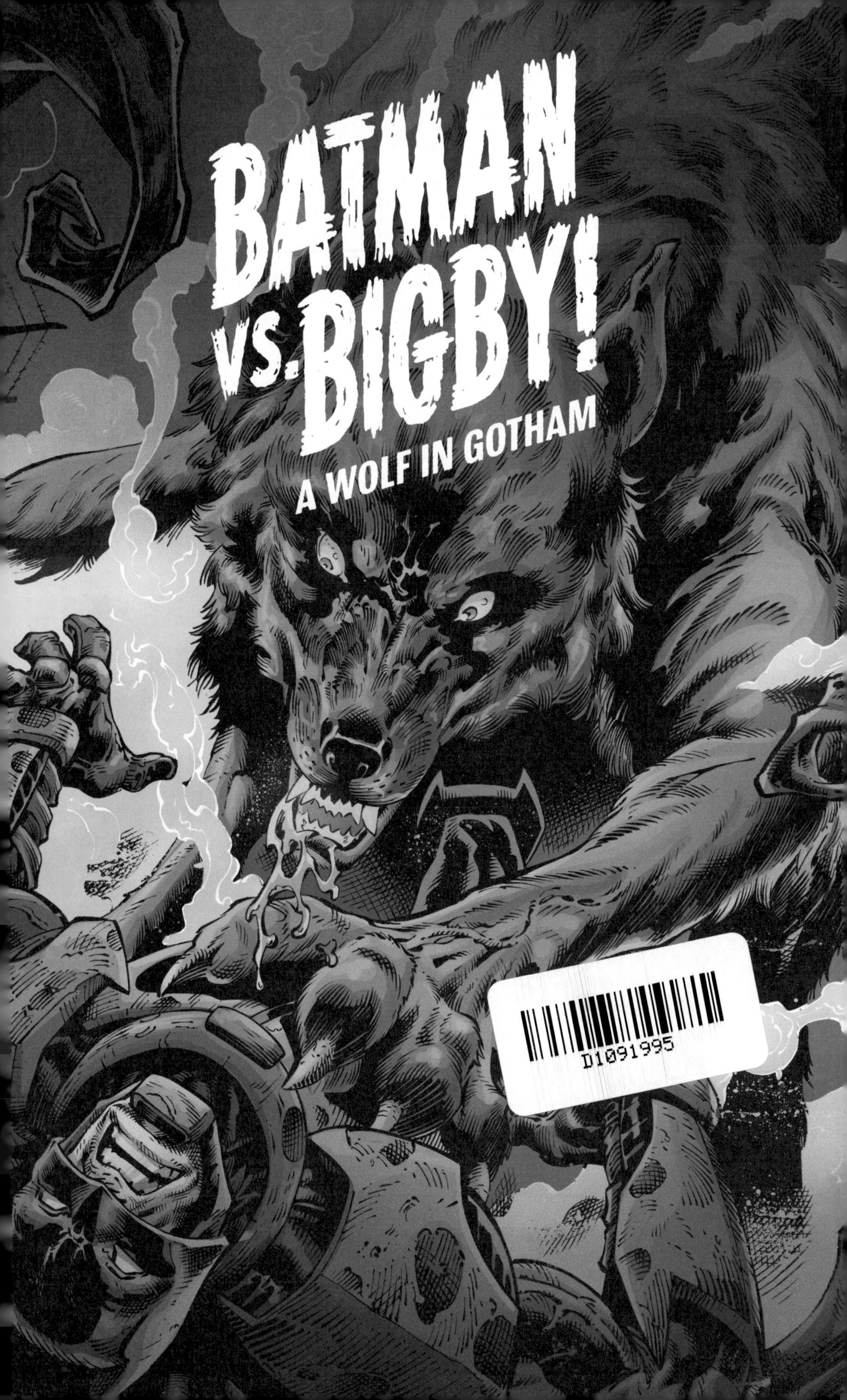
BATMAN VS. BIGBY!
A WOLF IN GOTHAM

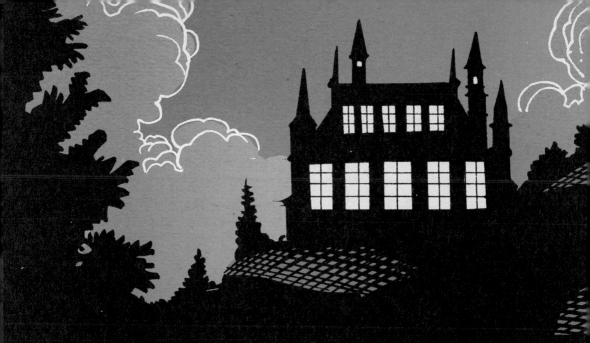

MAGGIE HOWELL	Editor – Original Series
MATTHEW LEVINE	Editor – Original Series & Collected Edition
STEVE COOK	Design Director – Books & Publication Design
ERIN VANOVER	Publication Production
MARIE JAVINS	Editor-in-Chief, DC Comics
ANNE DePIES	Senior VP – General Manager
JIM LEE	Publisher & Chief Creative Officer
DON FALLETTI	VP – Manufacturing Operations & Workflow Management
LAWRENCE GANEM	VP – Talent Services
ALISON GILL	Senior VP – Manufacturing & Operations
JEFFREY KAUFMAN	VP – Editorial Strategy & Programming
NICK J. NAPOLITANO	VP – Manufacturing Administration & Design
NANCY SPEARS	VP – Revenue

BATMAN VS. BIGBY! A WOLF IN GOTHAM

DC Comics, 2900 West Alameda Ave., Burbank, CA 91505
Printed by LSC Communications, Owensville, MO, USA. 4.1.22. First Printing.
ISBN: 978-1-77951-525-4

Library of Congress Cataloging-in-Publication Data is available.

PEFC Certified
This product is from sustainably managed forests and controlled sources
PEFC
PEFC/29-31-337
www.pefc.org

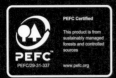

BATMAN vs. BIGBY!

A WOLF IN GOTHAM

BILL WILLINGHAM
Writer & creator of *Fables*

BRIAN LEVEL
Penciller

JAY LEISTEN
ANTHONY FOWLER JR.
Inkers

LEE LOUGHRIDGE
Colorist

STEVE WANDS
Letterer

YANICK PAQUETTE
& NATHAN FAIRBAIRN
Series & collection cover artists

Batman created by BOB KANE with BILL FINGER

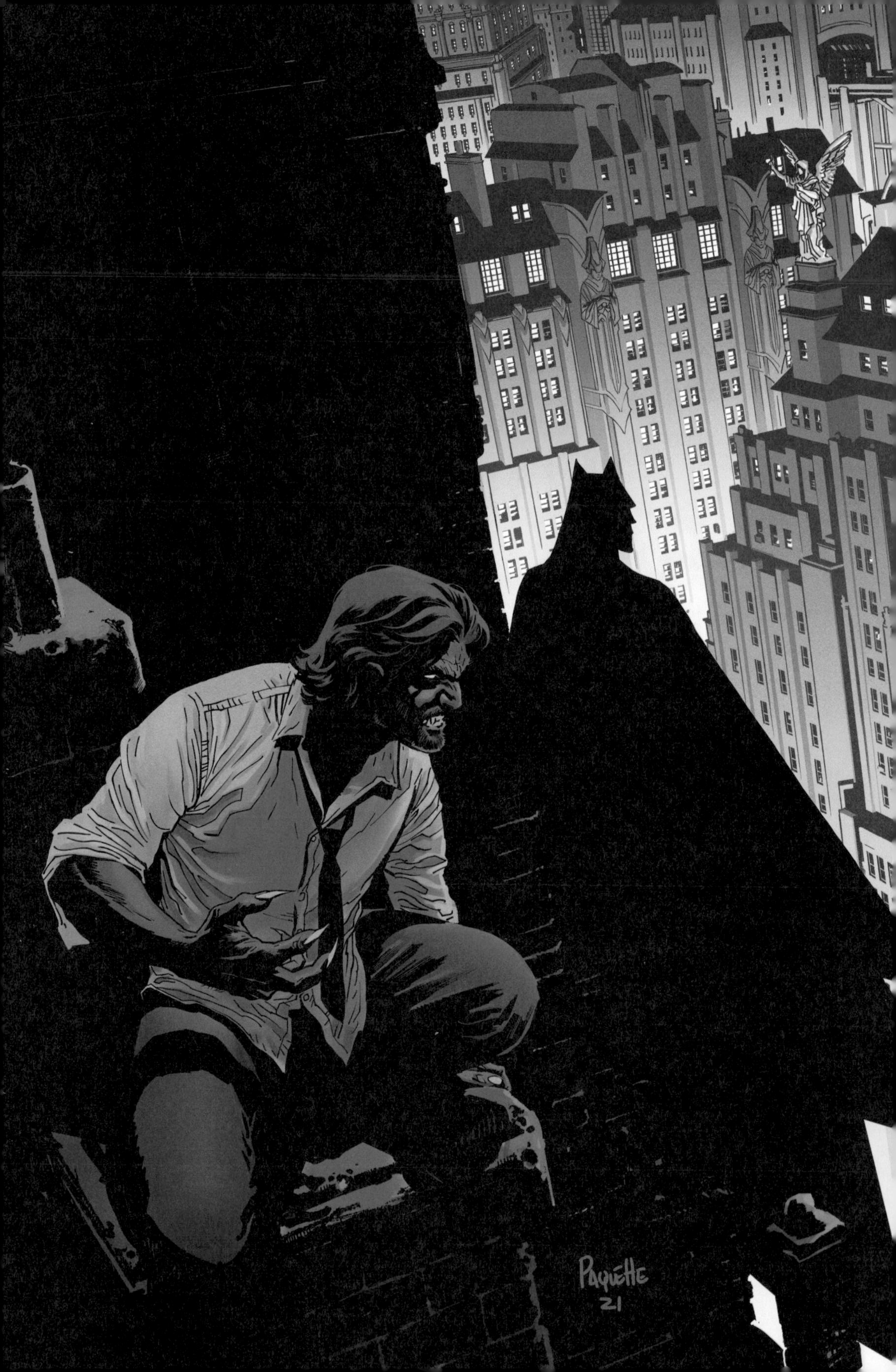
PAQUETTE
21

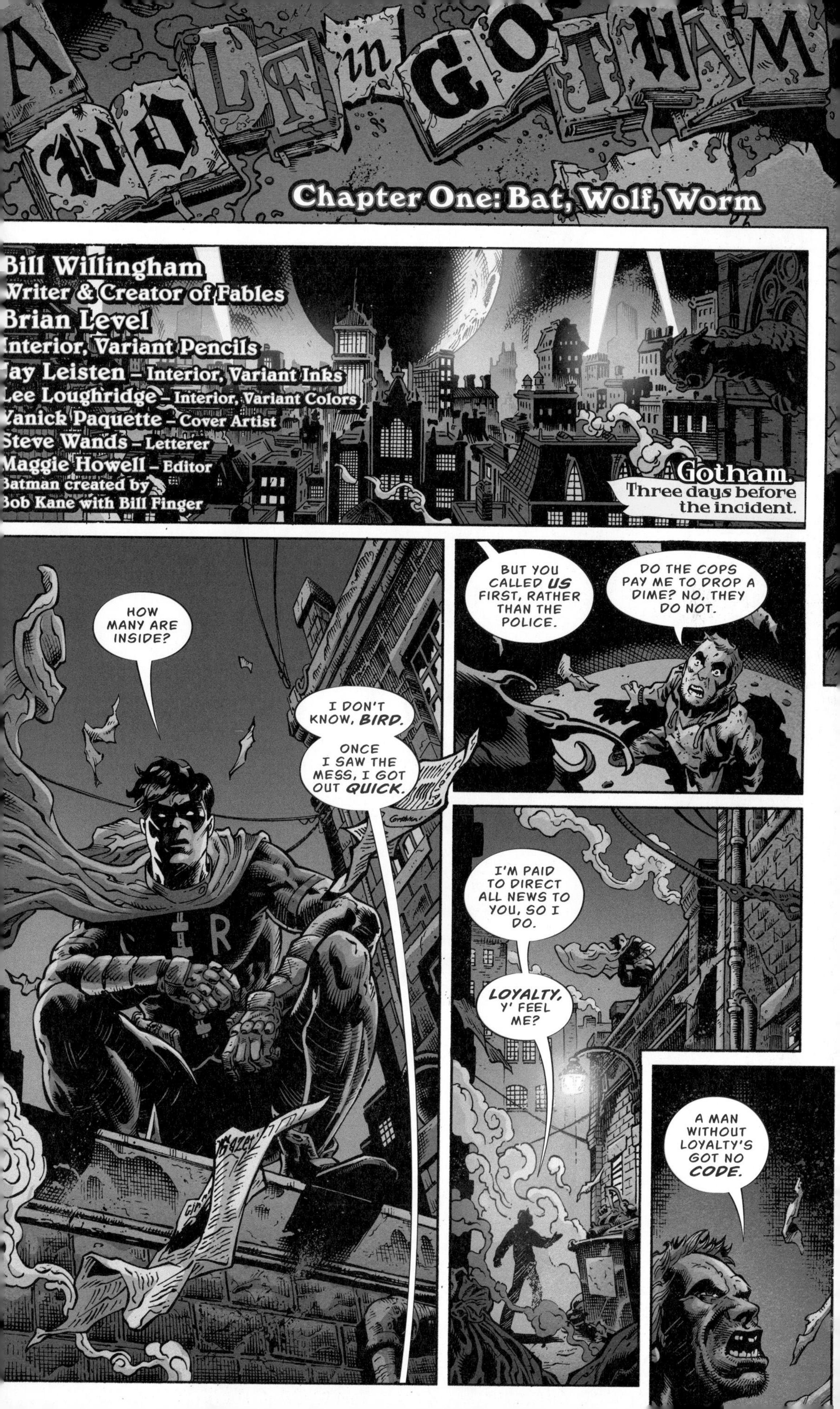

A WOLF in GOTHAM
Chapter One: Bat, Wolf, Worm
Bill Willingham
Writer & Creator of Fables
Brian Level
Interior, Variant Pencils
Jay Leisten – Interior, Variant Inks
Lee Loughridge – Interior, Variant Colors
Yanick Paquette – Cover Artist
Steve Wands – Letterer
Maggie Howell – Editor
Batman created by
Bob Kane with Bill Finger
Gotham. Three days before the incident.
HOW MANY ARE INSIDE?
I DON'T KNOW, BIRD.
ONCE I SAW THE MESS, I GOT OUT QUICK.
BUT YOU CALLED US FIRST, RATHER THAN THE POLICE.
DO THE COPS PAY ME TO DROP A DIME? NO, THEY DO NOT.
I'M PAID TO DIRECT ALL NEWS TO YOU, SO I DO.
LOYALTY, Y' FEEL ME?
A MAN WITHOUT LOYALTY'S GOT NO CODE.

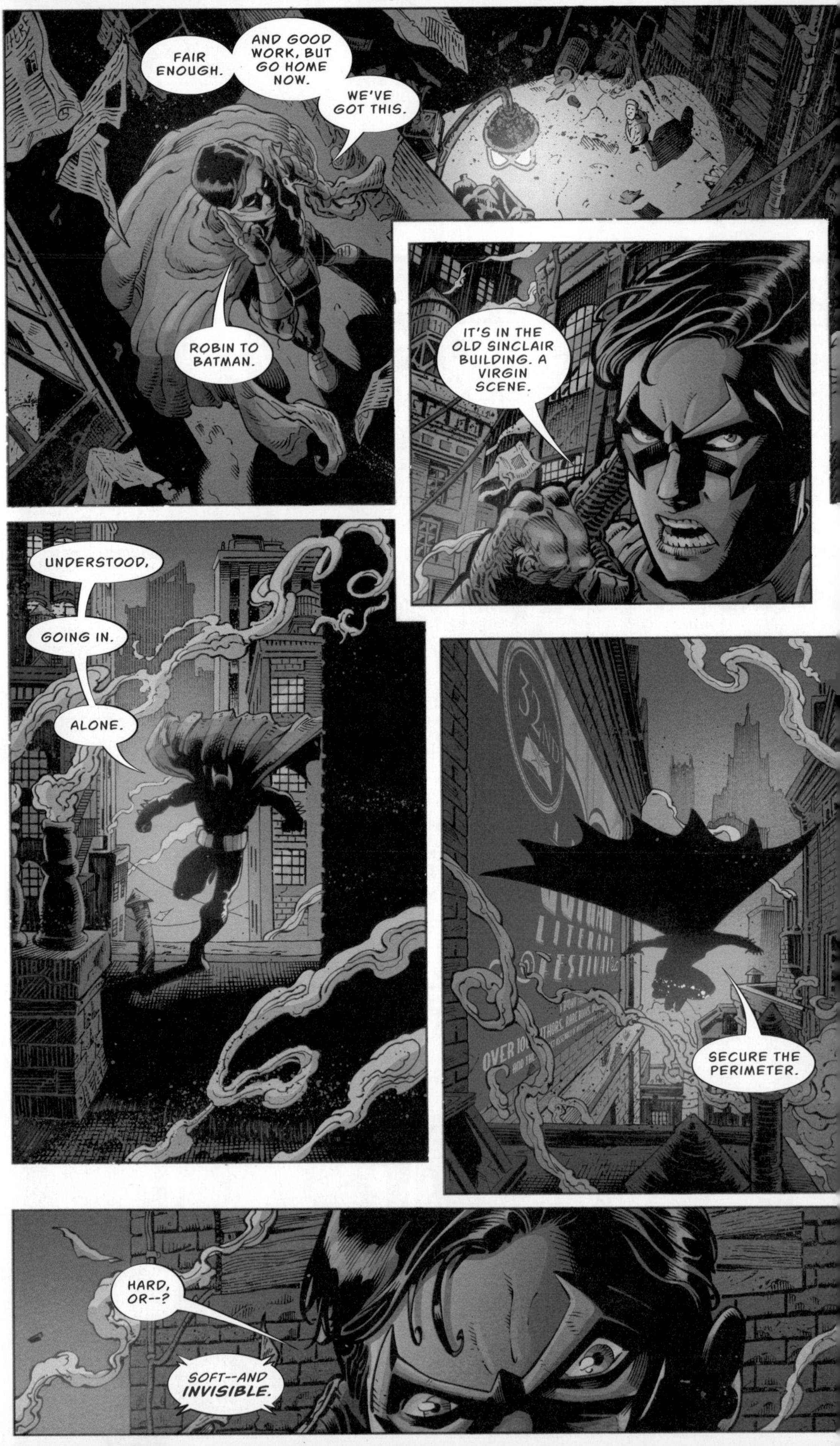
FAIR ENOUGH.
AND GOOD WORK, BUT GO HOME NOW.
WE'VE GOT THIS.
ROBIN TO BATMAN.
IT'S IN THE OLD SINCLAIR BUILDING. A VIRGIN SCENE.
UNDERSTOOD,
GOING IN.
ALONE.
SECURE THE PERIMETER.
HARD, OR--?
SOFT--AND *INVISIBLE*.

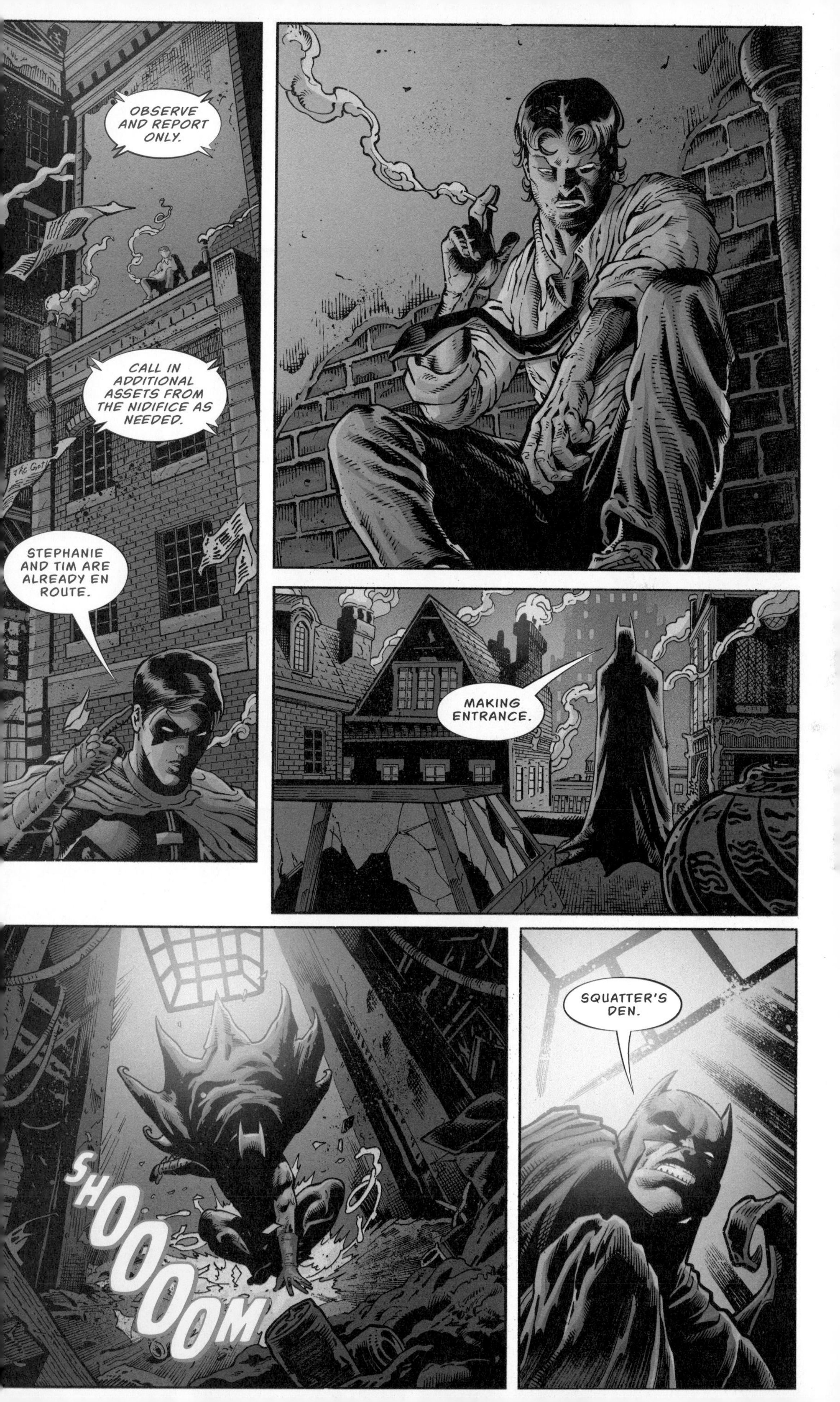
OBSERVE AND REPORT ONLY.
CALL IN ADDITIONAL ASSETS FROM THE NIDIFICE AS NEEDED.
STEPHANIE AND TIM ARE ALREADY EN ROUTE.
MAKING ENTRANCE.
SHOOOOM
SQUATTER'S DEN.

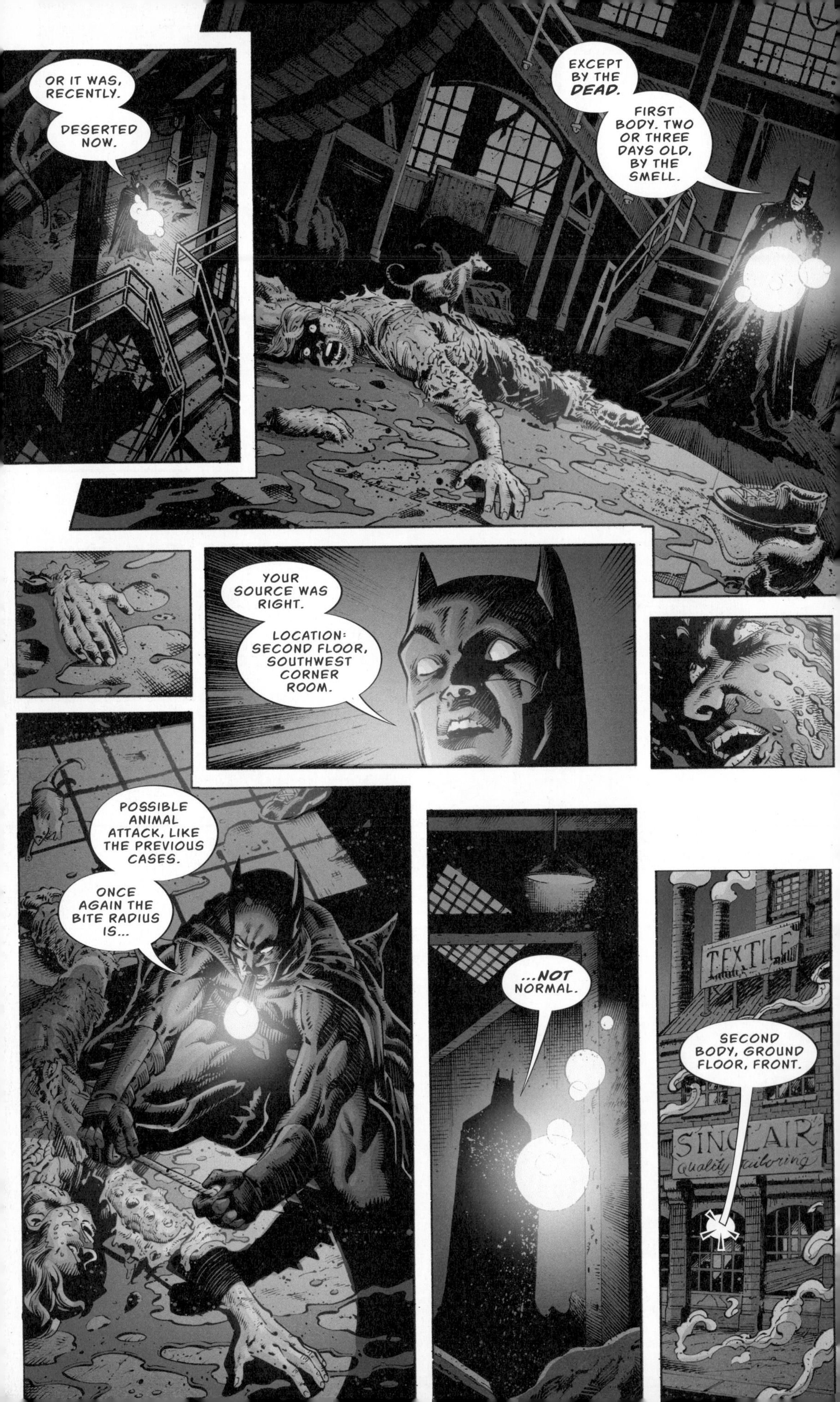
OR IT WAS, RECENTLY.
DESERTED NOW.
EXCEPT BY THE *DEAD.*
FIRST BODY. TWO OR THREE DAYS OLD, BY THE SMELL.
YOUR SOURCE WAS RIGHT.
LOCATION: SECOND FLOOR, SOUTHWEST CORNER ROOM.
POSSIBLE ANIMAL ATTACK, LIKE THE PREVIOUS CASES.
ONCE AGAIN THE BITE RADIUS IS...
...*NOT* NORMAL.
TEXTILE
SECOND BODY, GROUND FLOOR, FRONT.
SINCLAIR
Quality Tailoring

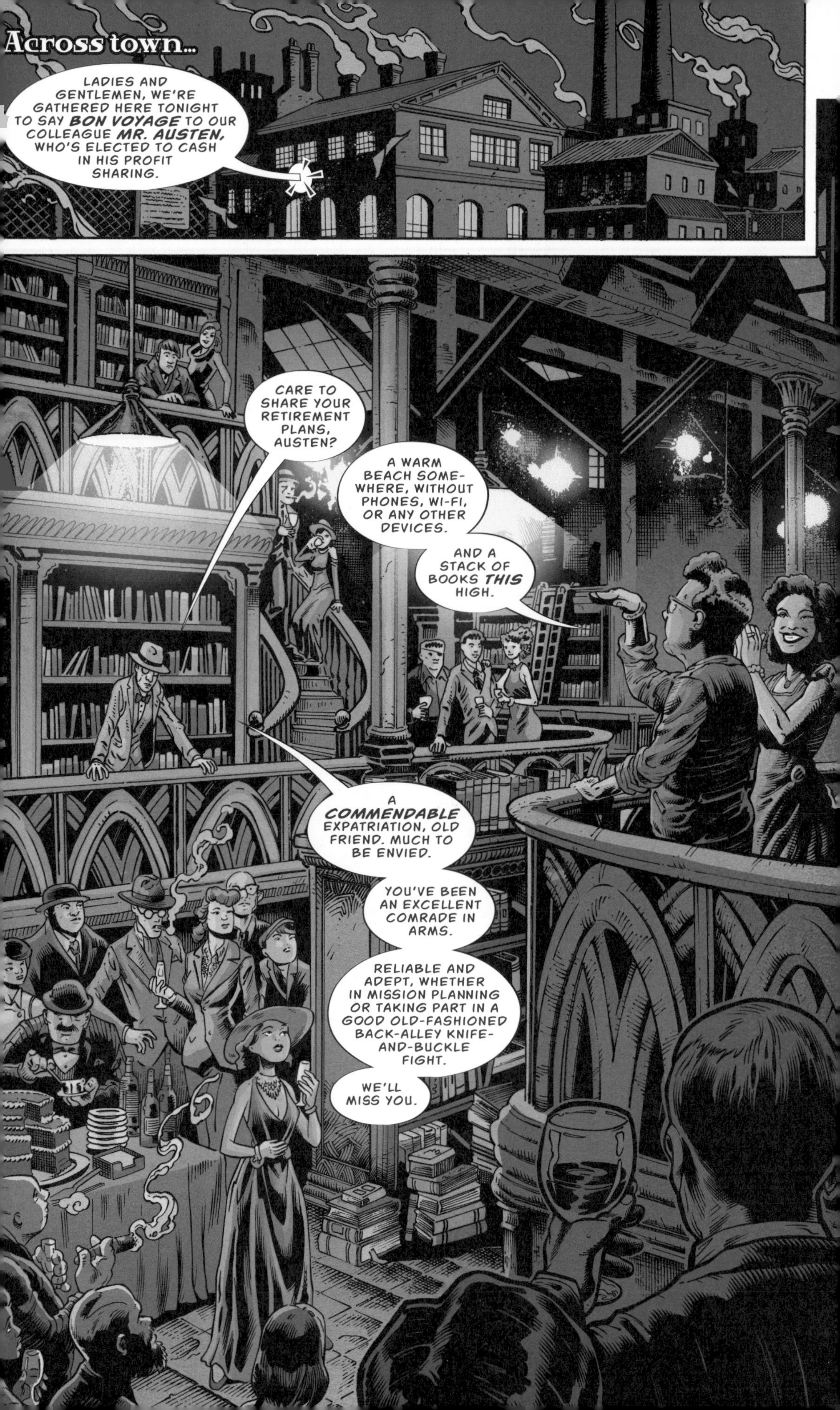
Across town...
LADIES AND GENTLEMEN, WE'RE GATHERED HERE TONIGHT TO SAY **BON VOYAGE** TO OUR COLLEAGUE **MR. AUSTEN,** WHO'S ELECTED TO CASH IN HIS PROFIT SHARING.
CARE TO SHARE YOUR RETIREMENT PLANS, AUSTEN?
A WARM BEACH SOME-WHERE, WITHOUT PHONES, WI-FI, OR ANY OTHER DEVICES.
AND A STACK OF BOOKS **THIS** HIGH.
A **COMMENDABLE** EXPATRIATION, OLD FRIEND. MUCH TO BE ENVIED.
YOU'VE BEEN AN EXCELLENT COMRADE IN ARMS.
RELIABLE AND ADEPT, WHETHER IN MISSION PLANNING OR TAKING PART IN A GOOD OLD-FASHIONED BACK-ALLEY KNIFE-AND-BUCKLE FIGHT.
WE'LL MISS YOU.

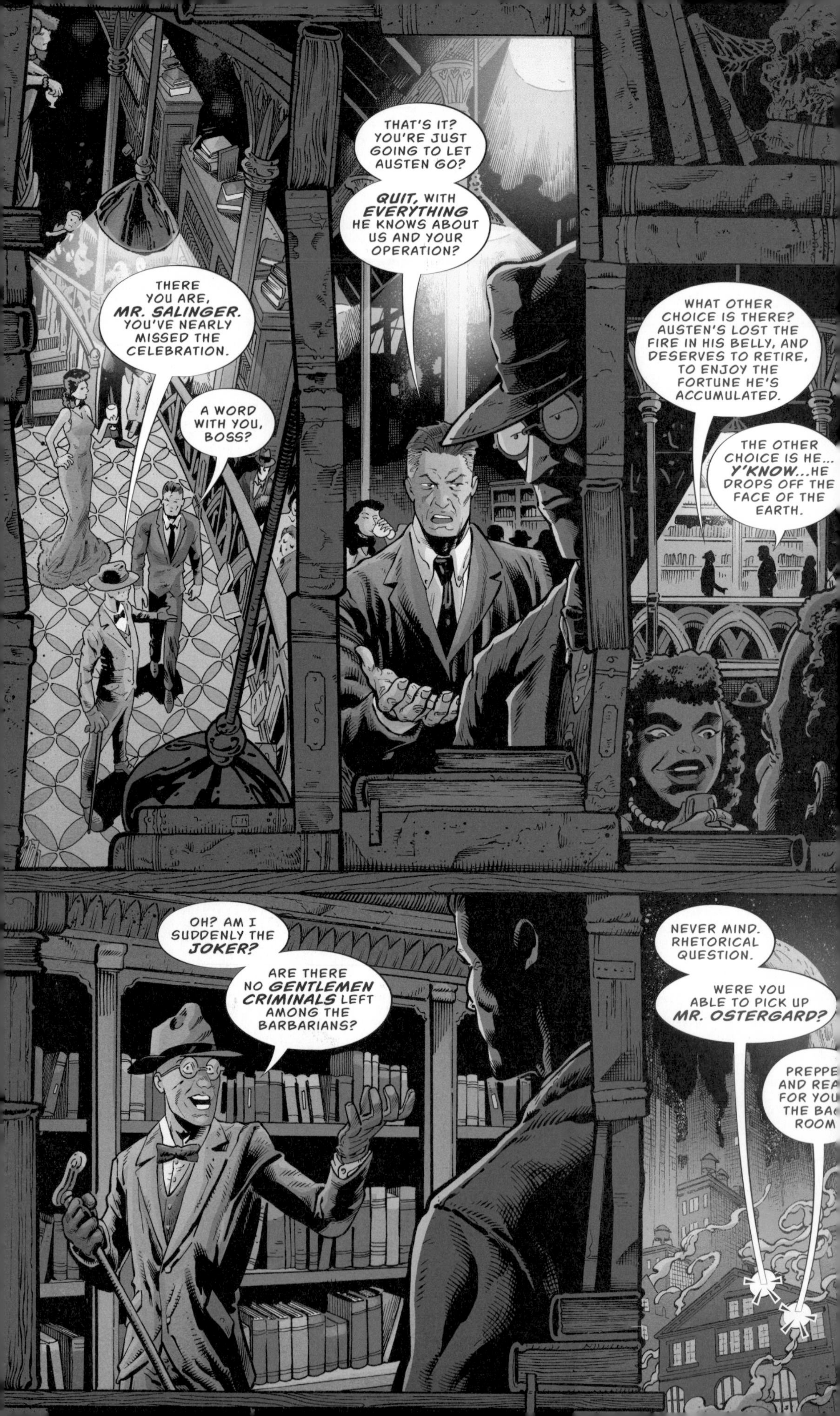
THERE YOU ARE, MR. SALINGER. YOU'VE NEARLY MISSED THE CELEBRATION.
A WORD WITH YOU, BOSS?
THAT'S IT? YOU'RE JUST GOING TO LET AUSTEN GO?
QUIT, WITH EVERYTHING HE KNOWS ABOUT US AND YOUR OPERATION?
WHAT OTHER CHOICE IS THERE? AUSTEN'S LOST THE FIRE IN HIS BELLY, AND DESERVES TO RETIRE, TO ENJOY THE FORTUNE HE'S ACCUMULATED.
THE OTHER CHOICE IS HE... Y'KNOW...HE DROPS OFF THE FACE OF THE EARTH.
OH? AM I SUDDENLY THE JOKER?
ARE THERE NO GENTLEMEN CRIMINALS LEFT AMONG THE BARBARIANS?
NEVER MIND. RHETORICAL QUESTION.
WERE YOU ABLE TO PICK UP MR. OSTERGARD?

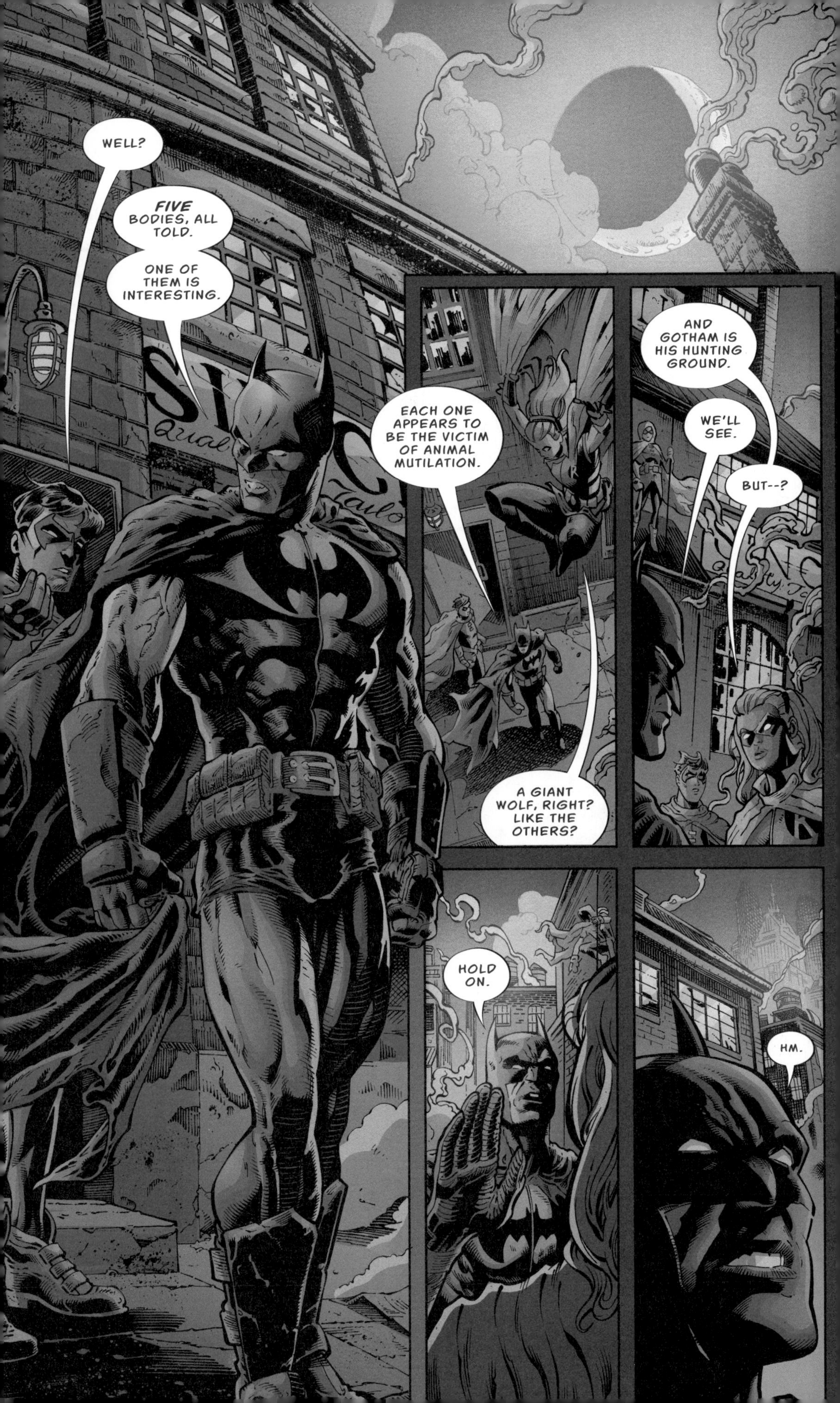
WELL?
FIVE BODIES, ALL TOLD.
ONE OF THEM IS INTERESTING.
EACH ONE APPEARS TO BE THE VICTIM OF ANIMAL MUTILATION.
A GIANT WOLF, RIGHT? LIKE THE OTHERS?
AND GOTHAM IS HIS HUNTING GROUND.
WE'LL SEE.
BUT--?
HOLD ON.
HM.

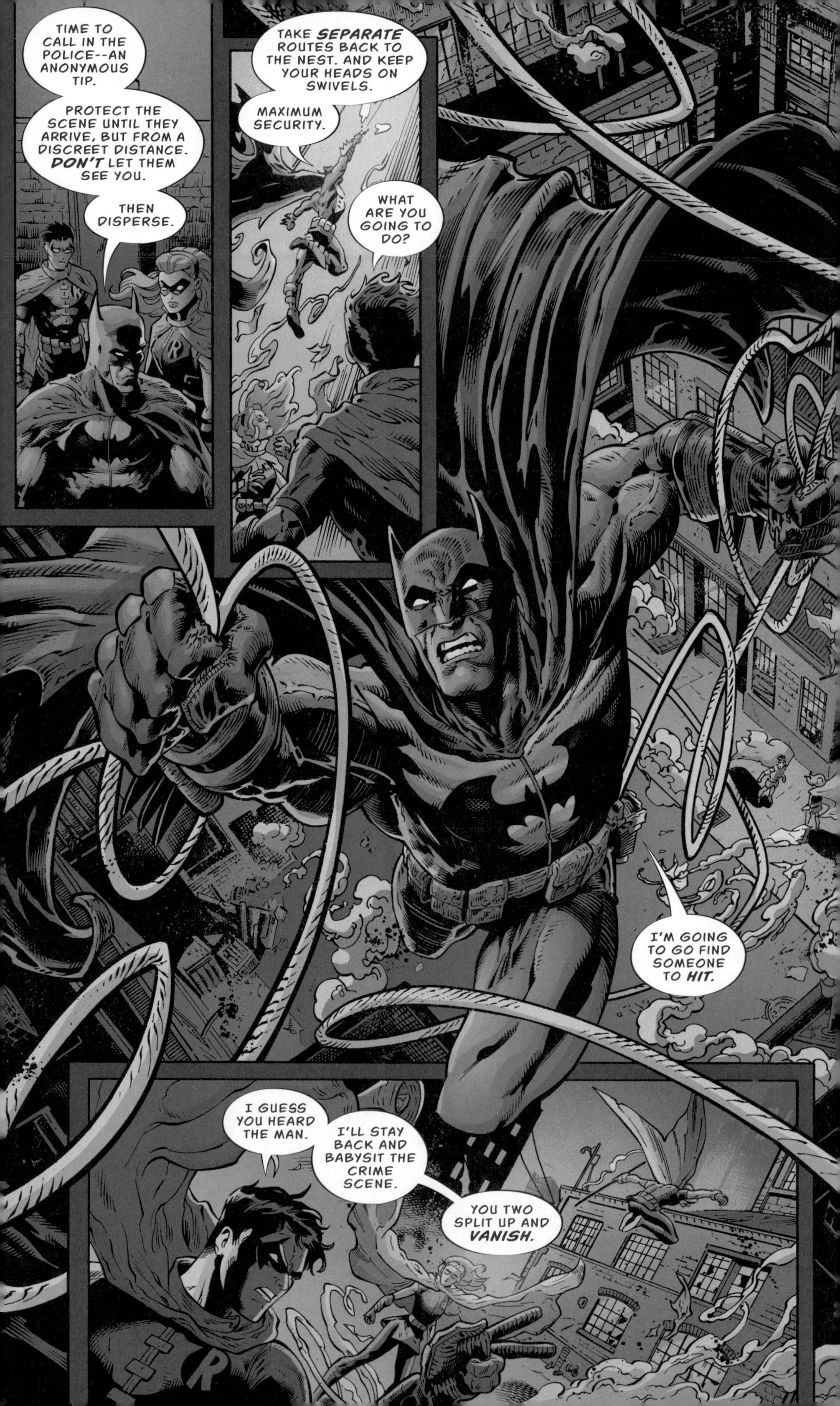
TIME TO CALL IN THE POLICE--AN ANONYMOUS TIP.
PROTECT THE SCENE UNTIL THEY ARRIVE, BUT FROM A DISCREET DISTANCE. DON'T LET THEM SEE YOU.
THEN DISPERSE.
TAKE SEPARATE ROUTES BACK TO THE NEST. AND KEEP YOUR HEADS ON SWIVELS.
MAXIMUM SECURITY.
WHAT ARE YOU GOING TO DO?
I'M GOING TO GO FIND SOMEONE TO HIT.
I GUESS YOU HEARD THE MAN.
I'LL STAY BACK AND BABYSIT THE CRIME SCENE.
YOU TWO SPLIT UP AND VANISH.

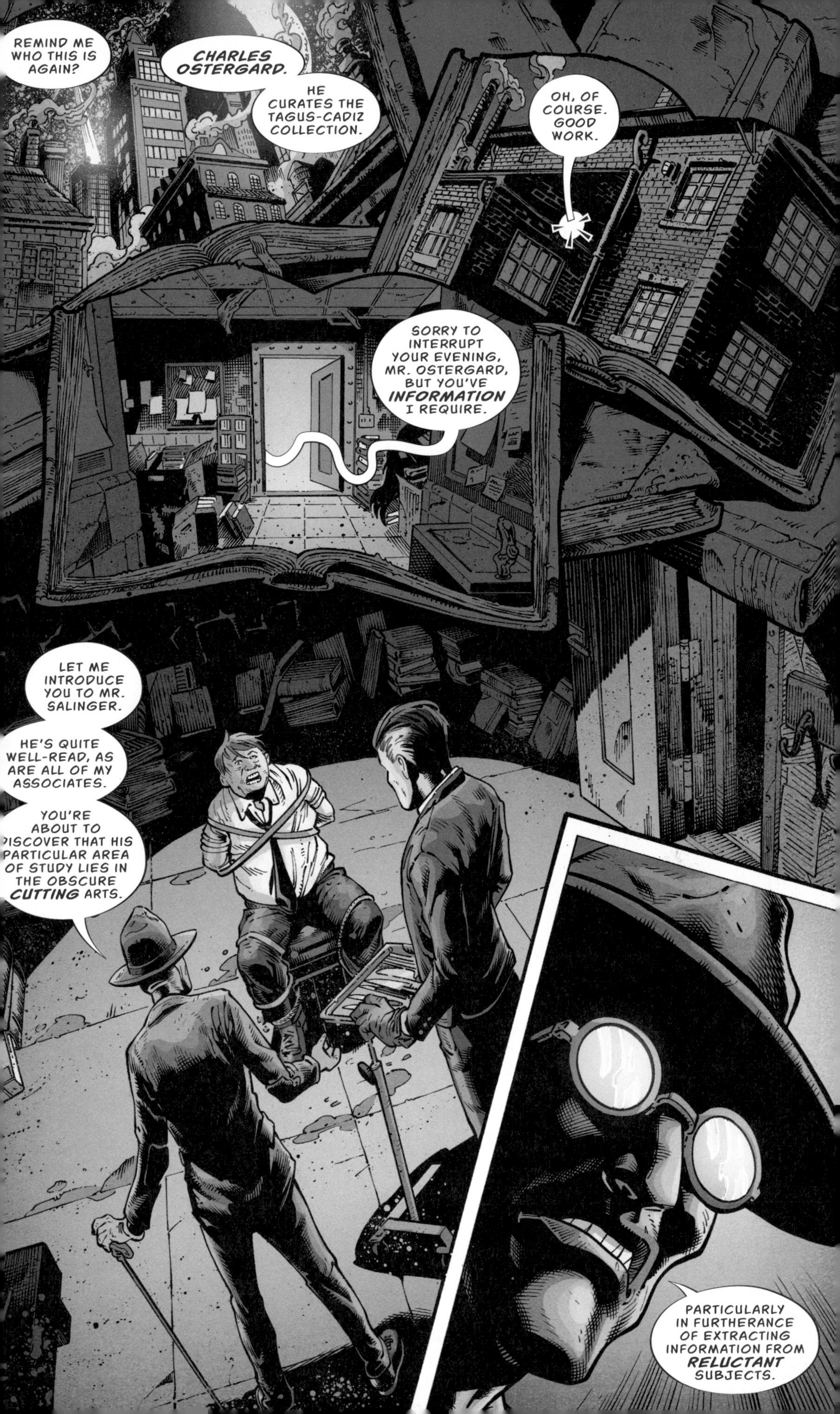
REMIND ME WHO THIS IS AGAIN?
CHARLES OSTERGARD.
HE CURATES THE TAGUS-CADIZ COLLECTION.
OH, OF COURSE. GOOD WORK.
SORRY TO INTERRUPT YOUR EVENING, MR. OSTERGARD, BUT YOU'VE INFORMATION I REQUIRE.
LET ME INTRODUCE YOU TO MR. SALINGER.
HE'S QUITE WELL-READ, AS ARE ALL OF MY ASSOCIATES.
YOU'RE ABOUT TO DISCOVER THAT HIS PARTICULAR AREA OF STUDY LIES IN THE OBSCURE CUTTING ARTS.
PARTICULARLY IN FURTHERANCE OF EXTRACTING INFORMATION FROM RELUCTANT SUBJECTS.

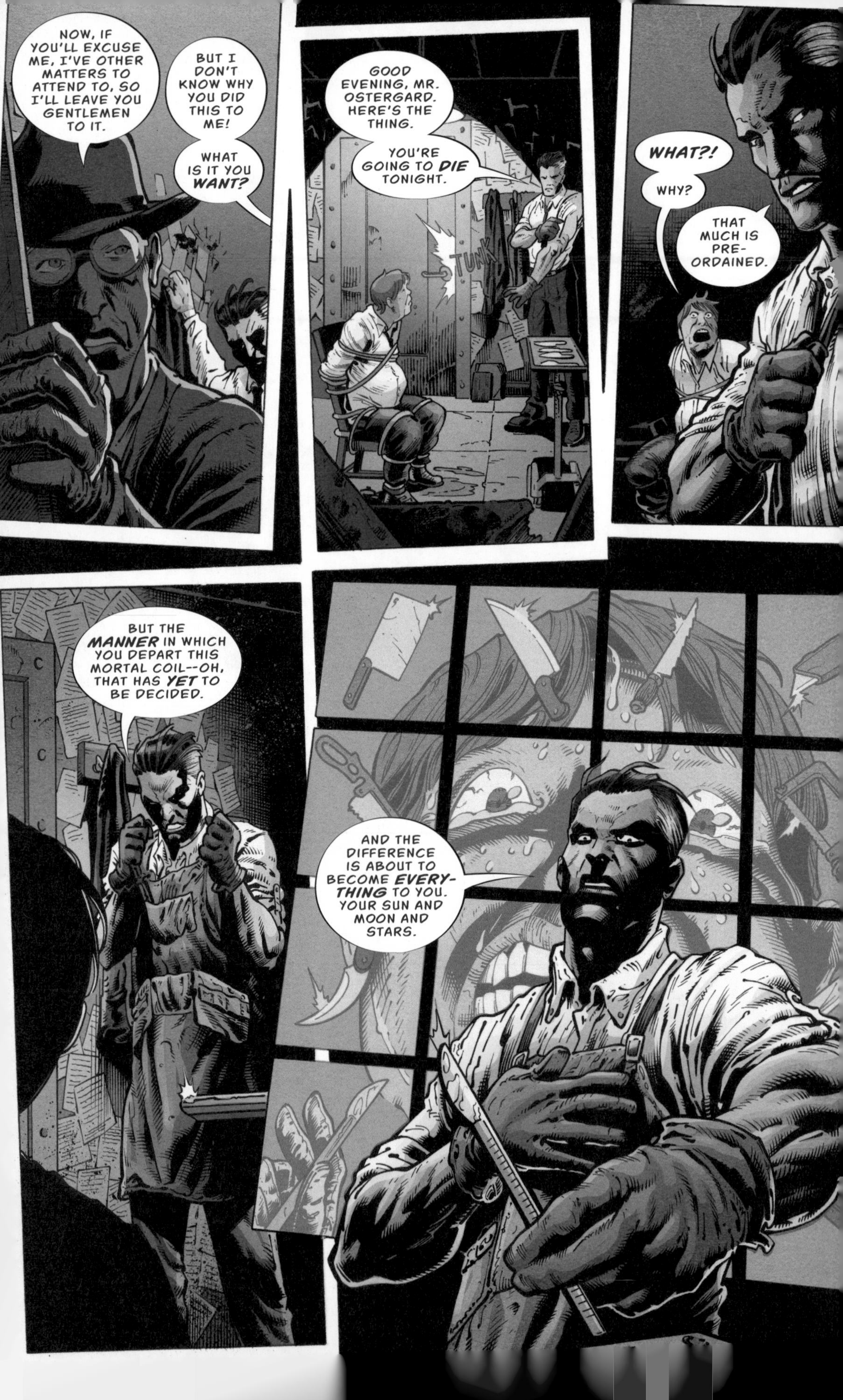
NOW, IF YOU'LL EXCUSE ME, I'VE OTHER MATTERS TO ATTEND TO, SO I'LL LEAVE YOU GENTLEMEN TO IT.
BUT I DON'T KNOW WHY YOU DID THIS TO ME!
WHAT IS IT YOU WANT?
GOOD EVENING, MR. OSTERGARD. HERE'S THE THING.
YOU'RE GOING TO DIE TONIGHT.
TUNK
WHAT?!
WHY?
THAT MUCH IS PRE-ORDAINED.
BUT THE MANNER IN WHICH YOU DEPART THIS MORTAL COIL--OH, THAT HAS YET TO BE DECIDED.
AND THE DIFFERENCE IS ABOUT TO BECOME EVERY-THING TO YOU. YOUR SUN AND MOON AND STARS.

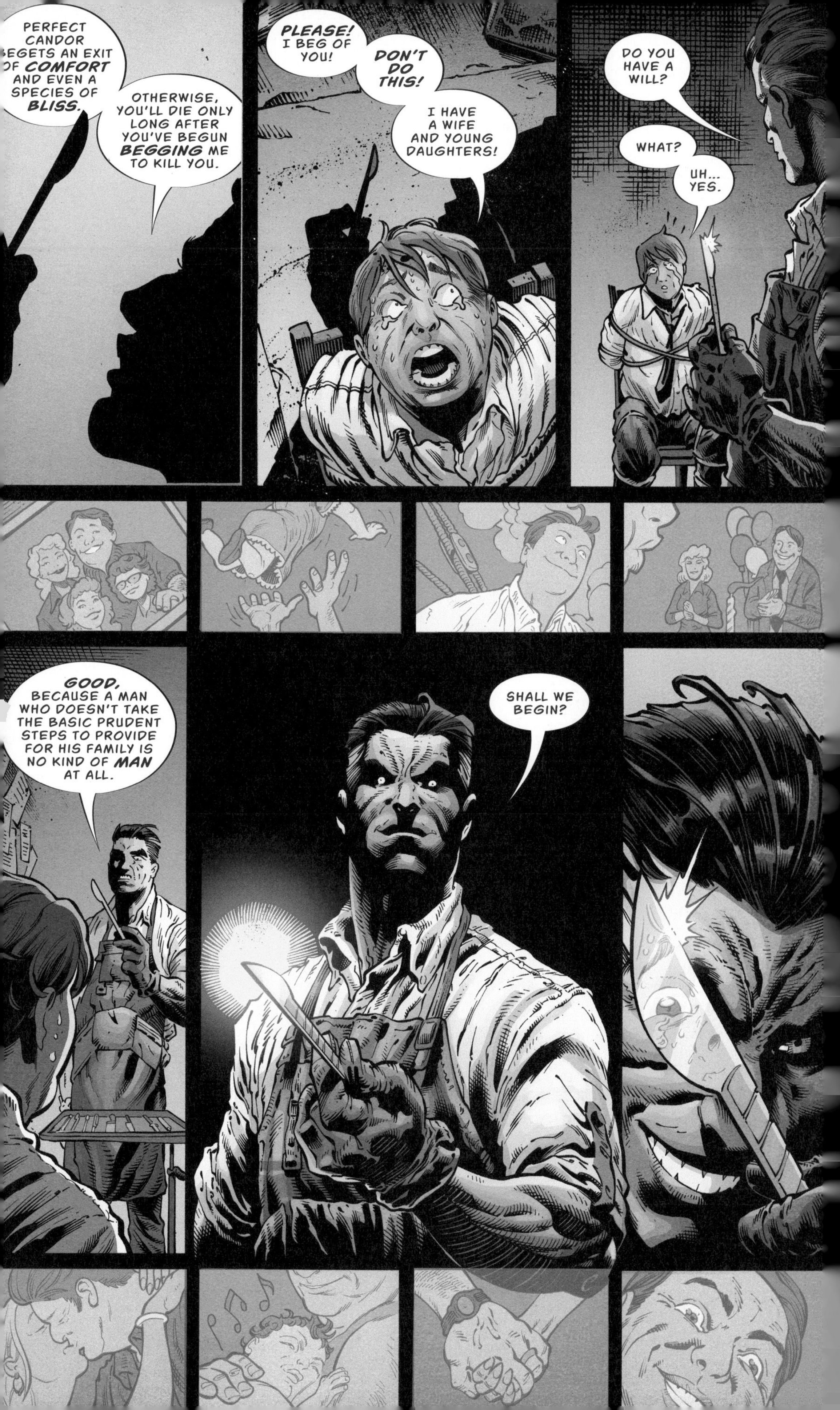
PERFECT CANDOR BEGETS AN EXIT OF COMFORT AND EVEN A SPECIES OF BLISS.
OTHERWISE, YOU'LL DIE ONLY LONG AFTER YOU'VE BEGUN BEGGING ME TO KILL YOU.
PLEASE! I BEG OF YOU!
DON'T DO THIS!
I HAVE A WIFE AND YOUNG DAUGHTERS!
DO YOU HAVE A WILL?
WHAT?
UH... YES.
GOOD, BECAUSE A MAN WHO DOESN'T TAKE THE BASIC PRUDENT STEPS TO PROVIDE FOR HIS FAMILY IS NO KIND OF MAN AT ALL.
SHALL WE BEGIN?

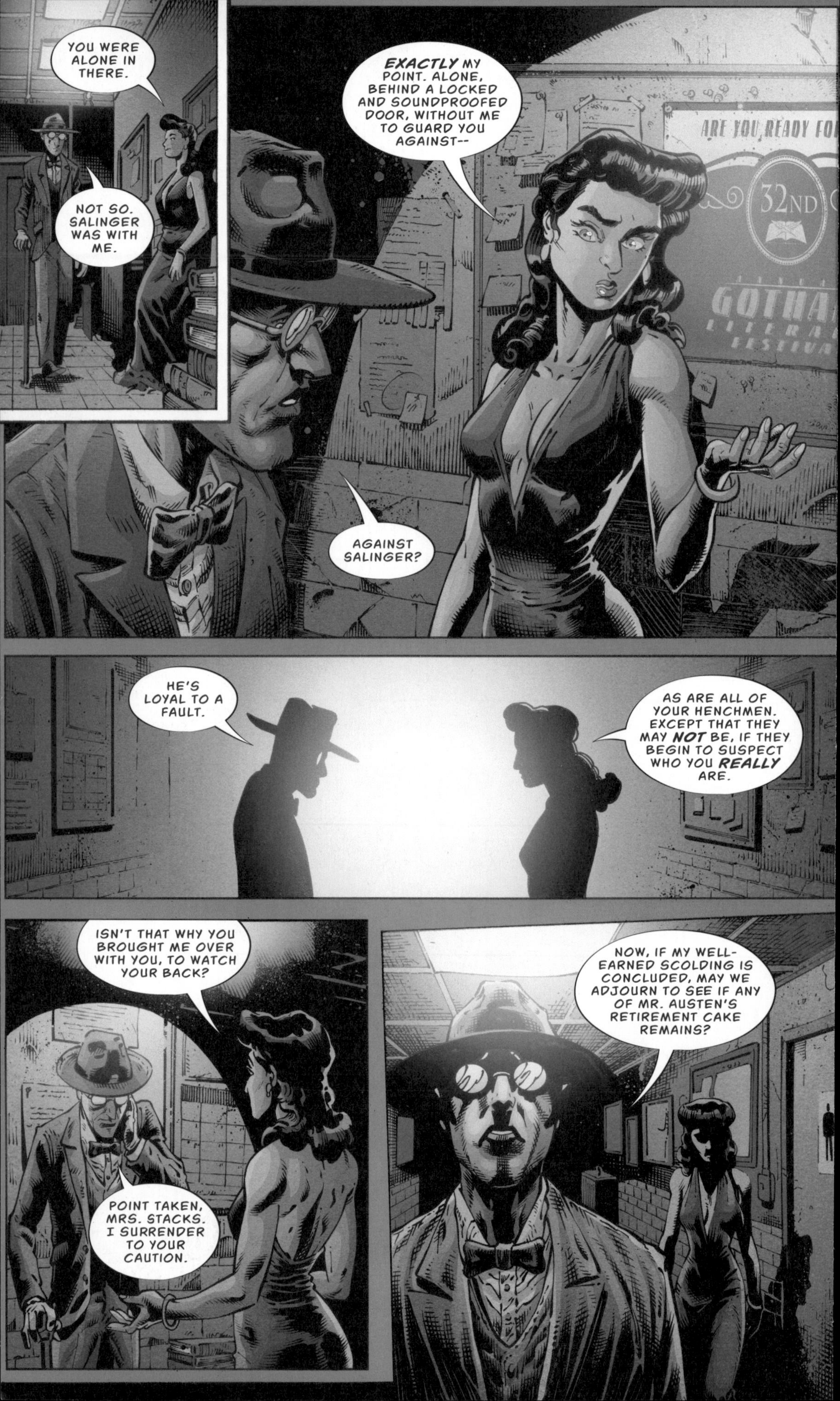

YOU WERE ALONE IN THERE.
NOT SO. SALINGER WAS WITH ME.
EXACTLY MY POINT. ALONE, BEHIND A LOCKED AND SOUNDPROOFED DOOR, WITHOUT ME TO GUARD YOU AGAINST--
ARE YOU READY FOR
32ND
GOTHA
AGAINST SALINGER?
HE'S LOYAL TO A FAULT.
AS ARE ALL OF YOUR HENCHMEN. EXCEPT THAT THEY MAY NOT BE, IF THEY BEGIN TO SUSPECT WHO YOU REALLY ARE.
ISN'T THAT WHY YOU BROUGHT ME OVER WITH YOU, TO WATCH YOUR BACK?
POINT TAKEN, MRS. STACKS. I SURRENDER TO YOUR CAUTION.
NOW, IF MY WELL-EARNED SCOLDING IS CONCLUDED, MAY WE ADJOURN TO SEE IF ANY OF MR. AUSTEN'S RETIREMENT CAKE REMAINS?

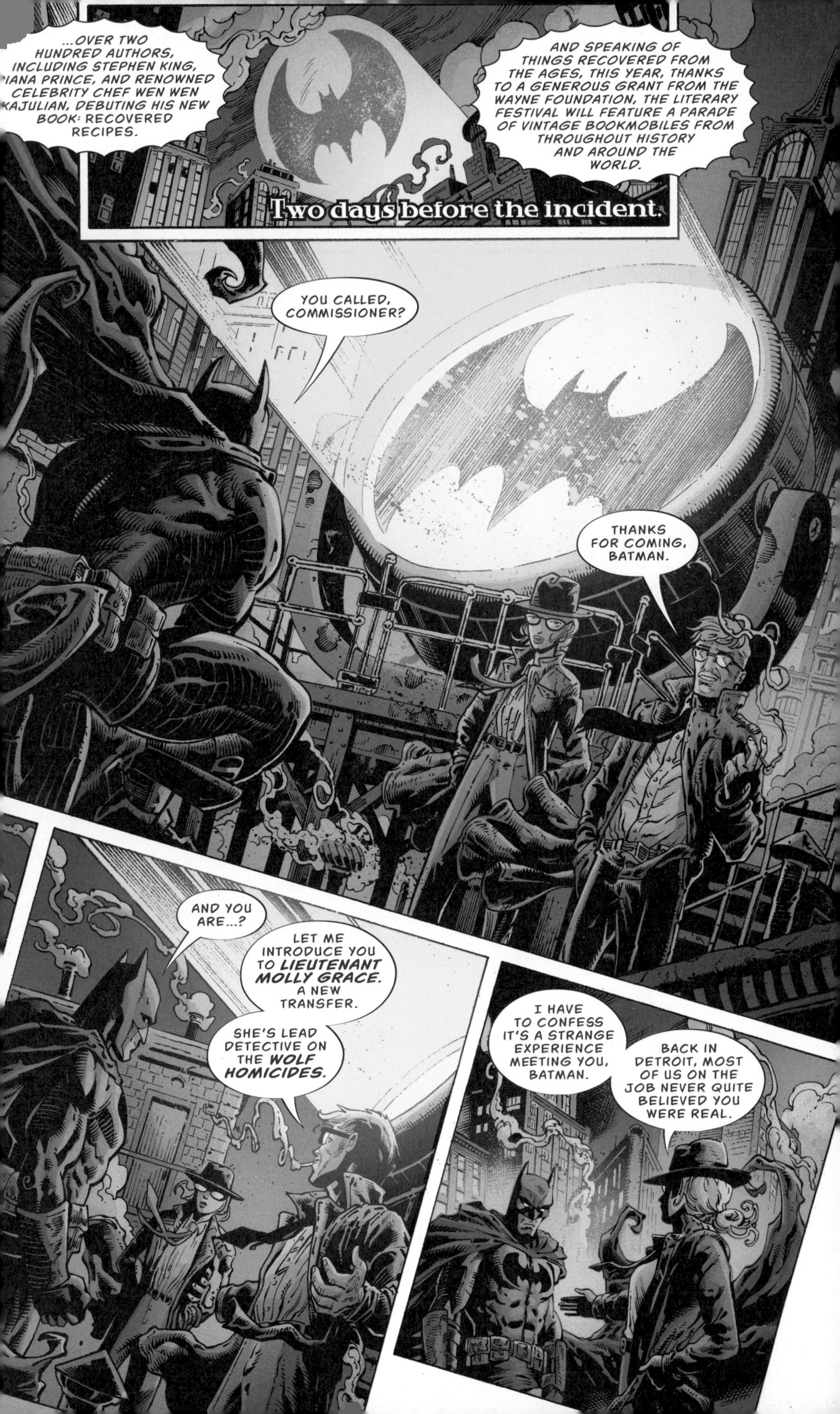
...OVER TWO HUNDRED AUTHORS, INCLUDING STEPHEN KING, IANA PRINCE, AND RENOWNED CELEBRITY CHEF WEN WEN AJULIAN, DEBUTING HIS NEW BOOK: RECOVERED RECIPES.
AND SPEAKING OF THINGS RECOVERED FROM THE AGES, THIS YEAR, THANKS TO A GENEROUS GRANT FROM THE WAYNE FOUNDATION, THE LITERARY FESTIVAL WILL FEATURE A PARADE OF VINTAGE BOOKMOBILES FROM THROUGHOUT HISTORY AND AROUND THE WORLD.
Two days before the incident.
YOU CALLED, COMMISSIONER?
THANKS FOR COMING, BATMAN.
AND YOU ARE...?
LET ME INTRODUCE YOU TO LIEUTENANT MOLLY GRACE. A NEW TRANSFER.
SHE'S LEAD DETECTIVE ON THE WOLF HOMICIDES.
I HAVE TO CONFESS IT'S A STRANGE EXPERIENCE MEETING YOU, BATMAN.
BACK IN DETROIT, MOST OF US ON THE JOB NEVER QUITE BELIEVED YOU WERE REAL.

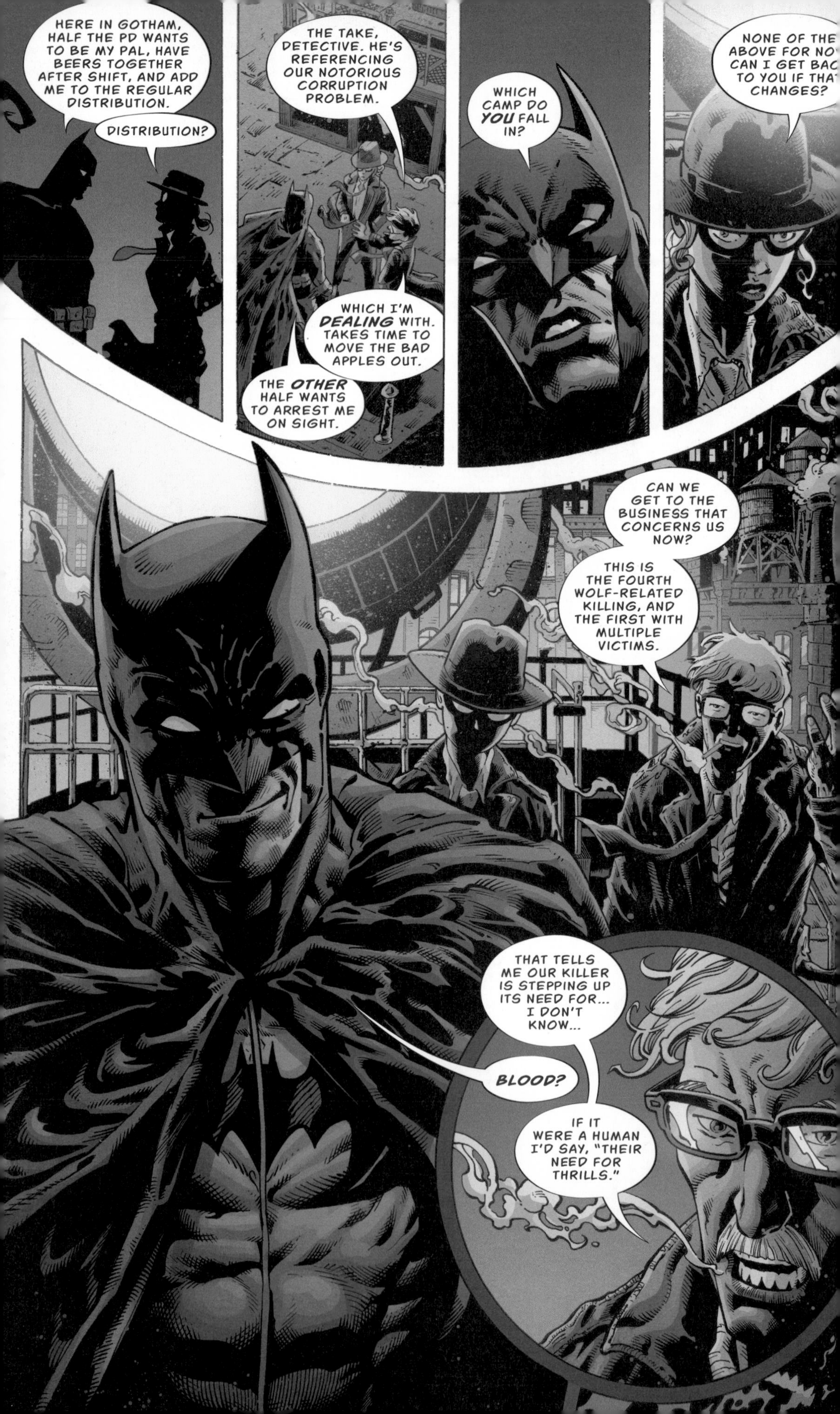

HERE IN GOTHAM, HALF THE PD WANTS TO BE MY PAL, HAVE BEERS TOGETHER AFTER SHIFT, AND ADD ME TO THE REGULAR DISTRIBUTION.
DISTRIBUTION?
THE TAKE, DETECTIVE. HE'S REFERENCING OUR NOTORIOUS CORRUPTION PROBLEM.
WHICH I'M DEALING WITH. TAKES TIME TO MOVE THE BAD APPLES OUT.
THE OTHER HALF WANTS TO ARREST ME ON SIGHT.
WHICH CAMP DO YOU FALL IN?
NONE OF THE ABOVE FOR NO CAN I GET BAC TO YOU IF THAT CHANGES?
CAN WE GET TO THE BUSINESS THAT CONCERNS US NOW?
THIS IS THE FOURTH WOLF-RELATED KILLING, AND THE FIRST WITH MULTIPLE VICTIMS.
THAT TELLS ME OUR KILLER IS STEPPING UP ITS NEED FOR... I DON'T KNOW...
BLOOD?
IF IT WERE A HUMAN I'D SAY, "THEIR NEED FOR THRILLS."

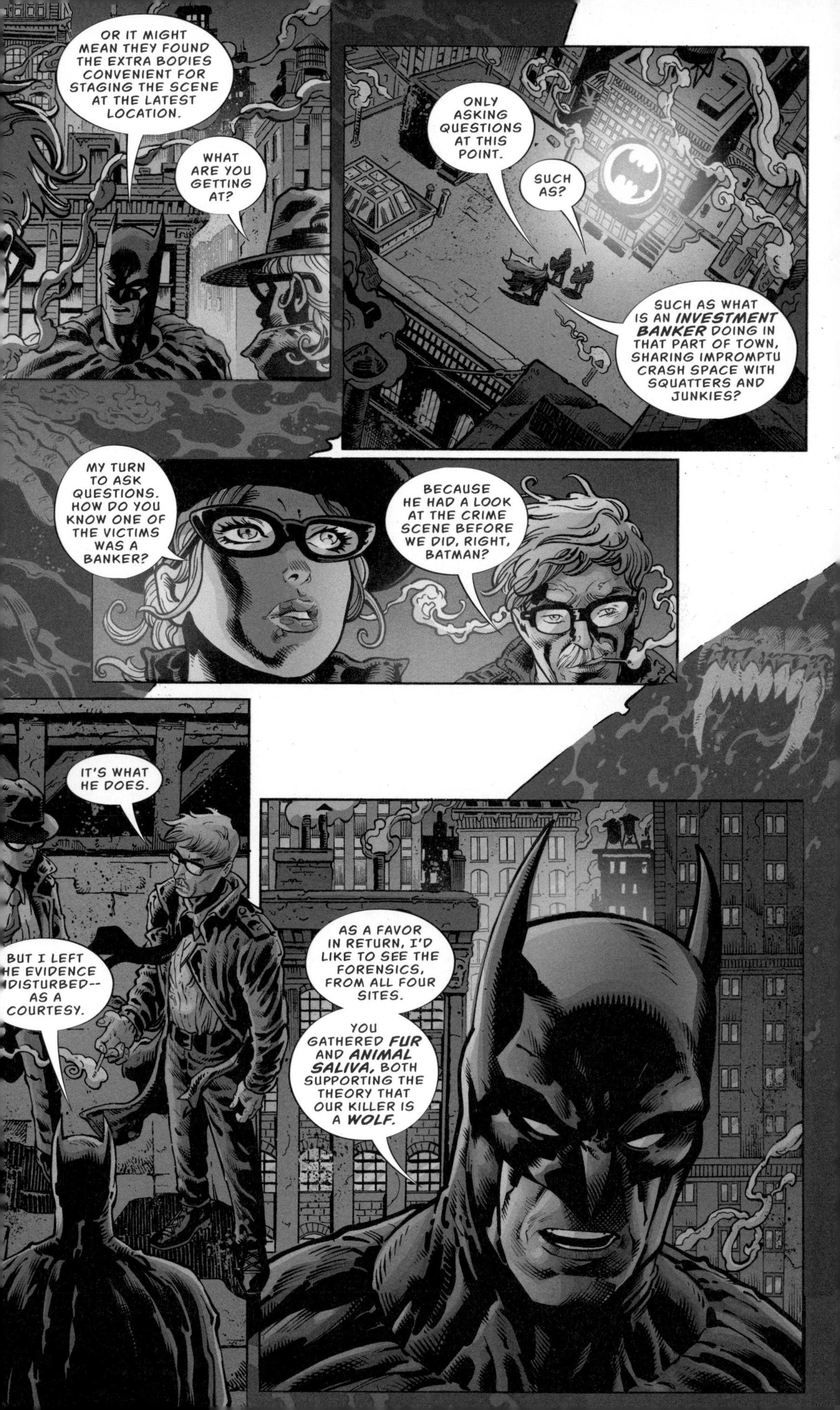
OR IT MIGHT MEAN THEY FOUND THE EXTRA BODIES CONVENIENT FOR STAGING THE SCENE AT THE LATEST LOCATION.
WHAT ARE YOU GETTING AT?
ONLY ASKING QUESTIONS AT THIS POINT.
SUCH AS?
SUCH AS WHAT IS AN INVESTMENT BANKER DOING IN THAT PART OF TOWN, SHARING IMPROMPTU CRASH SPACE WITH SQUATTERS AND JUNKIES?
MY TURN TO ASK QUESTIONS. HOW DO YOU KNOW ONE OF THE VICTIMS WAS A BANKER?
BECAUSE HE HAD A LOOK AT THE CRIME SCENE BEFORE WE DID, RIGHT, BATMAN?
IT'S WHAT HE DOES.
BUT I LEFT HE EVIDENCE IDISTURBED-- AS A COURTESY.
AS A FAVOR IN RETURN, I'D LIKE TO SEE THE FORENSICS, FROM ALL FOUR SITES.
YOU GATHERED FUR AND ANIMAL SALIVA, BOTH SUPPORTING THE THEORY THAT OUR KILLER IS A WOLF.

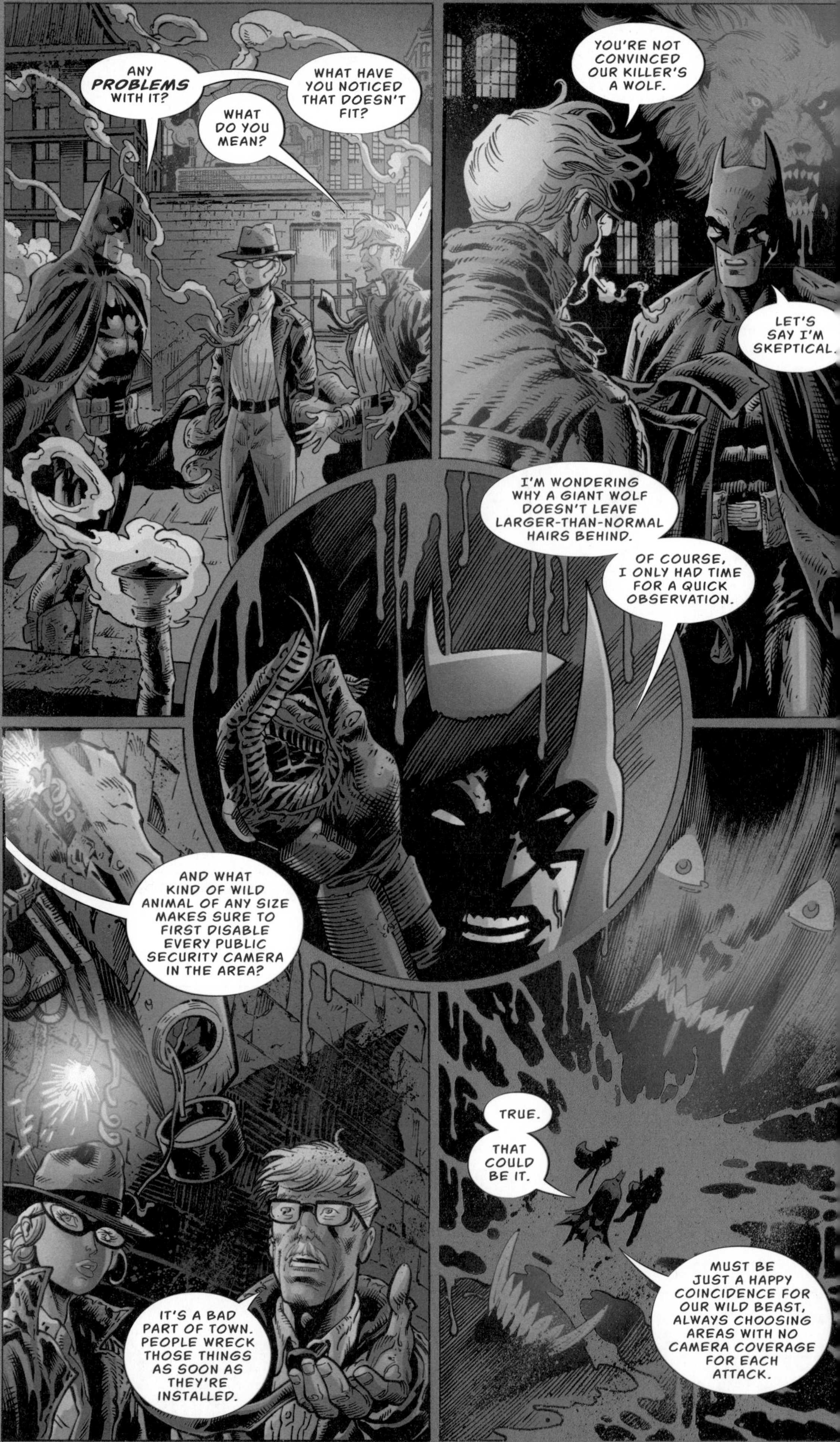
WHAT DO YOU MEAN?
WHAT HAVE YOU NOTICED THAT DOESN'T FIT?
ANY *PROBLEMS* WITH IT?
YOU'RE NOT CONVINCED OUR KILLER'S A WOLF.
LET'S SAY I'M SKEPTICAL.
I'M WONDERING WHY A GIANT WOLF DOESN'T LEAVE LARGER-THAN-NORMAL HAIRS BEHIND.
OF COURSE, I ONLY HAD TIME FOR A QUICK OBSERVATION.
AND WHAT KIND OF WILD ANIMAL OF ANY SIZE MAKES SURE TO FIRST DISABLE EVERY PUBLIC SECURITY CAMERA IN THE AREA?
IT'S A BAD PART OF TOWN. PEOPLE WRECK THOSE THINGS AS SOON AS THEY'RE INSTALLED.
TRUE.
THAT COULD BE IT.
MUST BE JUST A HAPPY COINCIDENCE FOR OUR WILD BEAST, ALWAYS CHOOSING AREAS WITH NO CAMERA COVERAGE FOR EACH ATTACK.

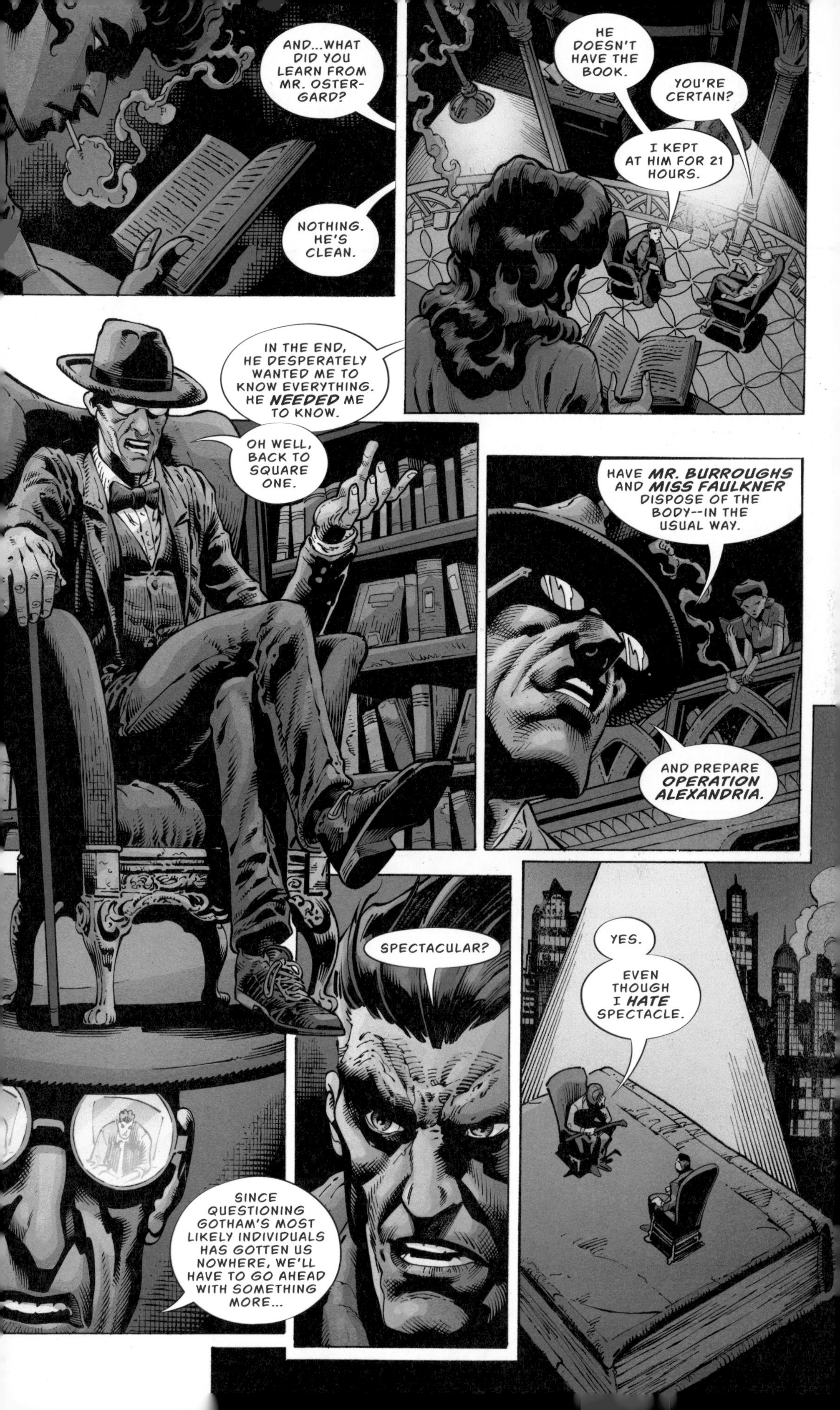

AND...WHAT DID YOU LEARN FROM MR. OSTER-GARD?
NOTHING. HE'S CLEAN.
HE DOESN'T HAVE THE BOOK.
YOU'RE CERTAIN?
I KEPT AT HIM FOR 21 HOURS.
IN THE END, HE DESPERATELY WANTED ME TO KNOW EVERYTHING. HE NEEDED ME TO KNOW.
OH WELL, BACK TO SQUARE ONE.
HAVE MR. BURROUGHS AND MISS FAULKNER DISPOSE OF THE BODY--IN THE USUAL WAY.
AND PREPARE OPERATION ALEXANDRIA.
SINCE QUESTIONING GOTHAM'S MOST LIKELY INDIVIDUALS HAS GOTTEN US NOWHERE, WE'LL HAVE TO GO AHEAD WITH SOMETHING MORE...
SPECTACULAR?
YES.
EVEN THOUGH I HATE SPECTACLE.

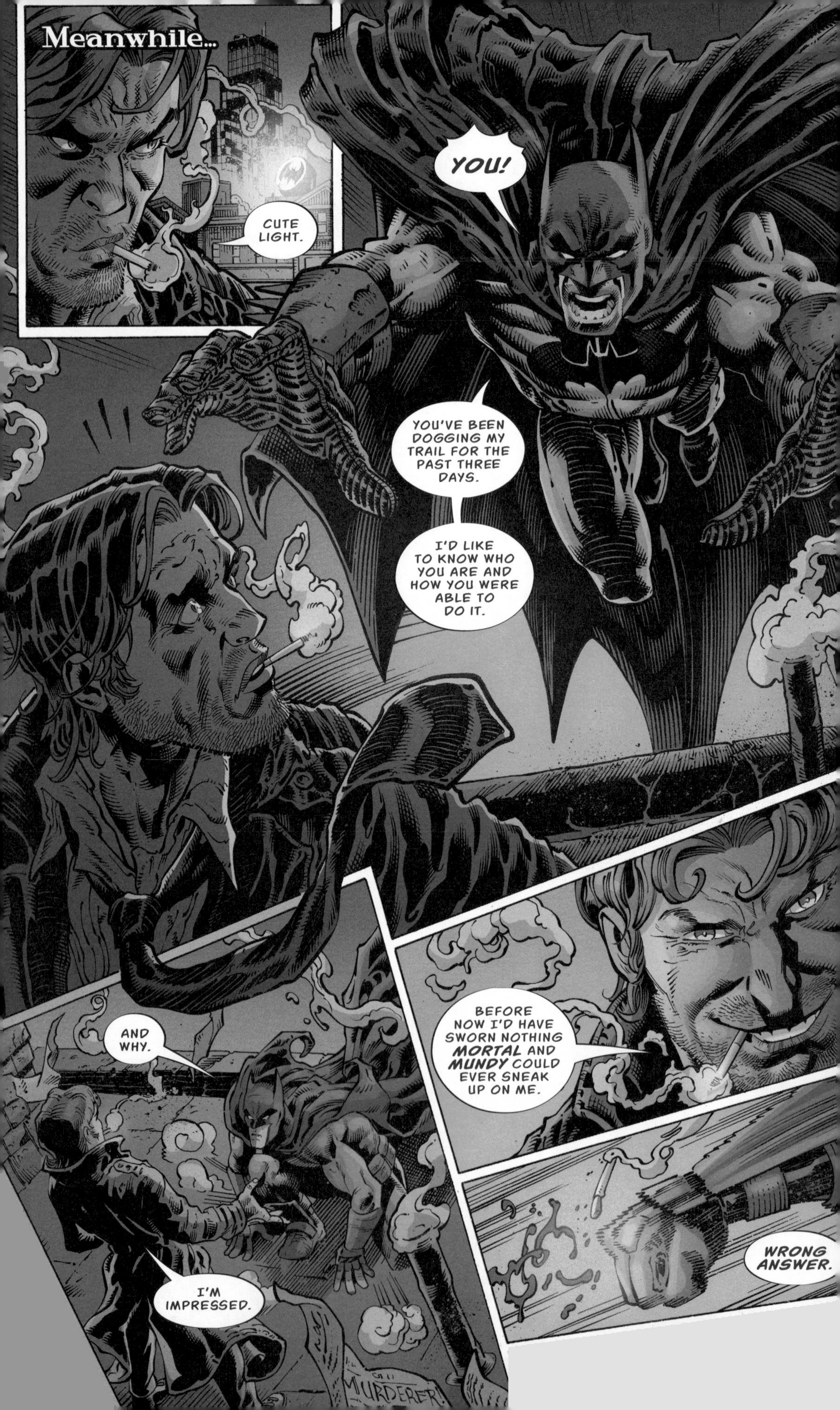
Meanwhile...
CUTE LIGHT.
YOU!
YOU'VE BEEN DOGGING MY TRAIL FOR THE PAST THREE DAYS.
I'D LIKE TO KNOW WHO YOU ARE AND HOW YOU WERE ABLE TO DO IT.
AND WHY.
I'M IMPRESSED.
BEFORE NOW I'D HAVE SWORN NOTHING MORTAL AND MUNDY COULD EVER SNEAK UP ON ME.
WRONG ANSWER.
MURDERER!

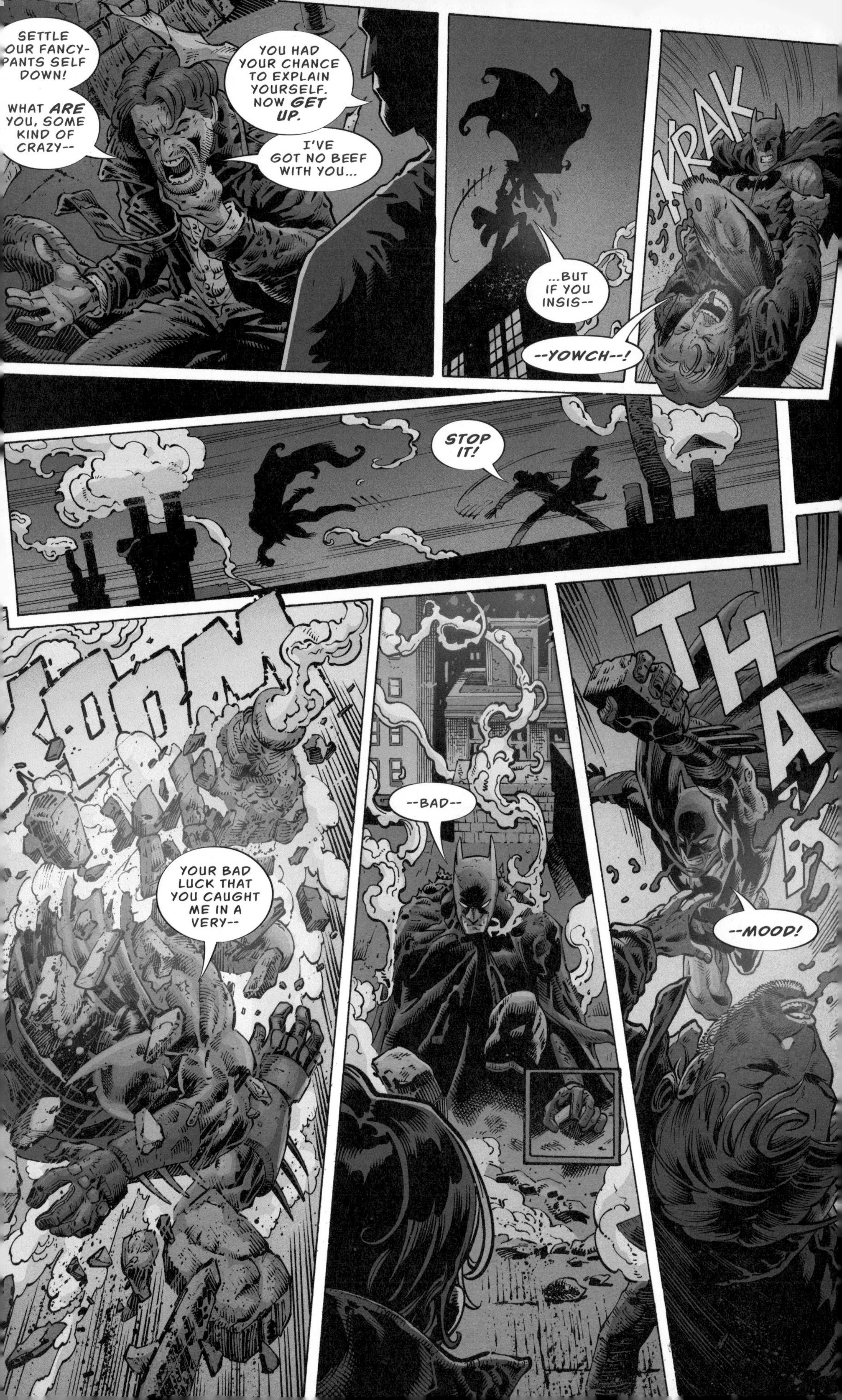
SETTLE OUR FANCY-PANTS SELF DOWN!
WHAT ARE YOU, SOME KIND OF CRAZY--
YOU HAD YOUR CHANCE TO EXPLAIN YOURSELF. NOW GET UP.
I'VE GOT NO BEEF WITH YOU...
...BUT IF YOU INSIS--
KRAK
--YOWCH--!
STOP IT!
YOUR BAD LUCK THAT YOU CAUGHT ME IN A VERY--
--BAD--
THA
--MOOD!

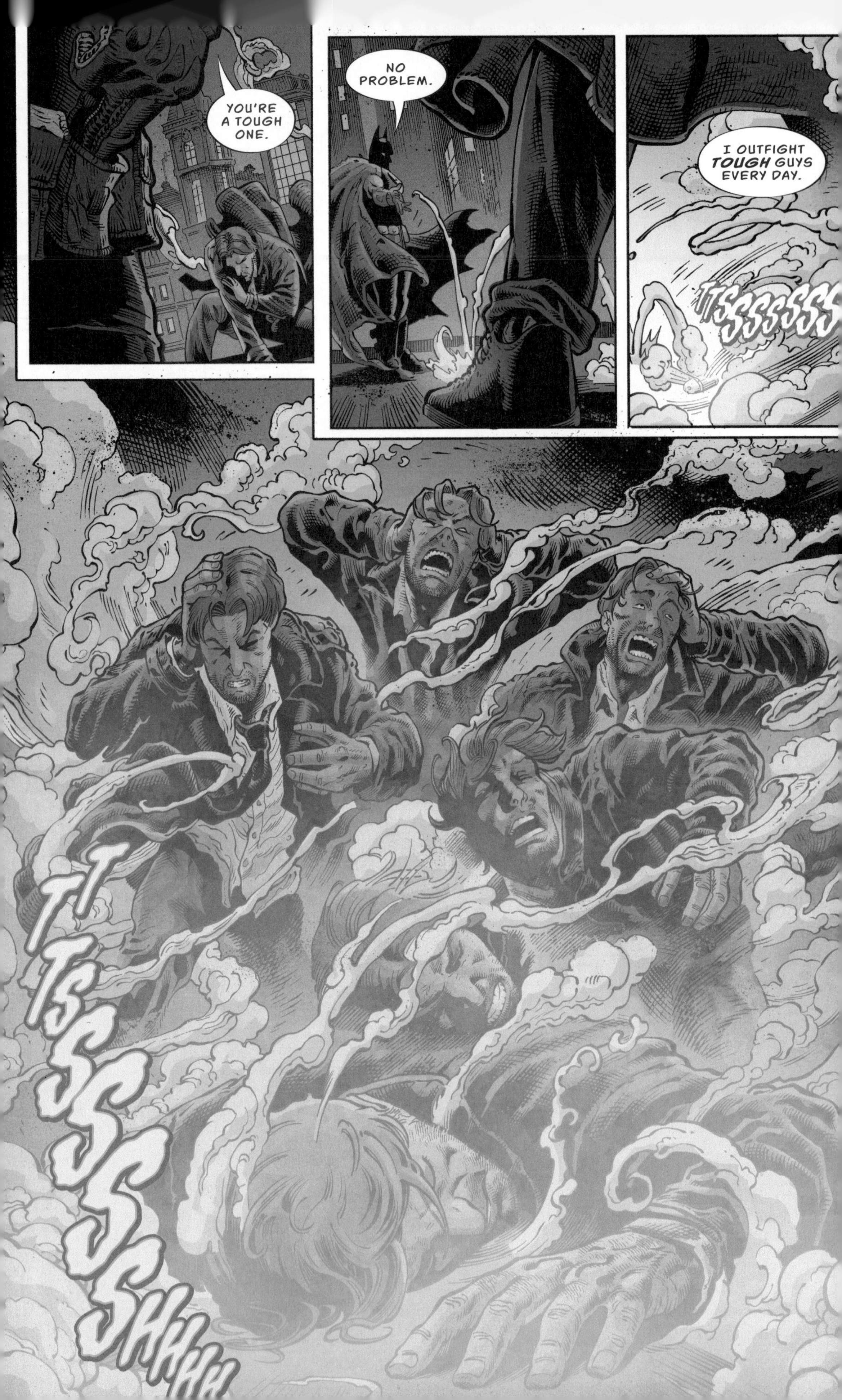
YOU'RE A TOUGH ONE.
NO PROBLEM.
I OUTFIGHT TOUGH GUYS EVERY DAY.
TTSSSSSSS
TTTSSSSSHHHH

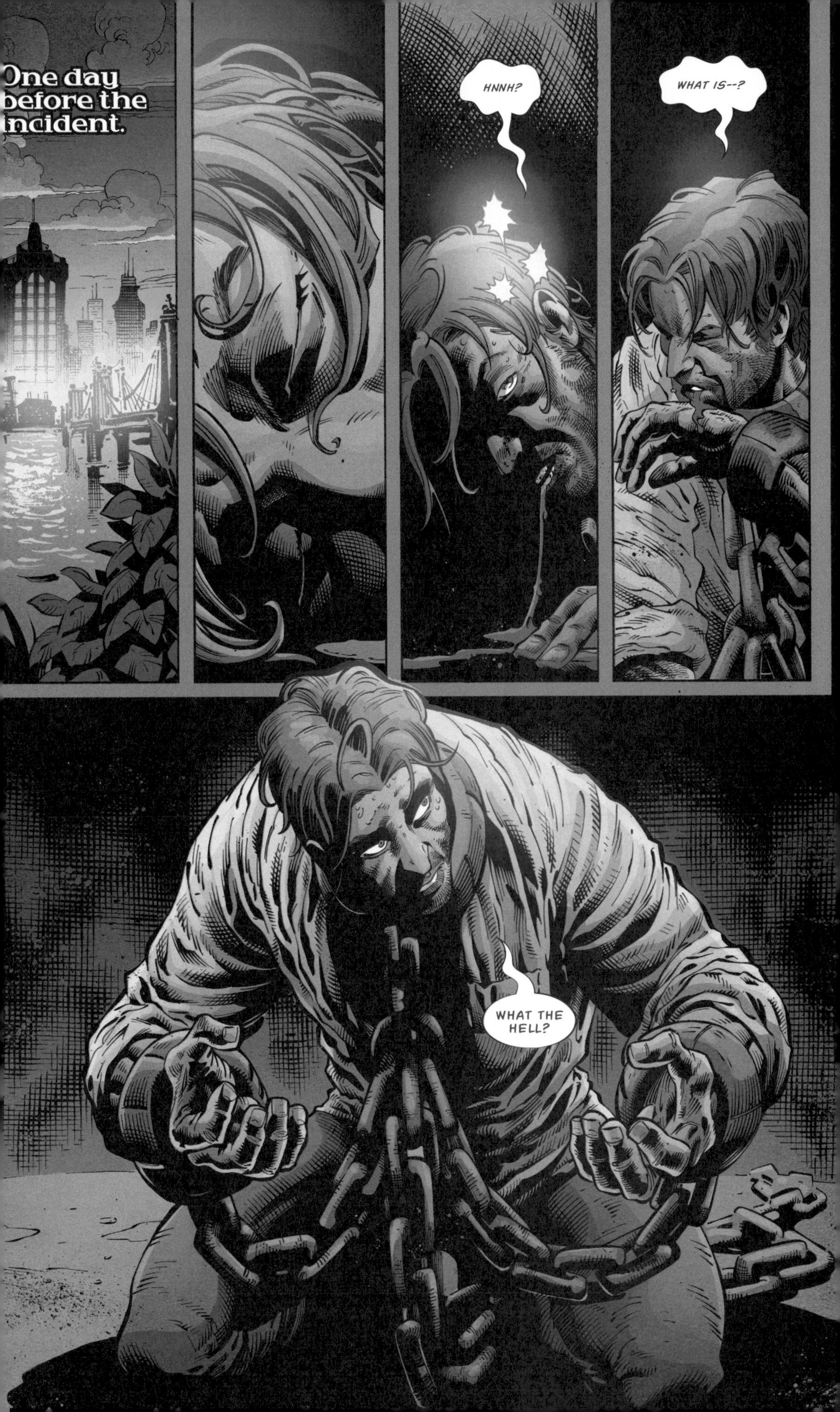
One day before the incident.
HNNH?
WHAT IS--?
WHAT THE HELL?

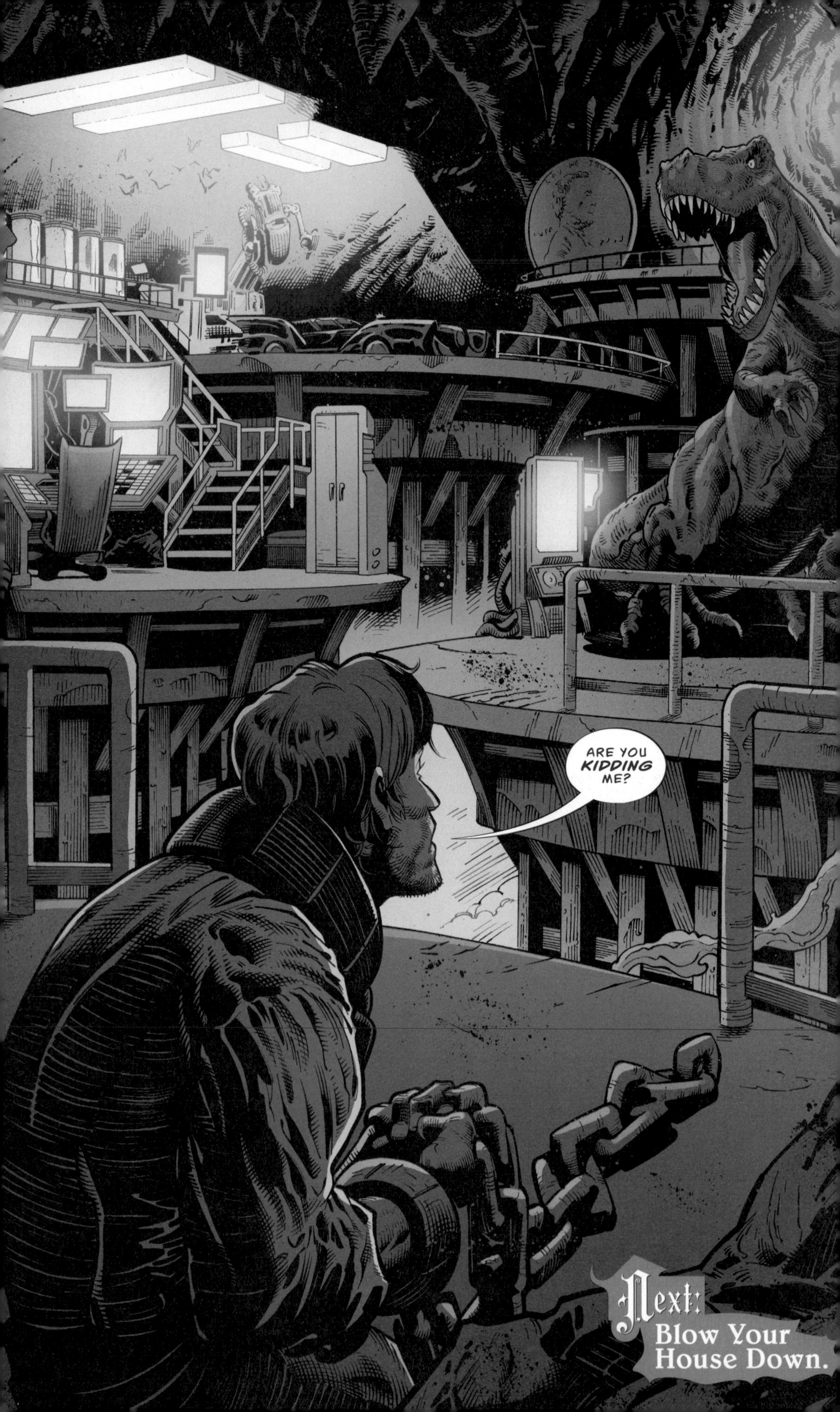
ARE YOU KIDDING ME?
Next: Blow Your House Down.

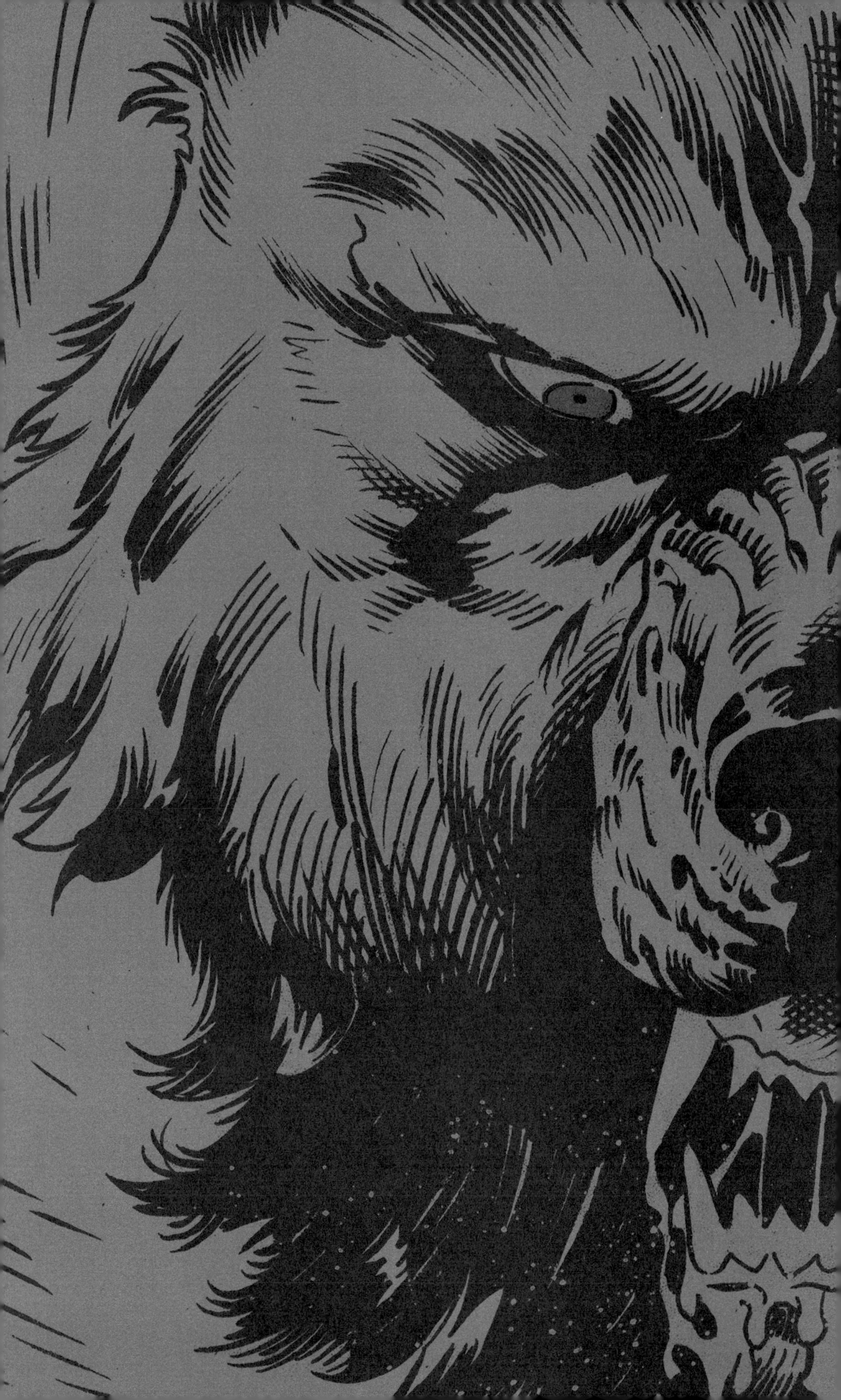

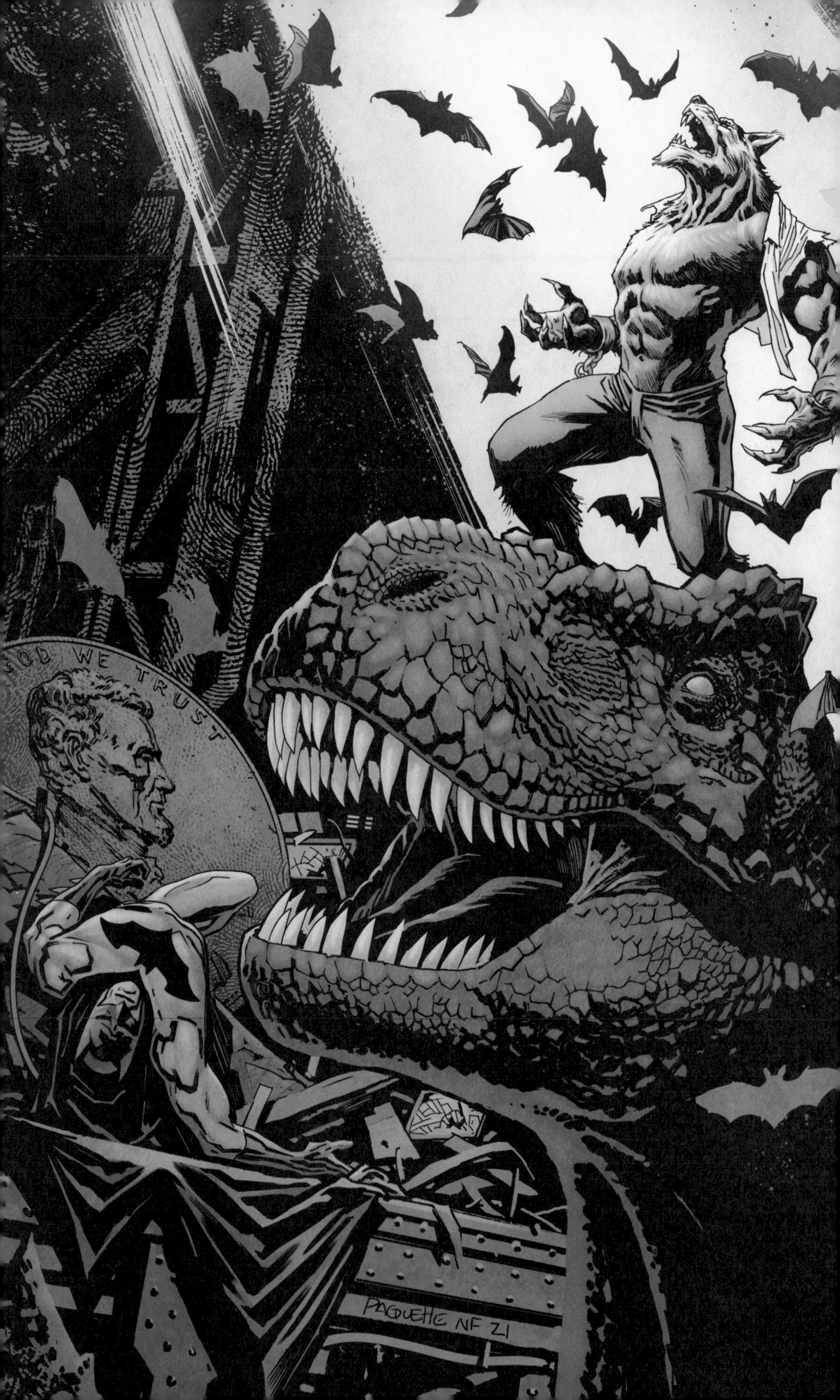
OD WE TRUST
PAQUETTE NF 21

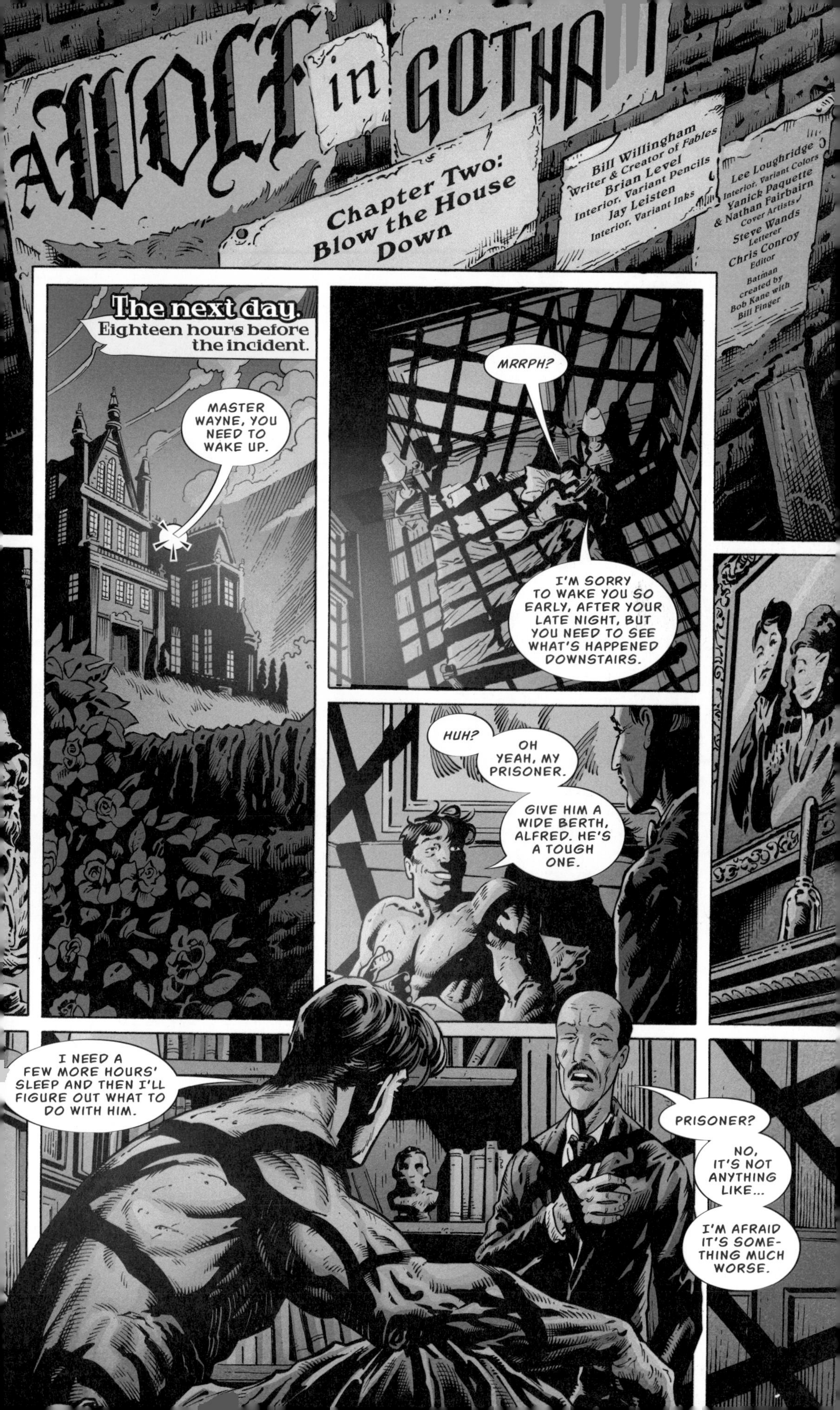
A WOLF in GOTHAM
Chapter Two: Blow the House Down
Bill Willingham Writer & Creator of Fables
Brian Level Interior, Variant Pencils
Jay Leisten Interior, Variant Inks
Lee Loughridge Interior, Variant Colors
Yanick Paquette & Nathan Fairbairn Cover Artists
Steve Wands Letterer
Chris Conroy Editor
Batman created by Bob Kane with Bill Finger
The next day.
Eighteen hours before the incident.
MASTER WAYNE, YOU NEED TO WAKE UP.
MRRPH?
I'M SORRY TO WAKE YOU SO EARLY, AFTER YOUR LATE NIGHT, BUT YOU NEED TO SEE WHAT'S HAPPENED DOWNSTAIRS.
HUH?
OH YEAH, MY PRISONER.
GIVE HIM A WIDE BERTH, ALFRED. HE'S A TOUGH ONE.
I NEED A FEW MORE HOURS' SLEEP AND THEN I'LL FIGURE OUT WHAT TO DO WITH HIM.
PRISONER?
NO, IT'S NOT ANYTHING LIKE...
I'M AFRAID IT'S SOME-THING MUCH WORSE.

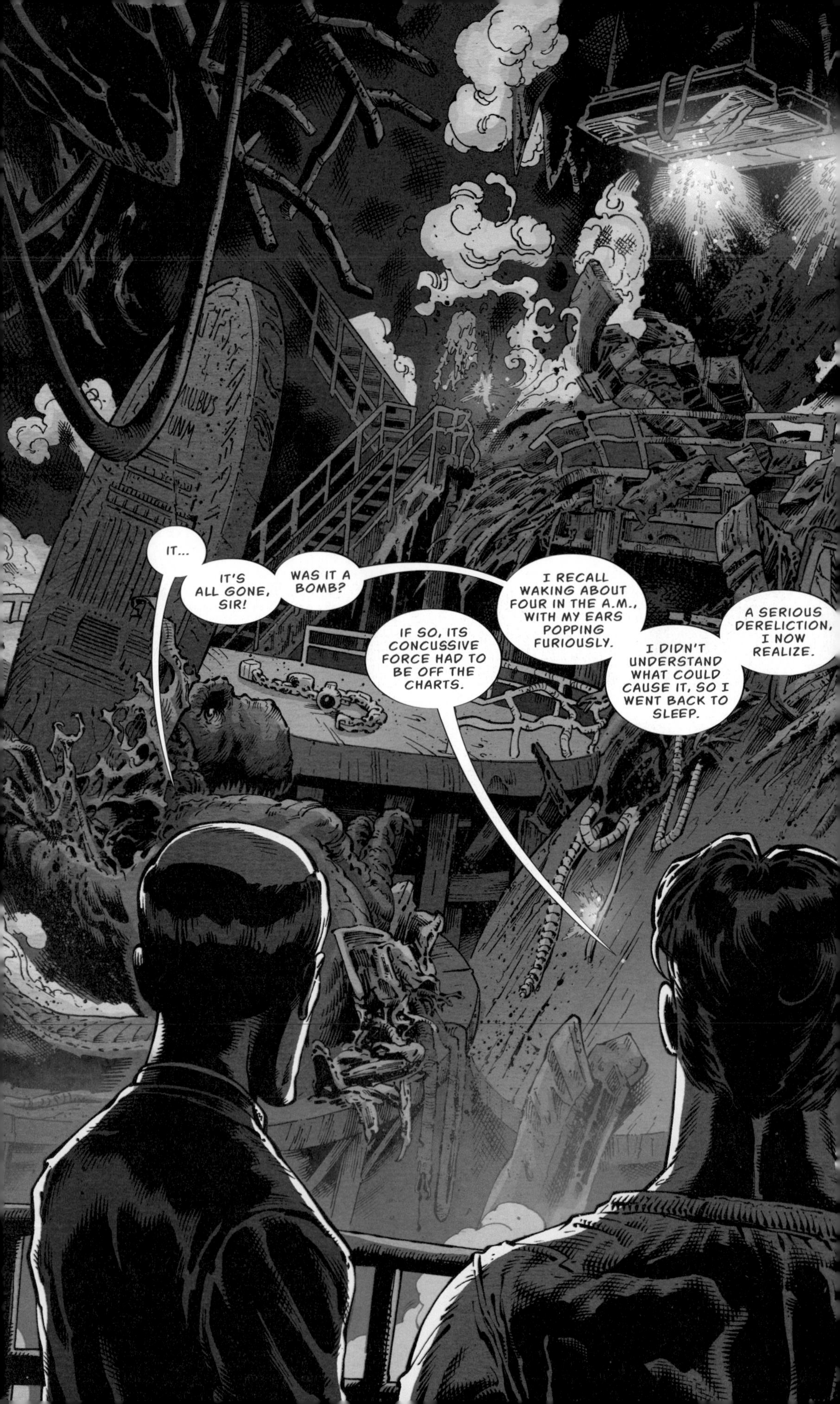
IT...
IT'S ALL GONE, SIR!
WAS IT A BOMB?
I RECALL WAKING ABOUT FOUR IN THE A.M., WITH MY EARS POPPING FURIOUSLY.
IF SO, ITS CONCUSSIVE FORCE HAD TO BE OFF THE CHARTS.
I DIDN'T UNDERSTAND WHAT COULD CAUSE IT, SO I WENT BACK TO SLEEP.
A SERIOUS DERELICTION, I NOW REALIZE.

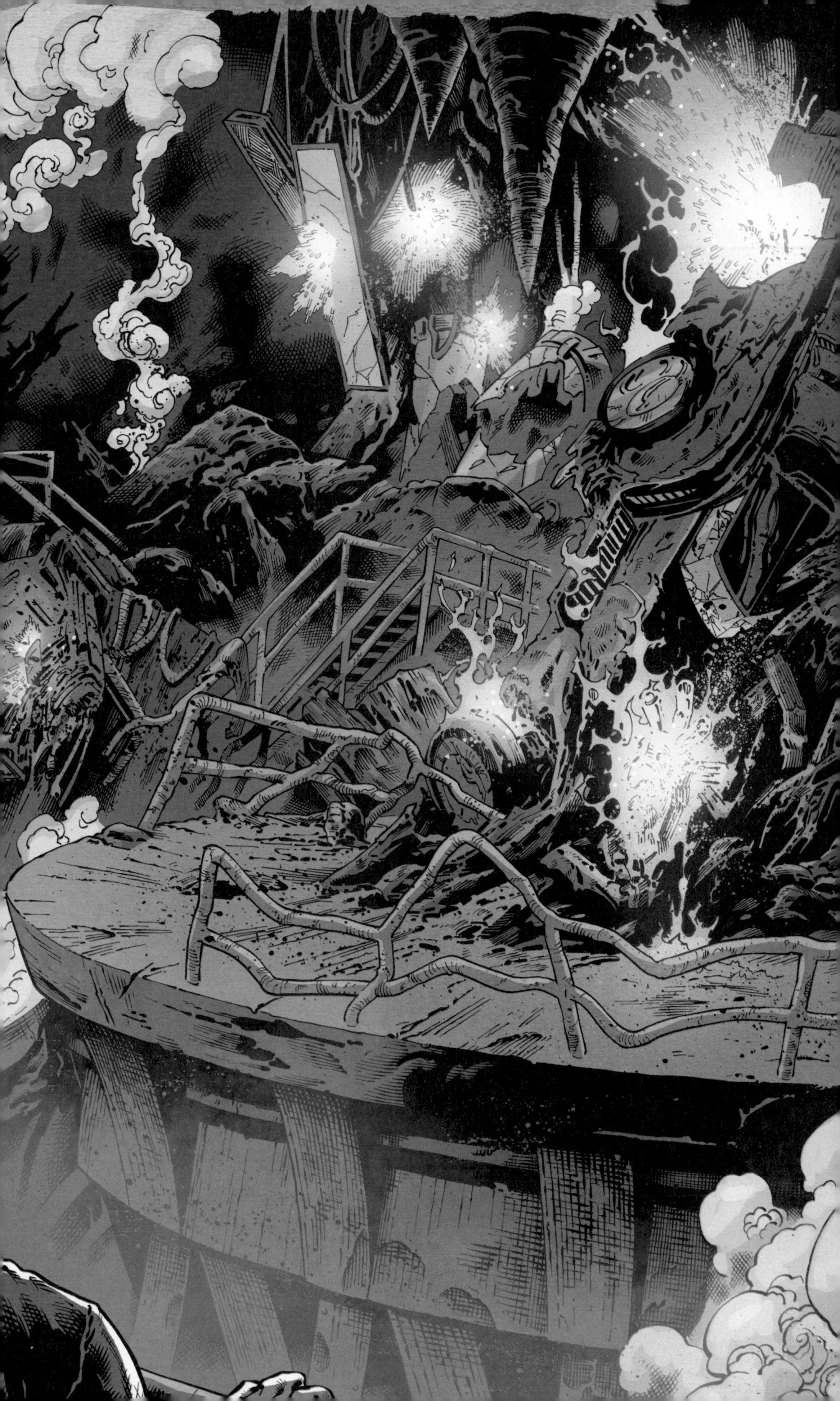

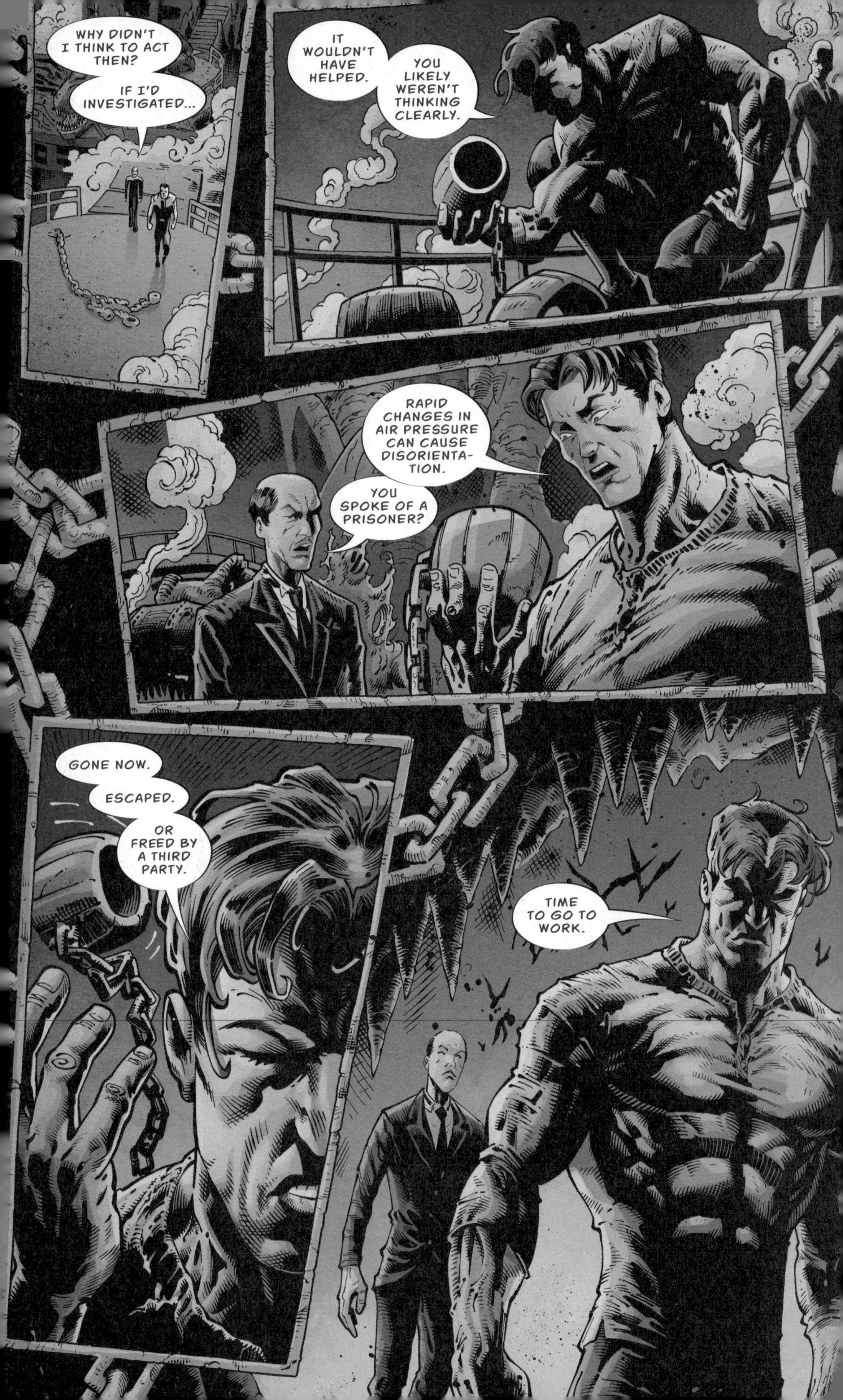

WHY DIDN'T I THINK TO ACT THEN?
IF I'D INVESTIGATED...
IT WOULDN'T HAVE HELPED.
YOU LIKELY WEREN'T THINKING CLEARLY.
RAPID CHANGES IN AIR PRESSURE CAN CAUSE DISORIENTATION.
YOU SPOKE OF A PRISONER?
GONE NOW.
ESCAPED.
OR FREED BY A THIRD PARTY.
TIME TO GO TO WORK.

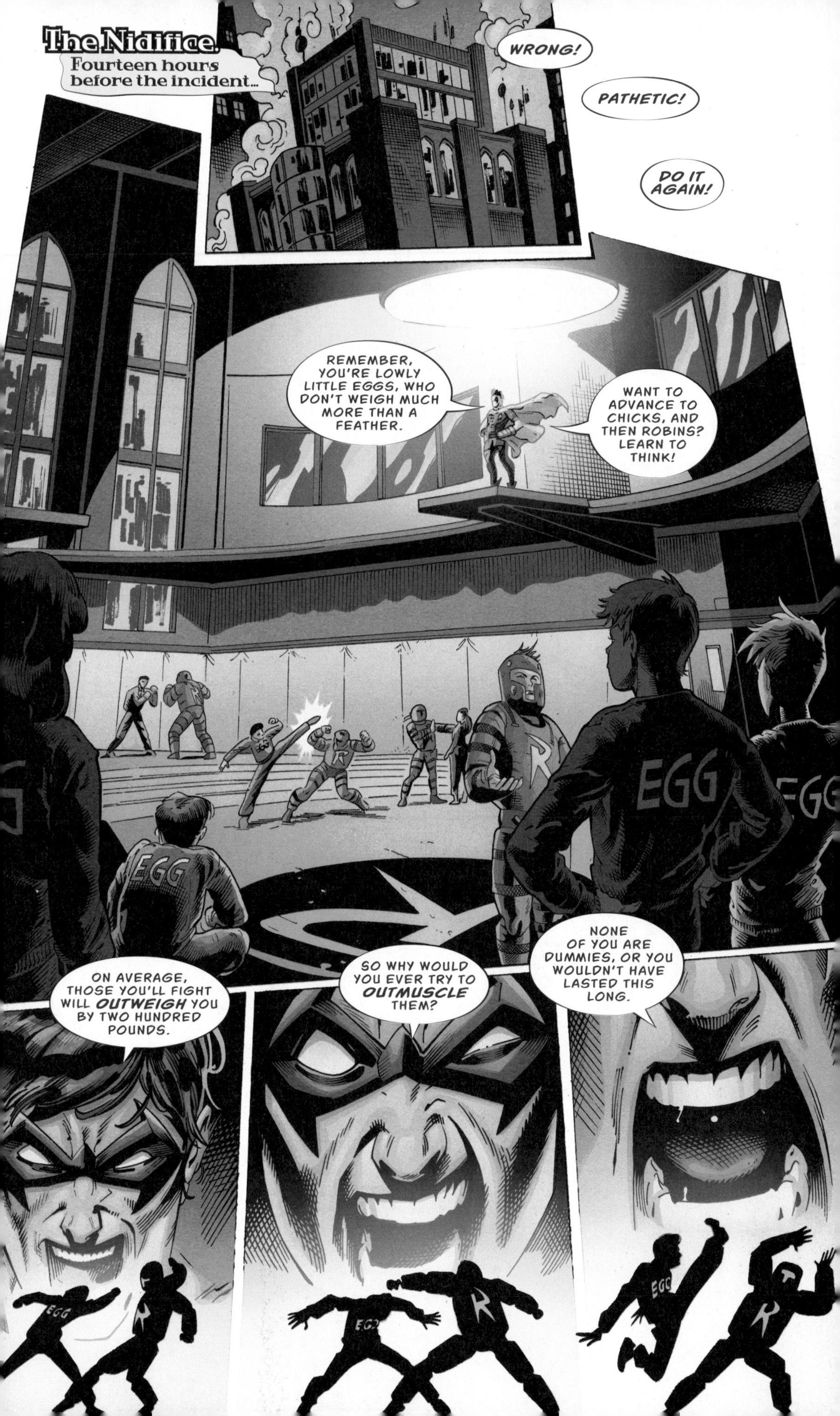
The Nidifice.
Fourteen hours before the incident...
WRONG!
PATHETIC!
DO IT AGAIN!
REMEMBER, YOU'RE LOWLY LITTLE EGGS, WHO DON'T WEIGH MUCH MORE THAN A FEATHER.
WANT TO ADVANCE TO CHICKS, AND THEN ROBINS? LEARN TO THINK!
EGG
EGG
EGG
ON AVERAGE, THOSE YOU'LL FIGHT WILL *OUTWEIGH* YOU BY TWO HUNDRED POUNDS.
SO WHY WOULD YOU EVER TRY TO *OUTMUSCLE* THEM?
NONE OF YOU ARE DUMMIES, OR YOU WOULDN'T HAVE LASTED THIS LONG.

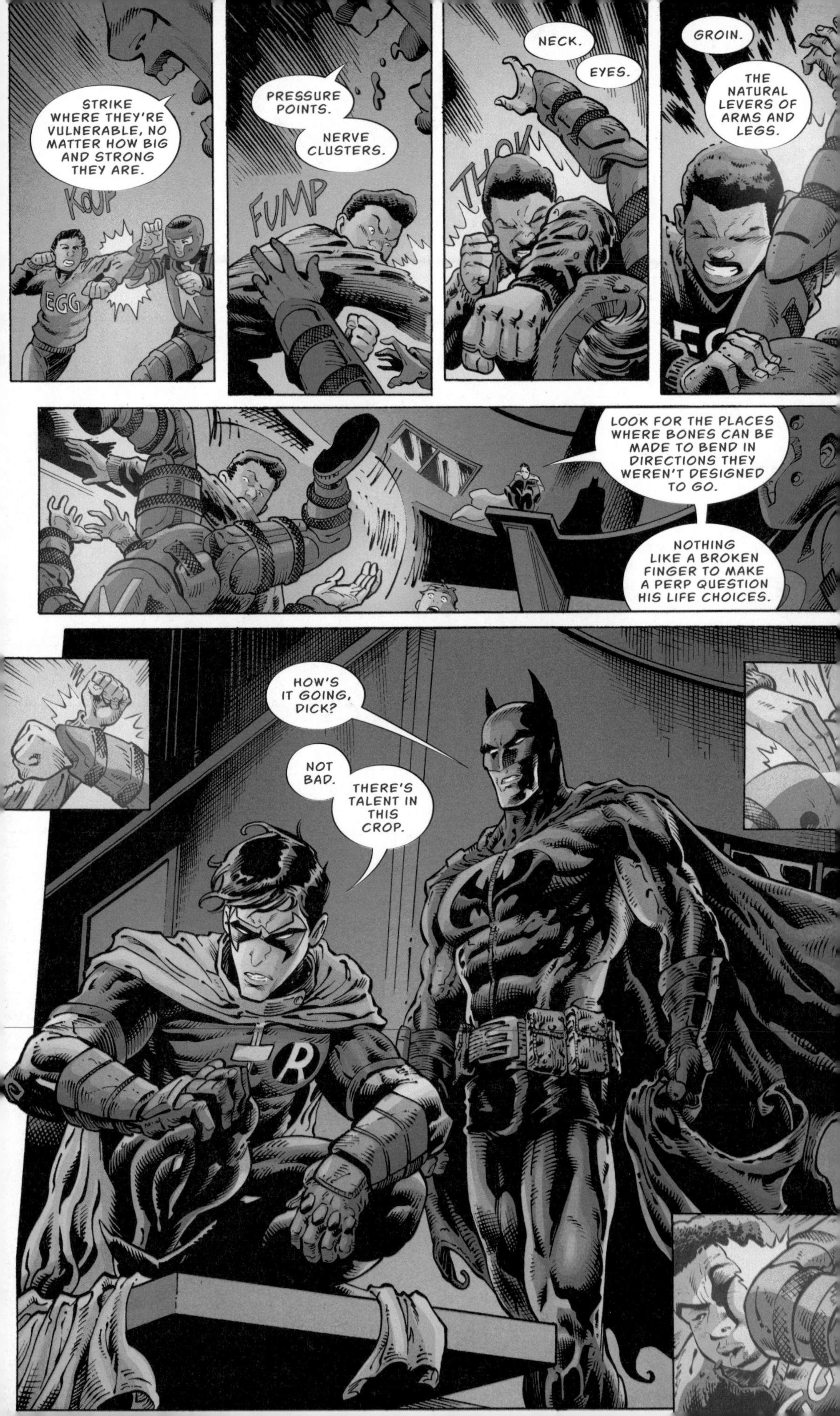
STRIKE WHERE THEY'RE VULNERABLE, NO MATTER HOW BIG AND STRONG THEY ARE.
KOOP
EGG
PRESSURE POINTS.
NERVE CLUSTERS.
FUMP
NECK.
EYES.
THOK
GROIN.
THE NATURAL LEVERS OF ARMS AND LEGS.
LOOK FOR THE PLACES WHERE BONES CAN BE MADE TO BEND IN DIRECTIONS THEY WEREN'T DESIGNED TO GO.
NOTHING LIKE A BROKEN FINGER TO MAKE A PERP QUESTION HIS LIFE CHOICES.
HOW'S IT GOING, DICK?
NOT BAD.
THERE'S TALENT IN THIS CROP.

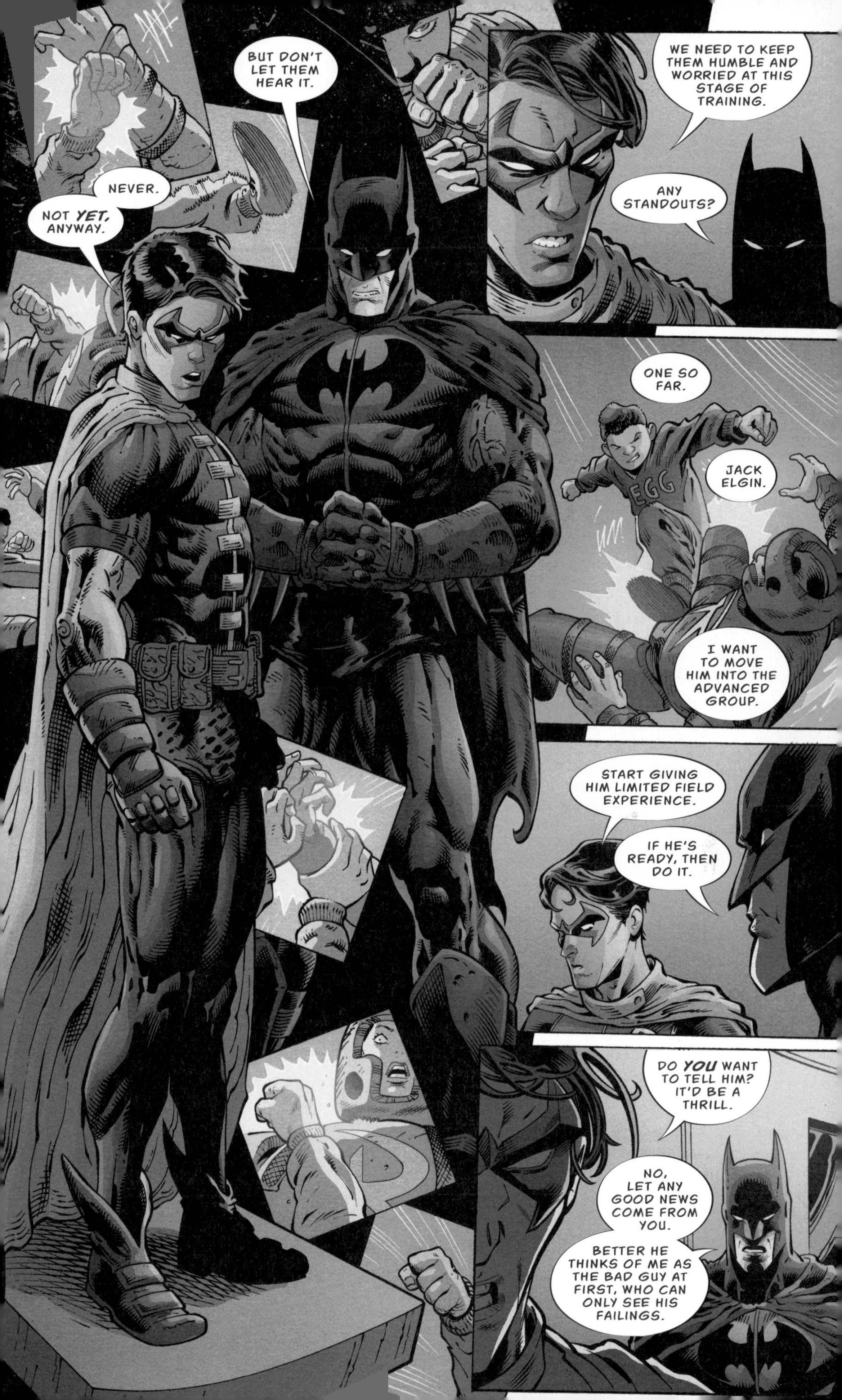

NEVER.
NOT *YET,* ANYWAY.
BUT DON'T LET THEM HEAR IT.
WE NEED TO KEEP THEM HUMBLE AND WORRIED AT THIS STAGE OF TRAINING.
ANY STANDOUTS?
ONE SO FAR.
EGG
JACK ELGIN.
I WANT TO MOVE HIM INTO THE ADVANCED GROUP.
START GIVING HIM LIMITED FIELD EXPERIENCE.
IF HE'S READY, THEN DO IT.
DO *YOU* WANT TO TELL HIM? IT'D BE A THRILL.
NO, LET ANY GOOD NEWS COME FROM YOU.
BETTER HE THINKS OF ME AS THE BAD GUY AT FIRST, WHO CAN ONLY SEE HIS FAILINGS.

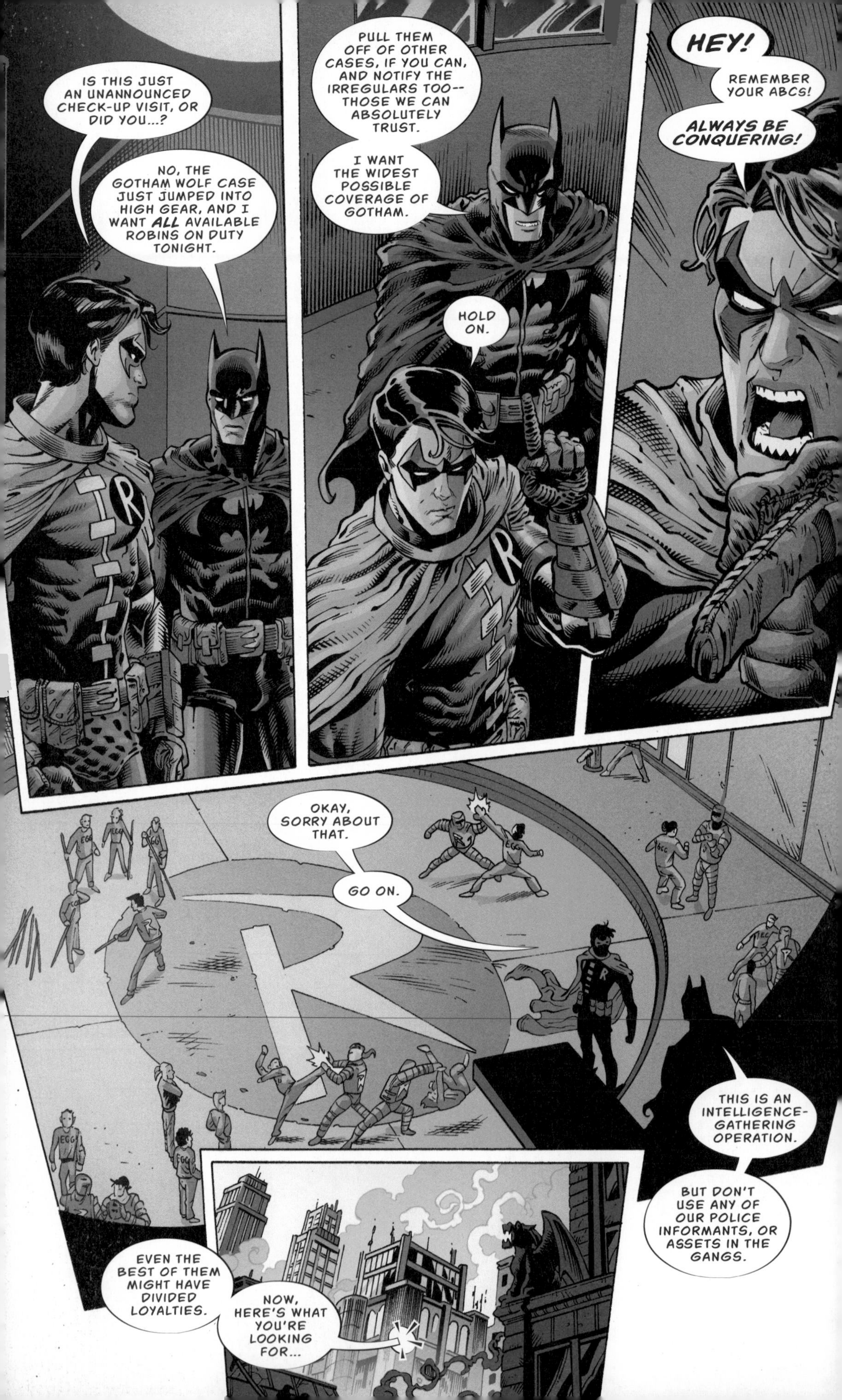
IS THIS JUST AN UNANNOUNCED CHECK-UP VISIT, OR DID YOU...?
NO, THE GOTHAM WOLF CASE JUST JUMPED INTO HIGH GEAR, AND I WANT **ALL** AVAILABLE ROBINS ON DUTY TONIGHT.
PULL THEM OFF OF OTHER CASES, IF YOU CAN, AND NOTIFY THE IRREGULARS TOO-- THOSE WE CAN ABSOLUTELY TRUST.
I WANT THE WIDEST POSSIBLE COVERAGE OF GOTHAM.
HOLD ON.
HEY!
REMEMBER YOUR ABCS!
ALWAYS BE CONQUERING!
OKAY, SORRY ABOUT THAT.
GO ON.
THIS IS AN INTELLIGENCE-GATHERING OPERATION.
BUT DON'T USE ANY OF OUR POLICE INFORMANTS, OR ASSETS IN THE GANGS.
EVEN THE BEST OF THEM MIGHT HAVE DIVIDED LOYALTIES.
NOW, HERE'S WHAT YOU'RE LOOKING FOR...

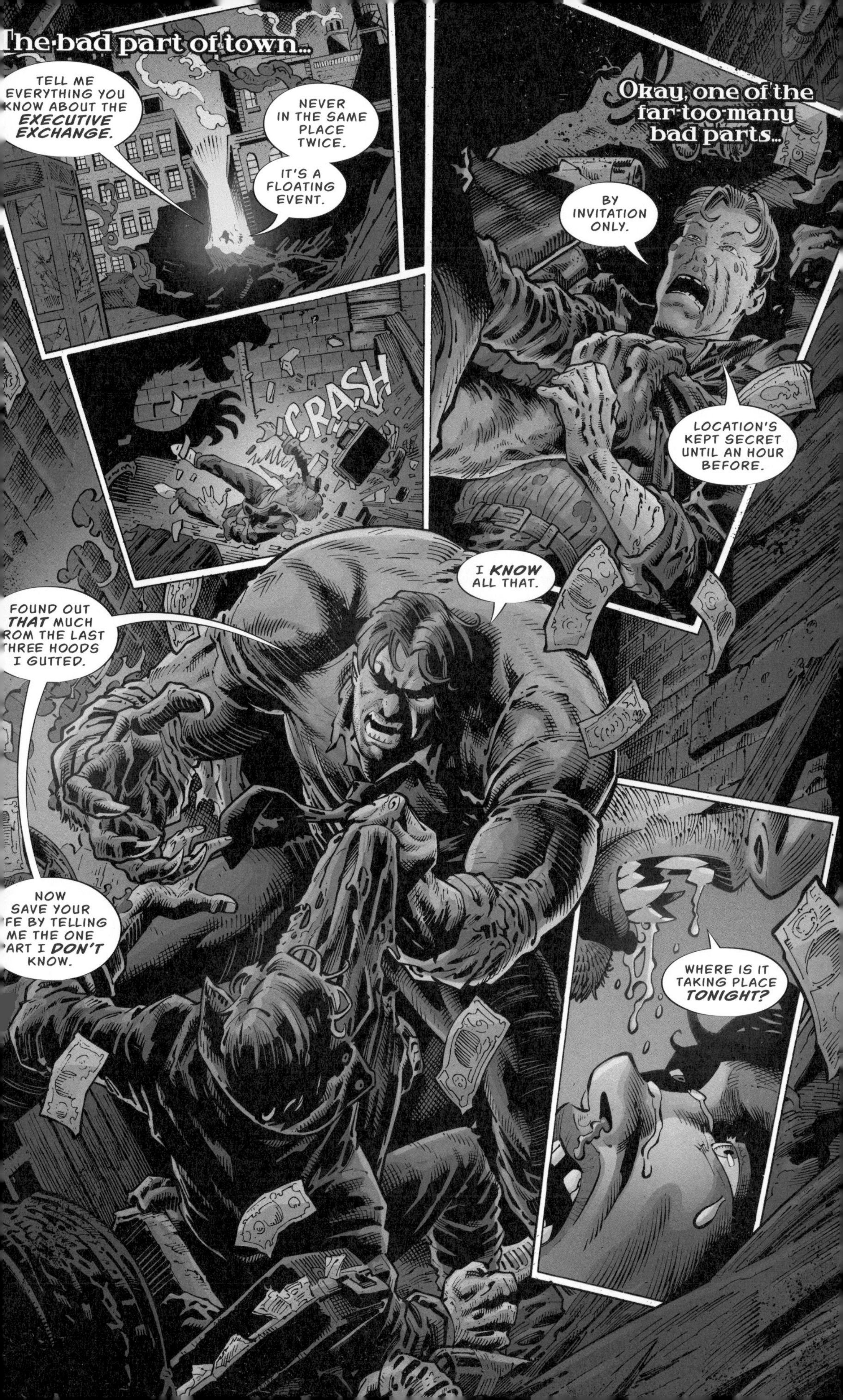

The bad part of town...
TELL ME EVERYTHING YOU KNOW ABOUT THE ***EXECUTIVE EXCHANGE.***
NEVER IN THE SAME PLACE TWICE.
IT'S A FLOATING EVENT.
CRASH
Okay, one of the far-too-many bad parts...
BY INVITATION ONLY.
LOCATION'S KEPT SECRET UNTIL AN HOUR BEFORE.
I ***KNOW*** ALL THAT.
FOUND OUT ***THAT*** MUCH ROM THE LAST THREE HOODS I GUTTED.
NOW SAVE YOUR FE BY TELLING ME THE ONE ART I ***DON'T*** KNOW.
WHERE IS IT TAKING PLACE ***TONIGHT?***

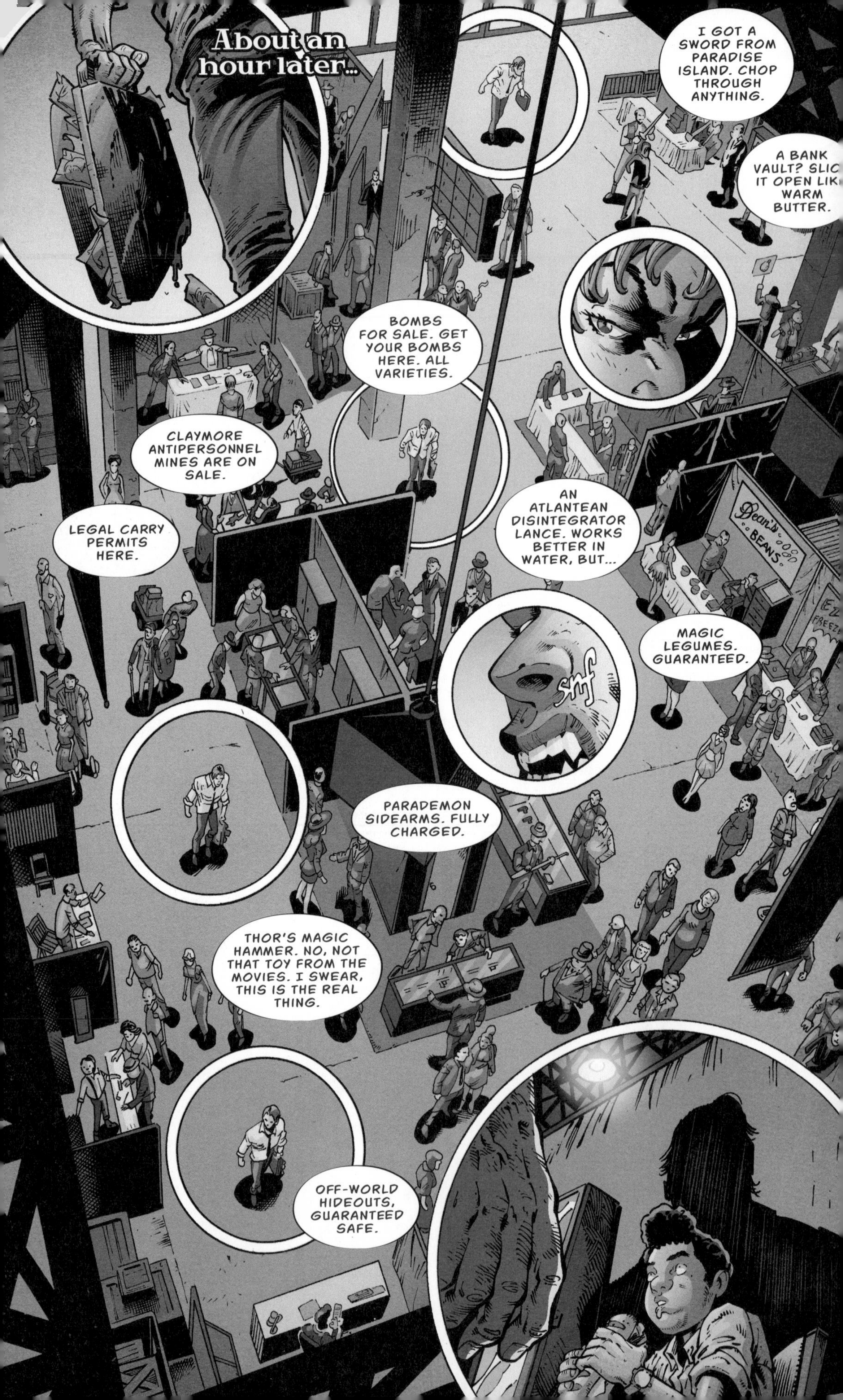
About an hour later...
I GOT A SWORD FROM PARADISE ISLAND. CHOP THROUGH ANYTHING.
A BANK VAULT? SLIC IT OPEN LIK WARM BUTTER.
BOMBS FOR SALE. GET YOUR BOMBS HERE. ALL VARIETIES.
CLAYMORE ANTIPERSONNEL MINES ARE ON SALE.
LEGAL CARRY PERMITS HERE.
AN ATLANTEAN DISINTEGRATOR LANCE. WORKS BETTER IN WATER, BUT...
Bean's BEANS
MAGIC LEGUMES. GUARANTEED.
snf
PARADEMON SIDEARMS. FULLY CHARGED.
THOR'S MAGIC HAMMER. NO, NOT THAT TOY FROM THE MOVIES. I SWEAR, THIS IS THE REAL THING.
OFF-WORLD HIDEOUTS, GUARANTEED SAFE.

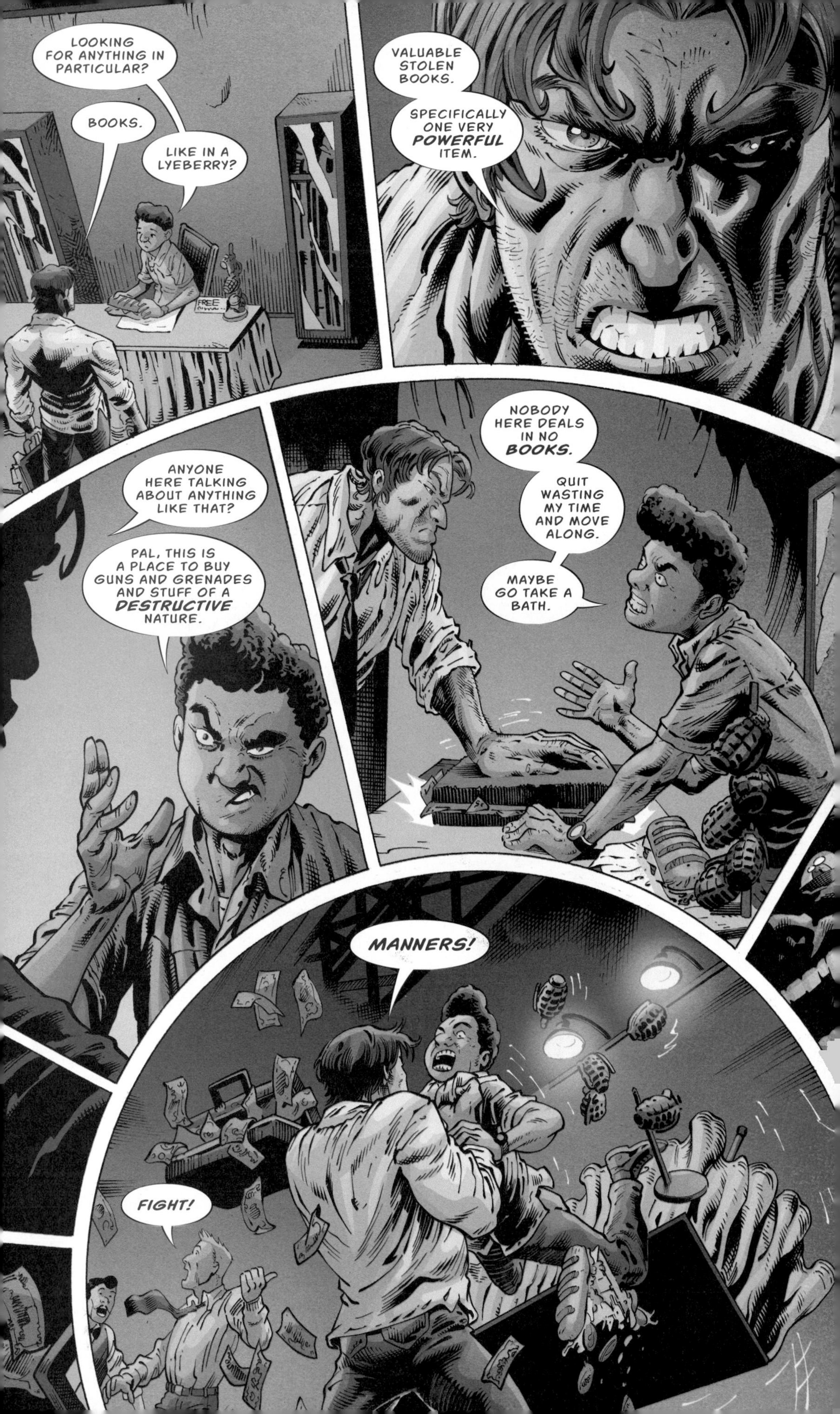
LOOKING FOR ANYTHING IN PARTICULAR?
BOOKS.
LIKE IN A LYEBERRY?
FREE
VALUABLE STOLEN BOOKS.
SPECIFICALLY ONE VERY POWERFUL ITEM.
ANYONE HERE TALKING ABOUT ANYTHING LIKE THAT?
PAL, THIS IS A PLACE TO BUY GUNS AND GRENADES AND STUFF OF A DESTRUCTIVE NATURE.
NOBODY HERE DEALS IN NO BOOKS.
QUIT WASTING MY TIME AND MOVE ALONG.
MAYBE GO TAKE A BATH.
MANNERS!
FIGHT!

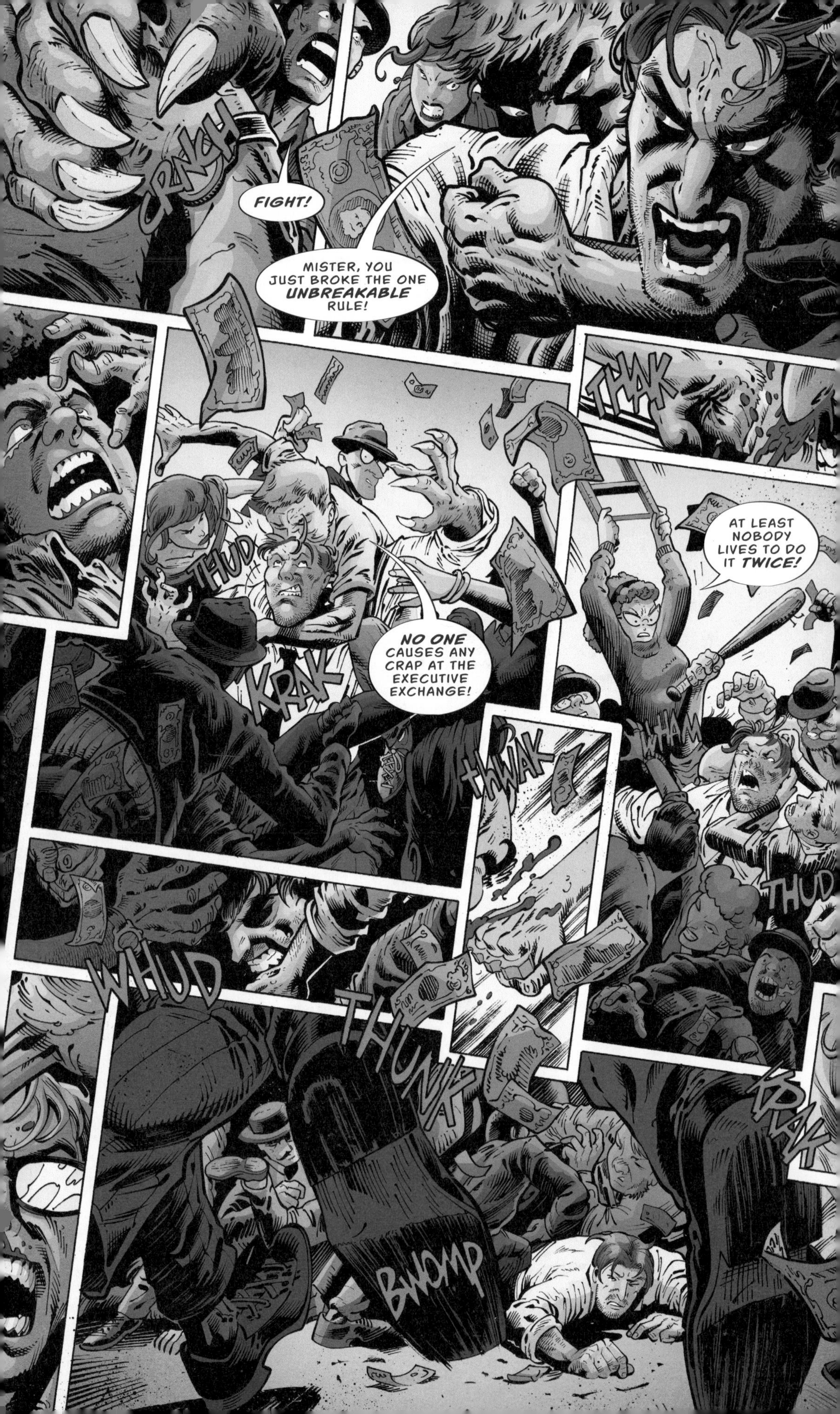
CRNCH
FIGHT!
MISTER, YOU JUST BROKE THE ONE UNBREAKABLE RULE!
THAK
AT LEAST NOBODY LIVES TO DO IT TWICE!
THUD
NO ONE CAUSES ANY CRAP AT THE EXECUTIVE EXCHANGE!
KRAK
WHAM
thWAK
THUD
WHUD
THUNK
KRAK
BWOMP

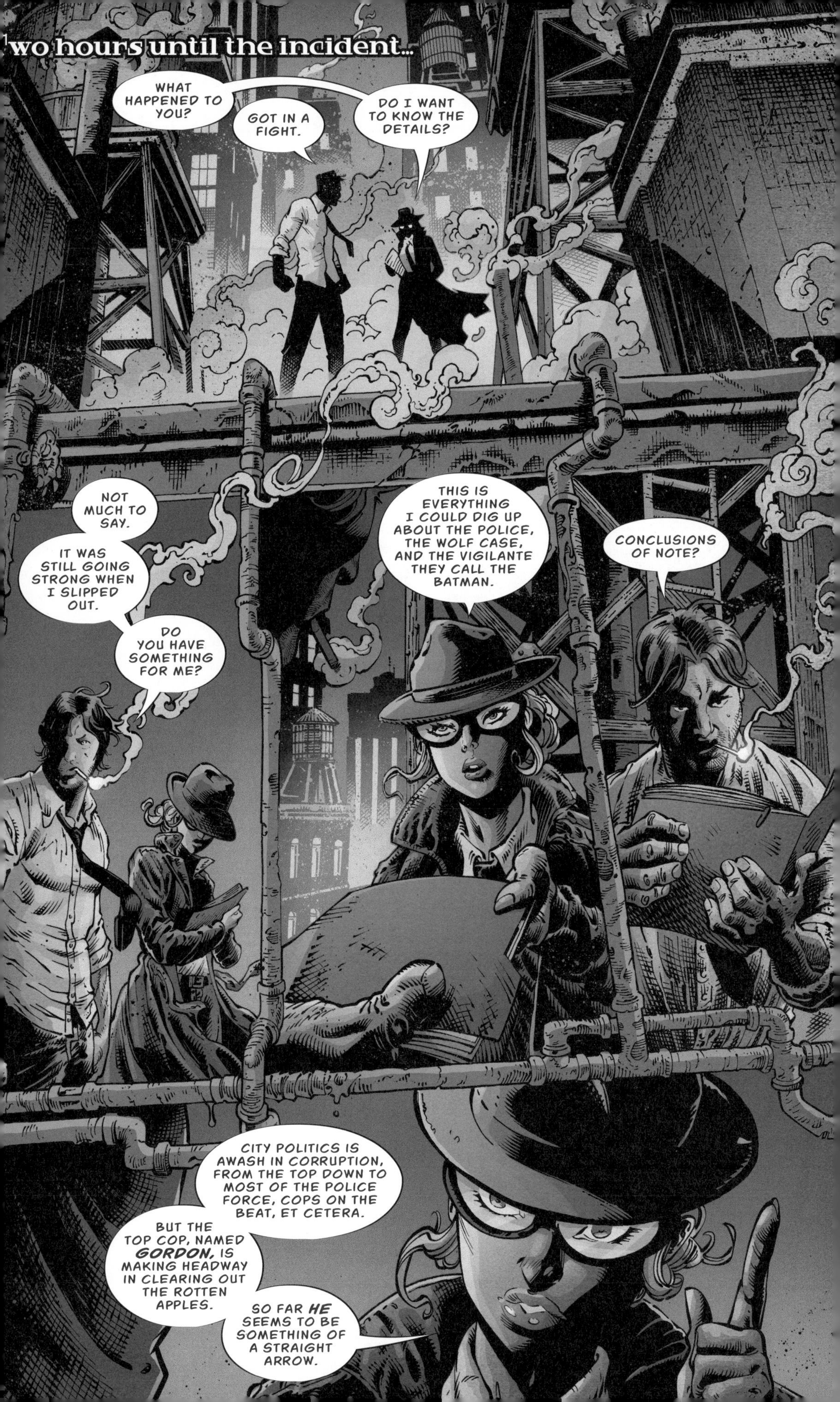
Two hours until the incident...
WHAT HAPPENED TO YOU?
GOT IN A FIGHT.
DO I WANT TO KNOW THE DETAILS?
NOT MUCH TO SAY.
IT WAS STILL GOING STRONG WHEN I SLIPPED OUT.
DO YOU HAVE SOMETHING FOR ME?
THIS IS EVERYTHING I COULD DIG UP ABOUT THE POLICE, THE WOLF CASE, AND THE VIGILANTE THEY CALL THE BATMAN.
CONCLUSIONS OF NOTE?
CITY POLITICS IS AWASH IN CORRUPTION, FROM THE TOP DOWN TO MOST OF THE POLICE FORCE, COPS ON THE BEAT, ET CETERA.
BUT THE TOP COP, NAMED GORDON, IS MAKING HEADWAY IN CLEARING OUT THE ROTTEN APPLES.
SO FAR HE SEEMS TO BE SOMETHING OF A STRAIGHT ARROW.

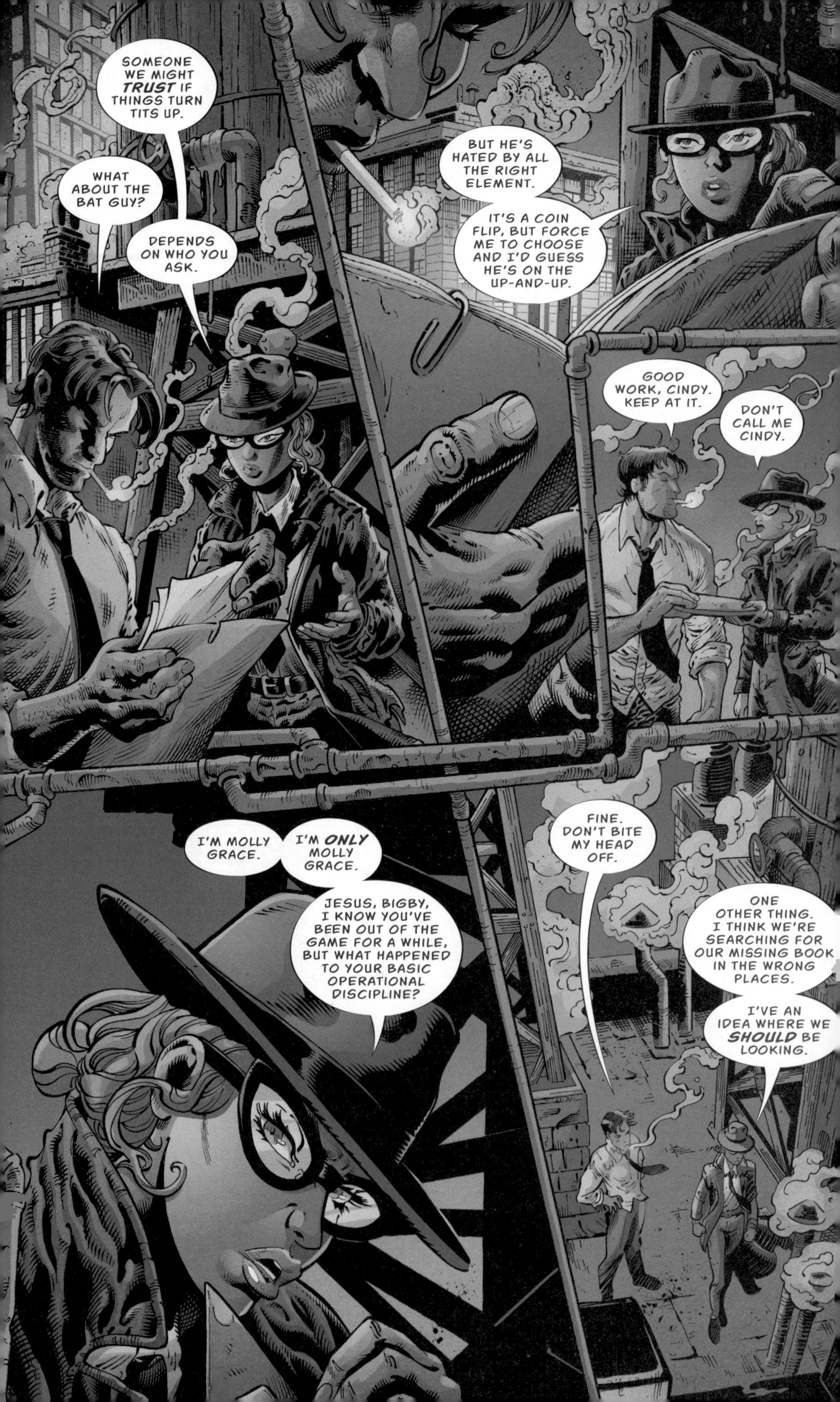
SOMEONE WE MIGHT TRUST IF THINGS TURN TITS UP.
WHAT ABOUT THE BAT GUY?
DEPENDS ON WHO YOU ASK.
BUT HE'S HATED BY ALL THE RIGHT ELEMENT.
IT'S A COIN FLIP, BUT FORCE ME TO CHOOSE AND I'D GUESS HE'S ON THE UP-AND-UP.
GOOD WORK, CINDY. KEEP AT IT.
DON'T CALL ME CINDY.
I'M MOLLY GRACE.
I'M ONLY MOLLY GRACE.
JESUS, BIGBY, I KNOW YOU'VE BEEN OUT OF THE GAME FOR A WHILE, BUT WHAT HAPPENED TO YOUR BASIC OPERATIONAL DISCIPLINE?
FINE. DON'T BITE MY HEAD OFF.
ONE OTHER THING. I THINK WE'RE SEARCHING FOR OUR MISSING BOOK IN THE WRONG PLACES.
I'VE AN IDEA WHERE WE SHOULD BE LOOKING.

"MAYBE WE SHOULD GO WHERE EVERYONE'S CURRENTLY INTERESTED IN BOOKS."

Gotham City Hall.
Less than an hour until the incident...

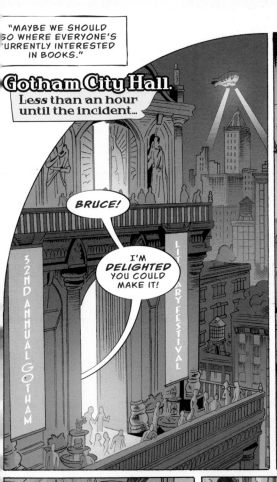

BRUCE!

I'M DELIGHTED YOU COULD MAKE IT!

32ND ANNUAL GOTHAM

LITERARY FESTIVAL

WOULDN'T MISS IT, MR. MAYOR.

ESPECIALLY SINCE YOU SINGLE-HANDEDLY PAID FOR ALL THIS FANCY FOOD AND TOP-NOTCH BOOZE, HUH?

SURE. LET'S SAY THAT.

I SWEAR, BRUCE, THIS YEAR'S LITERARY FESTIVAL IS GOING TO BE LIT!

A REGULAR JOCULARITATOR. NOT DULL, LIKE PEOPLE SAY.

EXCUSE ME, YOUR HONOR, BUT I'M COMPELLED TO MINGLE.

HA! I MADE A FUNNY!

PEOPLE DON'T THINK I'M FUNNY, BUT I'M DELIGHTFULLY FUNNY!

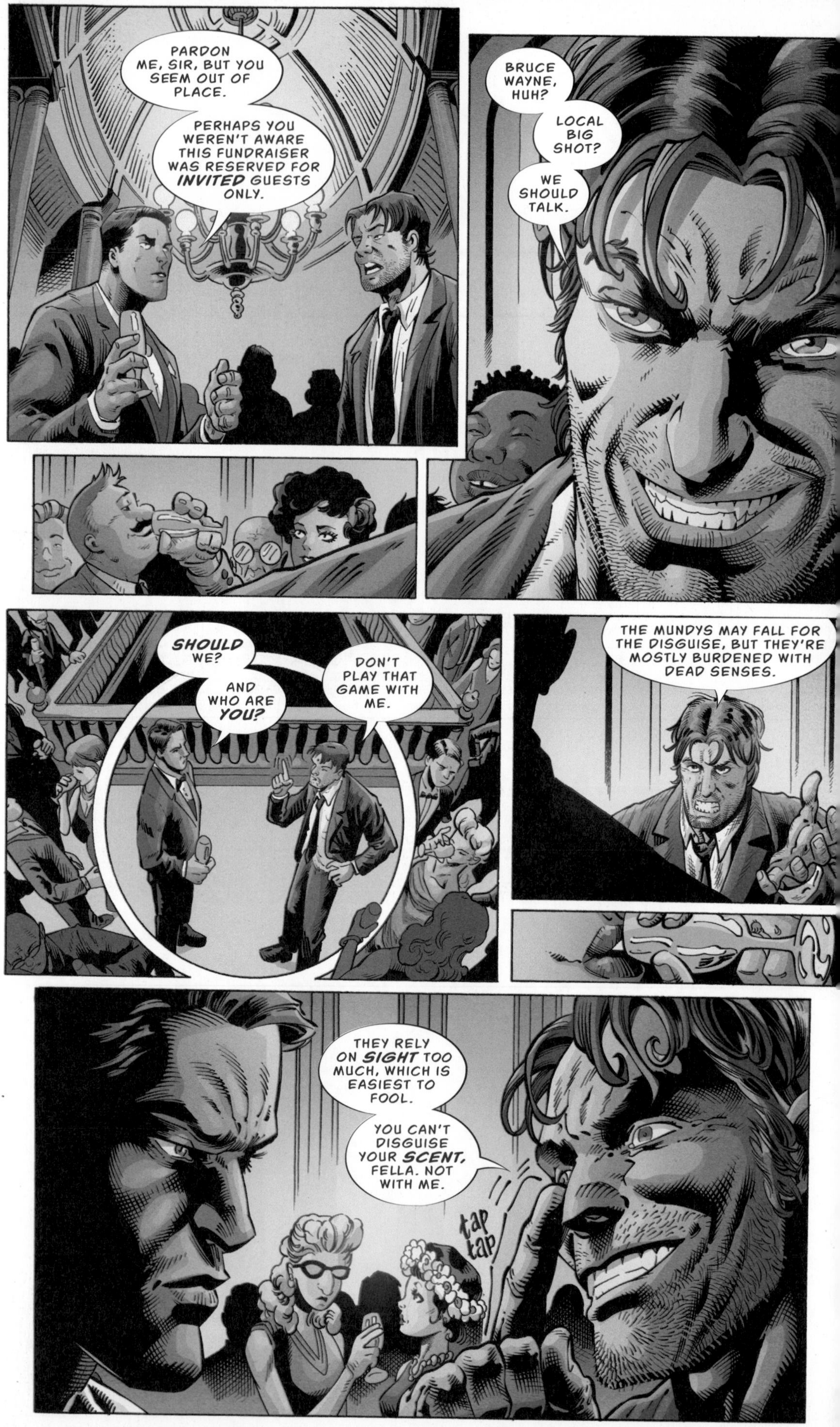
PARDON ME, SIR, BUT YOU SEEM OUT OF PLACE.
PERHAPS YOU WEREN'T AWARE THIS FUNDRAISER WAS RESERVED FOR INVITED GUESTS ONLY.
BRUCE WAYNE, HUH?
LOCAL BIG SHOT?
WE SHOULD TALK.
SHOULD WE?
AND WHO ARE YOU?
DON'T PLAY THAT GAME WITH ME.
THE MUNDYS MAY FALL FOR THE DISGUISE, BUT THEY'RE MOSTLY BURDENED WITH DEAD SENSES.
THEY RELY ON SIGHT TOO MUCH, WHICH IS EASIEST TO FOOL.
YOU CAN'T DISGUISE YOUR SCENT, FELLA. NOT WITH ME.
tap tap

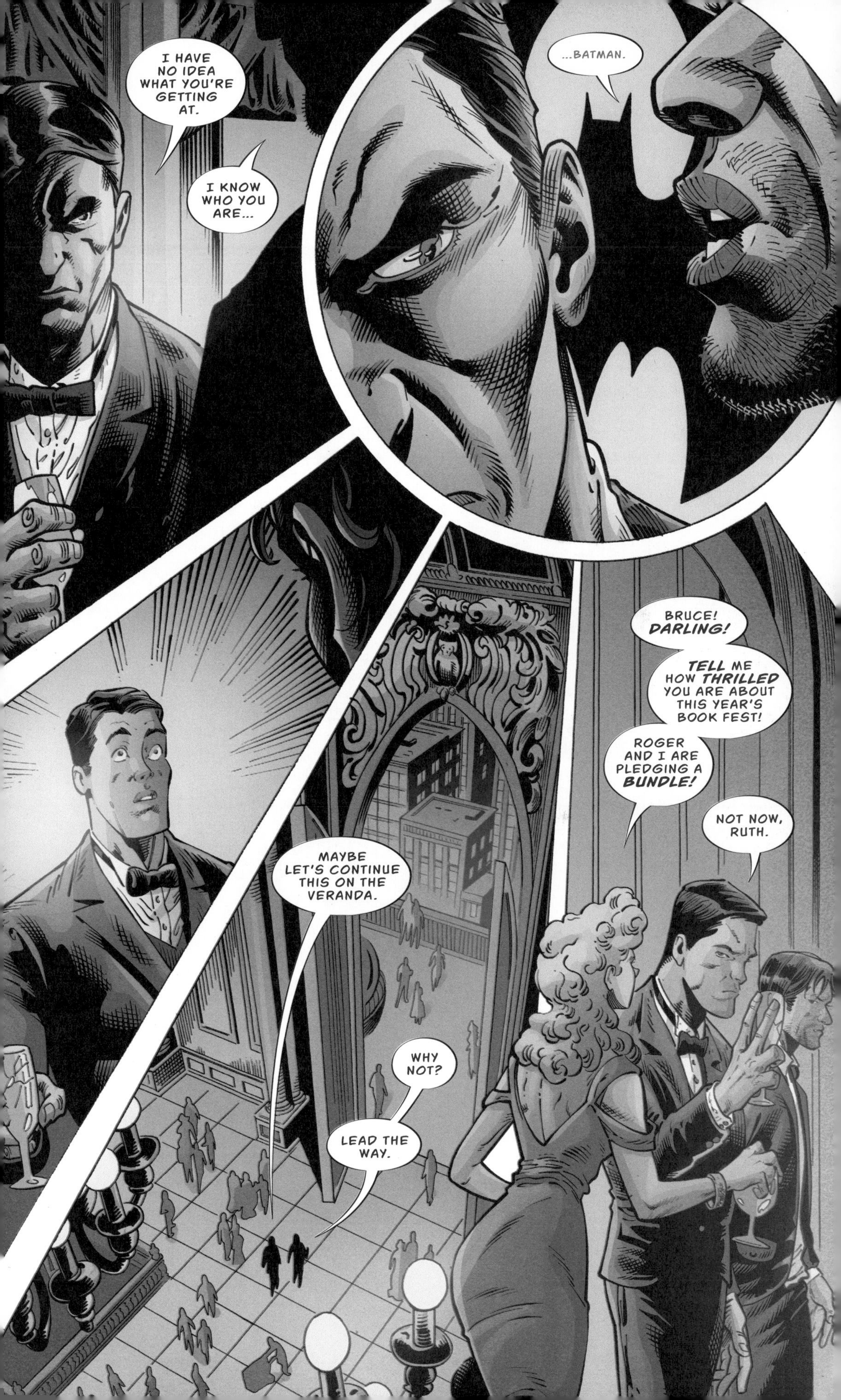
I HAVE NO IDEA WHAT YOU'RE GETTING AT.
I KNOW WHO YOU ARE...
...BATMAN.
BRUCE! DARLING!
TELL ME HOW THRILLED YOU ARE ABOUT THIS YEAR'S BOOK FEST!
ROGER AND I ARE PLEDGING A BUNDLE!
NOT NOW, RUTH.
MAYBE LET'S CONTINUE THIS ON THE VERANDA.
WHY NOT?
LEAD THE WAY.

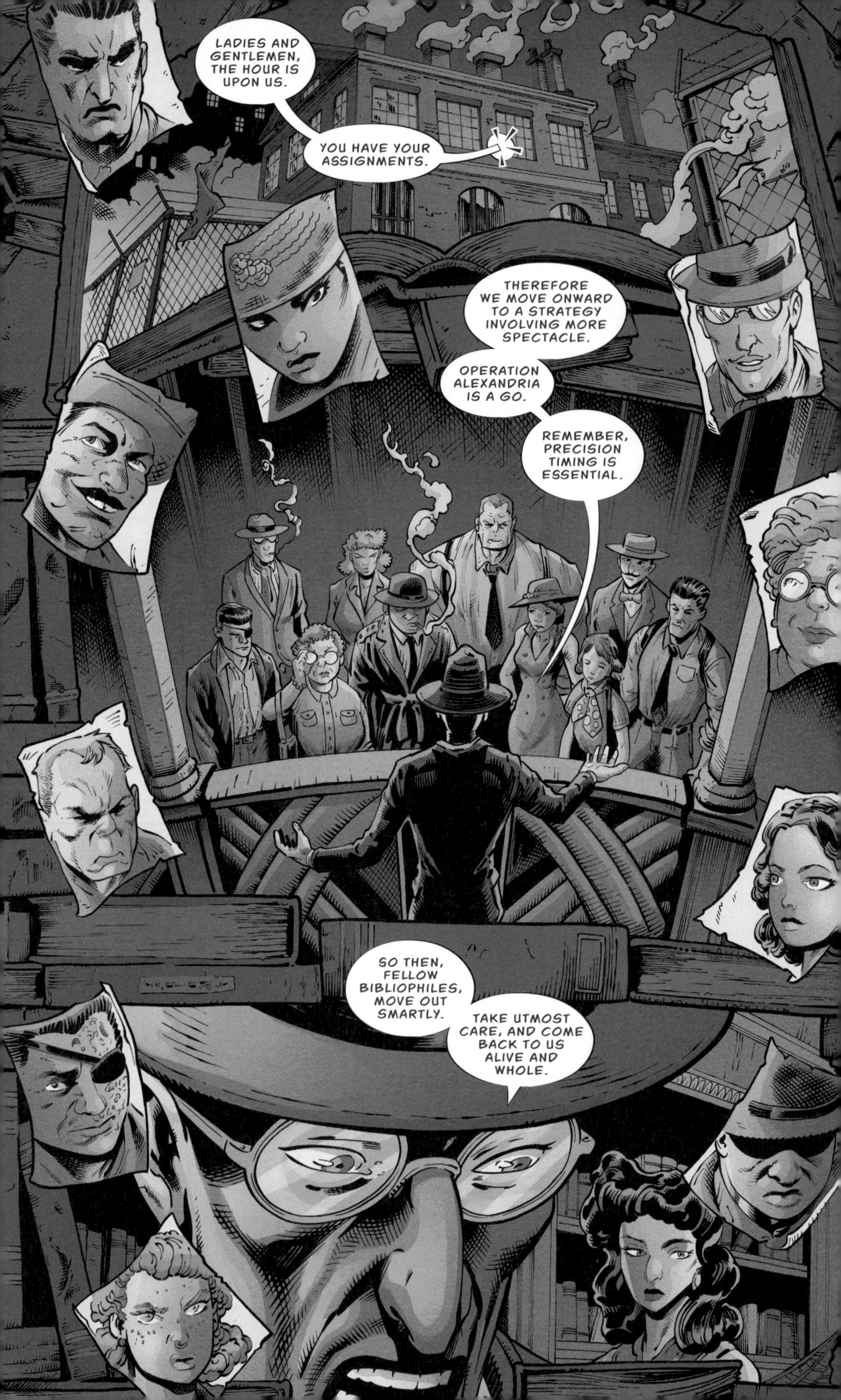

LADIES AND GENTLEMEN, THE HOUR IS UPON US.
YOU HAVE YOUR ASSIGNMENTS.
THEREFORE WE MOVE ONWARD TO A STRATEGY INVOLVING MORE SPECTACLE.
OPERATION ALEXANDRIA IS A GO.
REMEMBER, PRECISION TIMING IS ESSENTIAL.
SO THEN, FELLOW BIBLIOPHILES, MOVE OUT SMARTLY.
TAKE UTMOST CARE, AND COME BACK TO US ALIVE AND WHOLE.

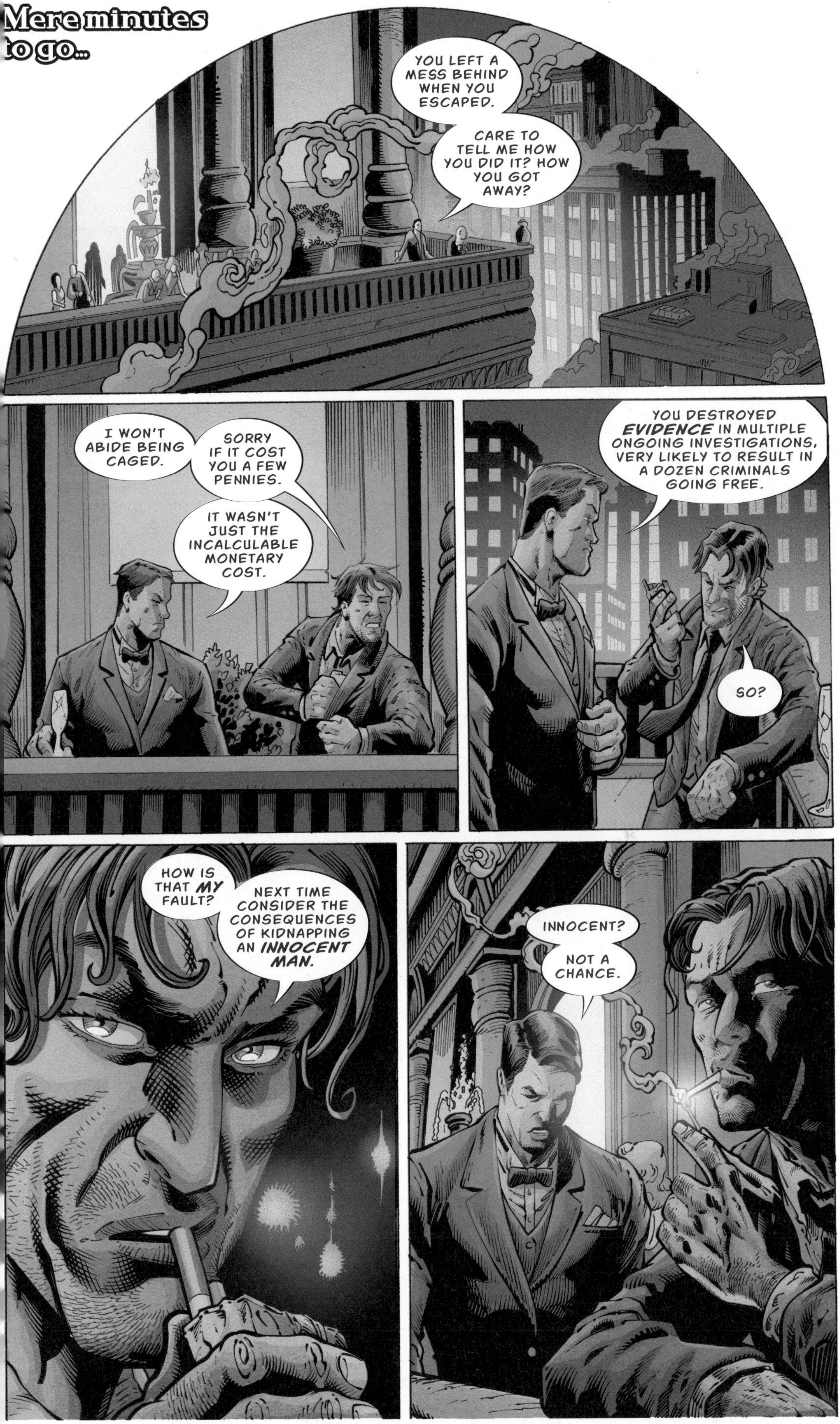
Mere minutes to go...
YOU LEFT A MESS BEHIND WHEN YOU ESCAPED.
CARE TO TELL ME HOW YOU DID IT? HOW YOU GOT AWAY?
I WON'T ABIDE BEING CAGED.
SORRY IF IT COST YOU A FEW PENNIES.
IT WASN'T JUST THE INCALCULABLE MONETARY COST.
YOU DESTROYED EVIDENCE IN MULTIPLE ONGOING INVESTIGATIONS, VERY LIKELY TO RESULT IN A DOZEN CRIMINALS GOING FREE.
SO?
HOW IS THAT MY FAULT?
NEXT TIME CONSIDER THE CONSEQUENCES OF KIDNAPPING AN INNOCENT MAN.
INNOCENT?
NOT A CHANCE.

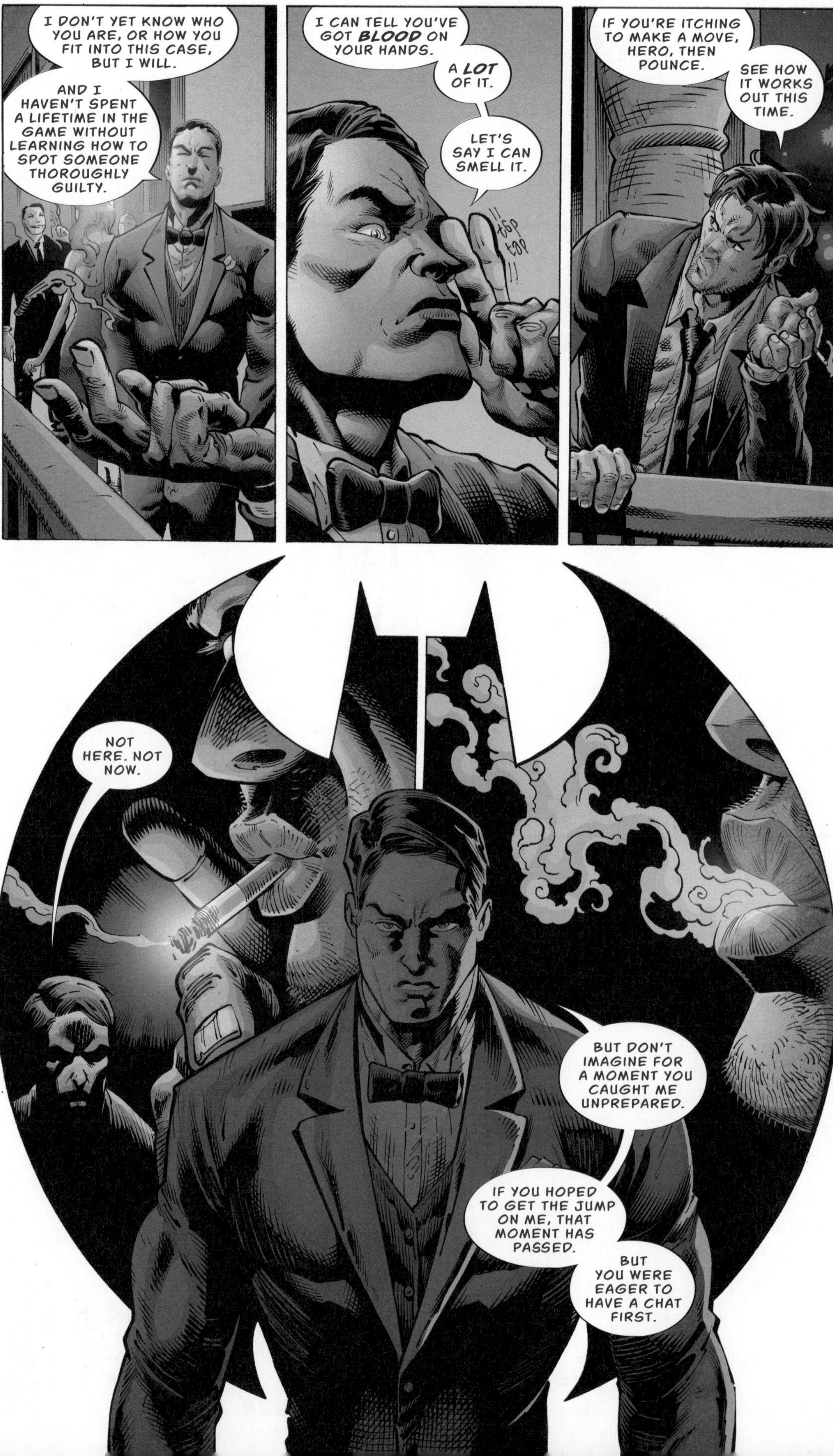
I DON'T YET KNOW WHO YOU ARE, OR HOW YOU FIT INTO THIS CASE, BUT I WILL.
AND I HAVEN'T SPENT A LIFETIME IN THE GAME WITHOUT LEARNING HOW TO SPOT SOMEONE THOROUGHLY GUILTY.
I CAN TELL YOU'VE GOT BLOOD ON YOUR HANDS.
A LOT OF IT.
LET'S SAY I CAN SMELL IT.
tap tap
IF YOU'RE ITCHING TO MAKE A MOVE, HERO, THEN POUNCE.
SEE HOW IT WORKS OUT THIS TIME.
NOT HERE. NOT NOW.
BUT DON'T IMAGINE FOR A MOMENT YOU CAUGHT ME UNPREPARED.
IF YOU HOPED TO GET THE JUMP ON ME, THAT MOMENT HAS PASSED.
BUT YOU WERE EAGER TO HAVE A CHAT FIRST.

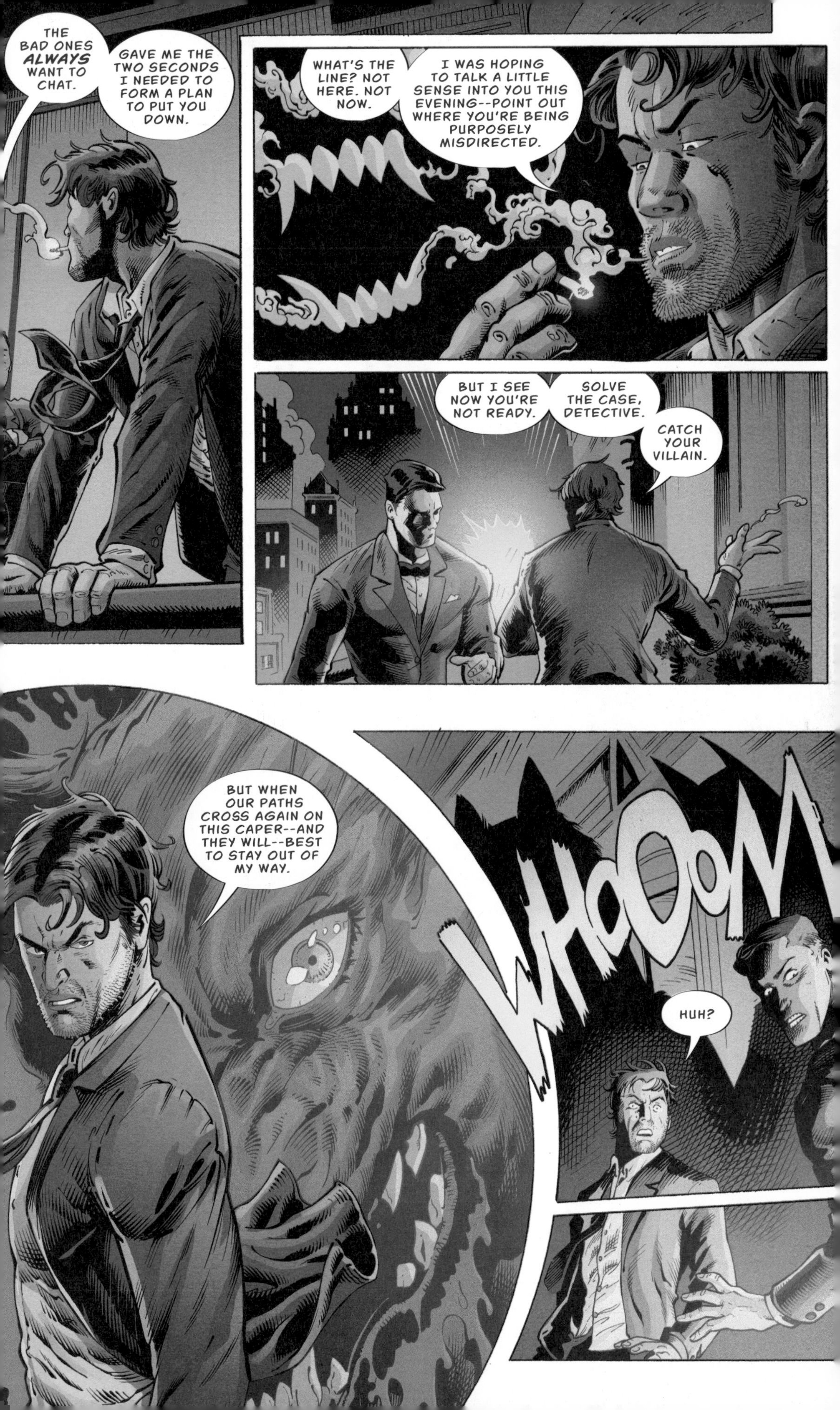

THE BAD ONES ALWAYS WANT TO CHAT.
GAVE ME THE TWO SECONDS I NEEDED TO FORM A PLAN TO PUT YOU DOWN.
WHAT'S THE LINE? NOT HERE. NOT NOW.
I WAS HOPING TO TALK A LITTLE SENSE INTO YOU THIS EVENING--POINT OUT WHERE YOU'RE BEING PURPOSELY MISDIRECTED.
BUT I SEE NOW YOU'RE NOT READY.
SOLVE THE CASE, DETECTIVE.
CATCH YOUR VILLAIN.
BUT WHEN OUR PATHS CROSS AGAIN ON THIS CAPER--AND THEY WILL--BEST TO STAY OUT OF MY WAY.
WHOOOM
HUH?

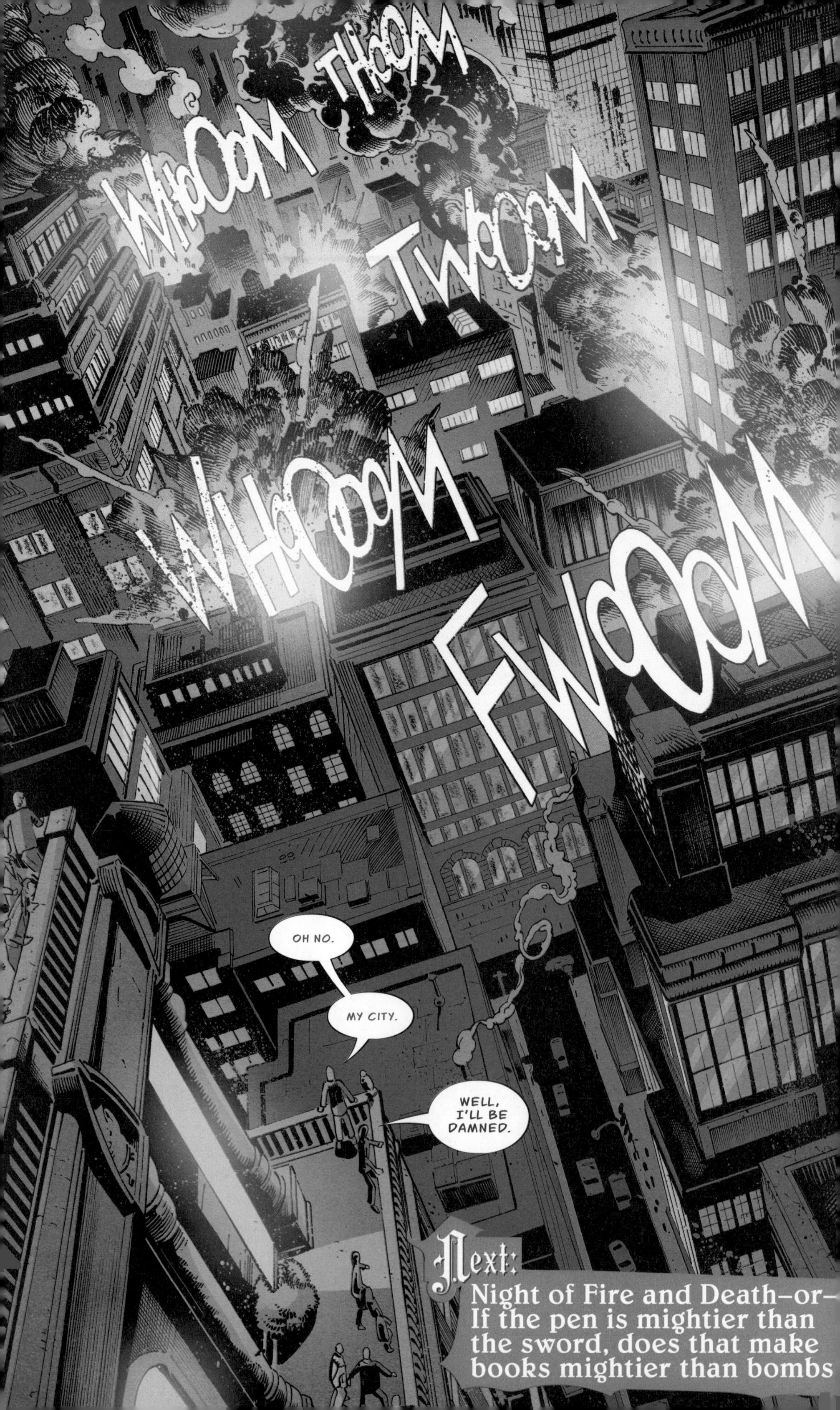
WHOOM
THOOM
TWOOM
WHOOM
FWOOM
OH NO.
MY CITY.
WELL, I'LL BE DAMNED.
Next:
Night of Fire and Death—or—
If the pen is mightier than the sword, does that make books mightier than bombs

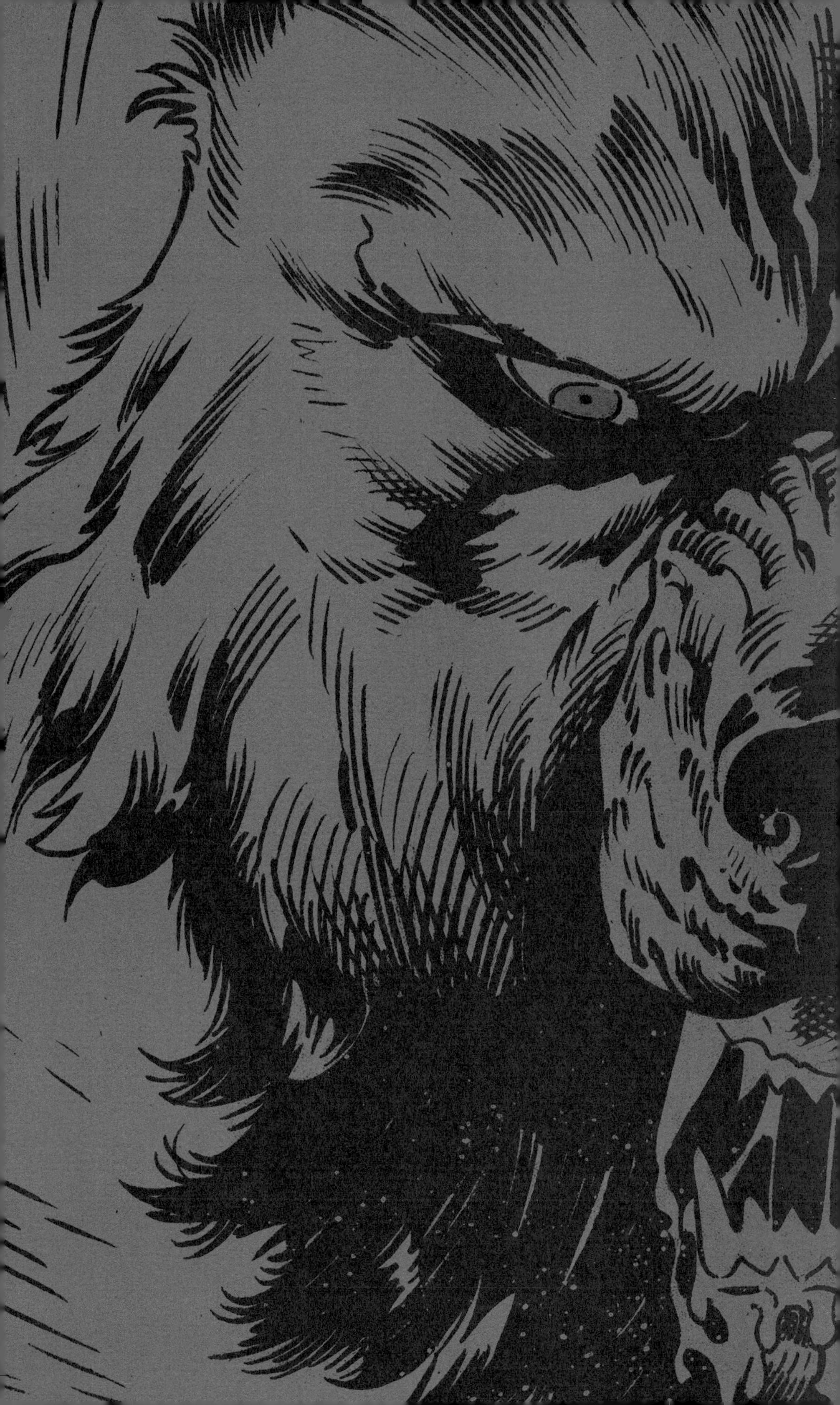

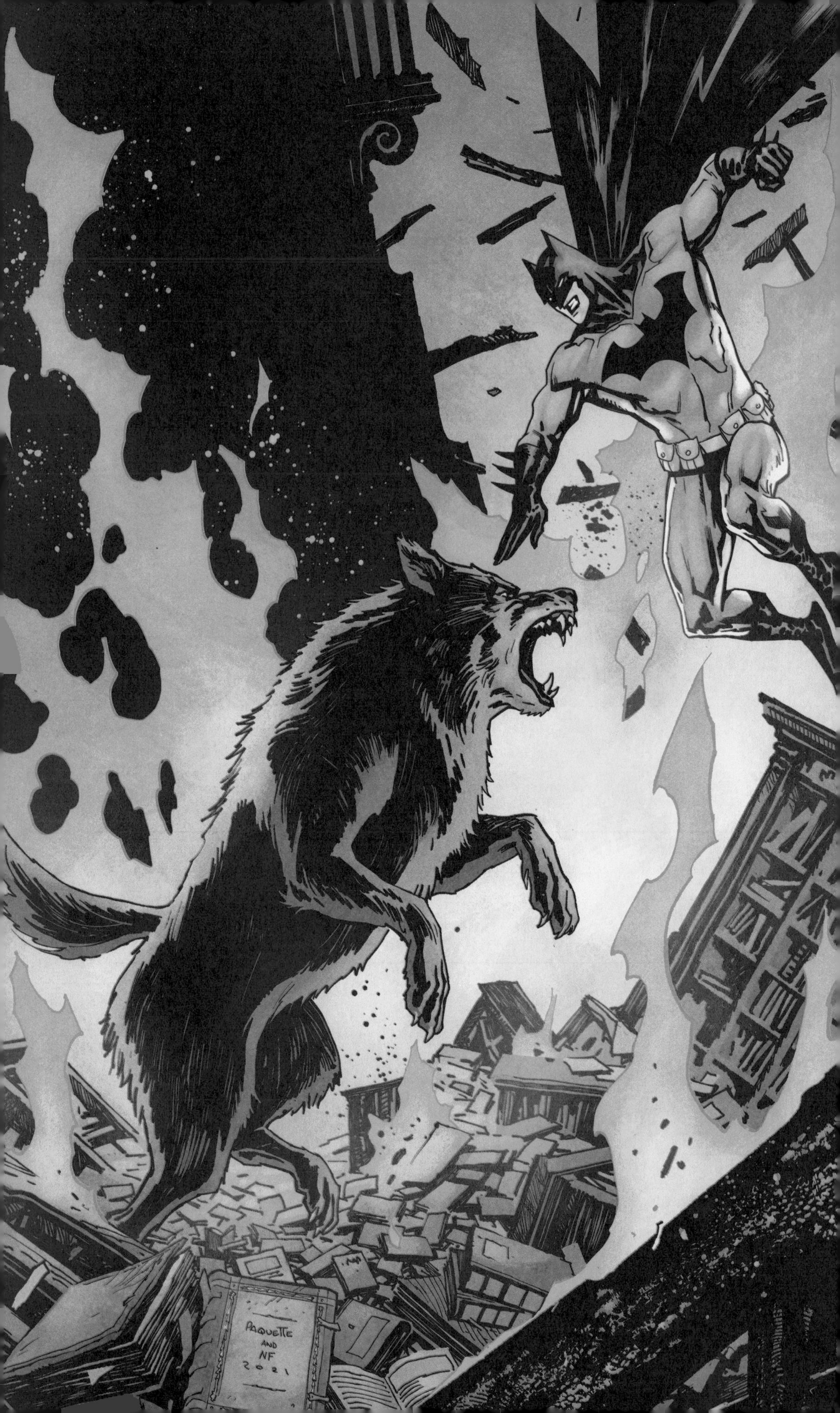
PAQUETTE
AND
NF
2021

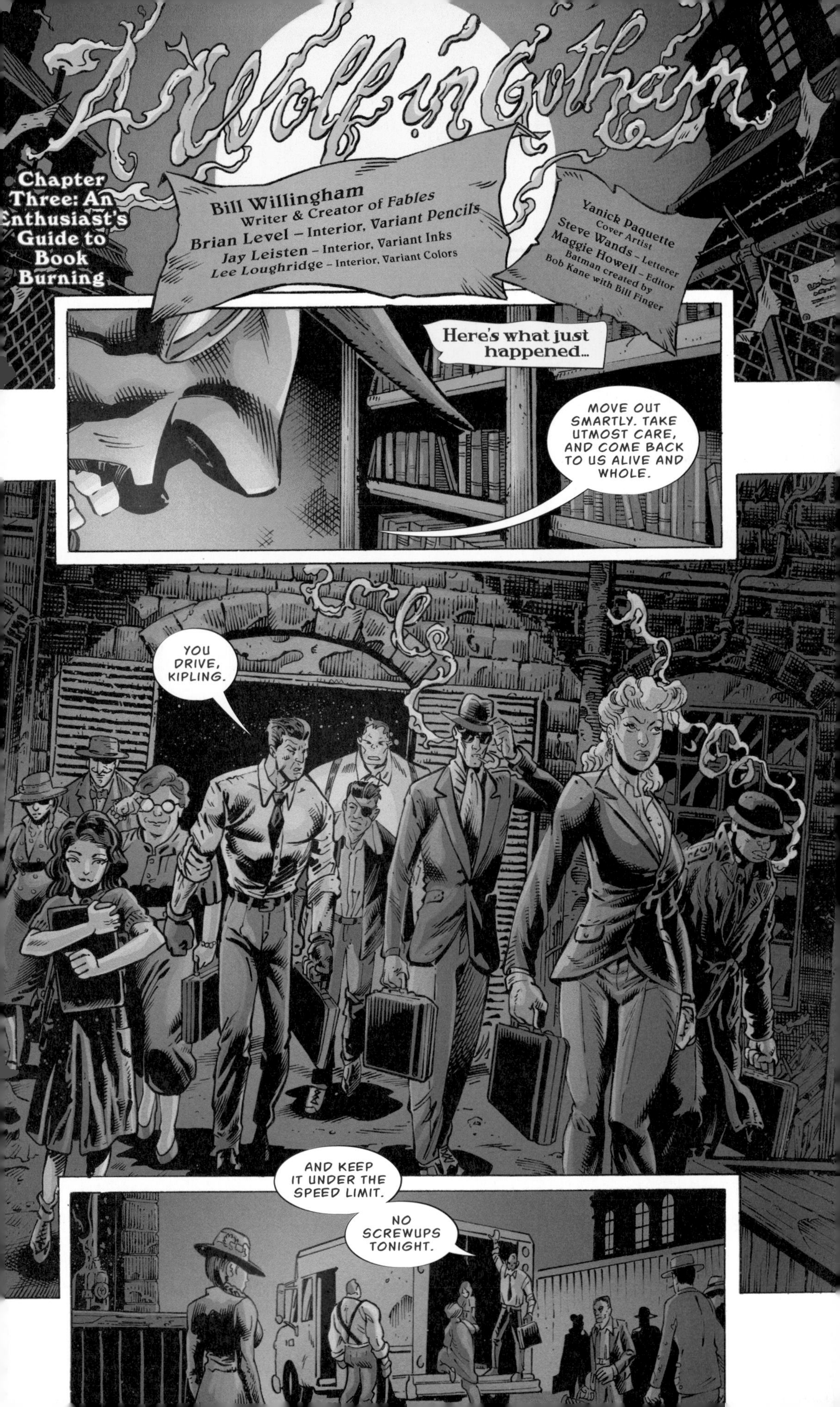
A Wolf in Gotham
Chapter Three: An Enthusiast's Guide to Book Burning
Bill Willingham Writer & Creator of Fables
Brian Level – Interior, Variant Pencils
Jay Leisten – Interior, Variant Inks
Lee Loughridge – Interior, Variant Colors
Yanick Paquette Cover Artist
Steve Wands – Letterer
Maggie Howell – Editor
Batman created by Bob Kane with Bill Finger
Here's what just happened...
MOVE OUT SMARTLY. TAKE UTMOST CARE, AND COME BACK TO US ALIVE AND WHOLE.
YOU DRIVE, KIPLING.
AND KEEP IT UNDER THE SPEED LIMIT.
NO SCREWUPS TONIGHT.

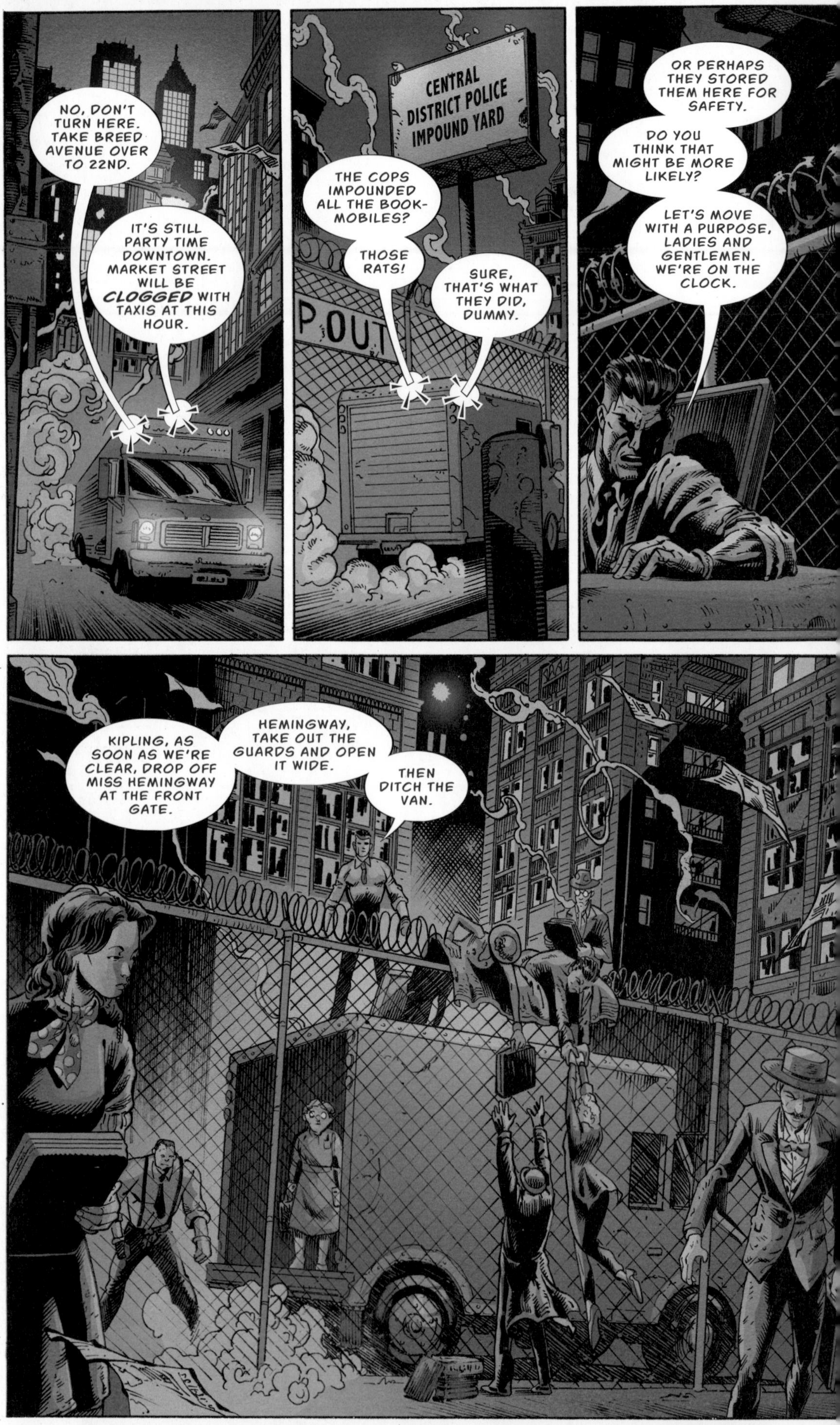
NO, DON'T TURN HERE. TAKE BREED AVENUE OVER TO 22ND.
IT'S STILL PARTY TIME DOWNTOWN. MARKET STREET WILL BE *CLOGGED* WITH TAXIS AT THIS HOUR.
CENTRAL DISTRICT POLICE IMPOUND YARD
THE COPS IMPOUNDED ALL THE BOOK-MOBILES?
THOSE RATS!
SURE, THAT'S WHAT THEY DID, DUMMY.
POUT
OR PERHAPS THEY STORED THEM HERE FOR SAFETY.
DO YOU THINK THAT MIGHT BE MORE LIKELY?
LET'S MOVE WITH A PURPOSE, LADIES AND GENTLEMEN. WE'RE ON THE CLOCK.
KIPLING, AS SOON AS WE'RE CLEAR, DROP OFF MISS HEMINGWAY AT THE FRONT GATE.
HEMINGWAY, TAKE OUT THE GUARDS AND OPEN IT WIDE.
THEN DITCH THE VAN.

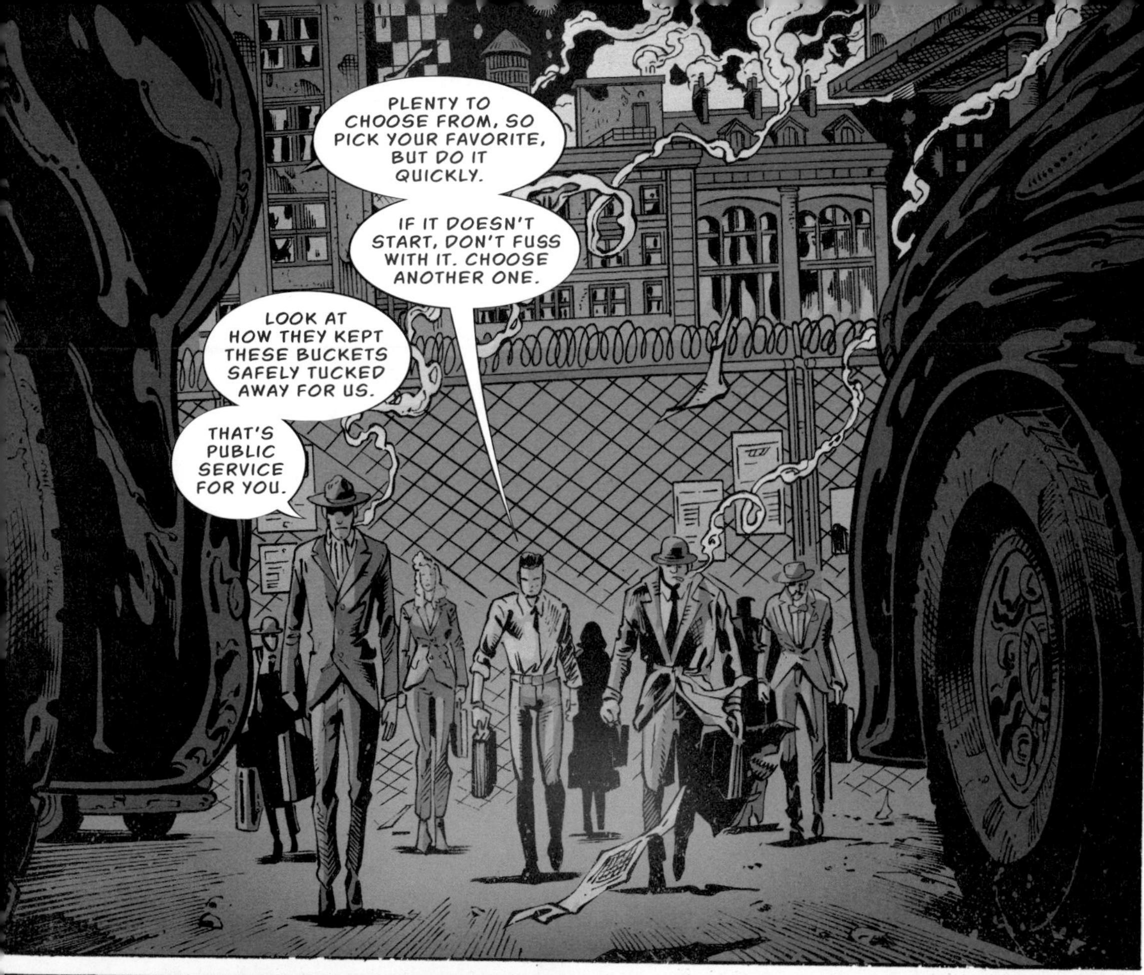
PLENTY TO CHOOSE FROM, SO PICK YOUR FAVORITE, BUT DO IT QUICKLY.
IF IT DOESN'T START, DON'T FUSS WITH IT. CHOOSE ANOTHER ONE.
LOOK AT HOW THEY KEPT THESE BUCKETS SAFELY TUCKED AWAY FOR US.
THAT'S PUBLIC SERVICE FOR YOU.

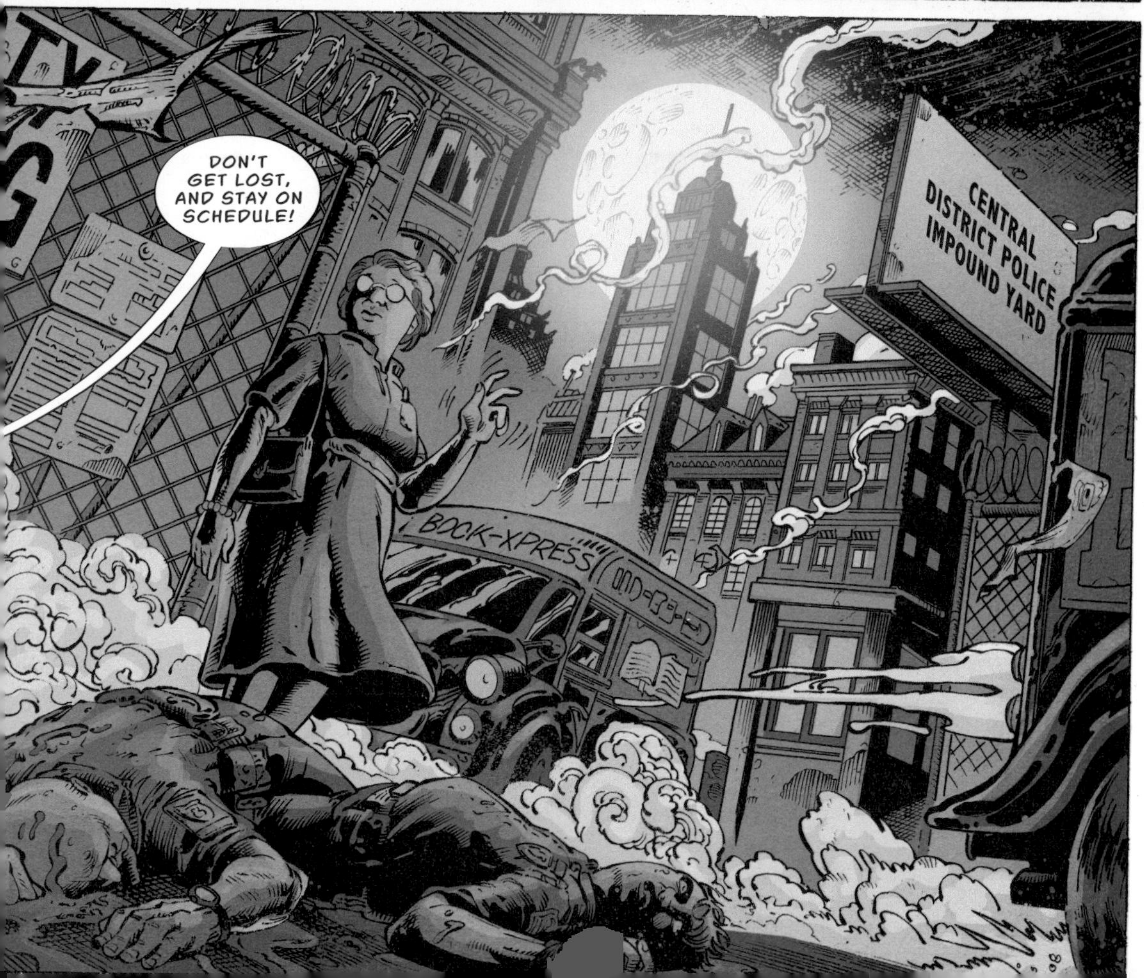
DON'T GET LOST, AND STAY ON SCHEDULE!
CENTRAL DISTRICT POLICE IMPOUND YARD
BOOK-XPRESS

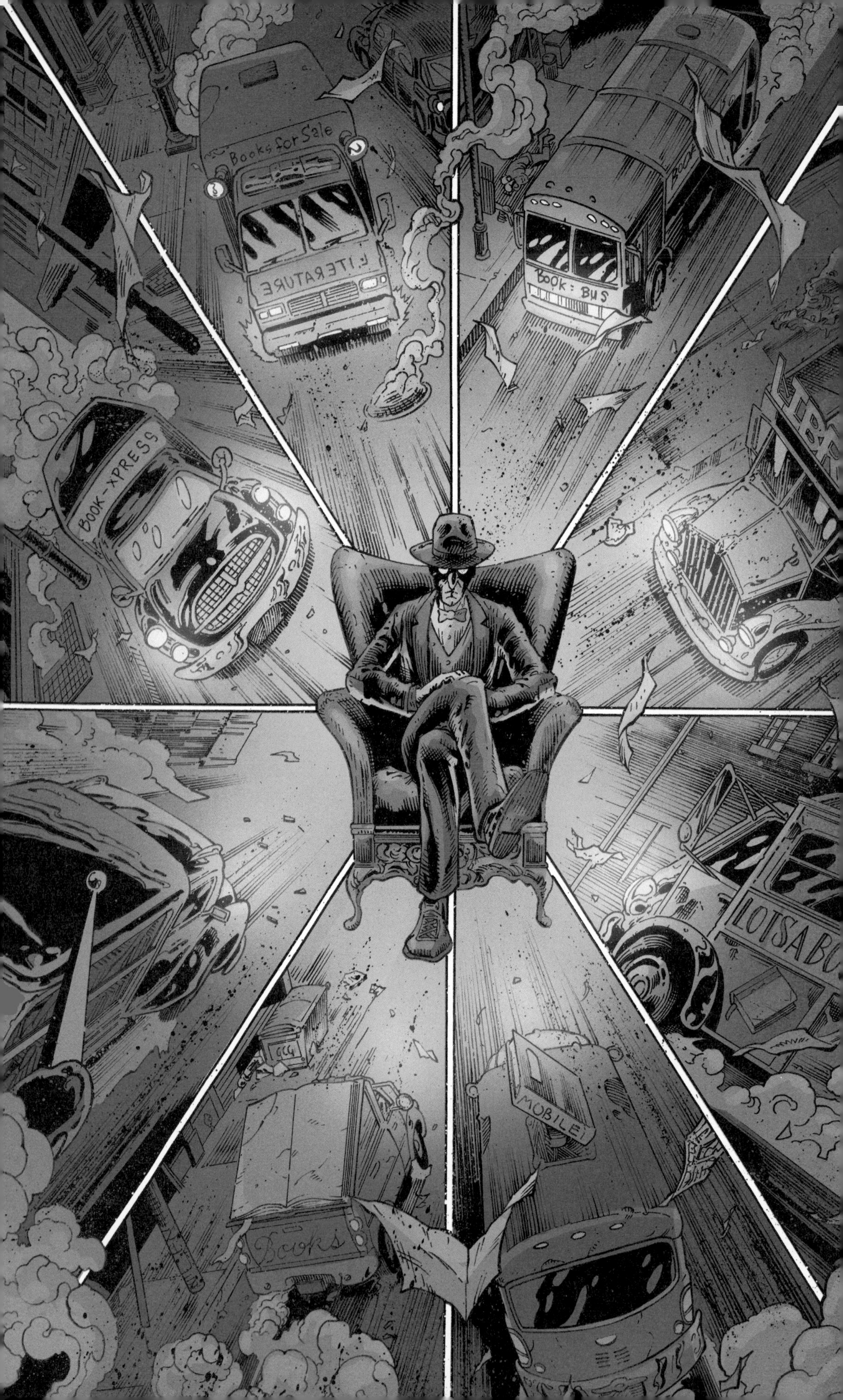
Books for Sale
LITERATURE
BOOK : BUS
BOOK-XPRESS
MOBILE
Books

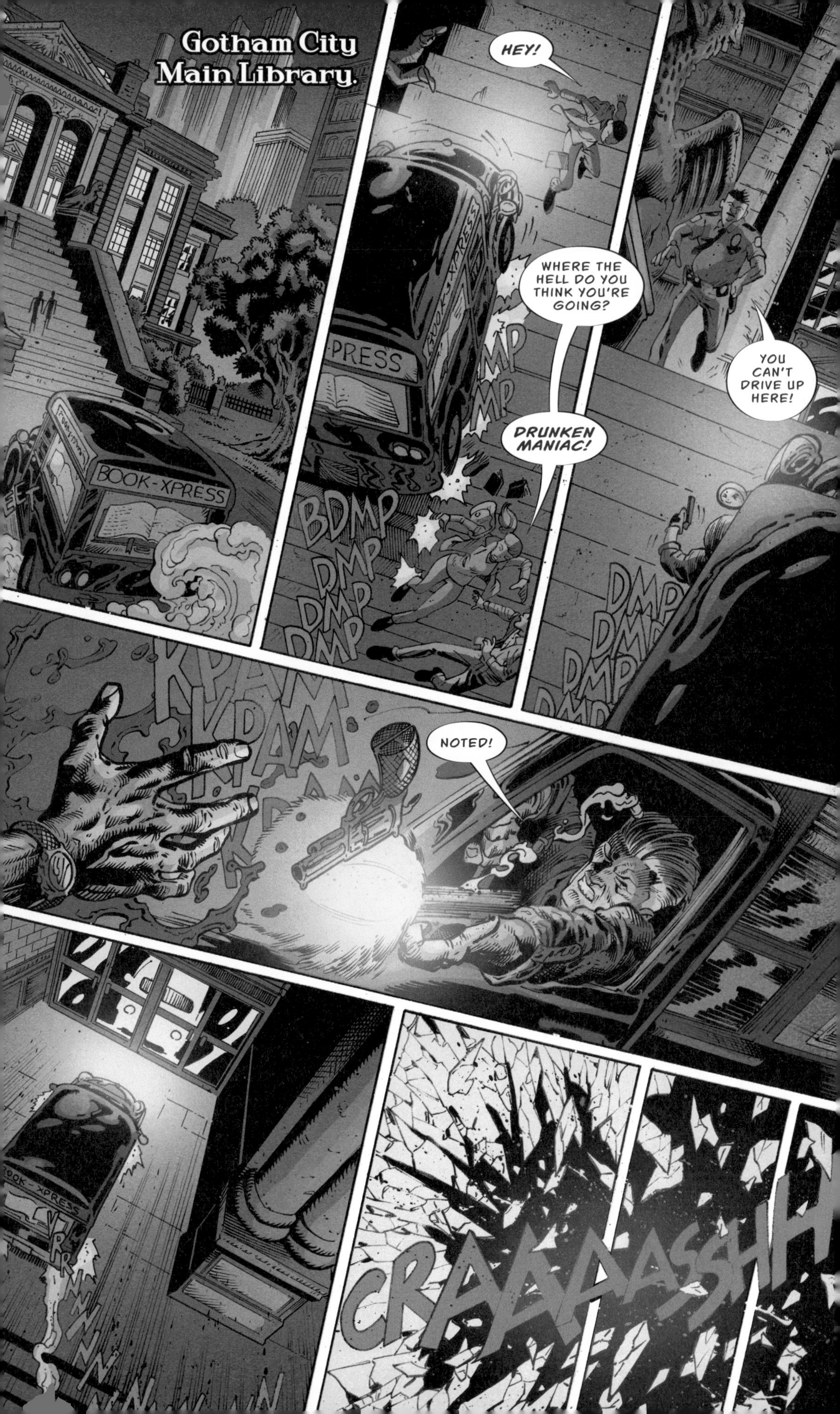
Gotham City Main Library.
BOOK-XPRESS
HEY!
WHERE THE HELL DO YOU THINK YOU'RE GOING?
DRUNKEN MANIAC!
BDMP DMP DMP DMP
YOU CAN'T DRIVE UP HERE!
DMP DMP DMP DMP
KPAM KPAM
NOTED!
BOOK-XPRESS
CRAAASHH

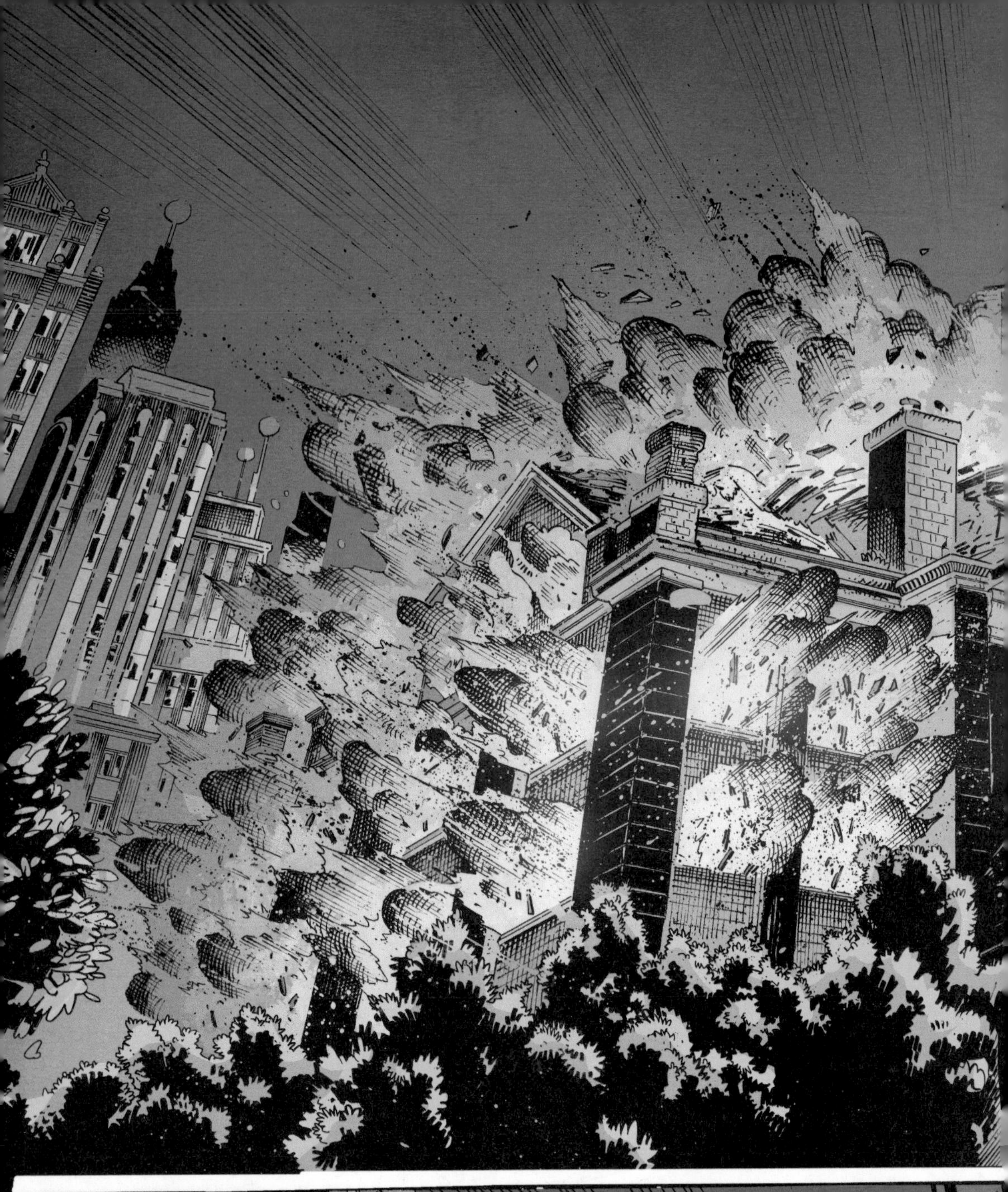

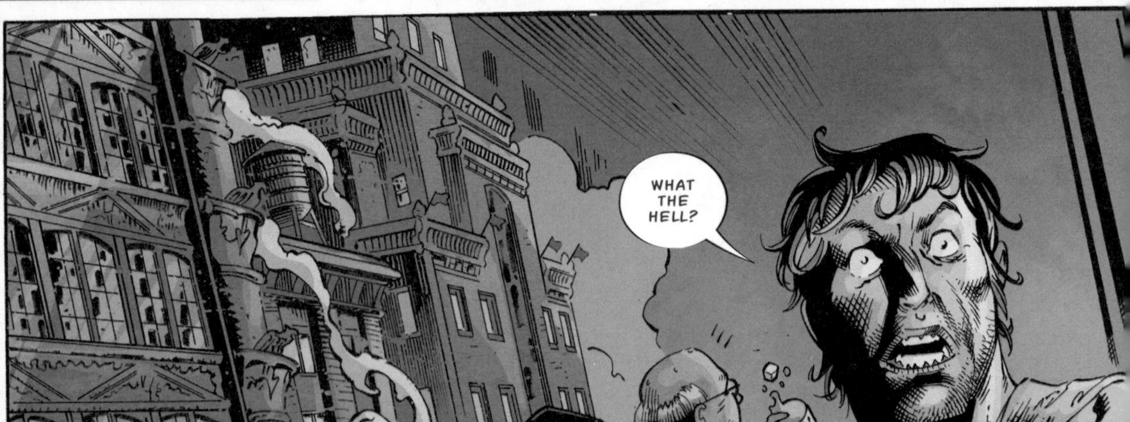
WHAT THE HELL?

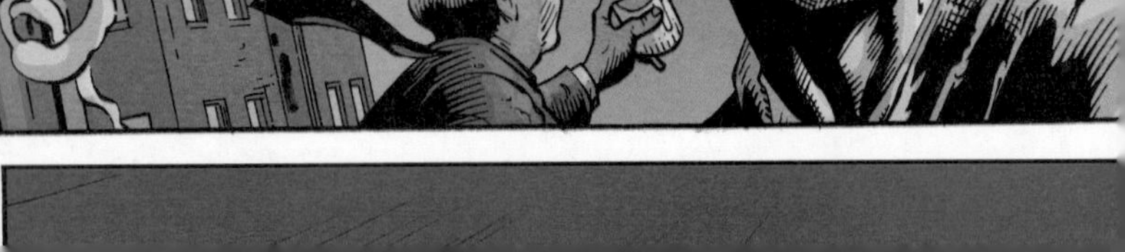

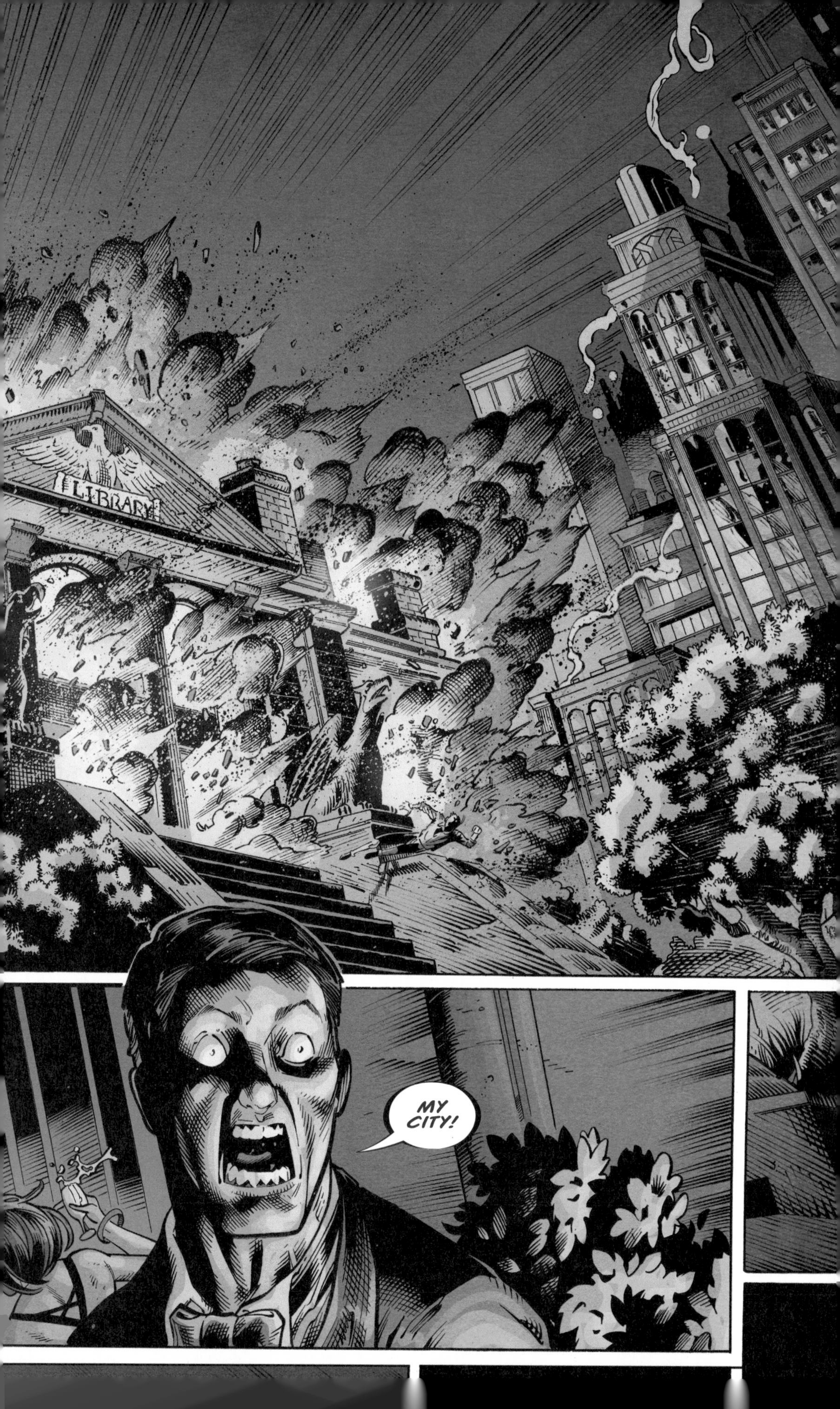

LIBRARY
MY CITY!

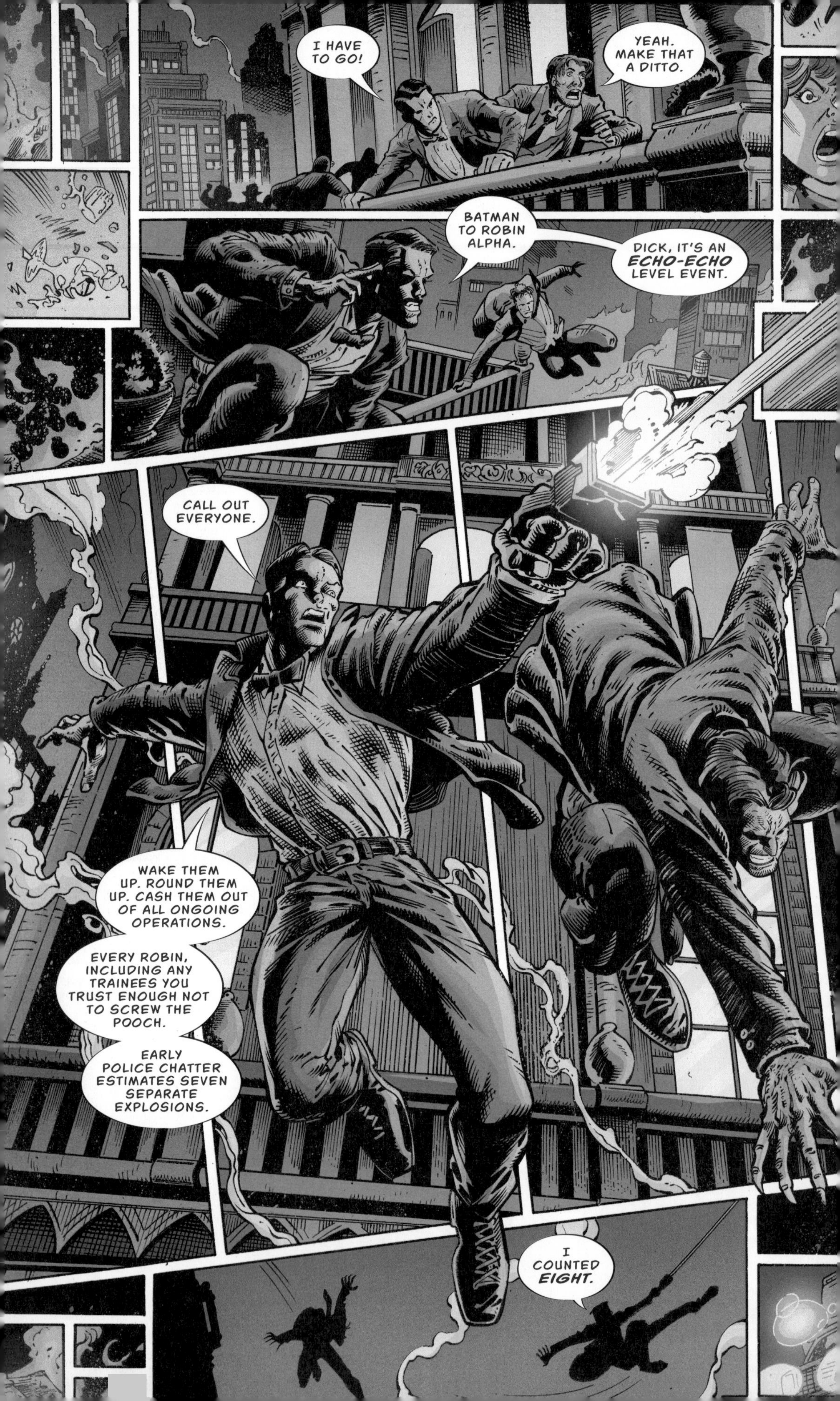
I HAVE TO GO!
YEAH. MAKE THAT A DITTO.
BATMAN TO ROBIN ALPHA.
DICK, IT'S AN *ECHO-ECHO* LEVEL EVENT.
CALL OUT EVERYONE.
WAKE THEM UP. ROUND THEM UP. CASH THEM OUT OF ALL ONGOING OPERATIONS.
EVERY ROBIN, INCLUDING ANY TRAINEES YOU TRUST ENOUGH NOT TO SCREW THE POOCH.
EARLY POLICE CHATTER ESTIMATES SEVEN SEPARATE EXPLOSIONS.
I COUNTED *EIGHT.*

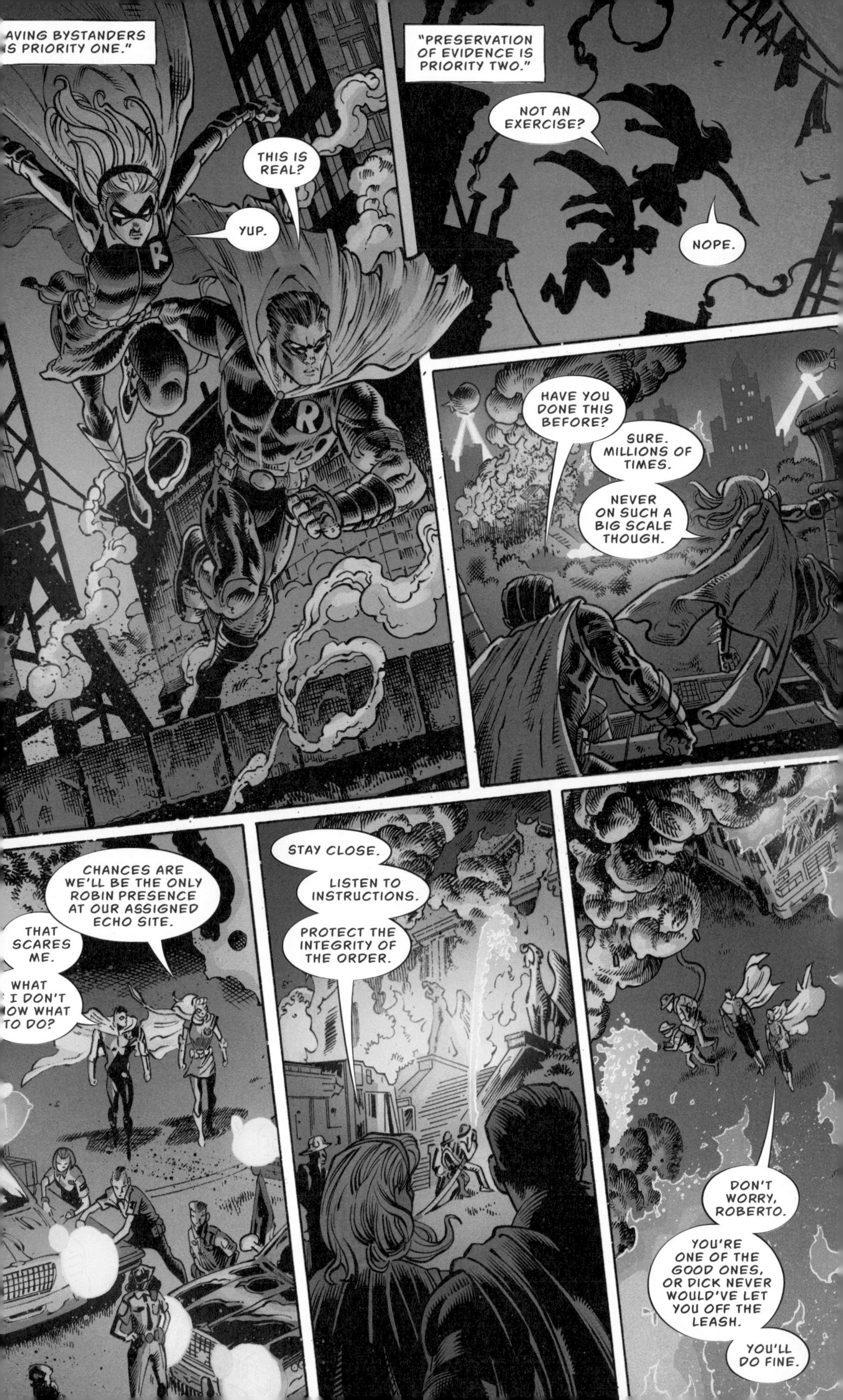

AVING BYSTANDERS
S PRIORITY ONE."
THIS IS REAL?
YUP.
"PRESERVATION OF EVIDENCE IS PRIORITY TWO."
NOT AN EXERCISE?
NOPE.
HAVE YOU DONE THIS BEFORE?
SURE. MILLIONS OF TIMES.
NEVER ON SUCH A BIG SCALE THOUGH.
CHANCES ARE WE'LL BE THE ONLY ROBIN PRESENCE AT OUR ASSIGNED ECHO SITE.
THAT SCARES ME.
WHAT I DON'T OW WHAT TO DO?
STAY CLOSE.
LISTEN TO INSTRUCTIONS.
PROTECT THE INTEGRITY OF THE ORDER.
DON'T WORRY, ROBERTO.
YOU'RE ONE OF THE GOOD ONES, OR DICK NEVER WOULD'VE LET YOU OFF THE LEASH.
YOU'LL DO FINE.

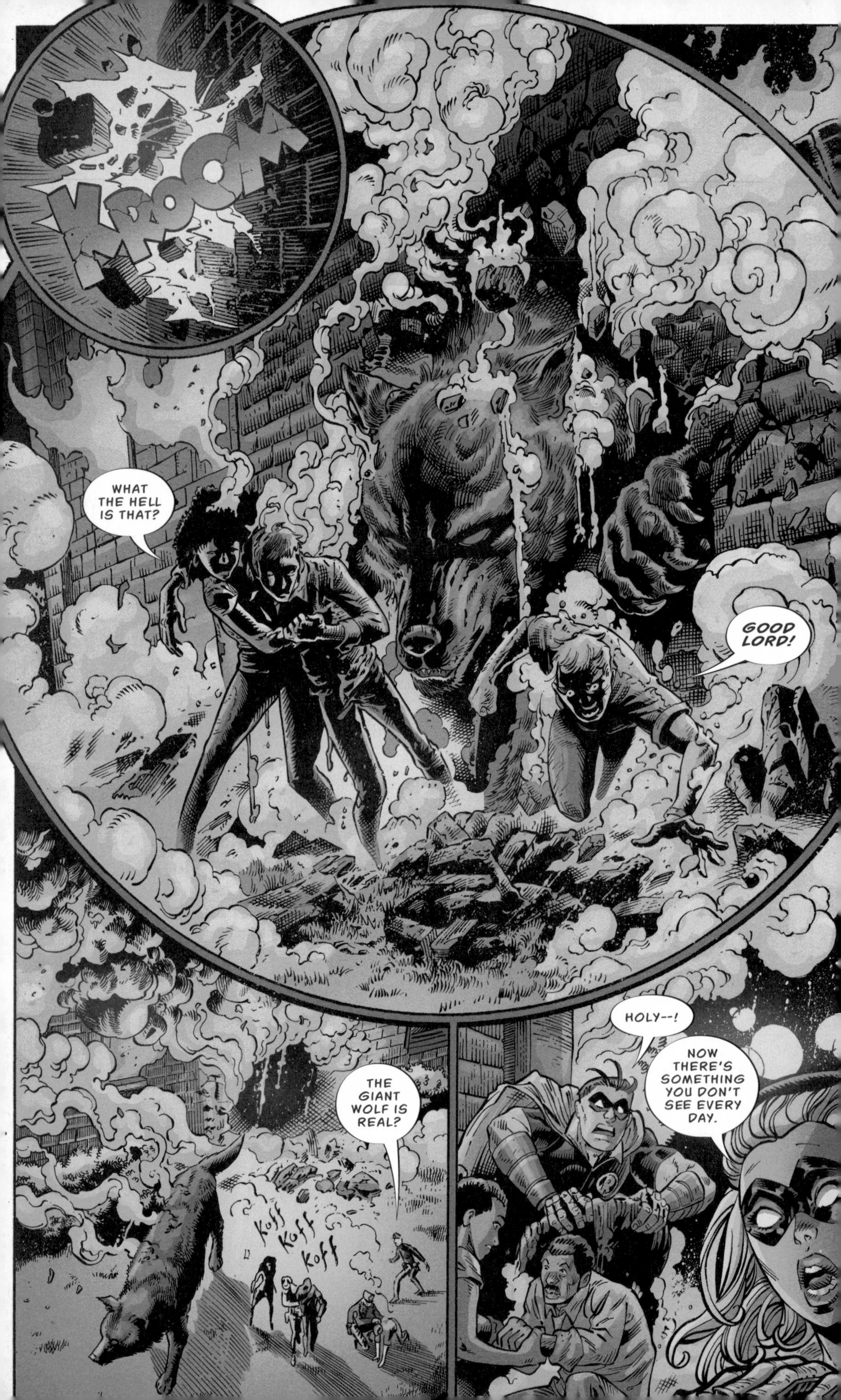
KROOM
WHAT THE HELL IS THAT?
GOOD LORD!
THE GIANT WOLF IS REAL?
KOFF KOFF KOFF
HOLY--!
NOW THERE'S SOMETHING YOU DON'T SEE EVERY DAY.

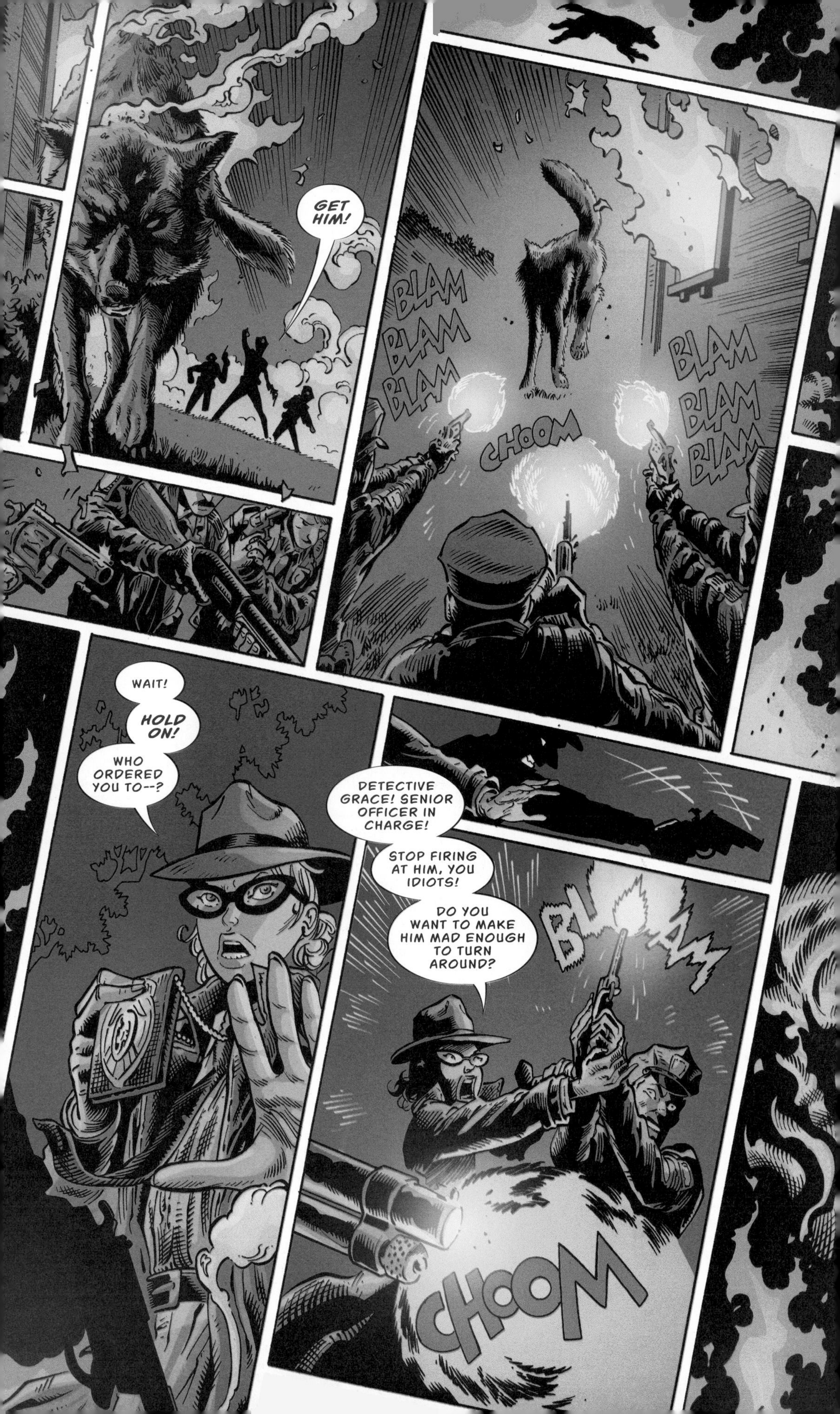

GET HIM!
BLAM BLAM BLAM
CHOOM
BLAM BLAM BLAM
WAIT!
HOLD ON!
WHO ORDERED YOU TO--?
DETECTIVE GRACE! SENIOR OFFICER IN CHARGE!
STOP FIRING AT HIM, YOU IDIOTS!
DO YOU WANT TO MAKE HIM MAD ENOUGH TO TURN AROUND?
CHOOM

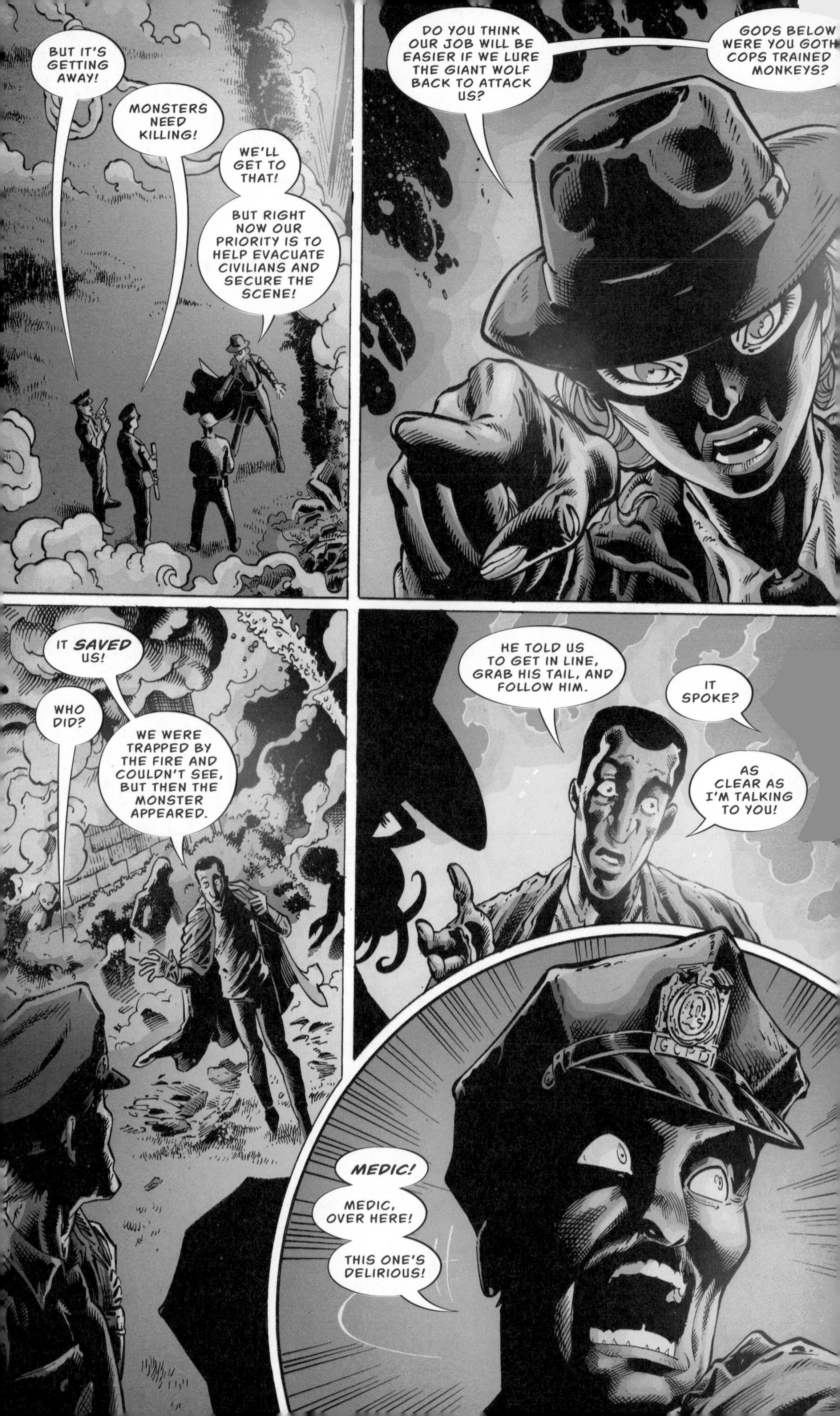
BUT IT'S GETTING AWAY!
MONSTERS NEED KILLING!
WE'LL GET TO THAT!
BUT RIGHT NOW OUR PRIORITY IS TO HELP EVACUATE CIVILIANS AND SECURE THE SCENE!
DO YOU THINK OUR JOB WILL BE EASIER IF WE LURE THE GIANT WOLF BACK TO ATTACK US?
GODS BELOW WERE YOU GOTH COPS TRAINED MONKEYS?
IT SAVED US!
WHO DID?
WE WERE TRAPPED BY THE FIRE AND COULDN'T SEE, BUT THEN THE MONSTER APPEARED.
HE TOLD US TO GET IN LINE, GRAB HIS TAIL, AND FOLLOW HIM.
IT SPOKE?
AS CLEAR AS I'M TALKING TO YOU!
GCPD
MEDIC!
MEDIC, OVER HERE!
THIS ONE'S DELIRIOUS!

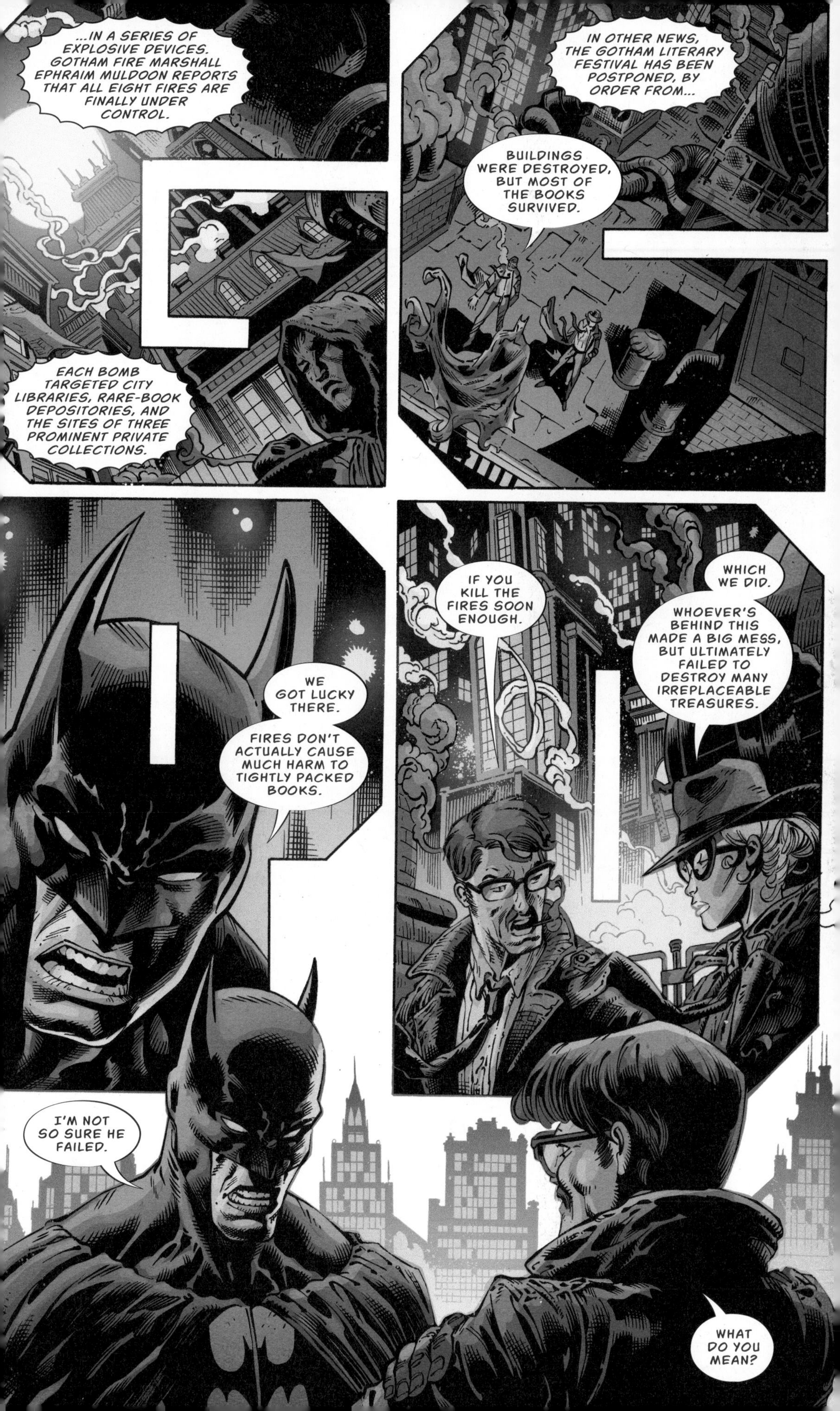
...IN A SERIES OF EXPLOSIVE DEVICES. GOTHAM FIRE MARSHALL EPHRAIM MULDOON REPORTS THAT ALL EIGHT FIRES ARE FINALLY UNDER CONTROL.
EACH BOMB TARGETED CITY LIBRARIES, RARE-BOOK DEPOSITORIES, AND THE SITES OF THREE PROMINENT PRIVATE COLLECTIONS.
IN OTHER NEWS, THE GOTHAM LITERARY FESTIVAL HAS BEEN POSTPONED, BY ORDER FROM...
BUILDINGS WERE DESTROYED, BUT MOST OF THE BOOKS SURVIVED.
WE GOT LUCKY THERE.
FIRES DON'T ACTUALLY CAUSE MUCH HARM TO TIGHTLY PACKED BOOKS.
IF YOU KILL THE FIRES SOON ENOUGH.
WHICH WE DID.
WHOEVER'S BEHIND THIS MADE A BIG MESS, BUT ULTIMATELY FAILED TO DESTROY MANY IRREPLACEABLE TREASURES.
I'M NOT SO SURE HE FAILED.
WHAT DO YOU MEAN?

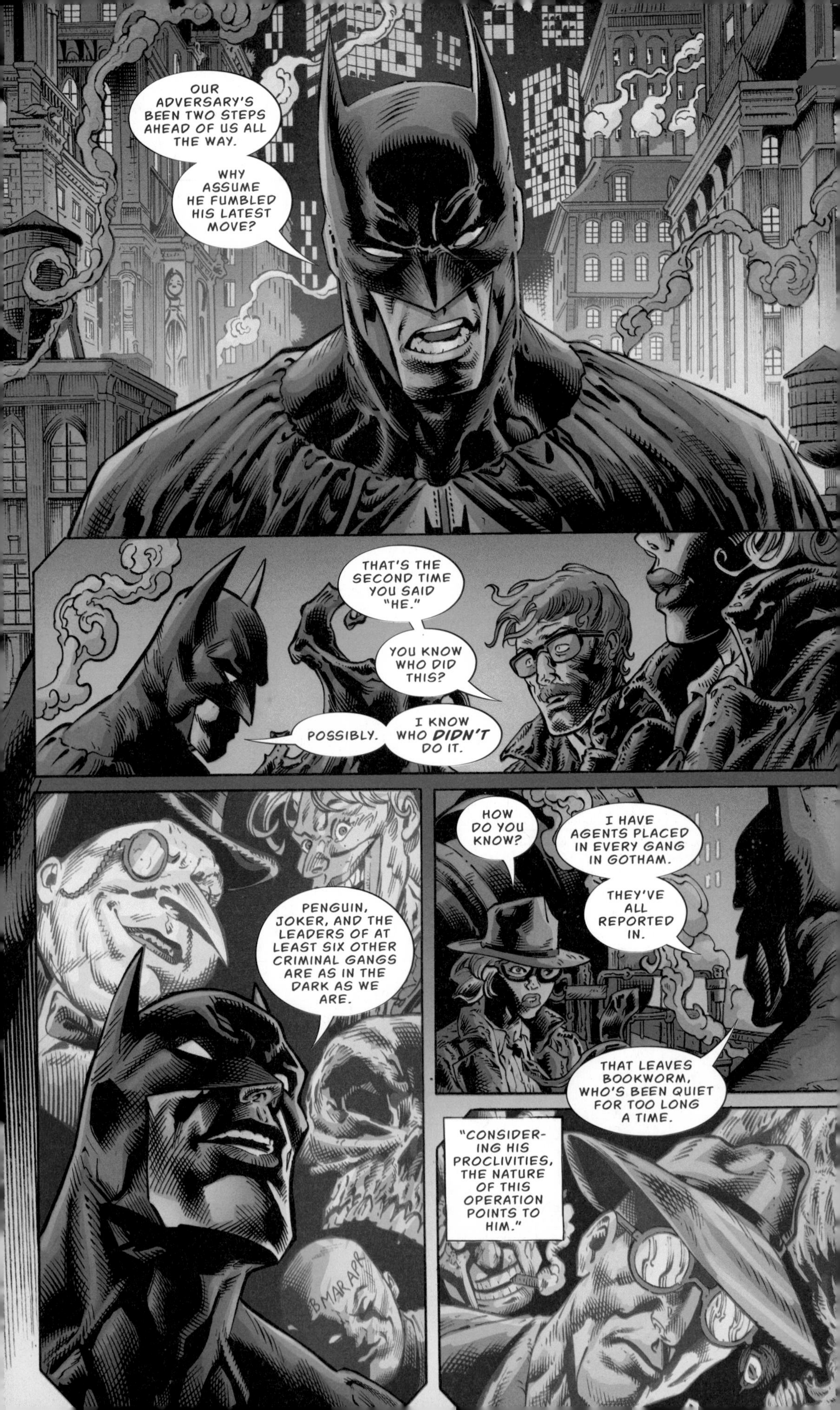

OUR ADVERSARY'S BEEN TWO STEPS AHEAD OF US ALL THE WAY.
WHY ASSUME HE FUMBLED HIS LATEST MOVE?
THAT'S THE SECOND TIME YOU SAID "HE."
YOU KNOW WHO DID THIS?
POSSIBLY.
I KNOW WHO *DIDN'T* DO IT.
PENGUIN, JOKER, AND THE LEADERS OF AT LEAST SIX OTHER CRIMINAL GANGS ARE AS IN THE DARK AS WE ARE.
HOW DO YOU KNOW?
I HAVE AGENTS PLACED IN EVERY GANG IN GOTHAM.
THEY'VE ALL REPORTED IN.
THAT LEAVES BOOKWORM, WHO'S BEEN QUIET FOR TOO LONG A TIME.
"CONSIDERING HIS PROCLIVITIES, THE NATURE OF THIS OPERATION POINTS TO HIM."

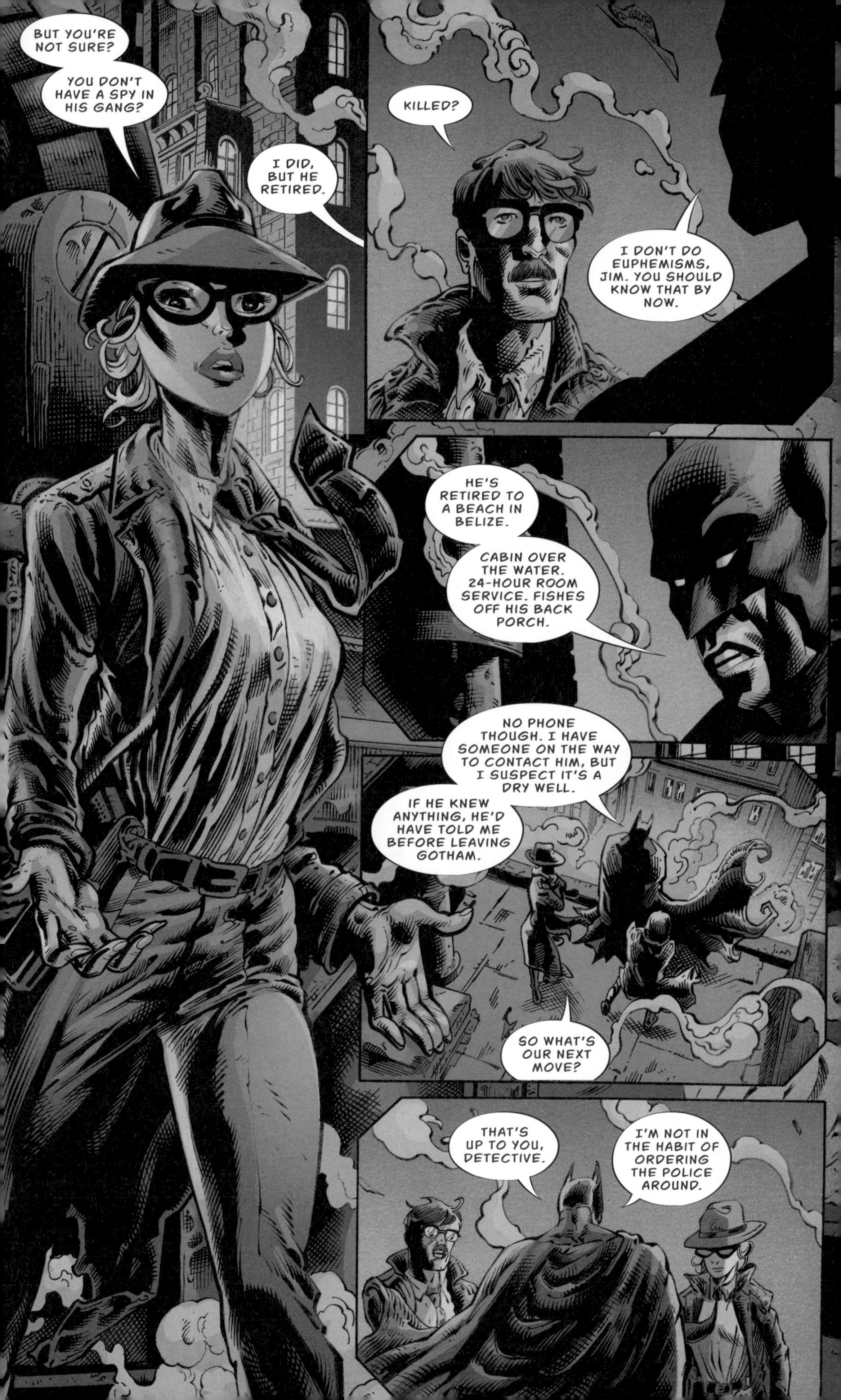

BUT YOU'RE NOT SURE?
YOU DON'T HAVE A SPY IN HIS GANG?
I DID, BUT HE RETIRED.
KILLED?
I DON'T DO EUPHEMISMS, JIM. YOU SHOULD KNOW THAT BY NOW.
HE'S RETIRED TO A BEACH IN BELIZE.
CABIN OVER THE WATER. 24-HOUR ROOM SERVICE. FISHES OFF HIS BACK PORCH.
NO PHONE THOUGH. I HAVE SOMEONE ON THE WAY TO CONTACT HIM, BUT I SUSPECT IT'S A DRY WELL.
IF HE KNEW ANYTHING, HE'D HAVE TOLD ME BEFORE LEAVING GOTHAM.
SO WHAT'S OUR NEXT MOVE?
THAT'S UP TO YOU, DETECTIVE.
I'M NOT IN THE HABIT OF ORDERING THE POLICE AROUND.

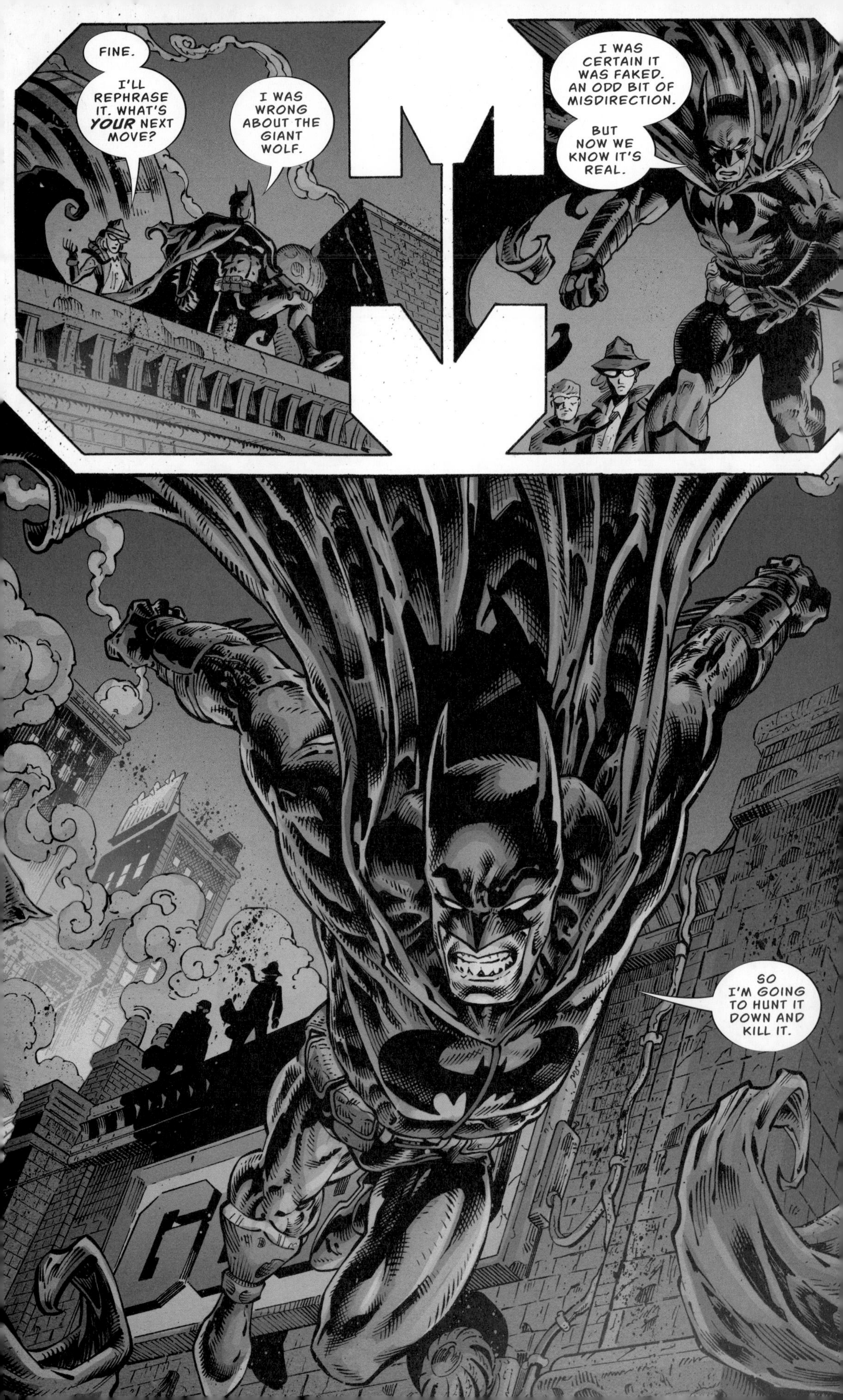
FINE.
I'LL REPHRASE IT. WHAT'S YOUR NEXT MOVE?
I WAS WRONG ABOUT THE GIANT WOLF.
I WAS CERTAIN IT WAS FAKED. AN ODD BIT OF MISDIRECTION.
BUT NOW WE KNOW IT'S REAL.
SO I'M GOING TO HUNT IT DOWN AND KILL IT.

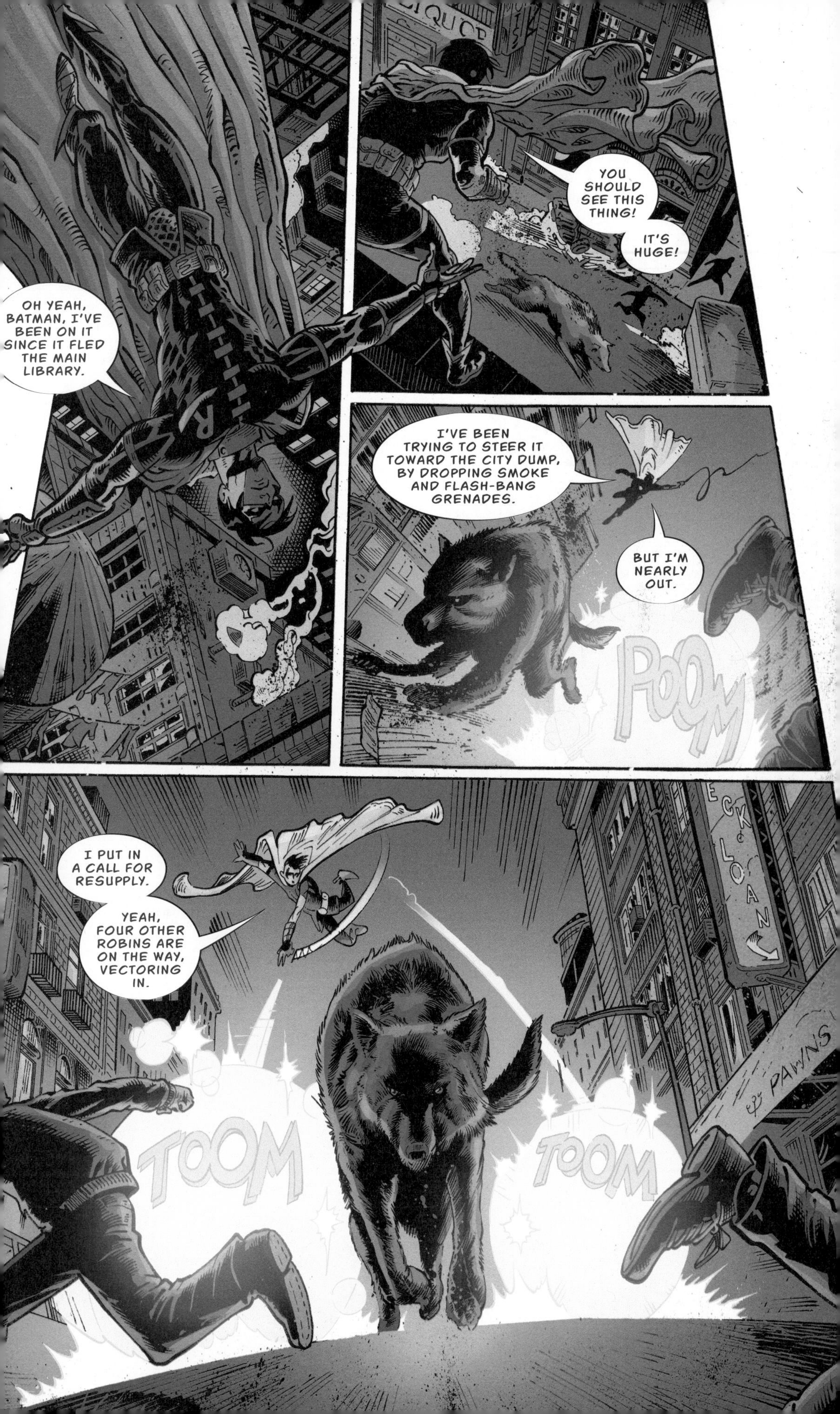
YOU SHOULD SEE THIS THING!
IT'S HUGE!
OH YEAH, BATMAN, I'VE BEEN ON IT SINCE IT FLED THE MAIN LIBRARY.
I'VE BEEN TRYING TO STEER IT TOWARD THE CITY DUMP, BY DROPPING SMOKE AND FLASH-BANG GRENADES.
BUT I'M NEARLY OUT.
POOM
I PUT IN A CALL FOR RESUPPLY.
YEAH, FOUR OTHER ROBINS ARE ON THE WAY, VECTORING IN.
LOAN
PAWNS
TOOM
TOOM

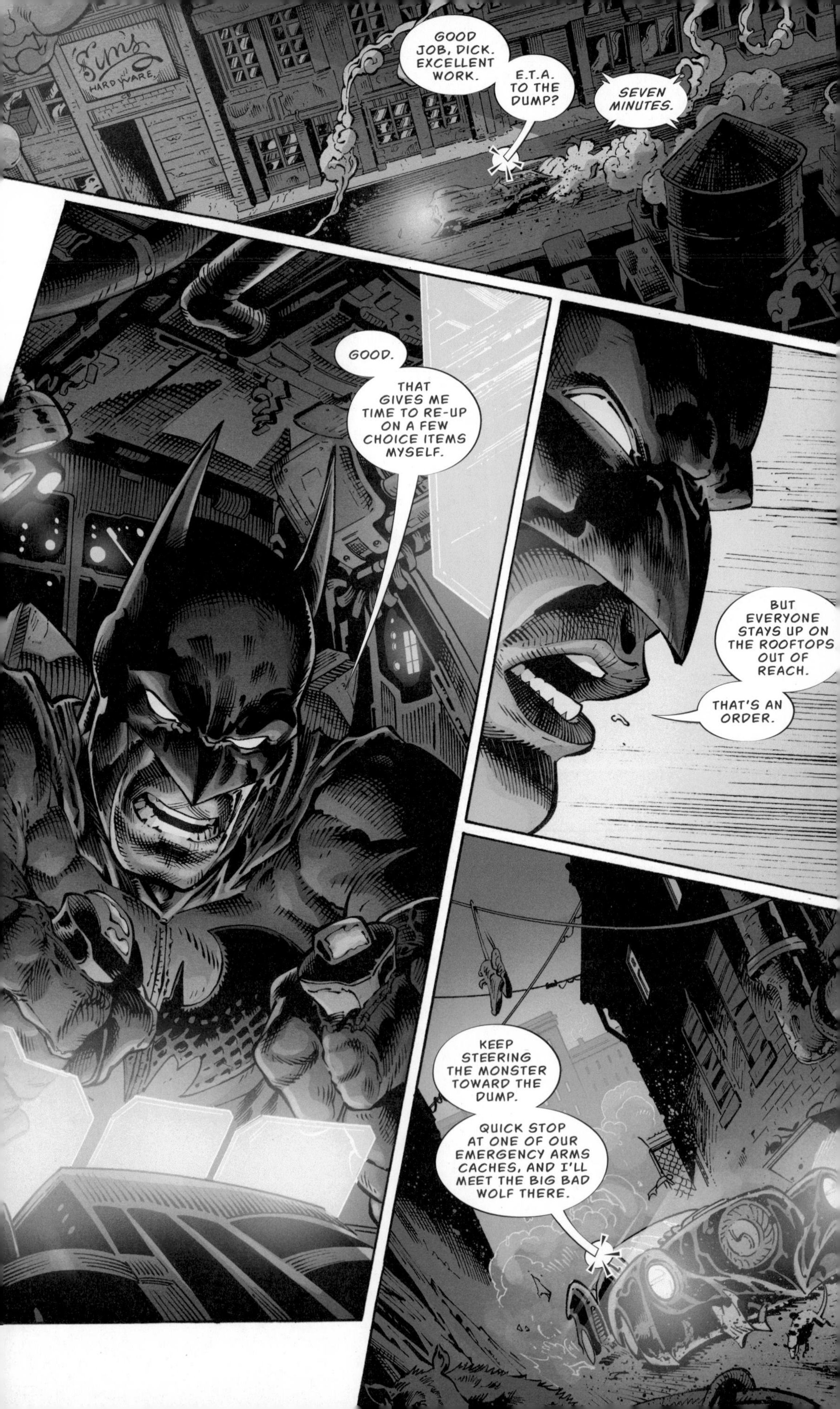

Sim's HARDWARE
GOOD JOB, DICK. EXCELLENT WORK.
E.T.A. TO THE DUMP?
SEVEN MINUTES.
GOOD.
THAT GIVES ME TIME TO RE-UP ON A FEW CHOICE ITEMS MYSELF.
BUT EVERYONE STAYS UP ON THE ROOFTOPS OUT OF REACH.
THAT'S AN ORDER.
KEEP STEERING THE MONSTER TOWARD THE DUMP.
QUICK STOP AT ONE OF OUR EMERGENCY ARMS CACHES, AND I'LL MEET THE BIG BAD WOLF THERE.

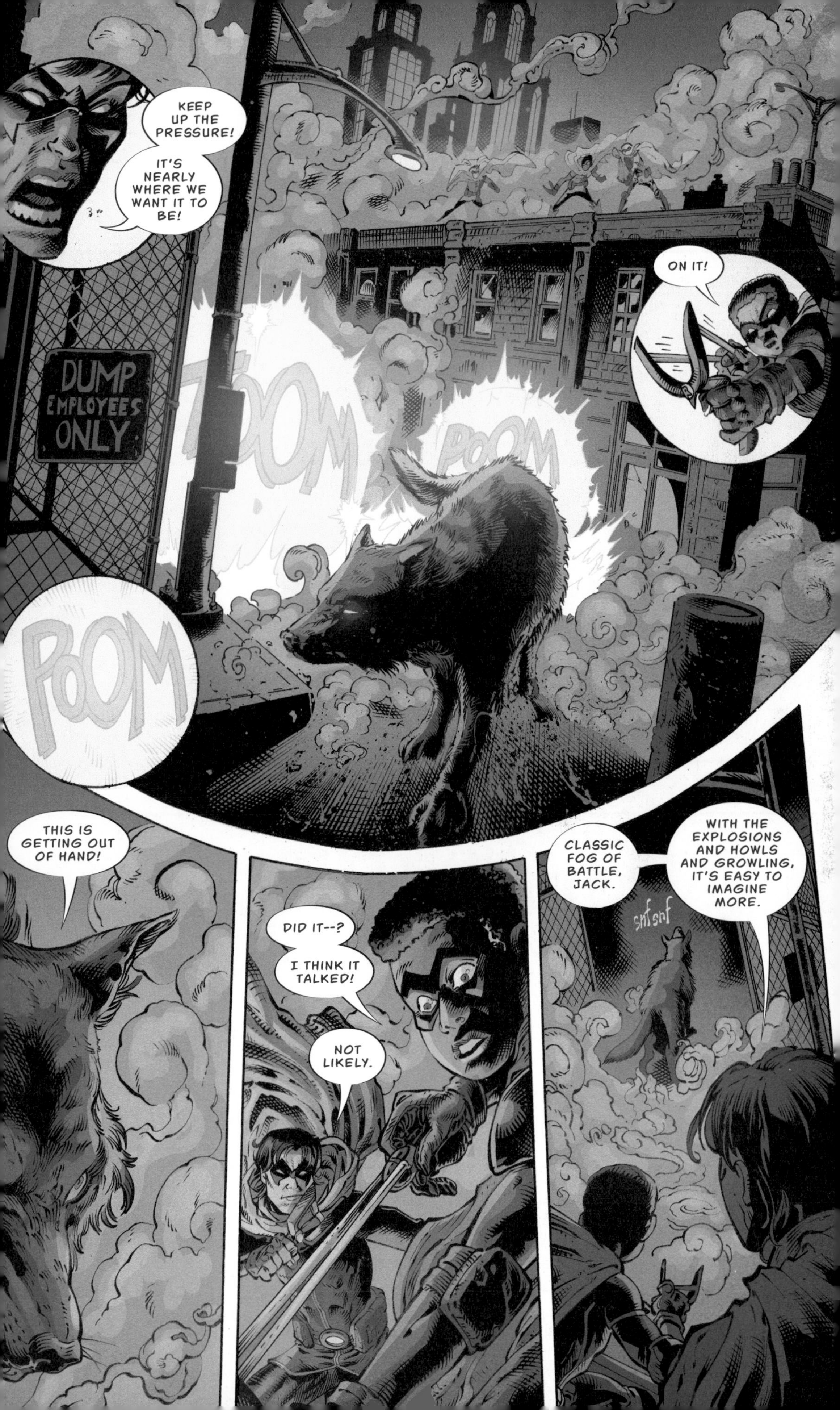
KEEP UP THE PRESSURE!
IT'S NEARLY WHERE WE WANT IT TO BE!
ON IT!
DUMP EMPLOYEES ONLY
FOOM
POOM
POOM
THIS IS GETTING OUT OF HAND!
DID IT--?
I THINK IT TALKED!
NOT LIKELY.
CLASSIC FOG OF BATTLE, JACK.
WITH THE EXPLOSIONS AND HOWLS AND GROWLING, IT'S EASY TO IMAGINE MORE.
snf snf

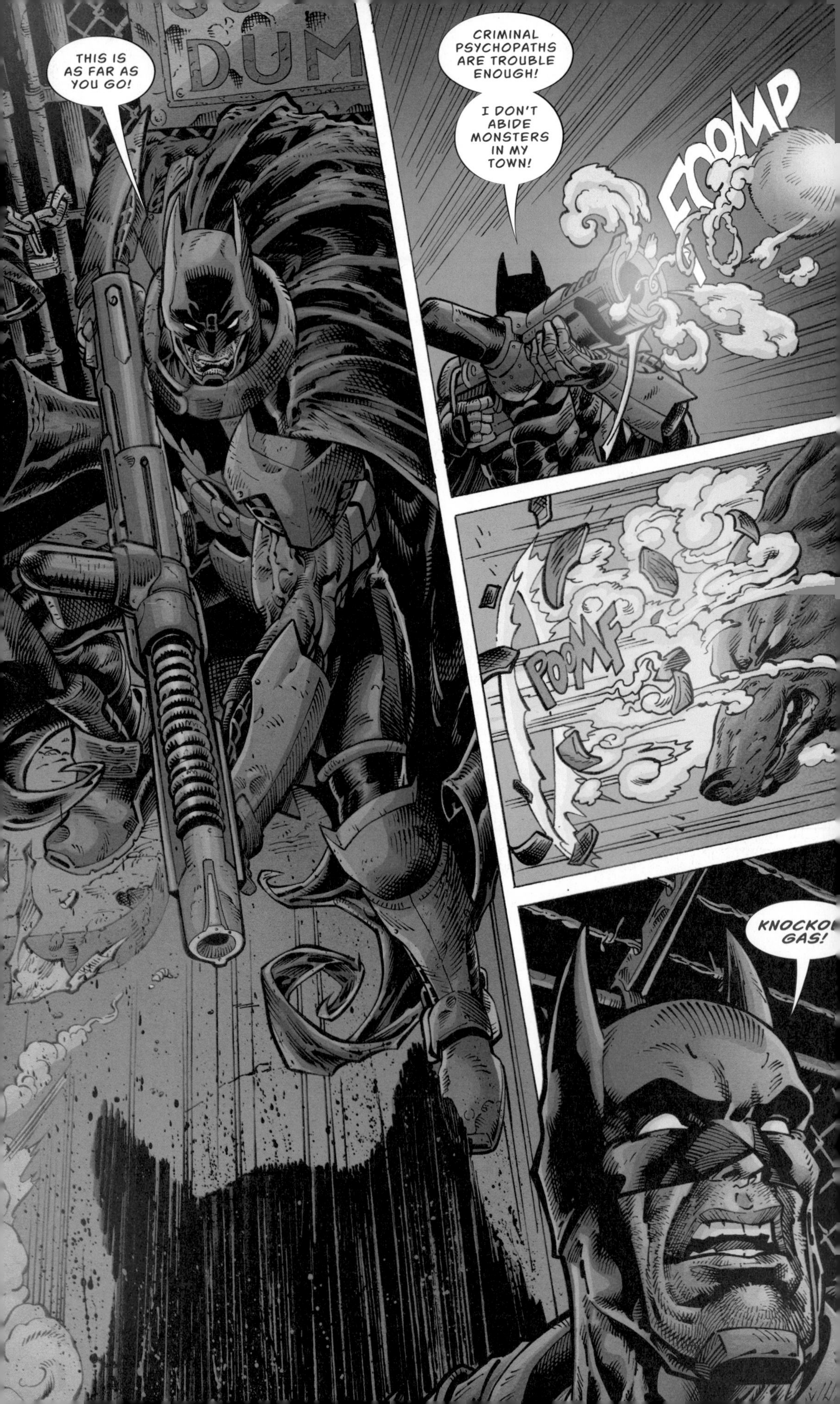
DUM
THIS IS AS FAR AS YOU GO!
CRIMINAL PSYCHOPATHS ARE TROUBLE ENOUGH!
I DON'T ABIDE MONSTERS IN MY TOWN!
FOOMP
POOMF
GAS!

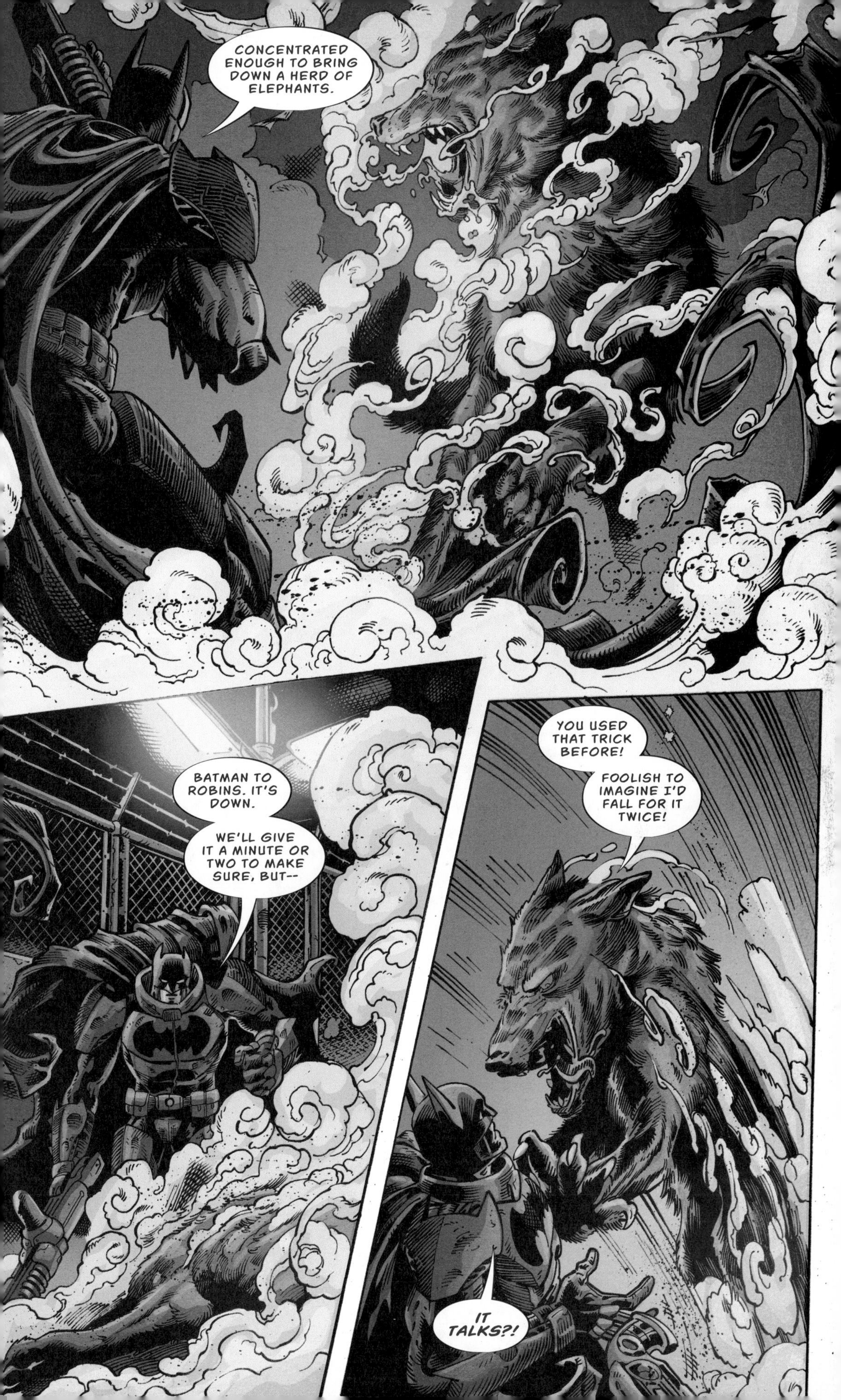
CONCENTRATED ENOUGH TO BRING DOWN A HERD OF ELEPHANTS.
BATMAN TO ROBINS. IT'S DOWN.
WE'LL GIVE IT A MINUTE OR TWO TO MAKE SURE, BUT--
YOU USED THAT TRICK BEFORE!
FOOLISH TO IMAGINE I'D FALL FOR IT TWICE!
IT TALKS?!

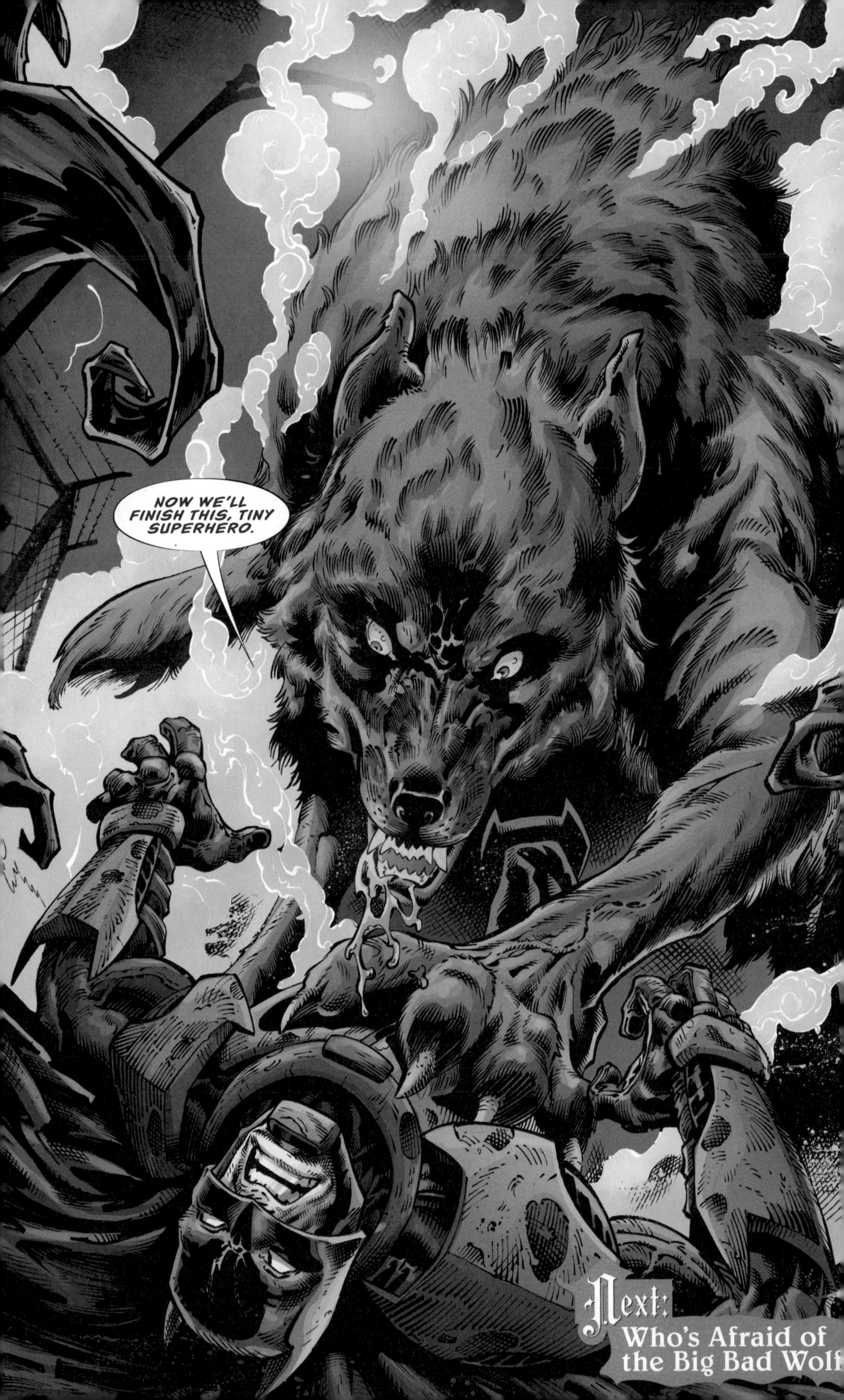
NOW WE'LL FINISH THIS, TINY SUPERHERO.
Next: Who's Afraid of the Big Bad Wolf

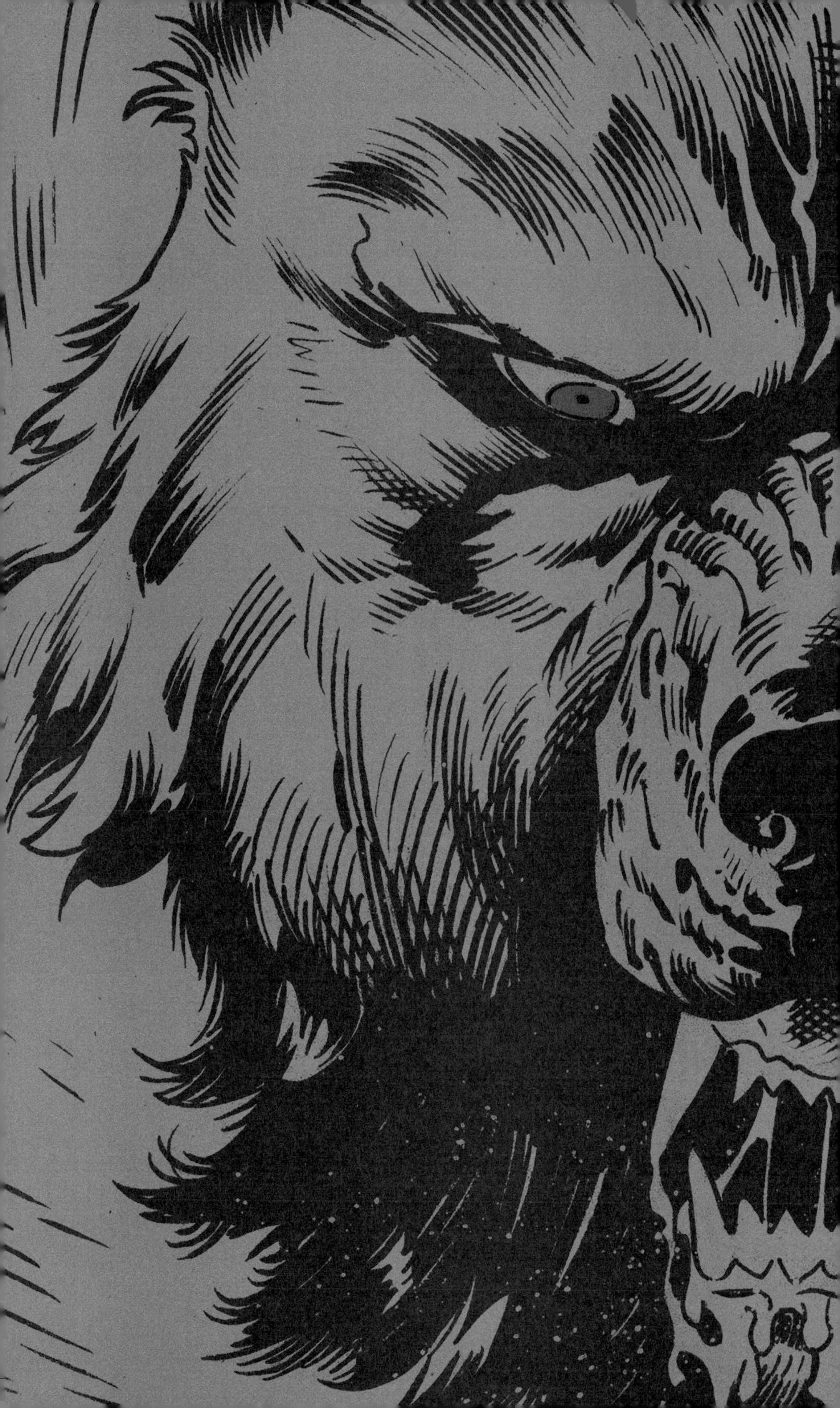

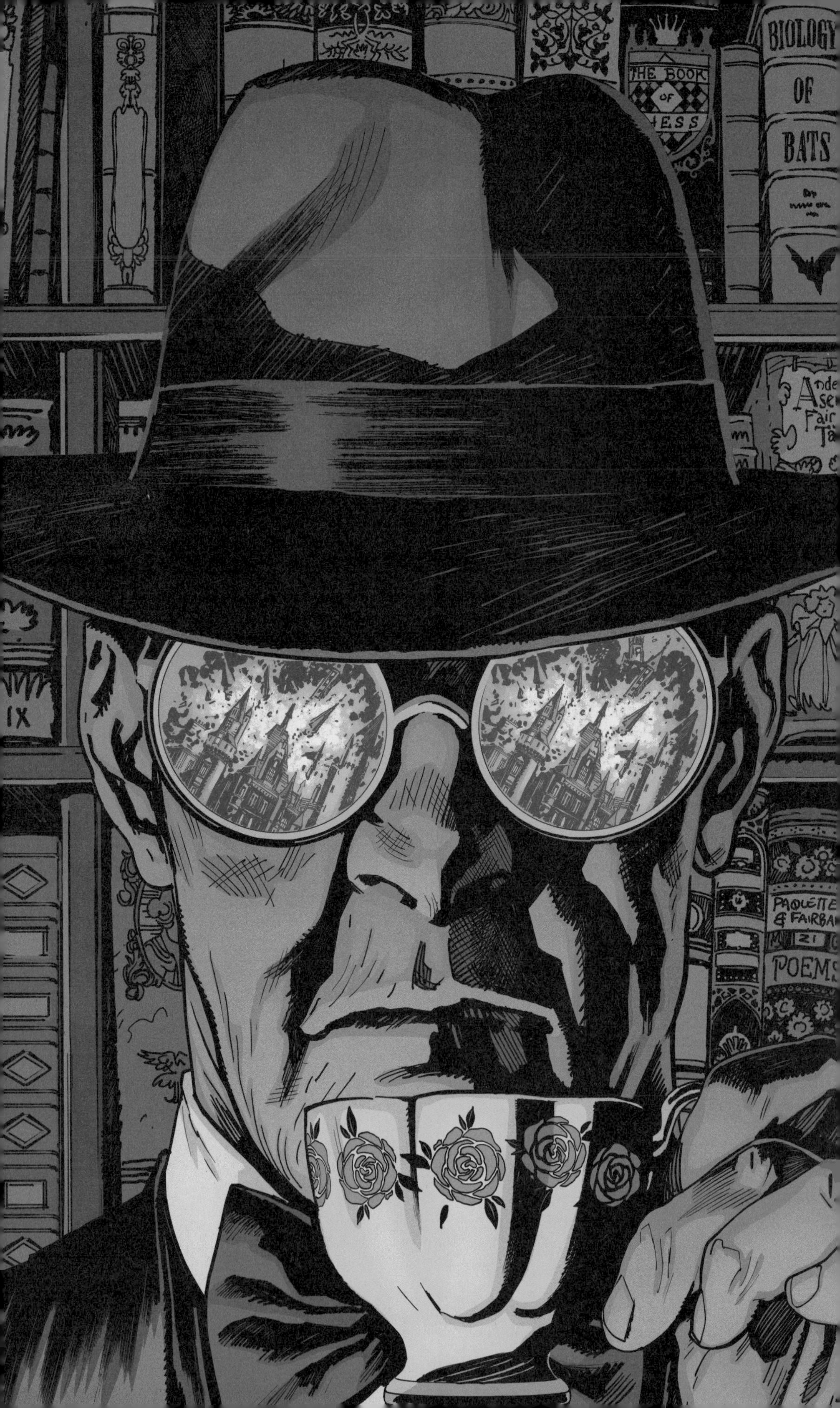
BIOLOGY OF BATS
THE BOOK OF
IX
POEMS

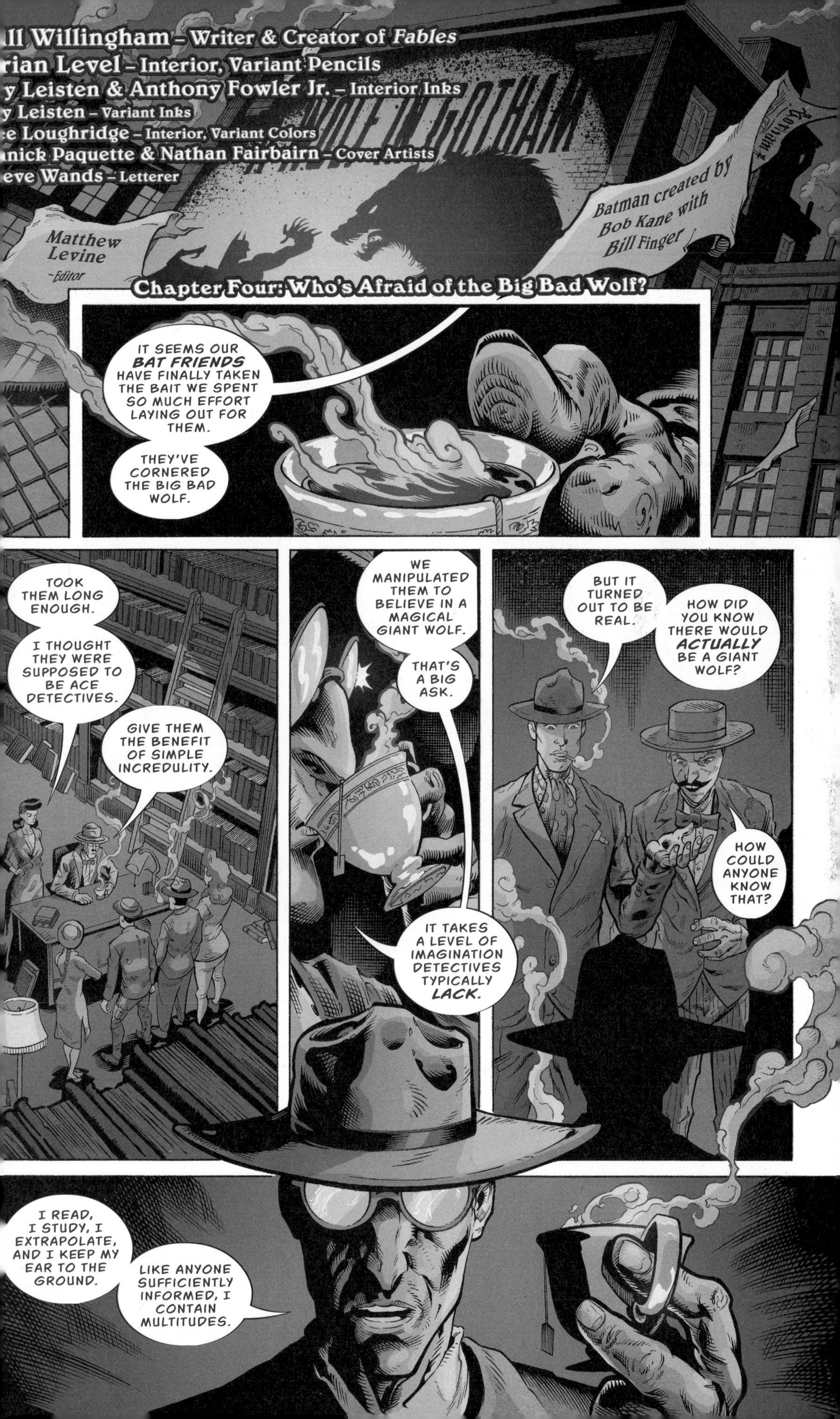

ll Willingham – Writer & Creator of Fables
rian Level – Interior, Variant Pencils
y Leisten & Anthony Fowler Jr. – Interior Inks
y Leisten – Variant Inks
e Loughridge – Interior, Variant Colors
nick Paquette & Nathan Fairbairn – Cover Artists
eve Wands – Letterer
Matthew Levine ~Editor
Batman created by Bob Kane with Bill Finger
Chapter Four: Who's Afraid of the Big Bad Wolf?
IT SEEMS OUR BAT FRIENDS HAVE FINALLY TAKEN THE BAIT WE SPENT SO MUCH EFFORT LAYING OUT FOR THEM.
THEY'VE CORNERED THE BIG BAD WOLF.
TOOK THEM LONG ENOUGH.
I THOUGHT THEY WERE SUPPOSED TO BE ACE DETECTIVES.
GIVE THEM THE BENEFIT OF SIMPLE INCREDULITY.
WE MANIPULATED THEM TO BELIEVE IN A MAGICAL GIANT WOLF.
THAT'S A BIG ASK.
IT TAKES A LEVEL OF IMAGINATION DETECTIVES TYPICALLY LACK.
BUT IT TURNED OUT TO BE REAL.
HOW DID YOU KNOW THERE WOULD ACTUALLY BE A GIANT WOLF?
HOW COULD ANYONE KNOW THAT?
I READ, I STUDY, I EXTRAPOLATE, AND I KEEP MY EAR TO THE GROUND.
LIKE ANYONE SUFFICIENTLY INFORMED, I CONTAIN MULTITUDES.

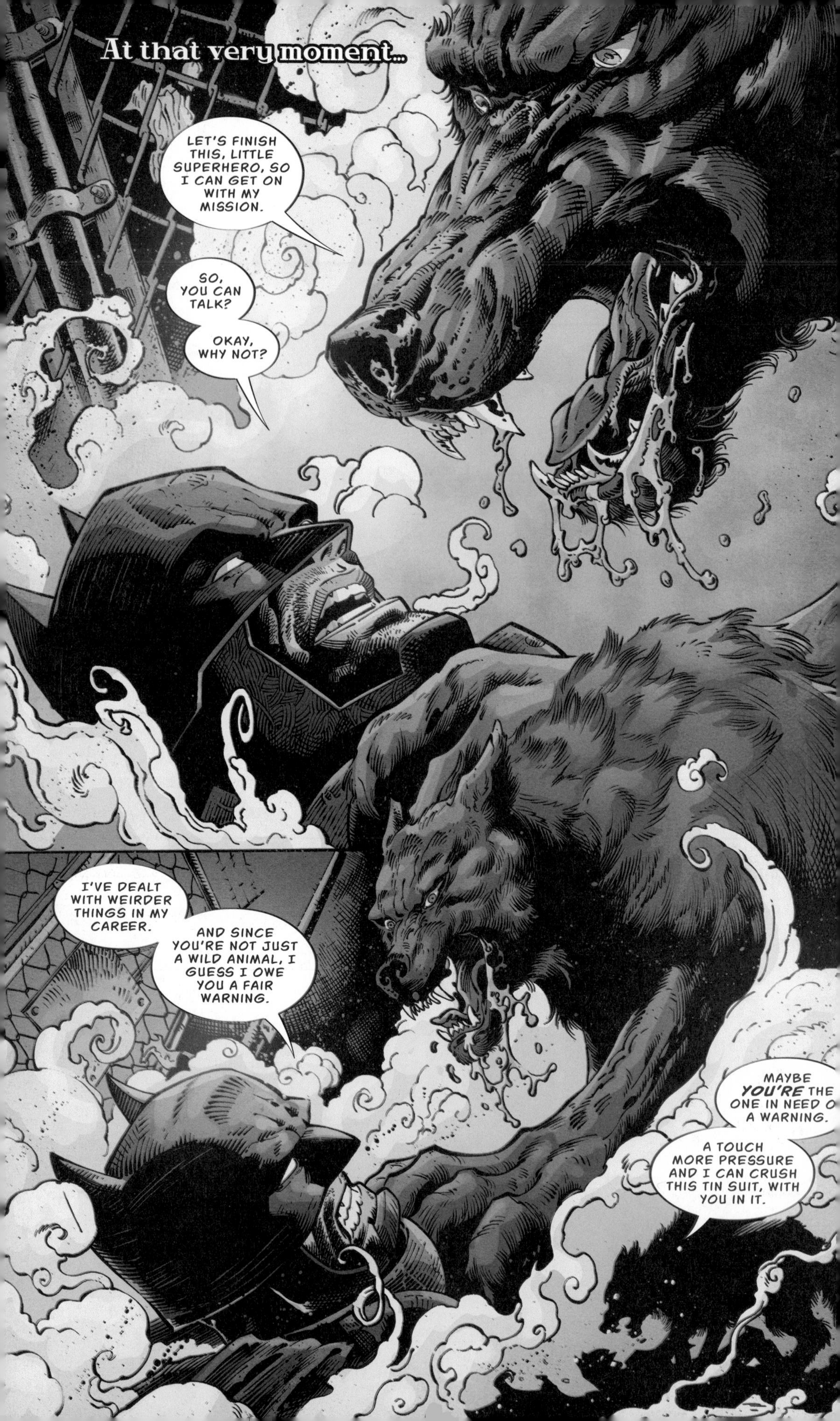
At that very moment...
LET'S FINISH THIS, LITTLE SUPERHERO, SO I CAN GET ON WITH MY MISSION.
SO, YOU CAN TALK?
OKAY, WHY NOT?
I'VE DEALT WITH WEIRDER THINGS IN MY CAREER.
AND SINCE YOU'RE NOT JUST A WILD ANIMAL, I GUESS I OWE YOU A FAIR WARNING.
MAYBE *YOU'RE* THE ONE IN NEED O A WARNING.
A TOUCH MORE PRESSURE AND I CAN CRUSH THIS TIN SUIT, WITH YOU IN IT.

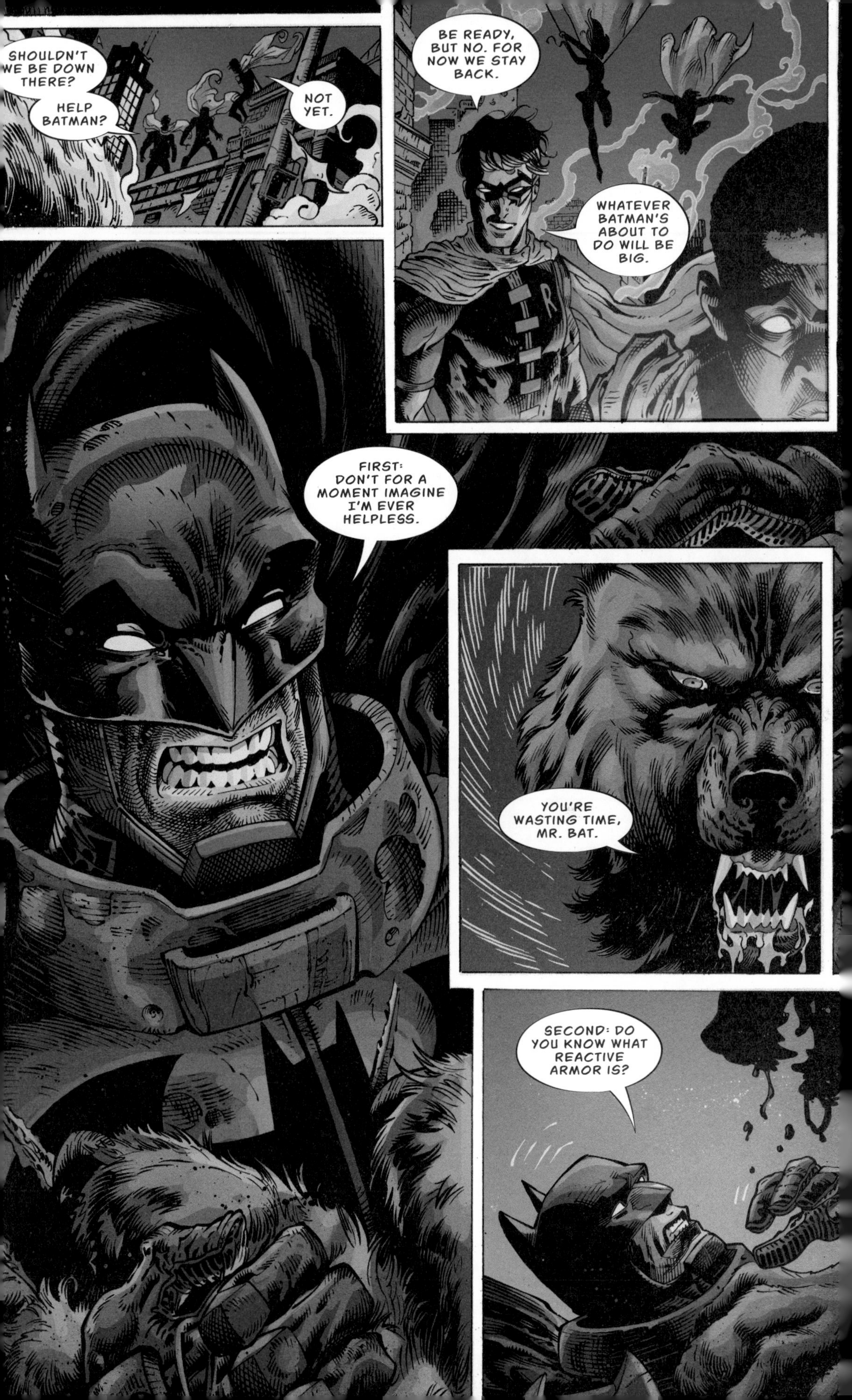
SHOULDN'T WE BE DOWN THERE?
HELP BATMAN?
NOT YET.
BE READY, BUT NO. FOR NOW WE STAY BACK.
WHATEVER BATMAN'S ABOUT TO DO WILL BE BIG.
FIRST: DON'T FOR A MOMENT IMAGINE I'M EVER HELPLESS.
YOU'RE WASTING TIME, MR. BAT.
SECOND: DO YOU KNOW WHAT REACTIVE ARMOR IS?

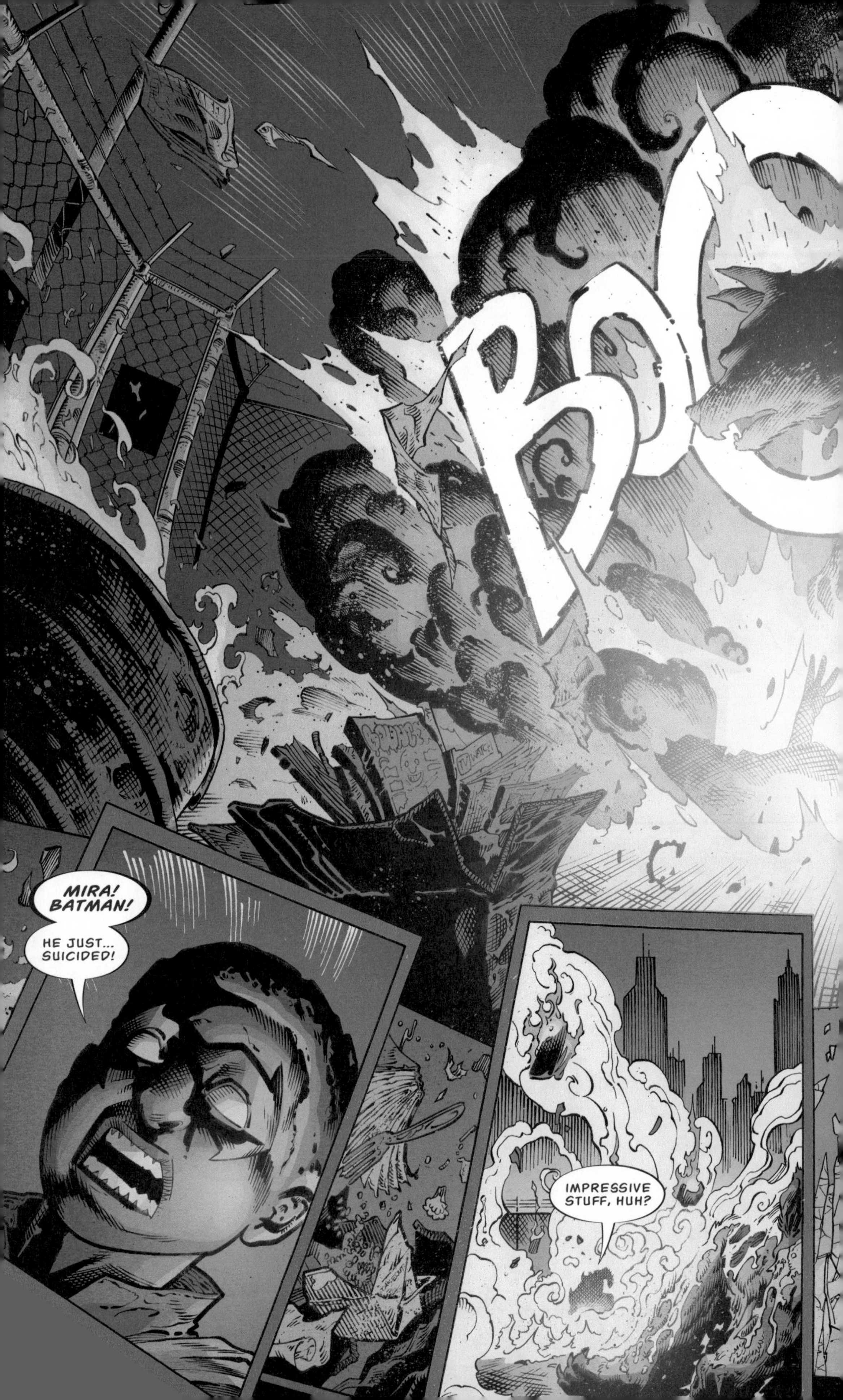
BOO
MIRA! BATMAN!
HE JUST... SUICIDED!
IMPRESSIVE STUFF, HUH?

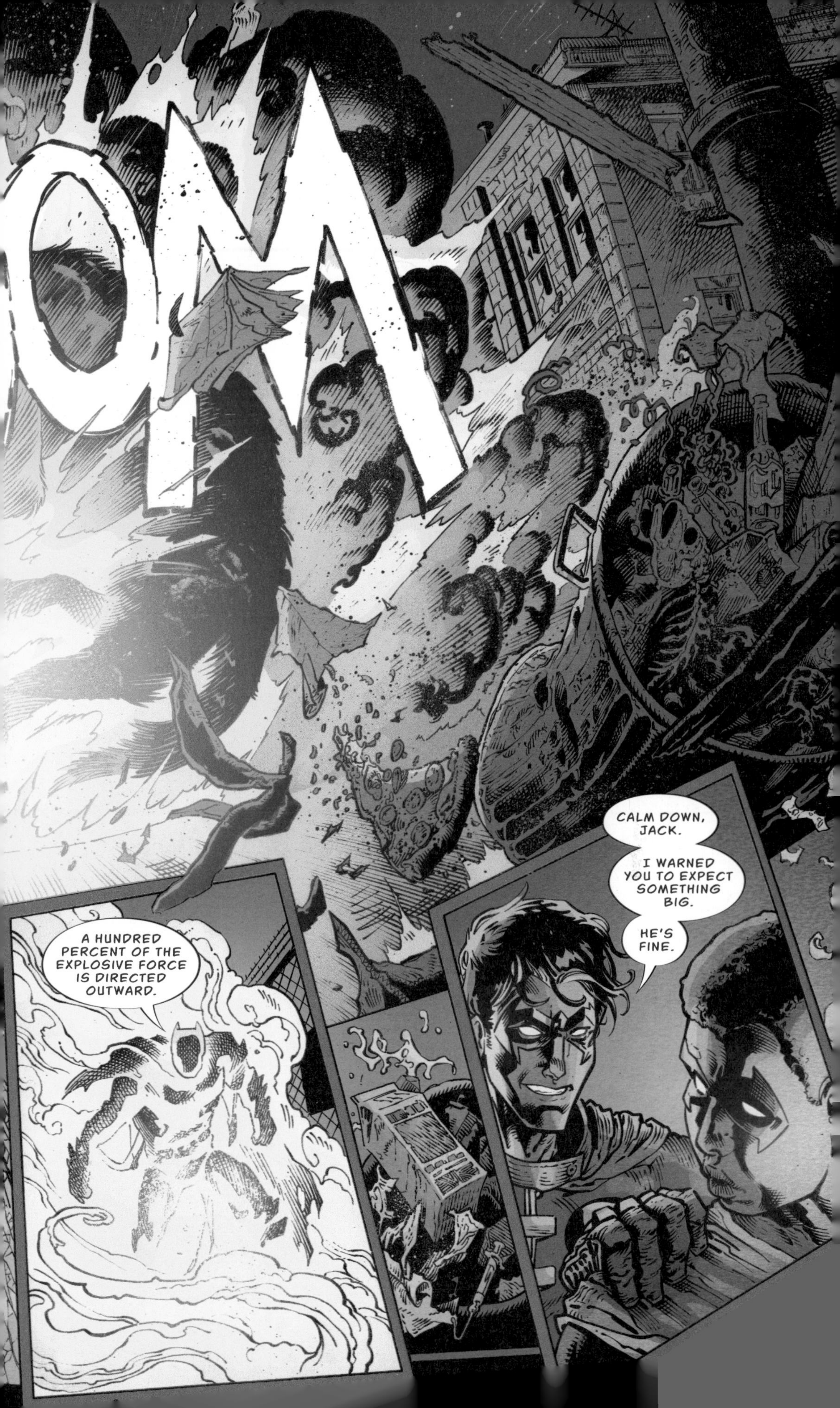

A HUNDRED PERCENT OF THE EXPLOSIVE FORCE IS DIRECTED OUTWARD.
CALM DOWN, JACK.
I WARNED YOU TO EXPECT SOMETHING BIG.
HE'S FINE.

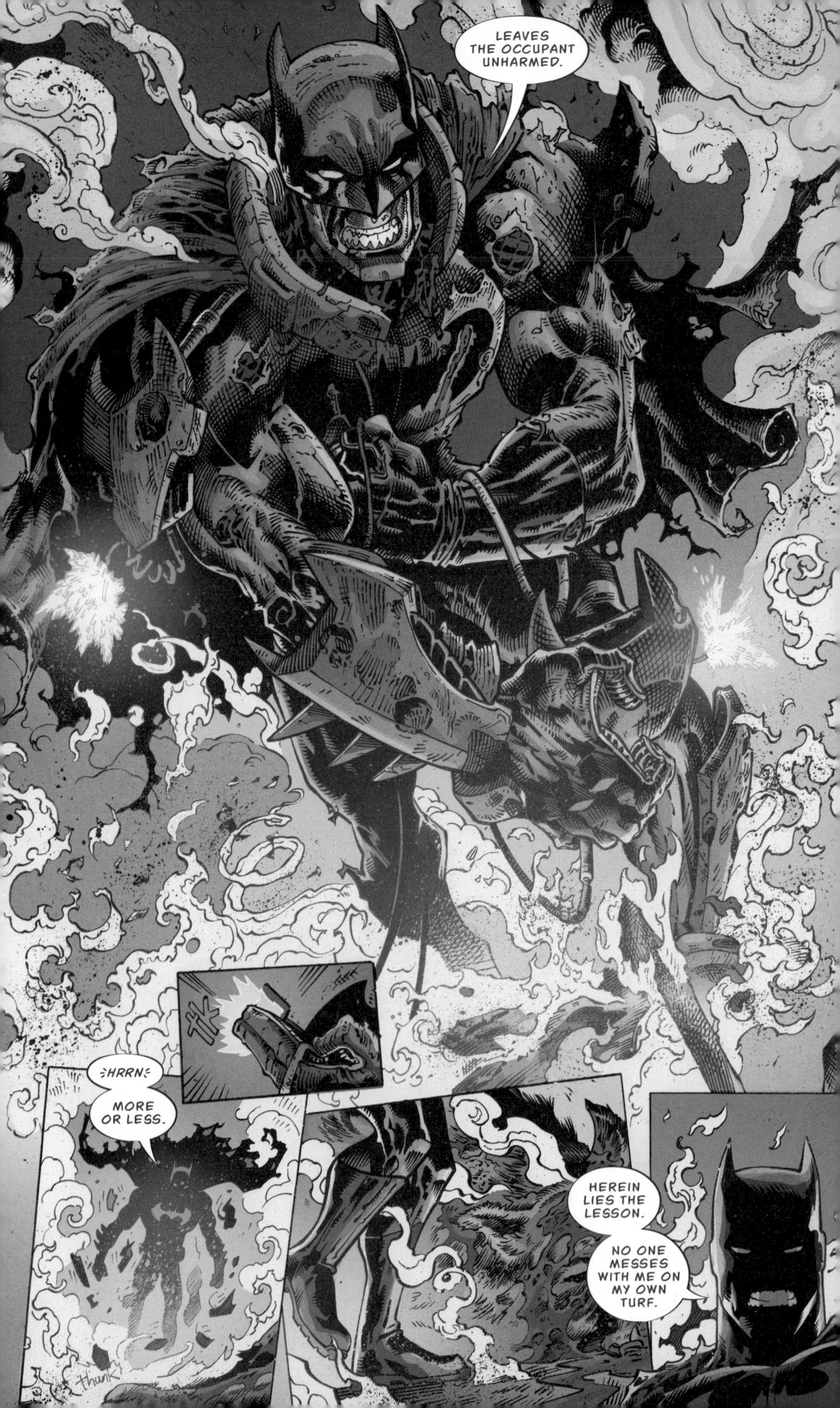
LEAVES THE OCCUPANT UNHARMED.
TK
HRRN
MORE OR LESS.
HEREIN LIES THE LESSON.
NO ONE MESSES WITH ME ON MY OWN TURF.

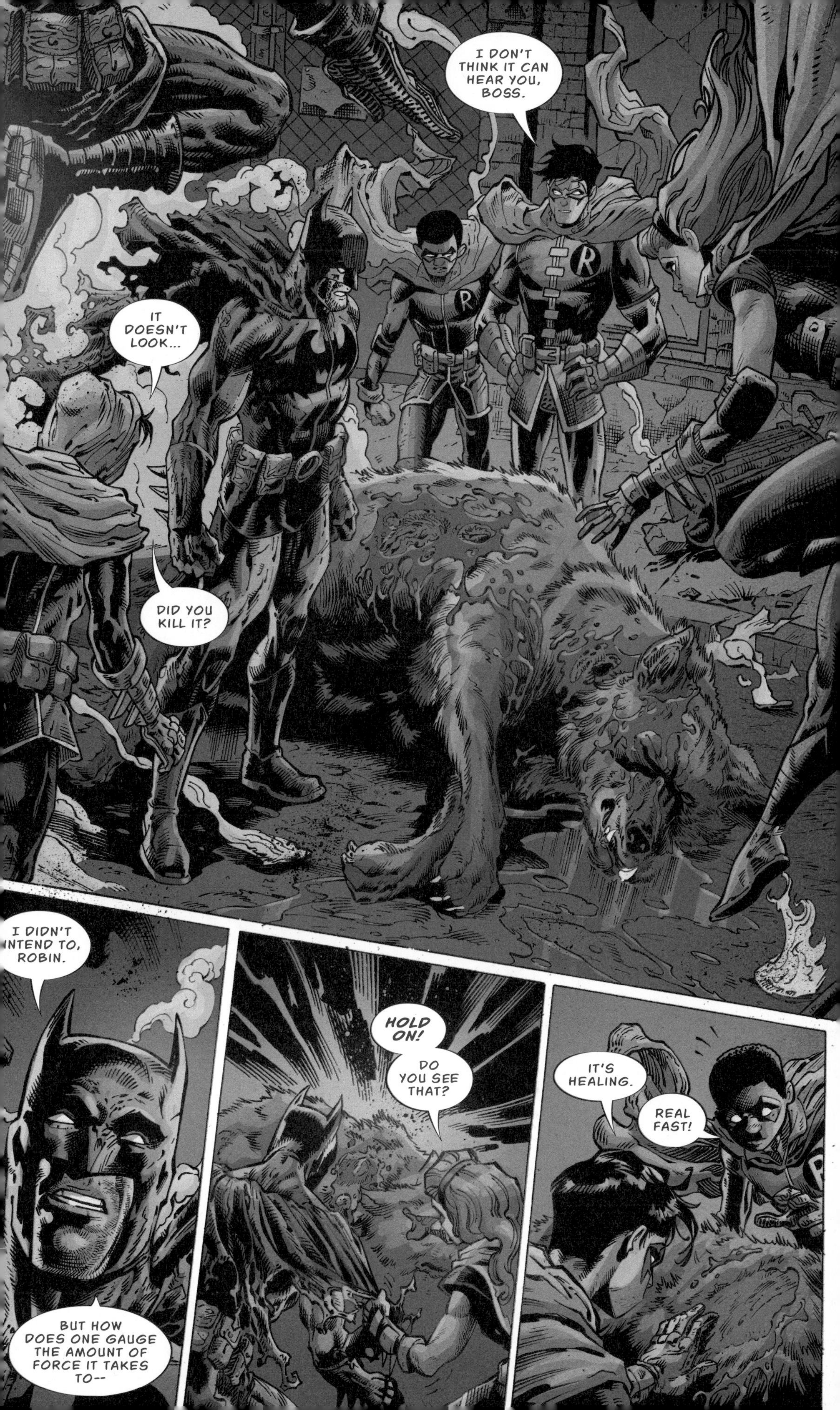
I DON'T THINK IT CAN HEAR YOU, BOSS.
IT DOESN'T LOOK...
DID YOU KILL IT?
I DIDN'T INTEND TO, ROBIN.
BUT HOW DOES ONE GAUGE THE AMOUNT OF FORCE IT TAKES TO--
HOLD ON!
DO YOU SEE THAT?
IT'S HEALING.
REAL FAST!

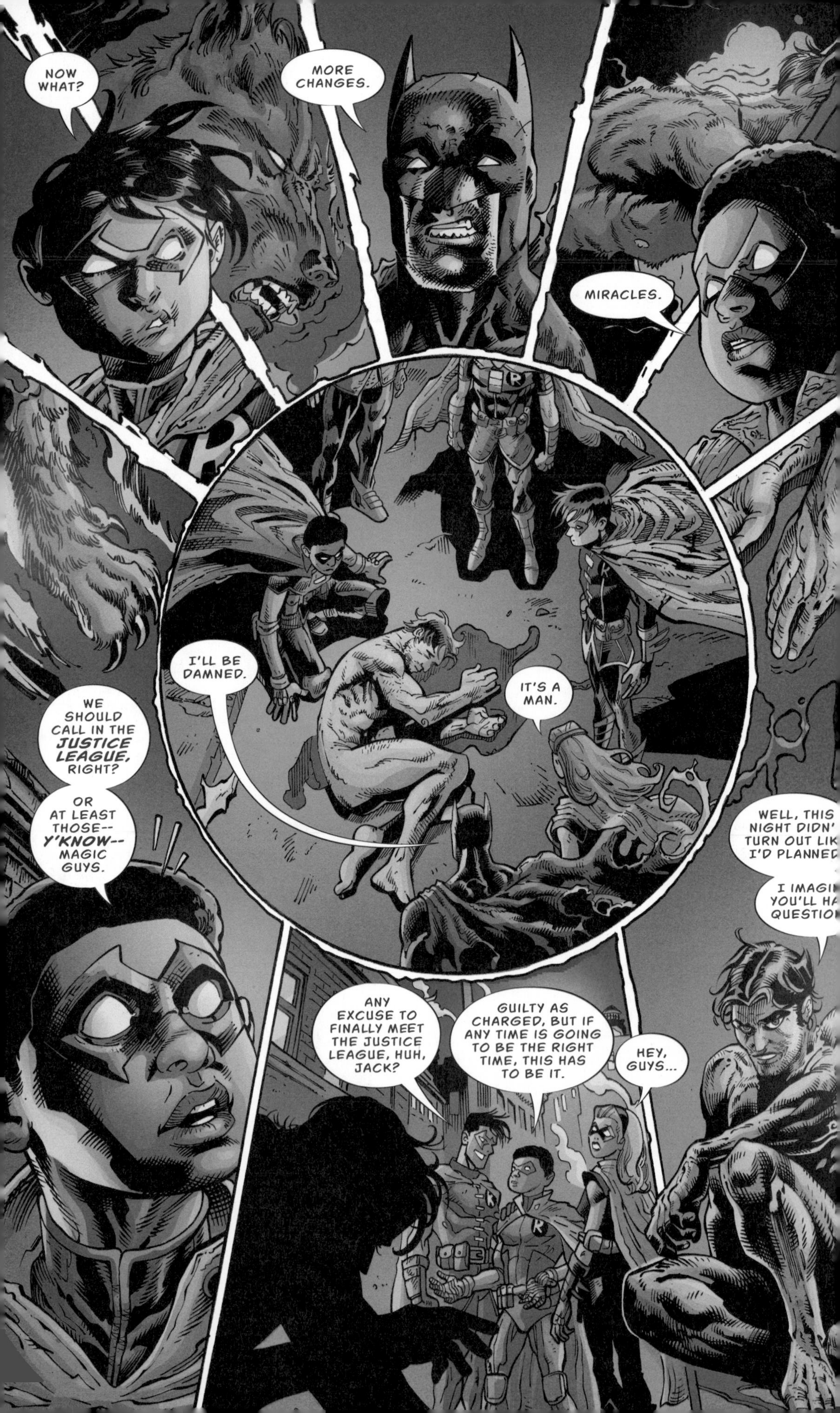

NOW WHAT?
MORE CHANGES.
MIRACLES.
I'LL BE DAMNED.
IT'S A MAN.
WE SHOULD CALL IN THE *JUSTICE LEAGUE,* RIGHT?
OR AT LEAST THOSE-- *Y'KNOW*-- MAGIC GUYS.
ANY EXCUSE TO FINALLY MEET THE JUSTICE LEAGUE, HUH, JACK?
GUILTY AS CHARGED, BUT IF ANY TIME IS GOING TO BE THE RIGHT TIME, THIS HAS TO BE IT.
HEY, GUYS...

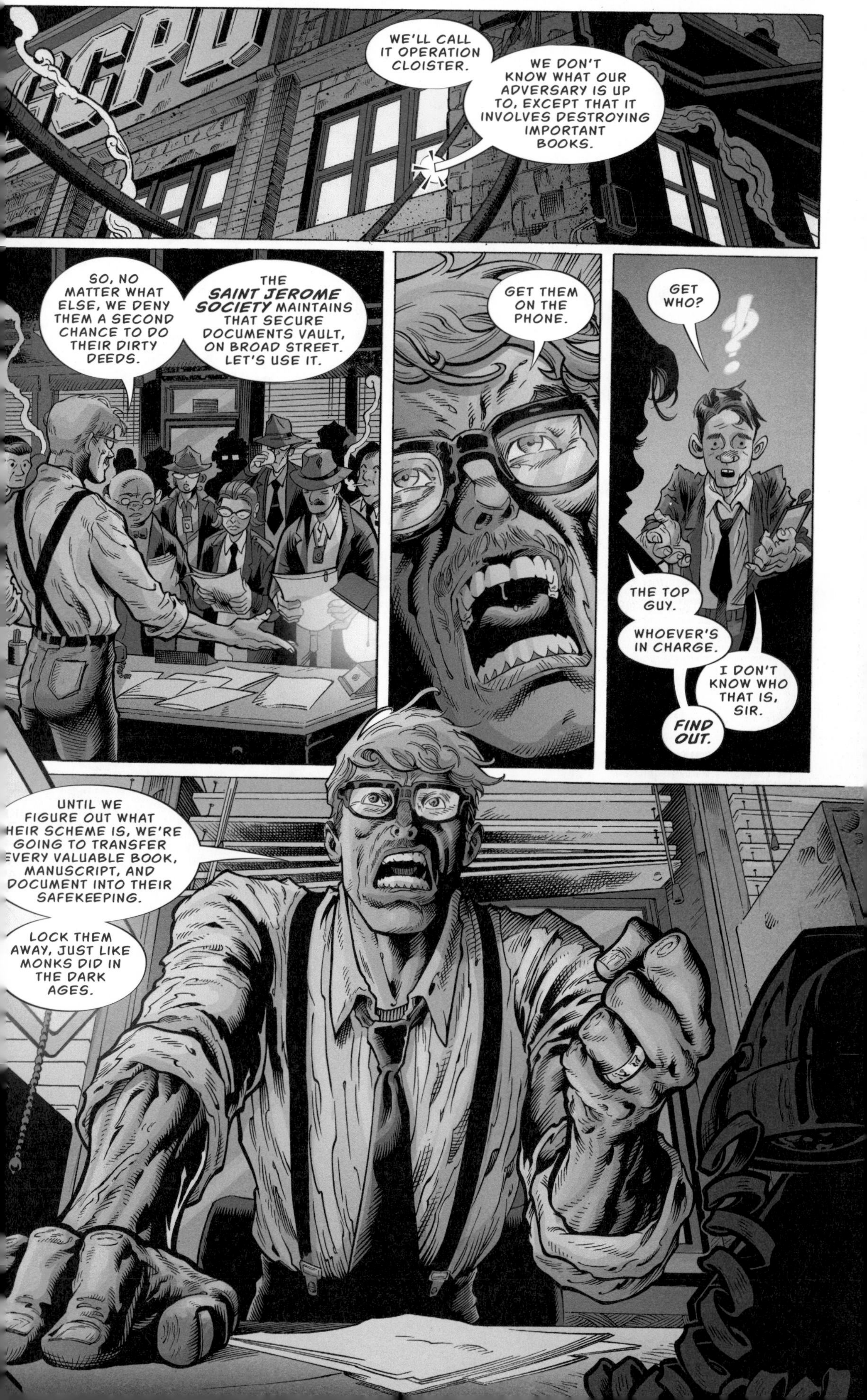
GCPD
WE'LL CALL IT OPERATION CLOISTER.
WE DON'T KNOW WHAT OUR ADVERSARY IS UP TO, EXCEPT THAT IT INVOLVES DESTROYING IMPORTANT BOOKS.
SO, NO MATTER WHAT ELSE, WE DENY THEM A SECOND CHANCE TO DO THEIR DIRTY DEEDS.
THE *SAINT JEROME SOCIETY* MAINTAINS THAT SECURE DOCUMENTS VAULT, ON BROAD STREET. LET'S USE IT.
GET THEM ON THE PHONE.
GET WHO?
?
THE TOP GUY.
WHOEVER'S IN CHARGE.
I DON'T KNOW WHO THAT IS, SIR.
FIND OUT.
UNTIL WE FIGURE OUT WHAT HEIR SCHEME IS, WE'RE GOING TO TRANSFER EVERY VALUABLE BOOK, MANUSCRIPT, AND DOCUMENT INTO THEIR SAFEKEEPING.
LOCK THEM AWAY, JUST LIKE MONKS DID IN THE DARK AGES.

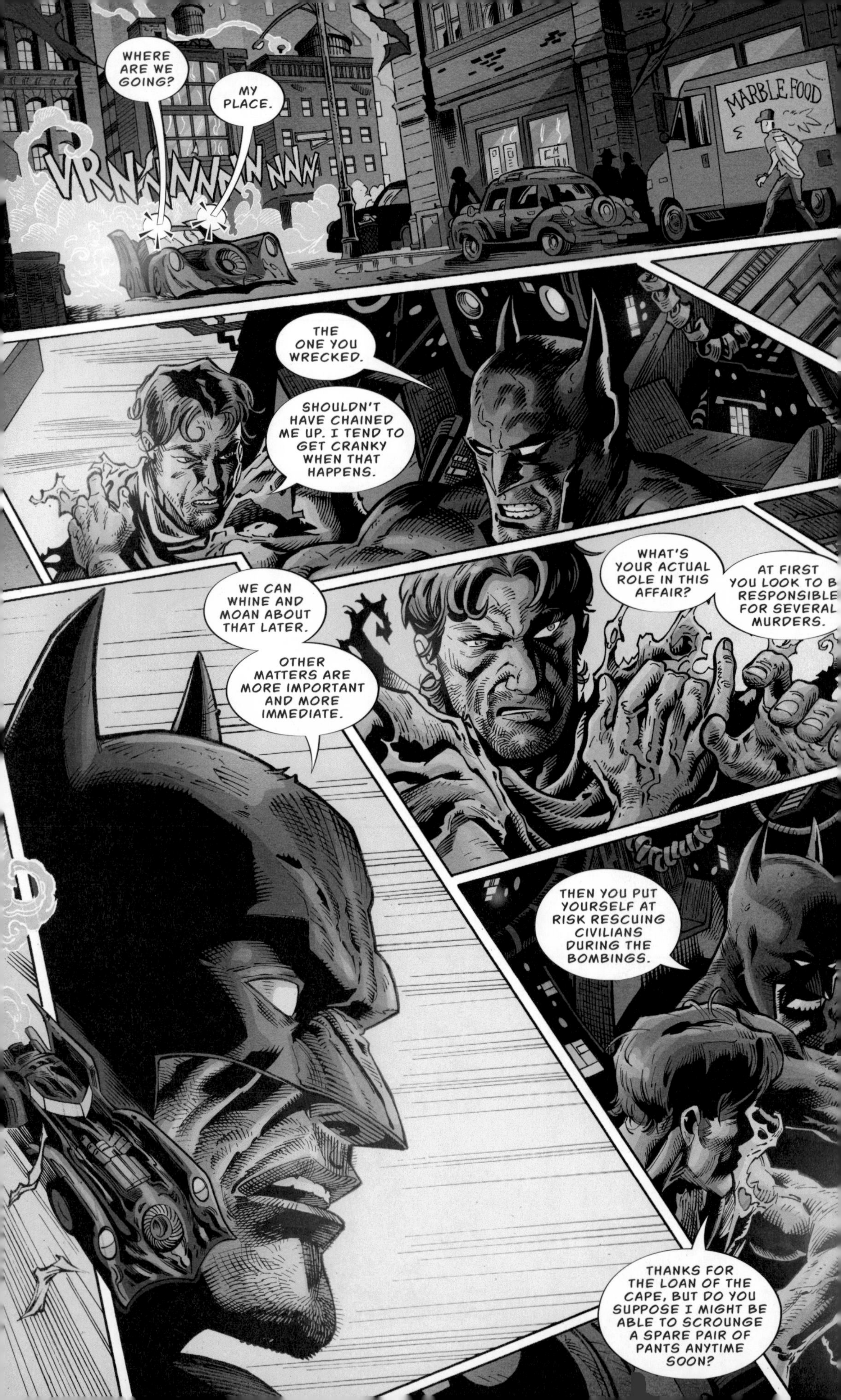

WHERE ARE WE GOING?
MY PLACE.
VRNNNNNNNNNN
THE ONE YOU WRECKED.
SHOULDN'T HAVE CHAINED ME UP. I TEND TO GET CRANKY WHEN THAT HAPPENS.
WE CAN WHINE AND MOAN ABOUT THAT LATER.
OTHER MATTERS ARE MORE IMPORTANT AND MORE IMMEDIATE.
WHAT'S YOUR ACTUAL ROLE IN THIS AFFAIR?
AT FIRST YOU LOOK TO BE RESPONSIBLE FOR SEVERAL MURDERS.
THEN YOU PUT YOURSELF AT RISK RESCUING CIVILIANS DURING THE BOMBINGS.
THANKS FOR THE LOAN OF THE CAPE, BUT DO YOU SUPPOSE I MIGHT BE ABLE TO SCROUNGE A SPARE PAIR OF PANTS ANYTIME SOON?

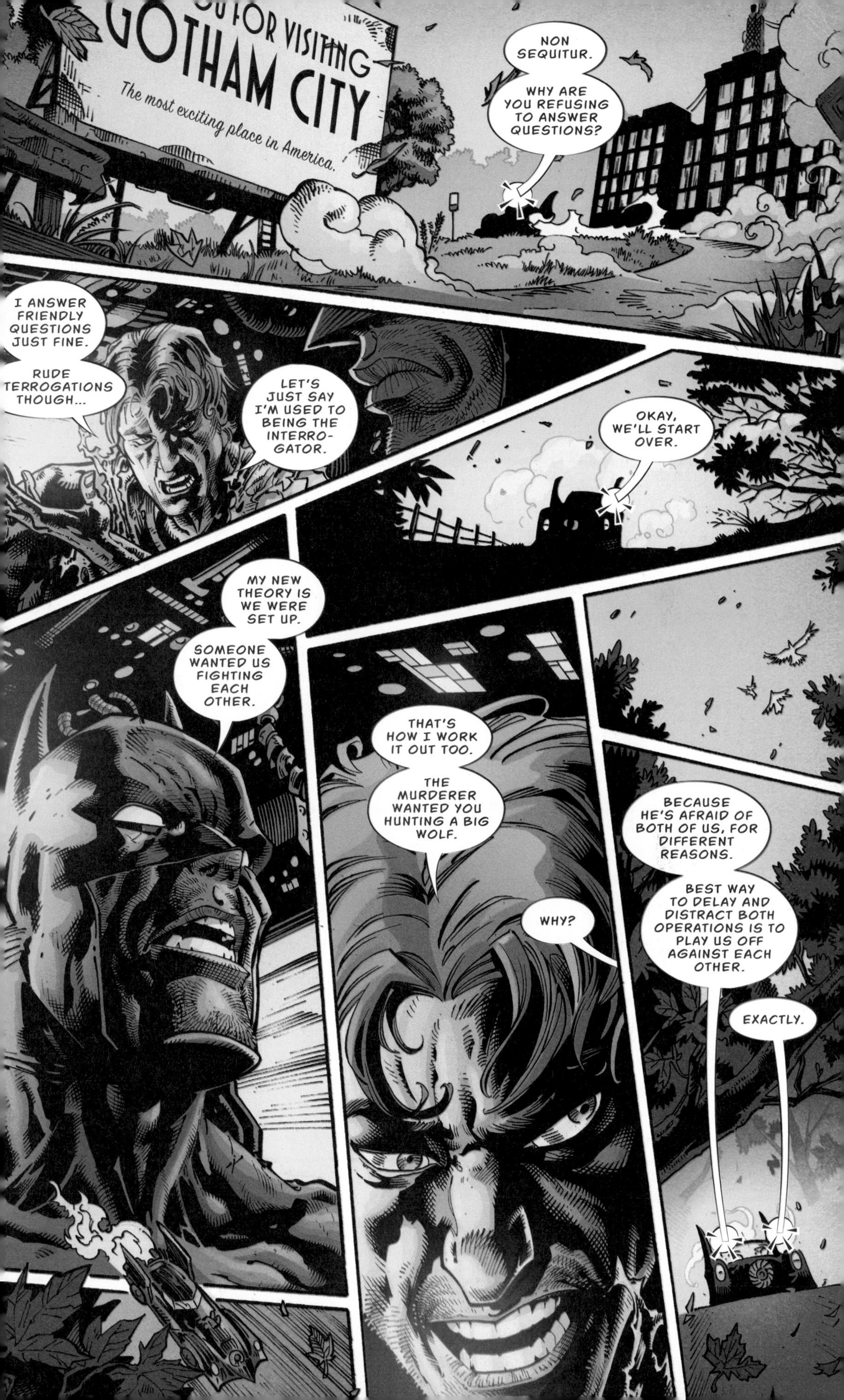

...OU FOR VISITING
GOTHAM CITY
The most exciting place in America.
NON SEQUITUR.
WHY ARE YOU REFUSING TO ANSWER QUESTIONS?
I ANSWER FRIENDLY QUESTIONS JUST FINE.
RUDE TERROGATIONS THOUGH...
LET'S JUST SAY I'M USED TO BEING THE INTERRO-GATOR.
OKAY, WE'LL START OVER.
MY NEW THEORY IS WE WERE SET UP.
SOMEONE WANTED US FIGHTING EACH OTHER.
THAT'S HOW I WORK IT OUT TOO.
THE MURDERER WANTED YOU HUNTING A BIG WOLF.
WHY?
BECAUSE HE'S AFRAID OF BOTH OF US, FOR DIFFERENT REASONS.
BEST WAY TO DELAY AND DISTRACT BOTH OPERATIONS IS TO PLAY US OFF AGAINST EACH OTHER.
EXACTLY.

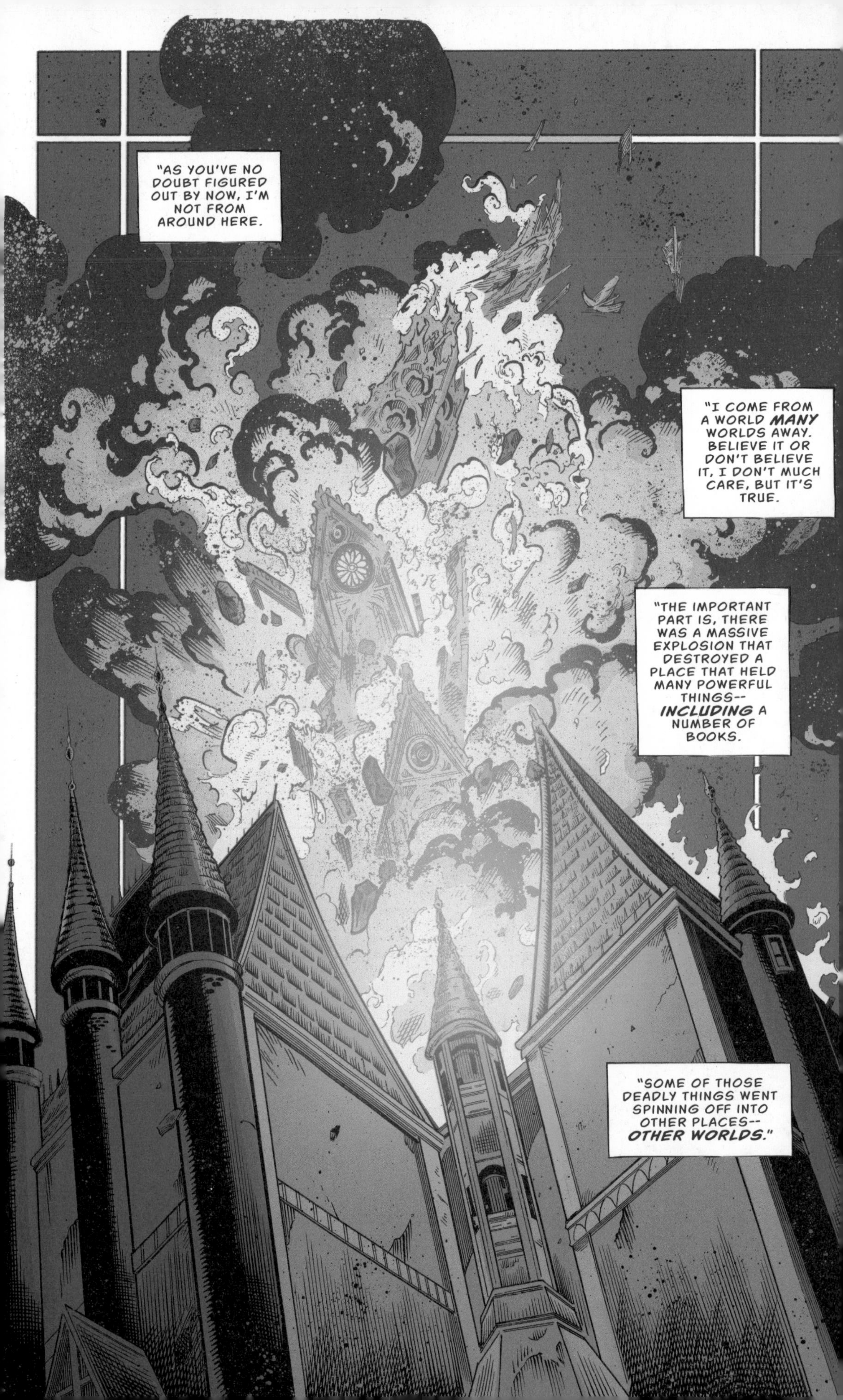
"AS YOU'VE NO DOUBT FIGURED OUT BY NOW, I'M NOT FROM AROUND HERE.
"I COME FROM A WORLD *MANY* WORLDS AWAY. BELIEVE IT OR DON'T BELIEVE IT, I DON'T MUCH CARE, BUT IT'S TRUE.
"THE IMPORTANT PART IS, THERE WAS A MASSIVE EXPLOSION THAT DESTROYED A PLACE THAT HELD MANY POWERFUL THINGS-- *INCLUDING* A NUMBER OF BOOKS.
"SOME OF THOSE DEADLY THINGS WENT SPINNING OFF INTO OTHER PLACES-- *OTHER WORLDS*."

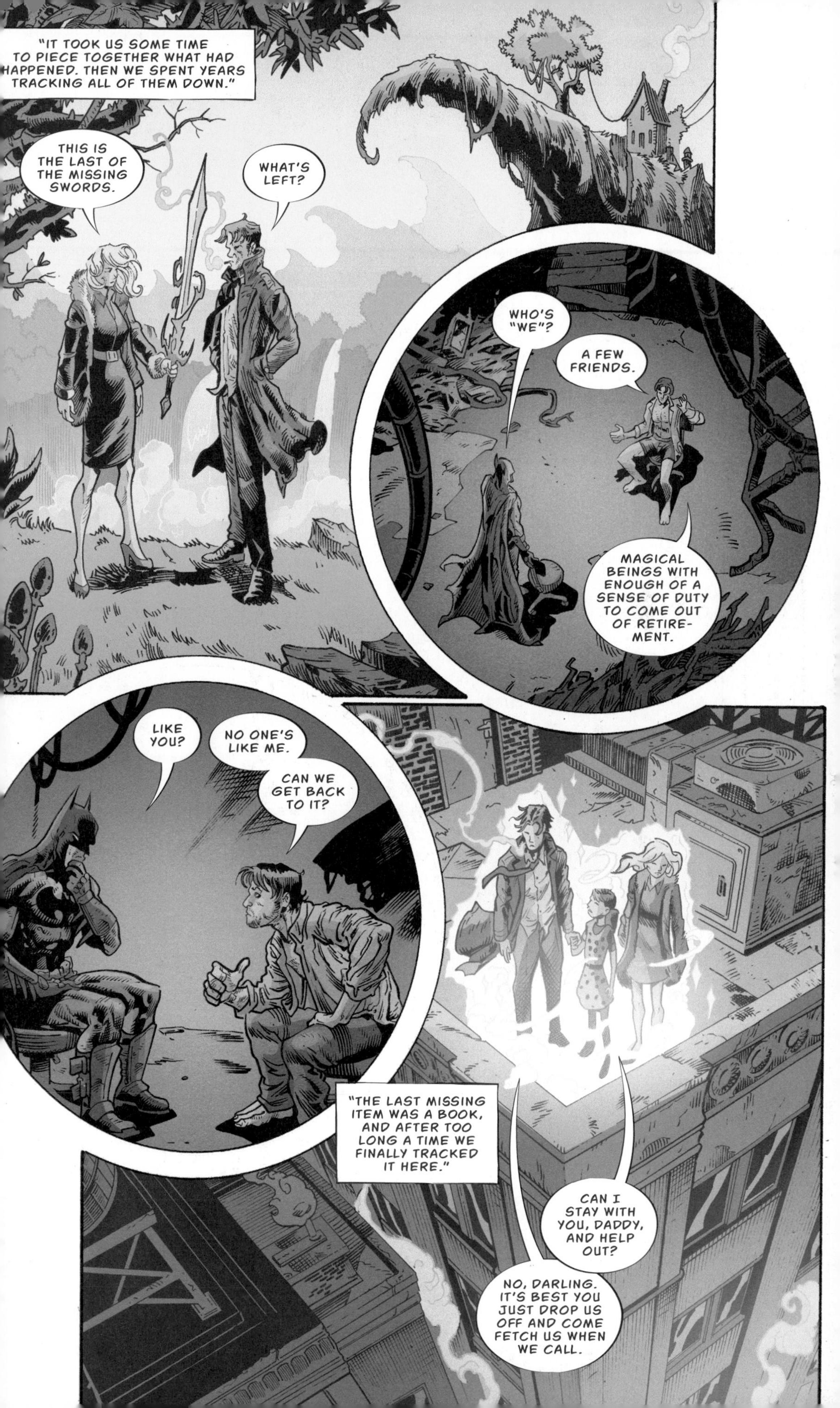
"IT TOOK US SOME TIME TO PIECE TOGETHER WHAT HAD HAPPENED. THEN WE SPENT YEARS TRACKING ALL OF THEM DOWN."
THIS IS THE LAST OF THE MISSING SWORDS.
WHAT'S LEFT?
WHO'S "WE"?
A FEW FRIENDS.
MAGICAL BEINGS WITH ENOUGH OF A SENSE OF DUTY TO COME OUT OF RETIRE-MENT.
LIKE YOU?
NO ONE'S LIKE ME.
CAN WE GET BACK TO IT?
"THE LAST MISSING ITEM WAS A BOOK, AND AFTER TOO LONG A TIME WE FINALLY TRACKED IT HERE."
CAN I STAY WITH YOU, DADDY, AND HELP OUT?
NO, DARLING. IT'S BEST YOU JUST DROP US OFF AND COME FETCH US WHEN WE CALL.

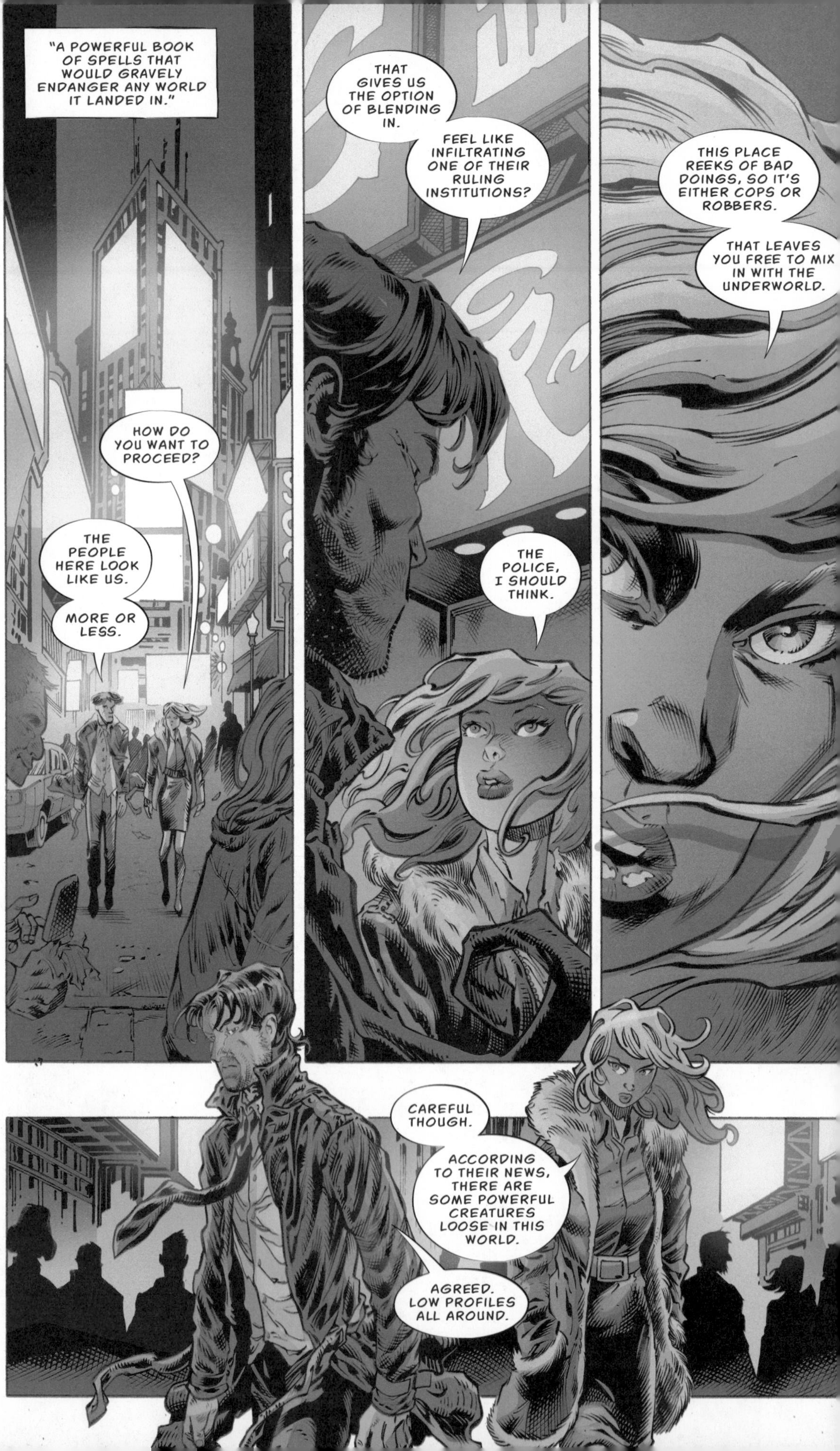
"A POWERFUL BOOK OF SPELLS THAT WOULD GRAVELY ENDANGER ANY WORLD IT LANDED IN."
HOW DO YOU WANT TO PROCEED?
THE PEOPLE HERE LOOK LIKE US.
MORE OR LESS.
THAT GIVES US THE OPTION OF BLENDING IN.
FEEL LIKE INFILTRATING ONE OF THEIR RULING INSTITUTIONS?
THE POLICE, I SHOULD THINK.
THIS PLACE REEKS OF BAD DOINGS, SO IT'S EITHER COPS OR ROBBERS.
THAT LEAVES YOU FREE TO MIX IN WITH THE UNDERWORLD.
CAREFUL THOUGH.
ACCORDING TO THEIR NEWS, THERE ARE SOME POWERFUL CREATURES LOOSE IN THIS WORLD.
AGREED. LOW PROFILES ALL AROUND.

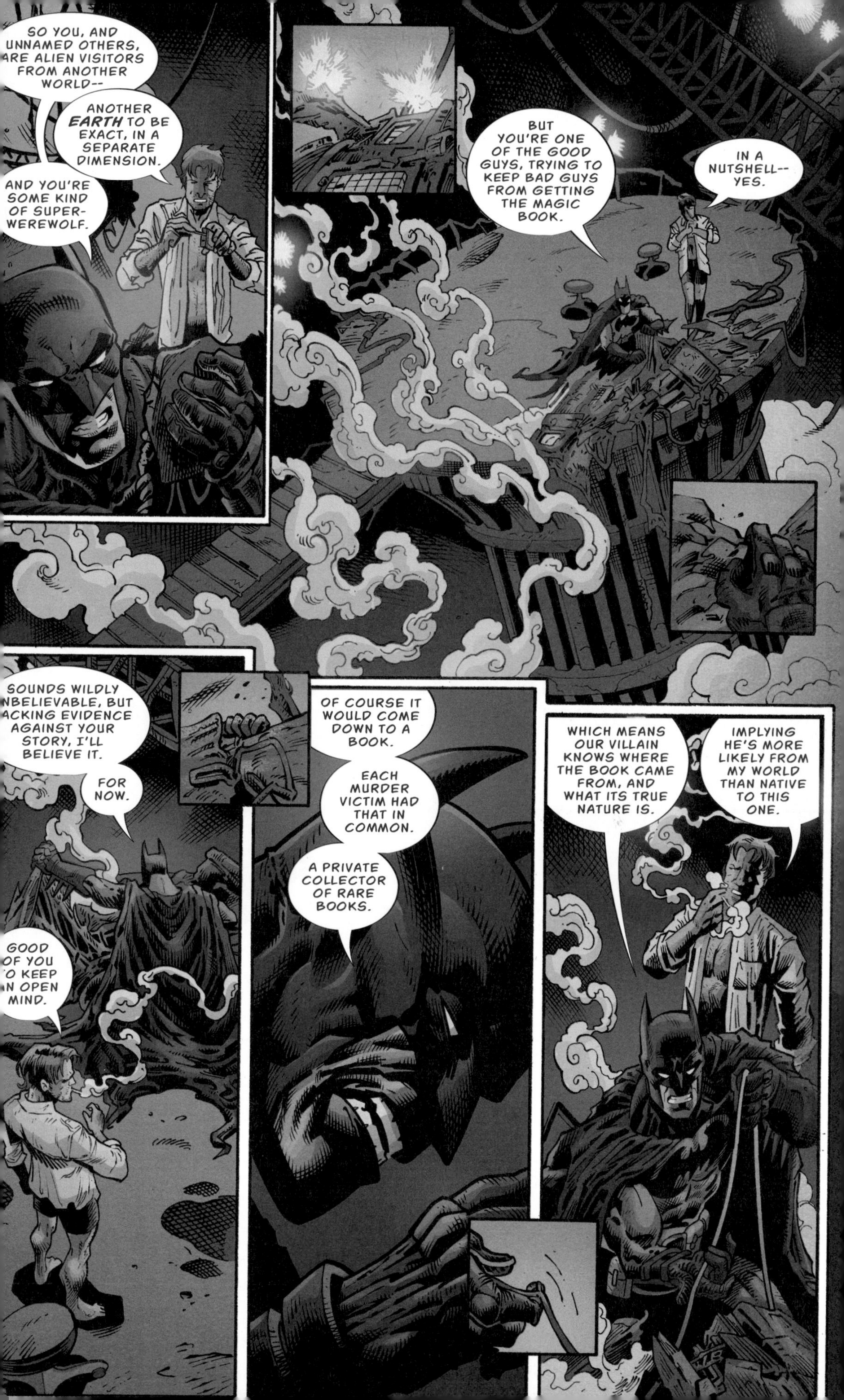
SO YOU, AND UNNAMED OTHERS, ARE ALIEN VISITORS FROM ANOTHER WORLD--
ANOTHER EARTH TO BE EXACT, IN A SEPARATE DIMENSION.
AND YOU'RE SOME KIND OF SUPER-WEREWOLF.
BUT YOU'RE ONE OF THE GOOD GUYS, TRYING TO KEEP BAD GUYS FROM GETTING THE MAGIC BOOK.
IN A NUTSHELL-- YES.
SOUNDS WILDLY NBELIEVABLE, BUT ACKING EVIDENCE AGAINST YOUR STORY, I'LL BELIEVE IT.
FOR NOW.
GOOD OF YOU O KEEP N OPEN MIND.
OF COURSE IT WOULD COME DOWN TO A BOOK.
EACH MURDER VICTIM HAD THAT IN COMMON.
A PRIVATE COLLECTOR OF RARE BOOKS.
WHICH MEANS OUR VILLAIN KNOWS WHERE THE BOOK CAME FROM, AND WHAT ITS TRUE NATURE IS.
IMPLYING HE'S MORE LIKELY FROM MY WORLD THAN NATIVE TO THIS ONE.

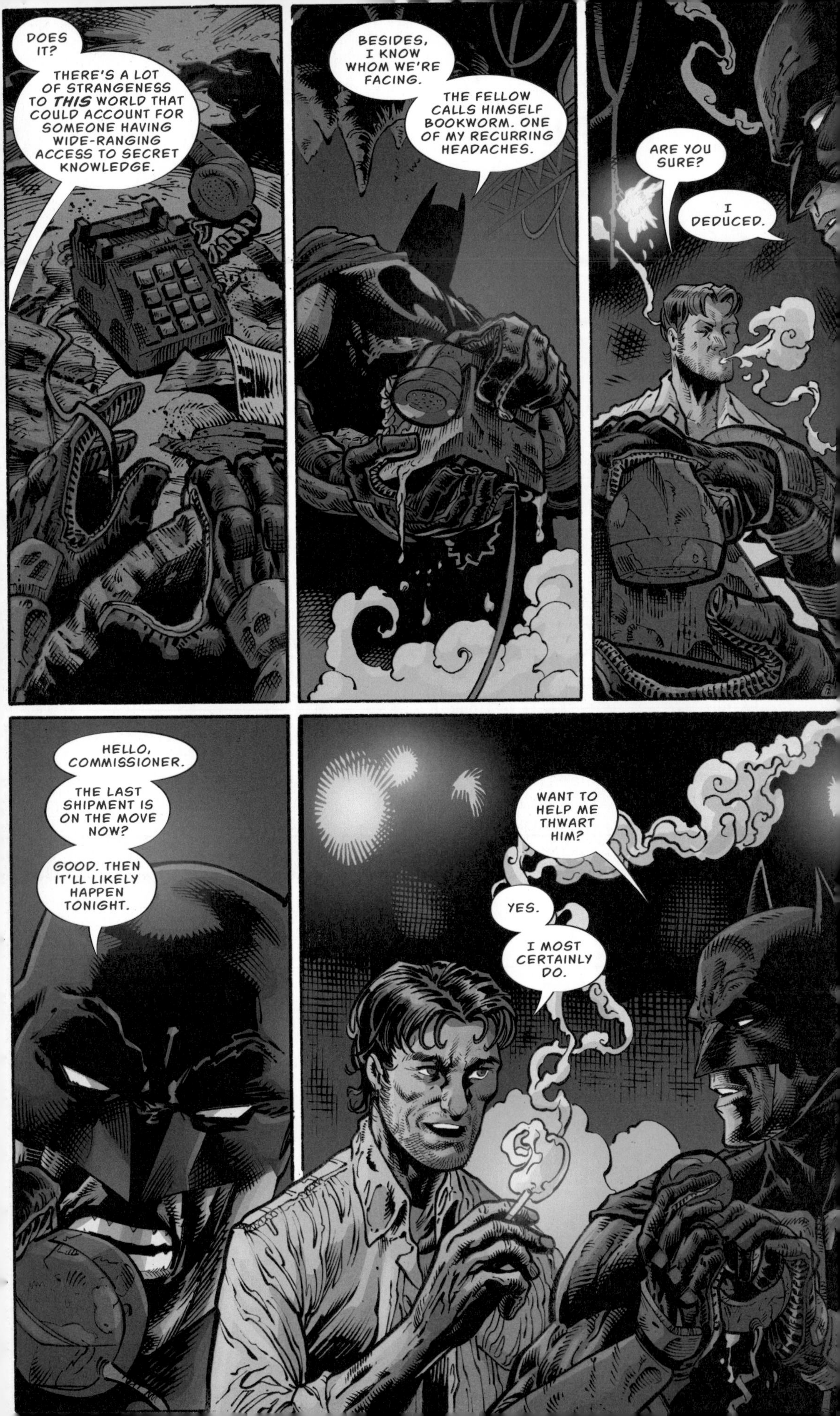
DOES IT?
THERE'S A LOT OF STRANGENESS TO *THIS* WORLD THAT COULD ACCOUNT FOR SOMEONE HAVING WIDE-RANGING ACCESS TO SECRET KNOWLEDGE.
BESIDES, I KNOW WHOM WE'RE FACING.
THE FELLOW CALLS HIMSELF BOOKWORM. ONE OF MY RECURRING HEADACHES.
ARE YOU SURE?
I DEDUCED.
HELLO, COMMISSIONER.
THE LAST SHIPMENT IS ON THE MOVE NOW?
GOOD. THEN IT'LL LIKELY HAPPEN TONIGHT.
WANT TO HELP ME THWART HIM?
YES.
I MOST CERTAINLY DO.

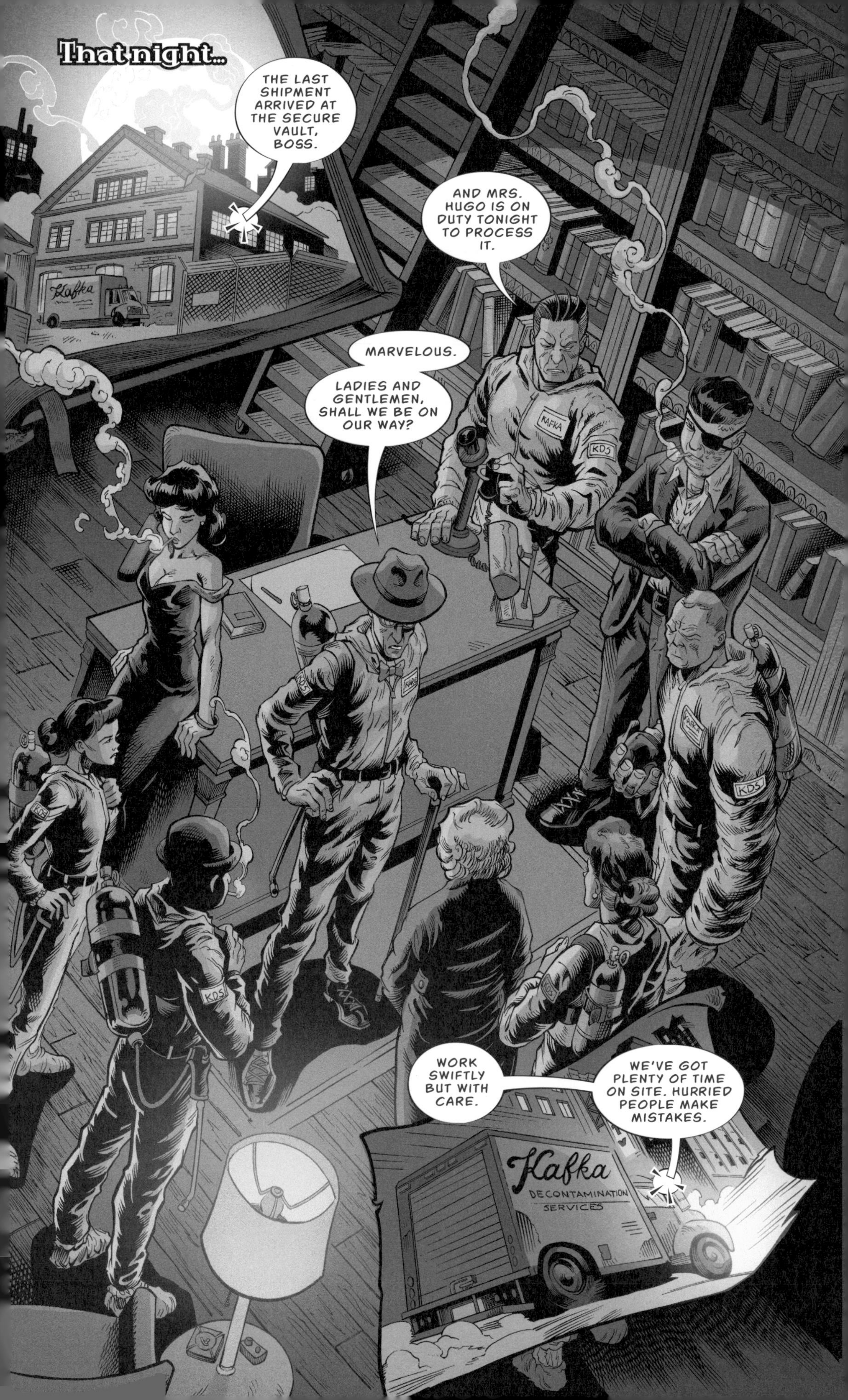
That night...
THE LAST SHIPMENT ARRIVED AT THE SECURE VAULT, BOSS.
AND MRS. HUGO IS ON DUTY TONIGHT TO PROCESS IT.
MARVELOUS.
LADIES AND GENTLEMEN, SHALL WE BE ON OUR WAY?
WORK SWIFTLY BUT WITH CARE.
WE'VE GOT PLENTY OF TIME ON SITE. HURRIED PEOPLE MAKE MISTAKES.
Kafka DECONTAMINATION SERVICES

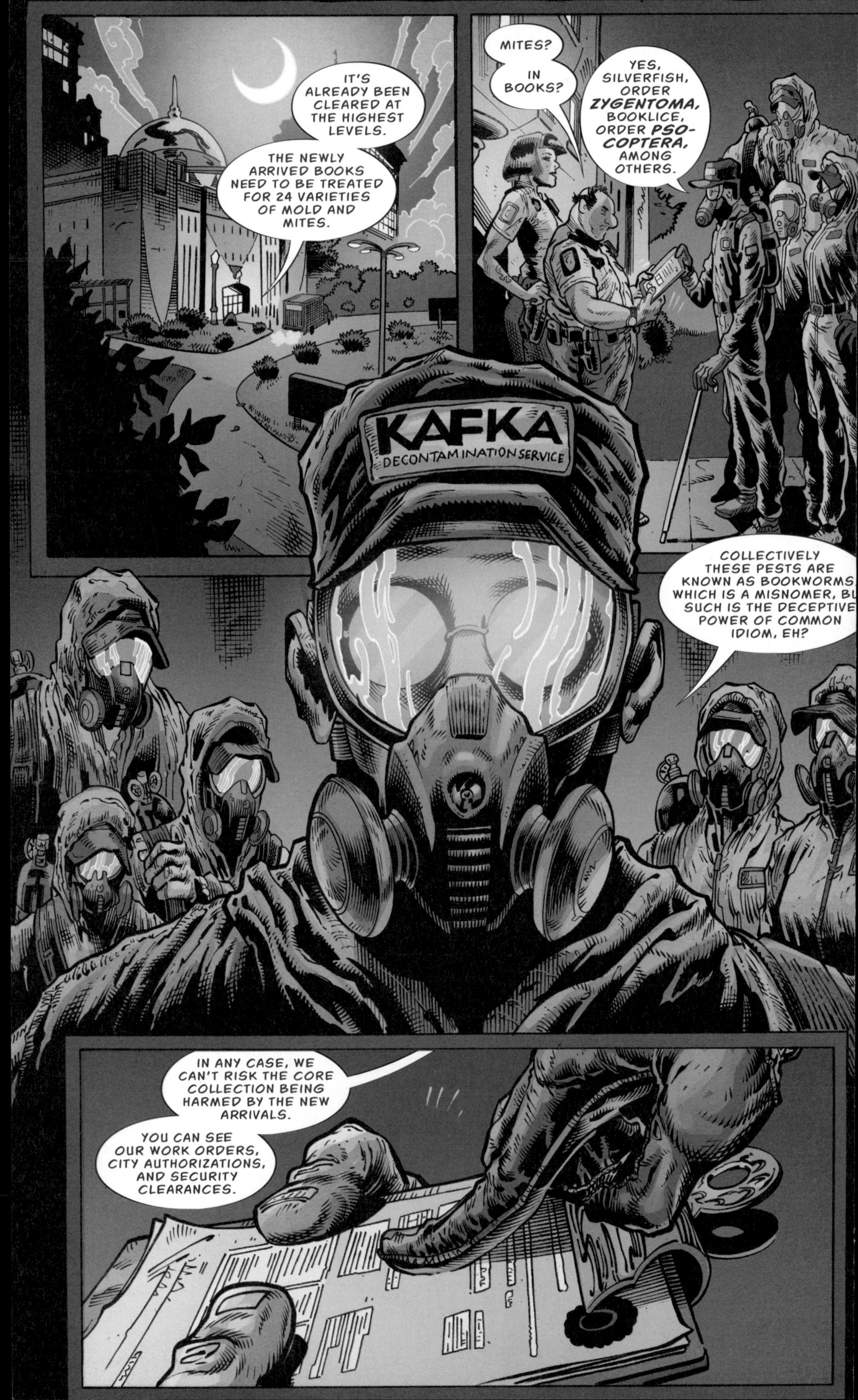
IT'S ALREADY BEEN CLEARED AT THE HIGHEST LEVELS.
THE NEWLY ARRIVED BOOKS NEED TO BE TREATED FOR 24 VARIETIES OF MOLD AND MITES.
MITES?
IN BOOKS?
YES, SILVERFISH, ORDER *ZYGENTOMA,* BOOKLICE, ORDER *PSO-COPTERA,* AMONG OTHERS.
KAFKA
DECONTAMINATION SERVICE
COLLECTIVELY THESE PESTS ARE KNOWN AS BOOKWORMS, WHICH IS A MISNOMER, BU SUCH IS THE DECEPTIVE POWER OF COMMON IDIOM, EH?
IN ANY CASE, WE CAN'T RISK THE CORE COLLECTION BEING HARMED BY THE NEW ARRIVALS.
YOU CAN SEE OUR WORK ORDERS, CITY AUTHORIZATIONS, AND SECURITY CLEARANCES.

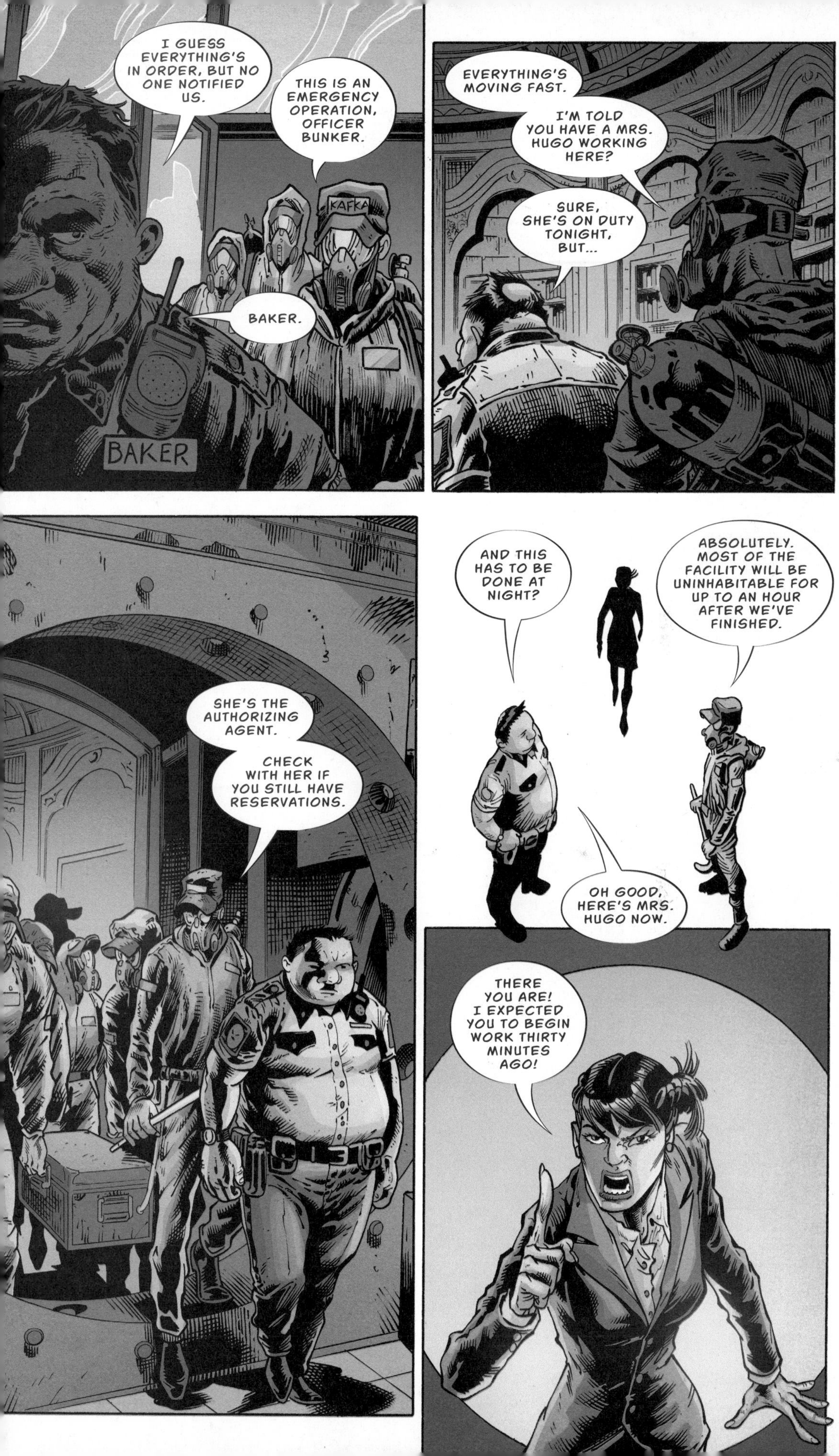
I GUESS EVERYTHING'S IN ORDER, BUT NO ONE NOTIFIED US.
THIS IS AN EMERGENCY OPERATION, OFFICER BUNKER.
KAFKA
BAKER.
BAKER
EVERYTHING'S MOVING FAST.
I'M TOLD YOU HAVE A MRS. HUGO WORKING HERE?
SURE, SHE'S ON DUTY TONIGHT, BUT...
SHE'S THE AUTHORIZING AGENT.
CHECK WITH HER IF YOU STILL HAVE RESERVATIONS.
AND THIS HAS TO BE DONE AT NIGHT?
ABSOLUTELY. MOST OF THE FACILITY WILL BE UNINHABITABLE FOR UP TO AN HOUR AFTER WE'VE FINISHED.
OH GOOD, HERE'S MRS. HUGO NOW.
THERE YOU ARE! I EXPECTED YOU TO BEGIN WORK THIRTY MINUTES AGO!

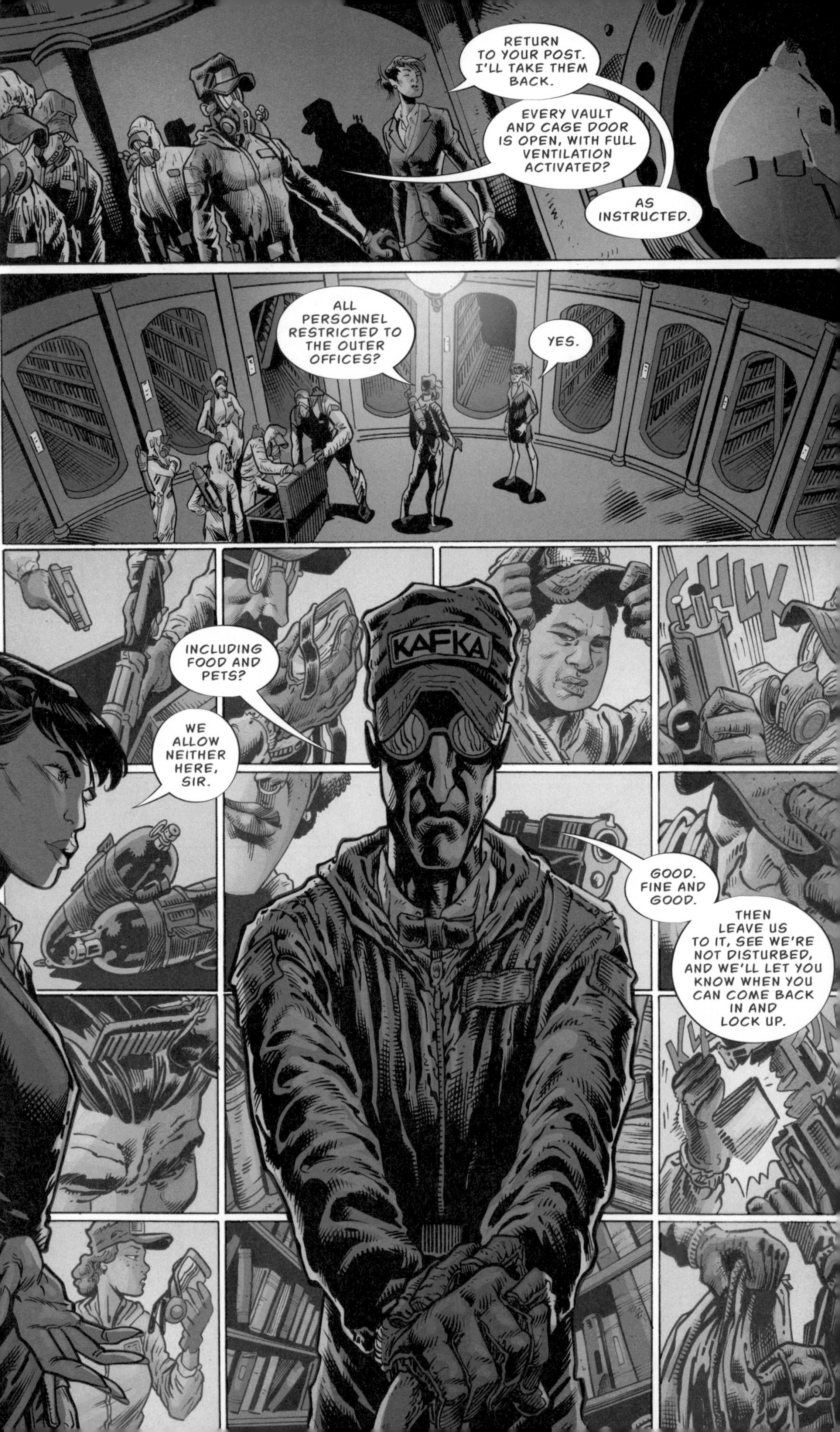

RETURN TO YOUR POST. I'LL TAKE THEM BACK.
EVERY VAULT AND CAGE DOOR IS OPEN, WITH FULL VENTILATION ACTIVATED?
AS INSTRUCTED.
ALL PERSONNEL RESTRICTED TO THE OUTER OFFICES?
YES.
KAFKA
INCLUDING FOOD AND PETS?
WE ALLOW NEITHER HERE, SIR.
CHLK
GOOD. FINE AND GOOD.
THEN LEAVE US TO IT, SEE WE'RE NOT DISTURBED, AND WE'LL LET YOU KNOW WHEN YOU CAN COME BACK IN AND LOCK UP.

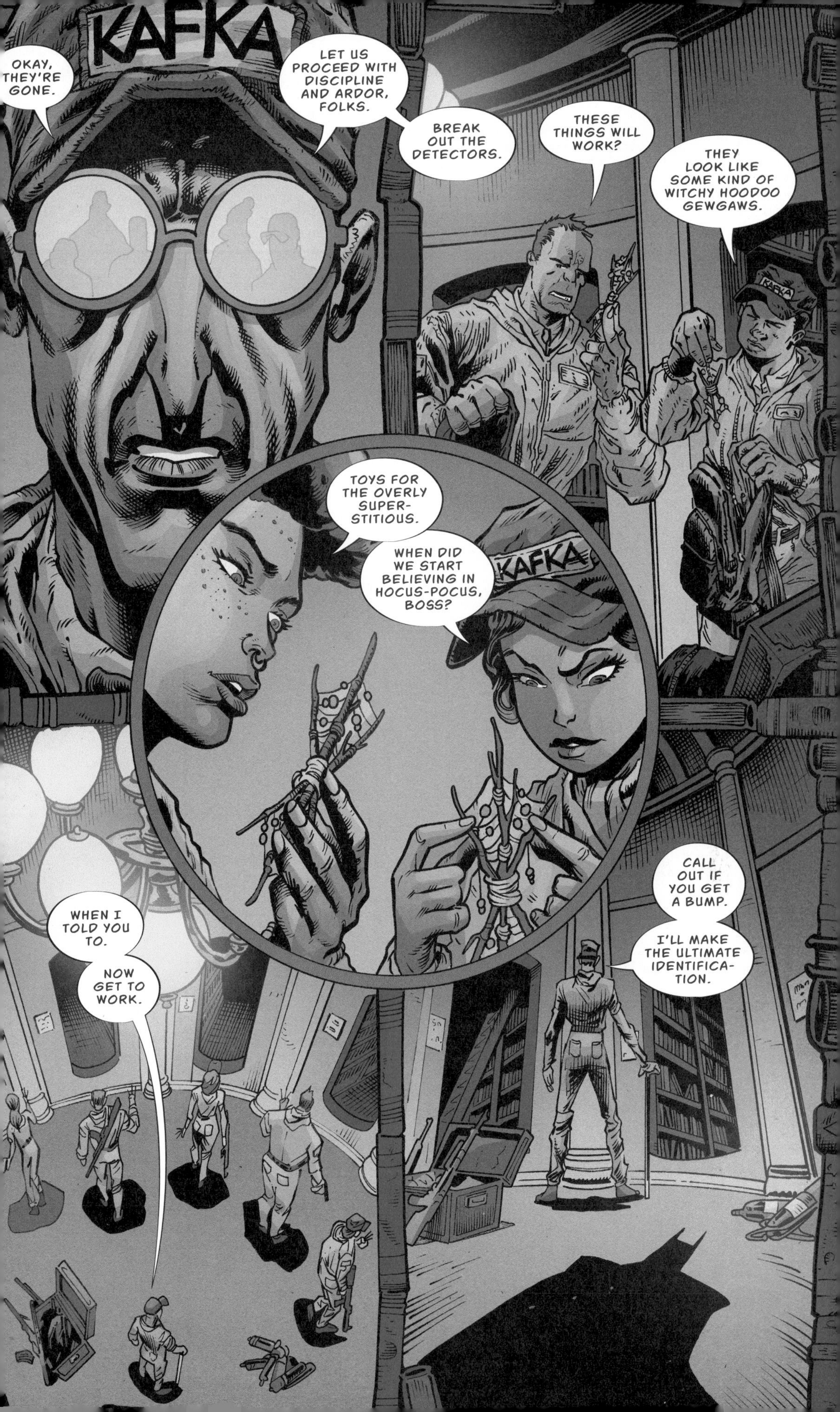

KAFKA
OKAY, THEY'RE GONE.
LET US PROCEED WITH DISCIPLINE AND ARDOR, FOLKS.
BREAK OUT THE DETECTORS.
THESE THINGS WILL WORK?
THEY LOOK LIKE SOME KIND OF WITCHY HOODOO GEWGAWS.
KAFKA
TOYS FOR THE OVERLY SUPER-STITIOUS.
WHEN DID WE START BELIEVING IN HOCUS-POCUS, BOSS?
KAFKA
WHEN I TOLD YOU TO.
NOW GET TO WORK.
CALL OUT IF YOU GET A BUMP.
I'LL MAKE THE ULTIMATE IDENTIFICA-TION.

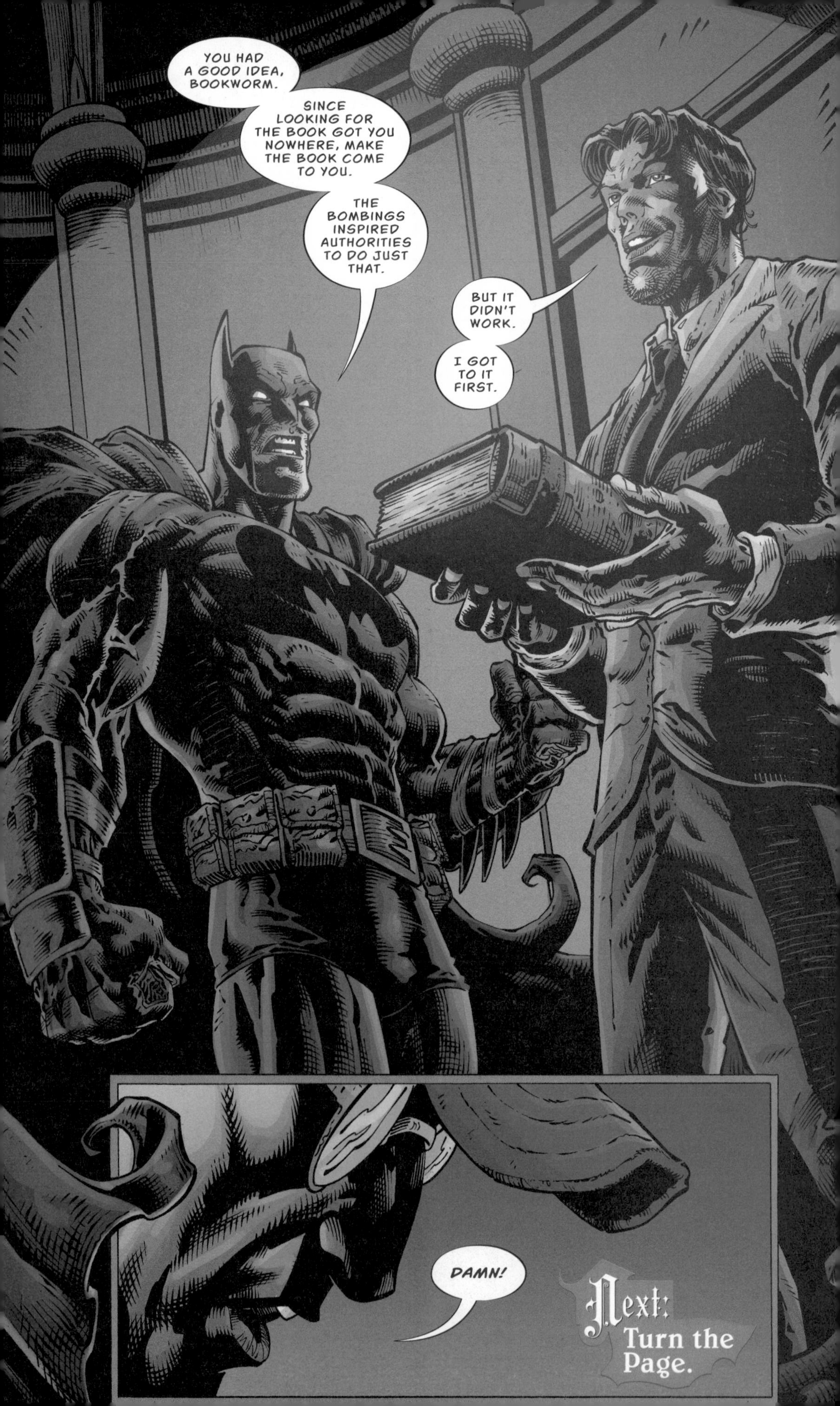

YOU HAD A GOOD IDEA, BOOKWORM.
SINCE LOOKING FOR THE BOOK GOT YOU NOWHERE, MAKE THE BOOK COME TO YOU.
THE BOMBINGS INSPIRED AUTHORITIES TO DO JUST THAT.
BUT IT DIDN'T WORK.
I GOT TO IT FIRST.
DAMN!
Next: Turn the Page.

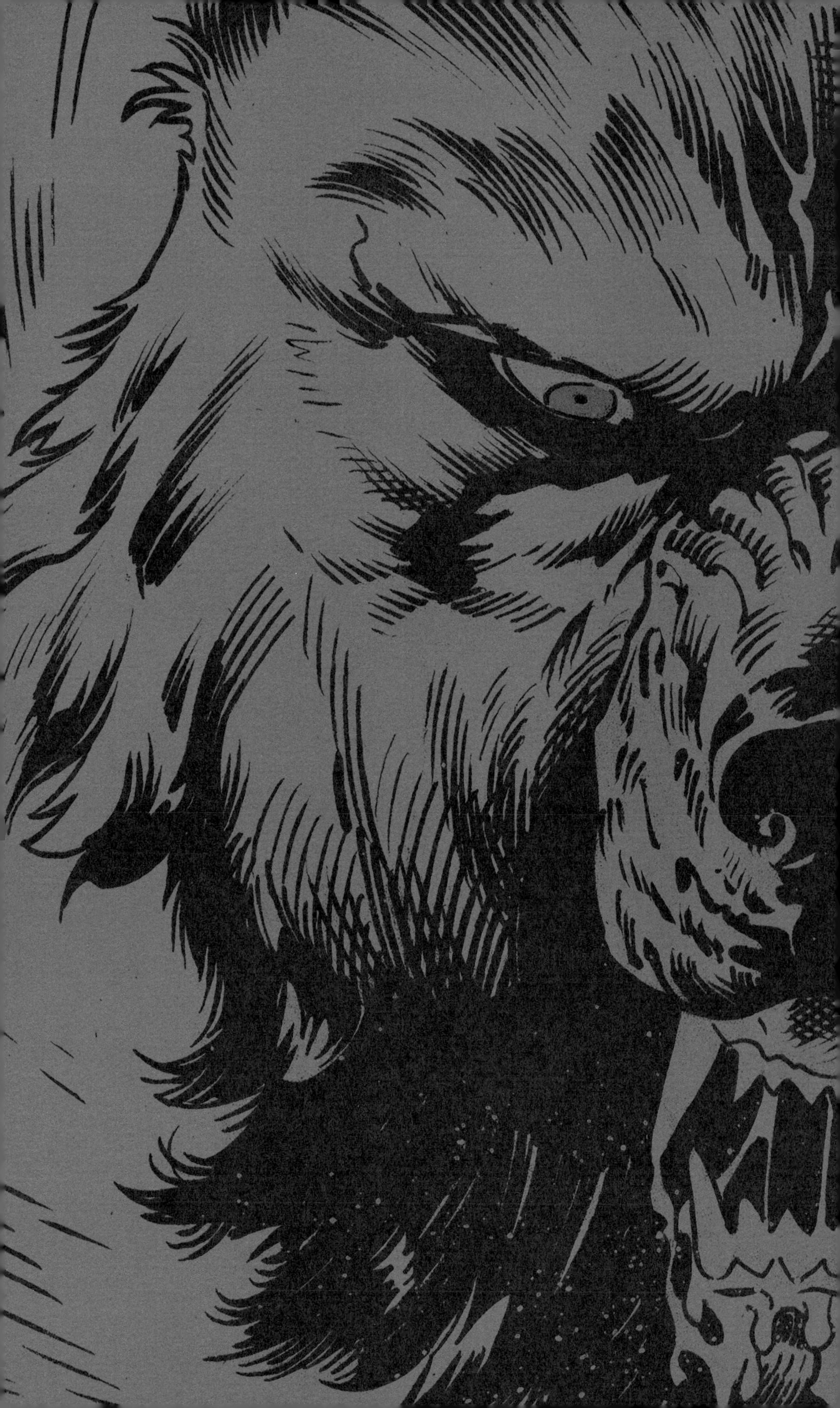

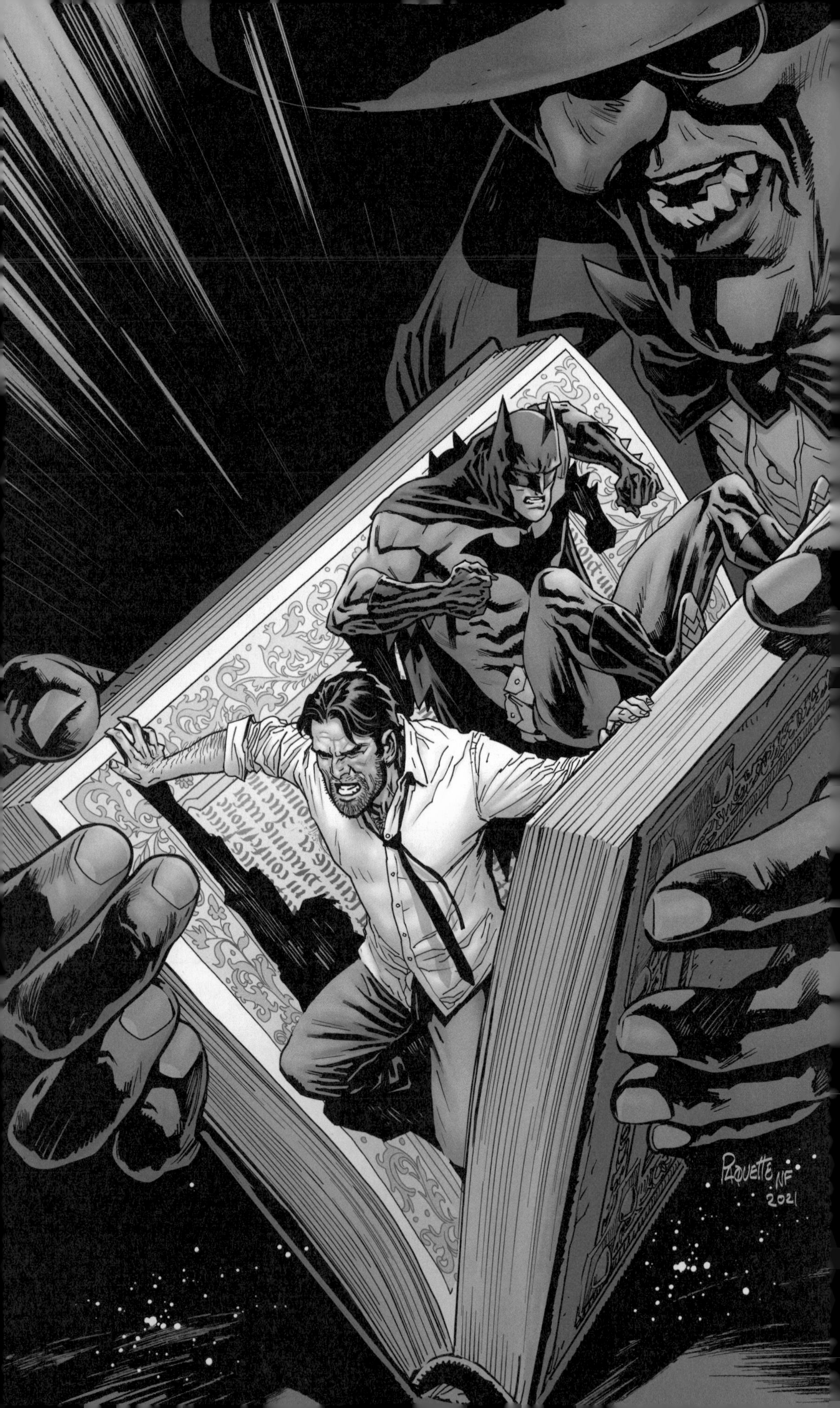
PAQUETTE NF
2021

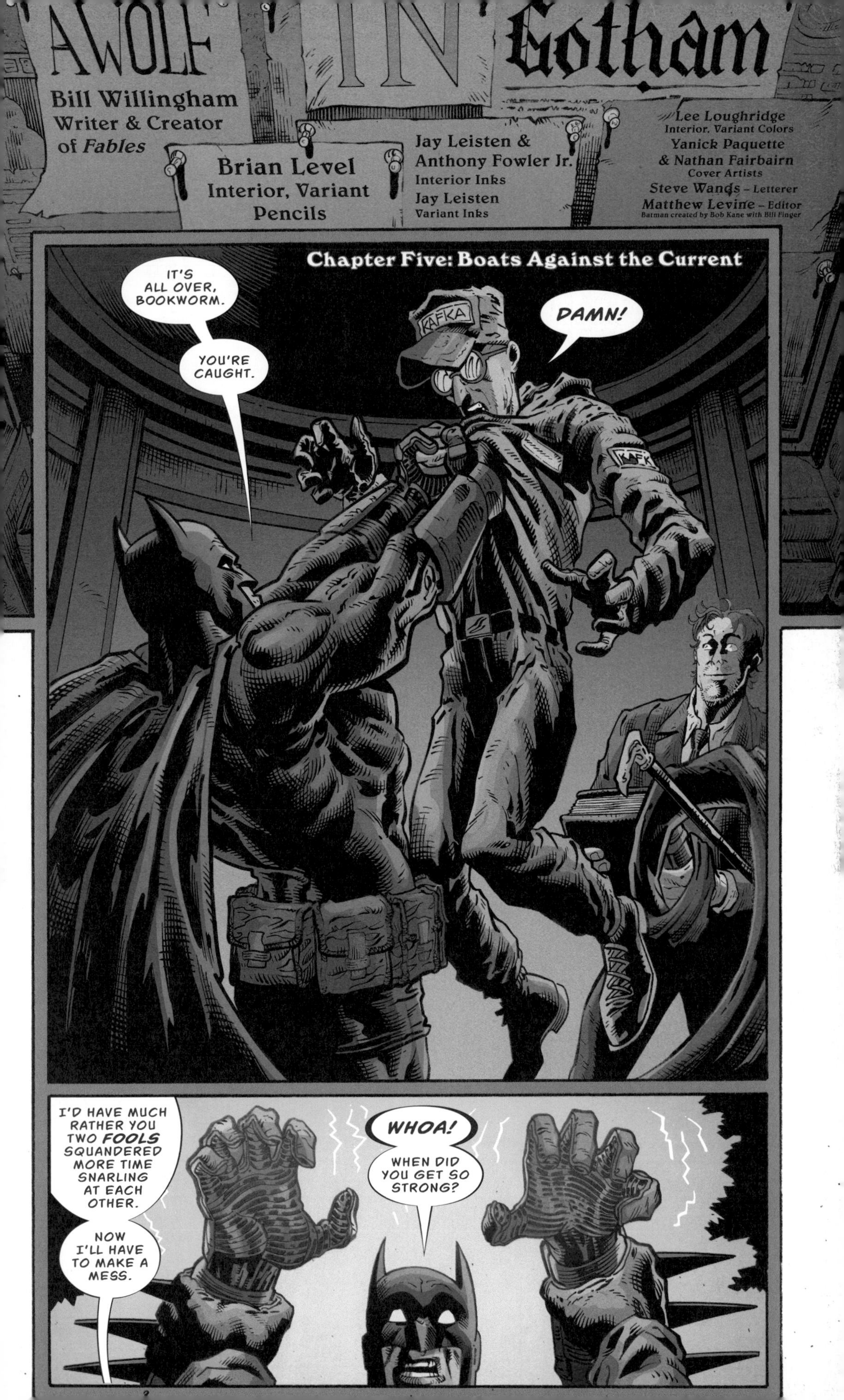

A WOLF IN Gotham
Bill Willingham Writer & Creator of Fables
Brian Level Interior, Variant Pencils
Jay Leisten & Anthony Fowler Jr. Interior Inks
Jay Leisten Variant Inks
Lee Loughridge Interior, Variant Colors
Yanick Paquette & Nathan Fairbairn Cover Artists
Steve Wands – Letterer
Matthew Levine – Editor
Batman created by Bob Kane with Bill Finger
Chapter Five: Boats Against the Current
IT'S ALL OVER, BOOKWORM.
YOU'RE CAUGHT.
DAMN!
KAFKA
KAFK
I'D HAVE MUCH RATHER YOU TWO FOOLS SQUANDERED MORE TIME SNARLING AT EACH OTHER.
NOW I'LL HAVE TO MAKE A MESS.
WHOA!
WHEN DID YOU GET SO STRONG?

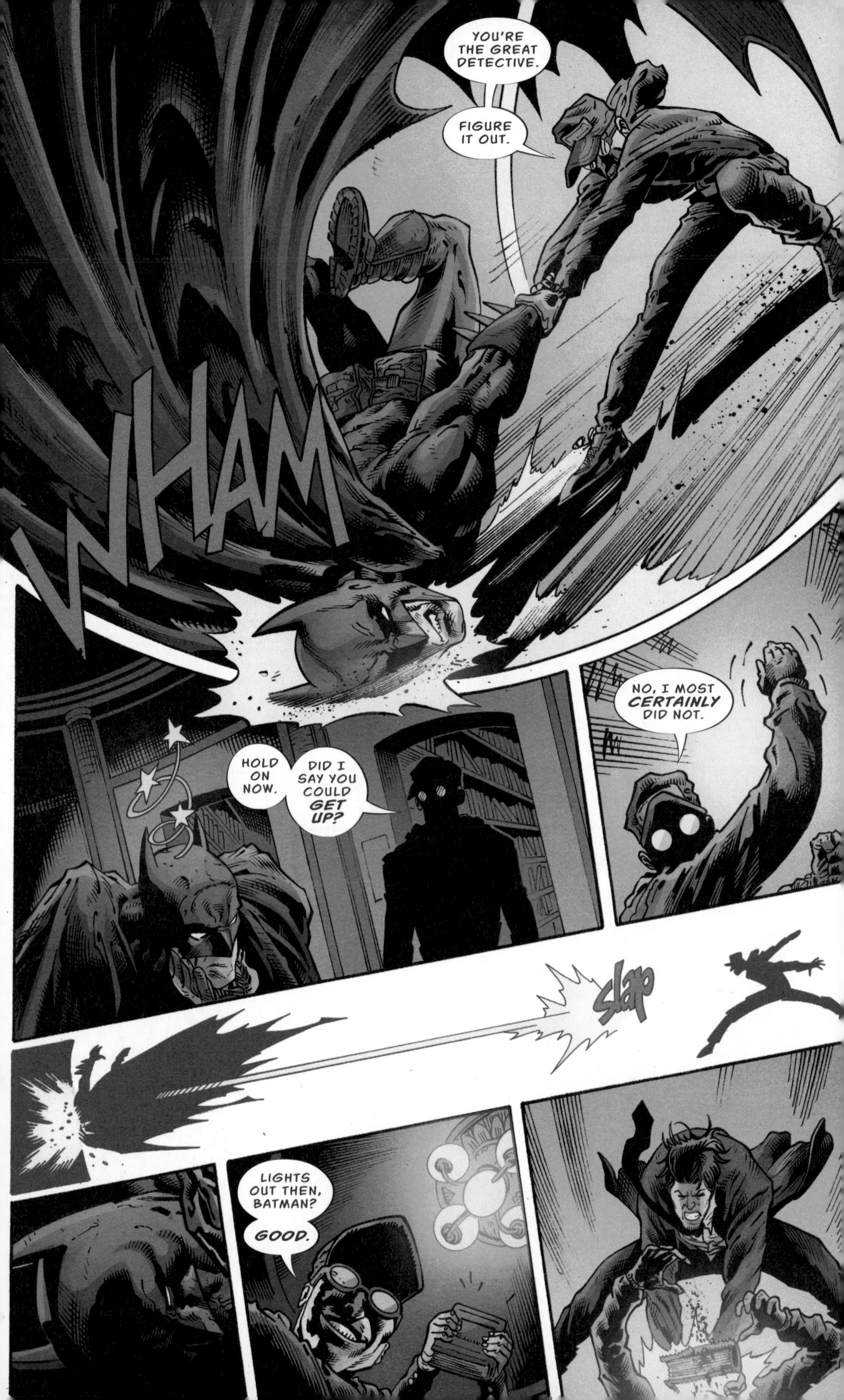
YOU'RE THE GREAT DETECTIVE.
FIGURE IT OUT.
WHAM
HOLD ON NOW.
DID I SAY YOU COULD GET UP?
NO, I MOST CERTAINLY DID NOT.
slap
LIGHTS OUT THEN, BATMAN?
GOOD.

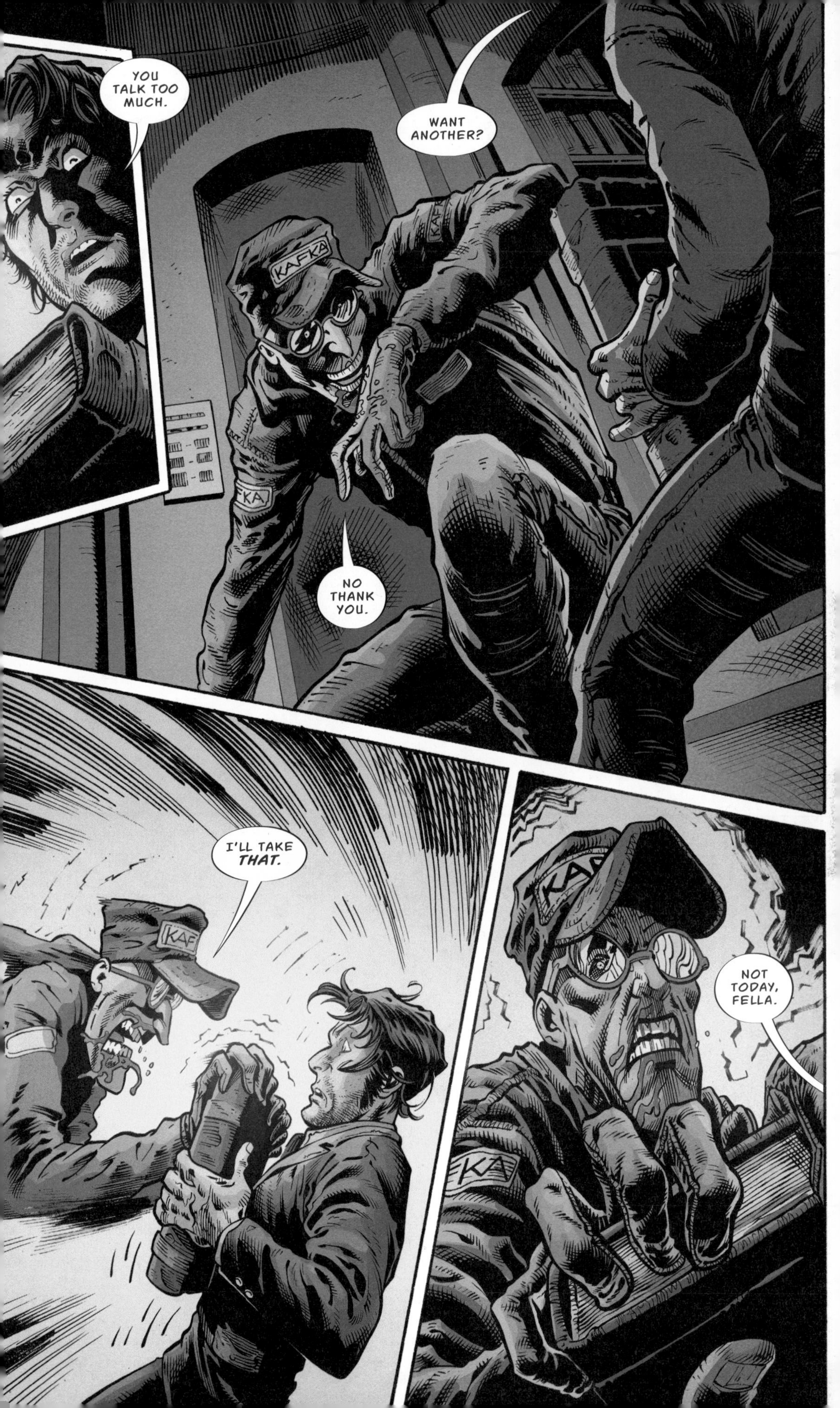
YOU TALK TOO MUCH.
WANT ANOTHER?
NO THANK YOU.
I'LL TAKE *THAT.*
NOT TODAY, FELLA.

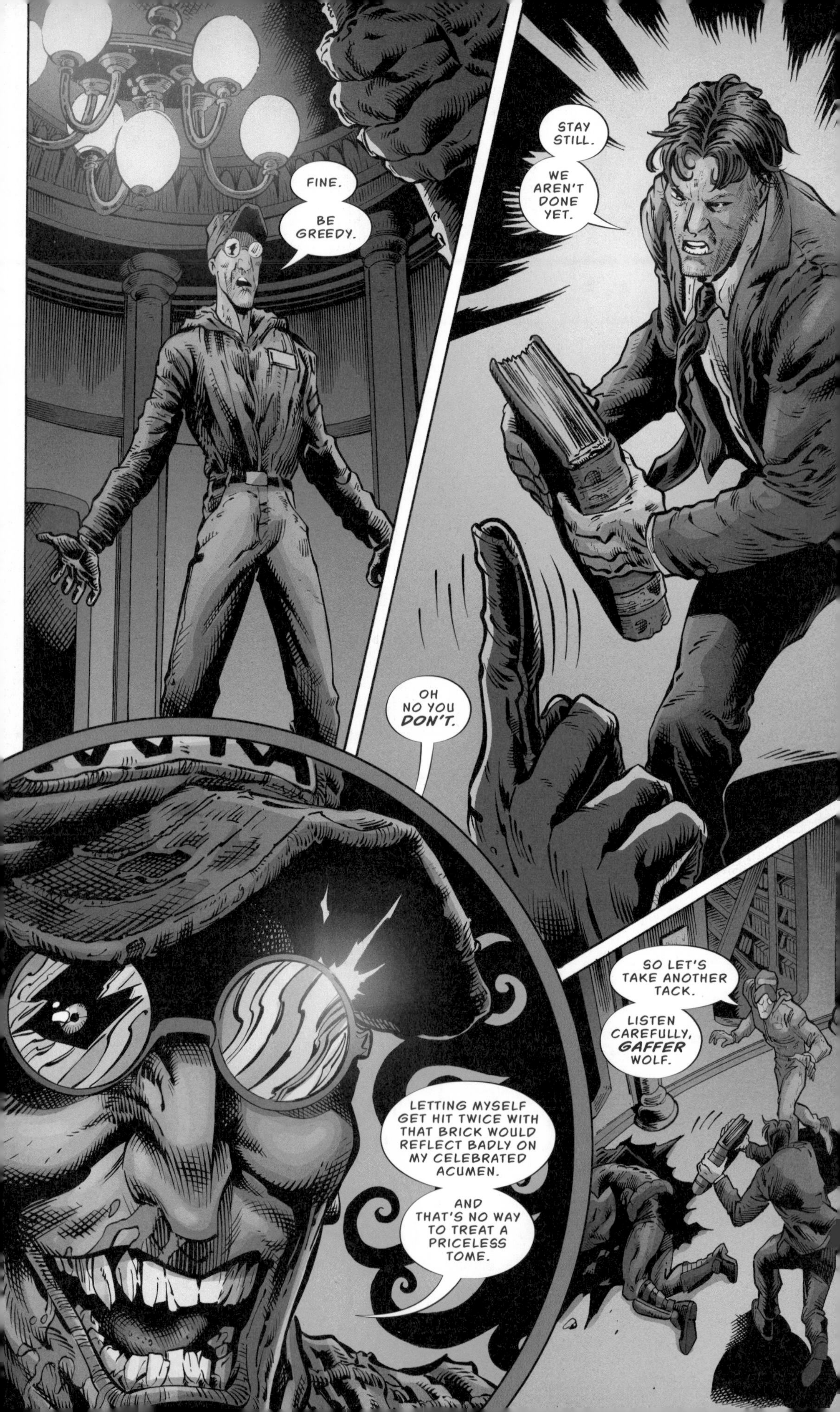
FINE.
BE GREEDY.
STAY STILL.
WE AREN'T DONE YET.
OH NO YOU **DON'T.**
LETTING MYSELF GET HIT TWICE WITH THAT BRICK WOULD REFLECT BADLY ON MY CELEBRATED ACUMEN.
AND THAT'S NO WAY TO TREAT A PRICELESS TOME.
SO LET'S TAKE ANOTHER TACK.
LISTEN CAREFULLY, ***GAFFER*** WOLF.

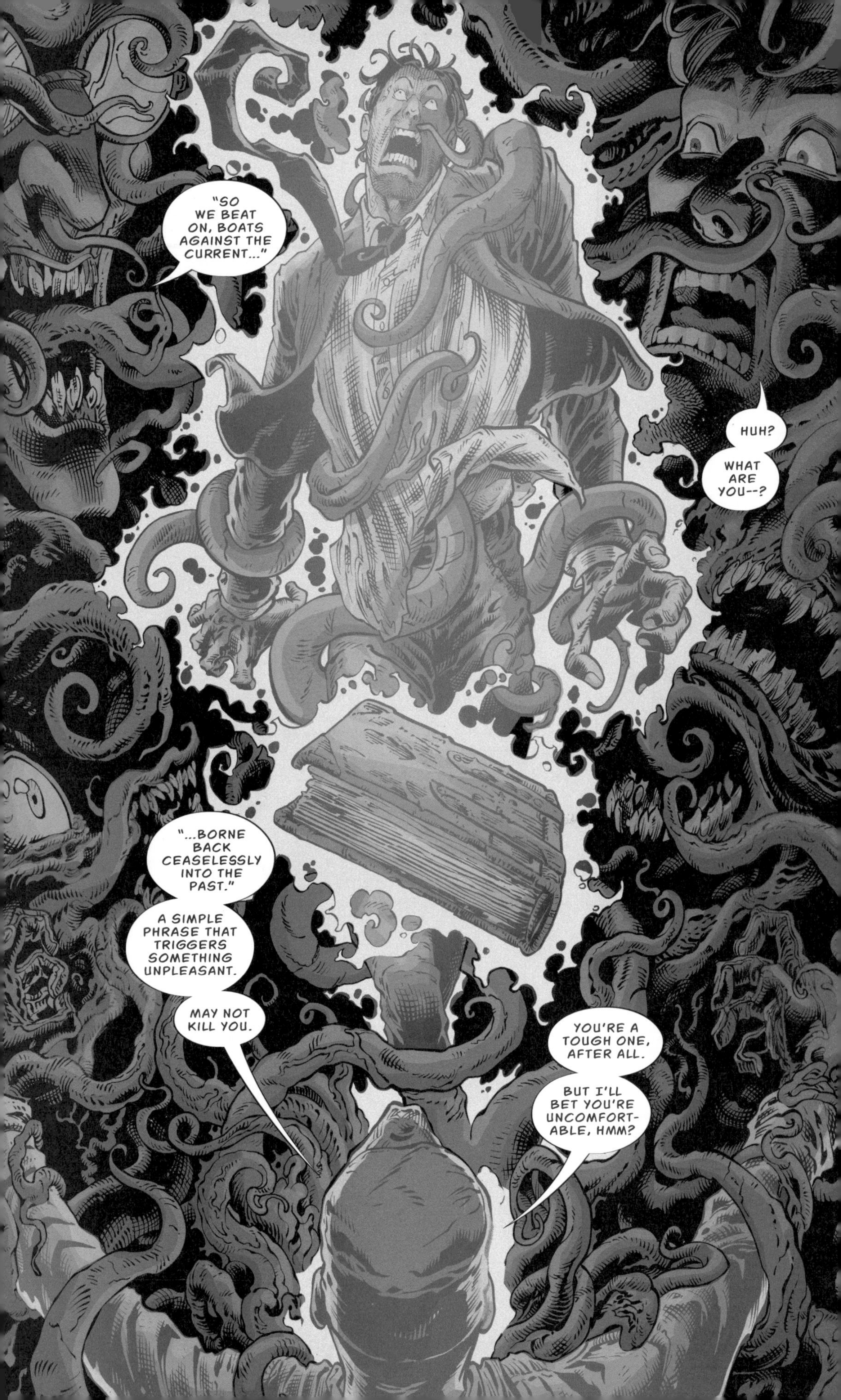
"SO WE BEAT ON, BOATS AGAINST THE CURRENT..."
HUH?
WHAT ARE YOU--?
"...BORNE BACK CEASELESSLY INTO THE PAST."
A SIMPLE PHRASE THAT TRIGGERS SOMETHING UNPLEASANT.
MAY NOT KILL YOU.
YOU'RE A TOUGH ONE, AFTER ALL.
BUT I'LL BET YOU'RE UNCOMFORT-ABLE, HMM?

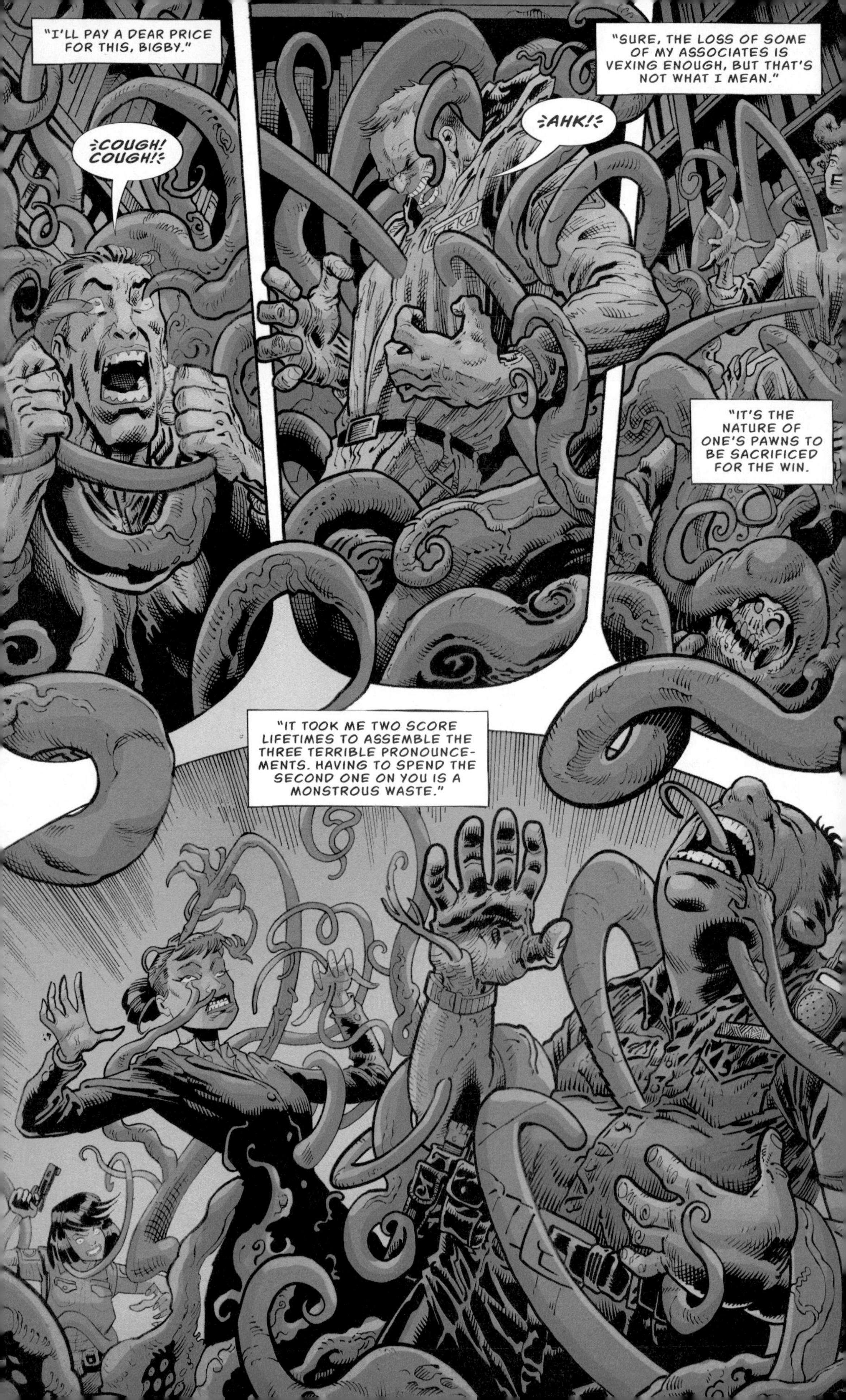
"I'LL PAY A DEAR PRICE FOR THIS, BIGBY."
COUGH! COUGH!
AHK!
"SURE, THE LOSS OF SOME OF MY ASSOCIATES IS VEXING ENOUGH, BUT THAT'S NOT WHAT I MEAN."
"IT'S THE NATURE OF ONE'S PAWNS TO BE SACRIFICED FOR THE WIN.
"IT TOOK ME TWO SCORE LIFETIMES TO ASSEMBLE THE THREE TERRIBLE PRONOUNCE-MENTS. HAVING TO SPEND THE SECOND ONE ON YOU IS A MONSTROUS WASTE."

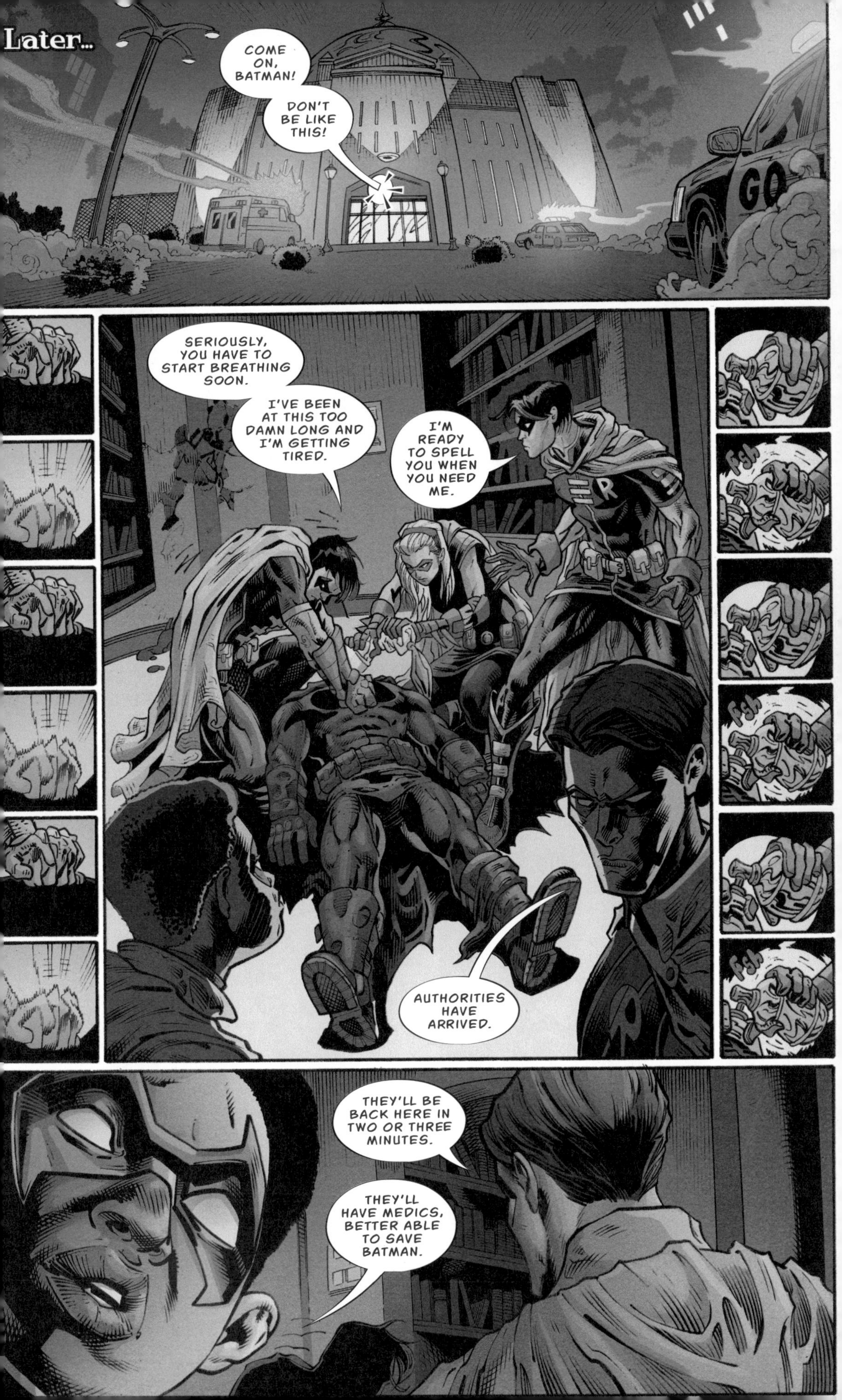
Later...
COME ON, BATMAN!
DON'T BE LIKE THIS!
GO
SERIOUSLY, YOU HAVE TO START BREATHING SOON.
I'VE BEEN AT THIS TOO DAMN LONG AND I'M GETTING TIRED.
I'M READY TO SPELL YOU WHEN YOU NEED ME.
AUTHORITIES HAVE ARRIVED.
THEY'LL BE BACK HERE IN TWO OR THREE MINUTES.
THEY'LL HAVE MEDICS, BETTER ABLE TO SAVE BATMAN.

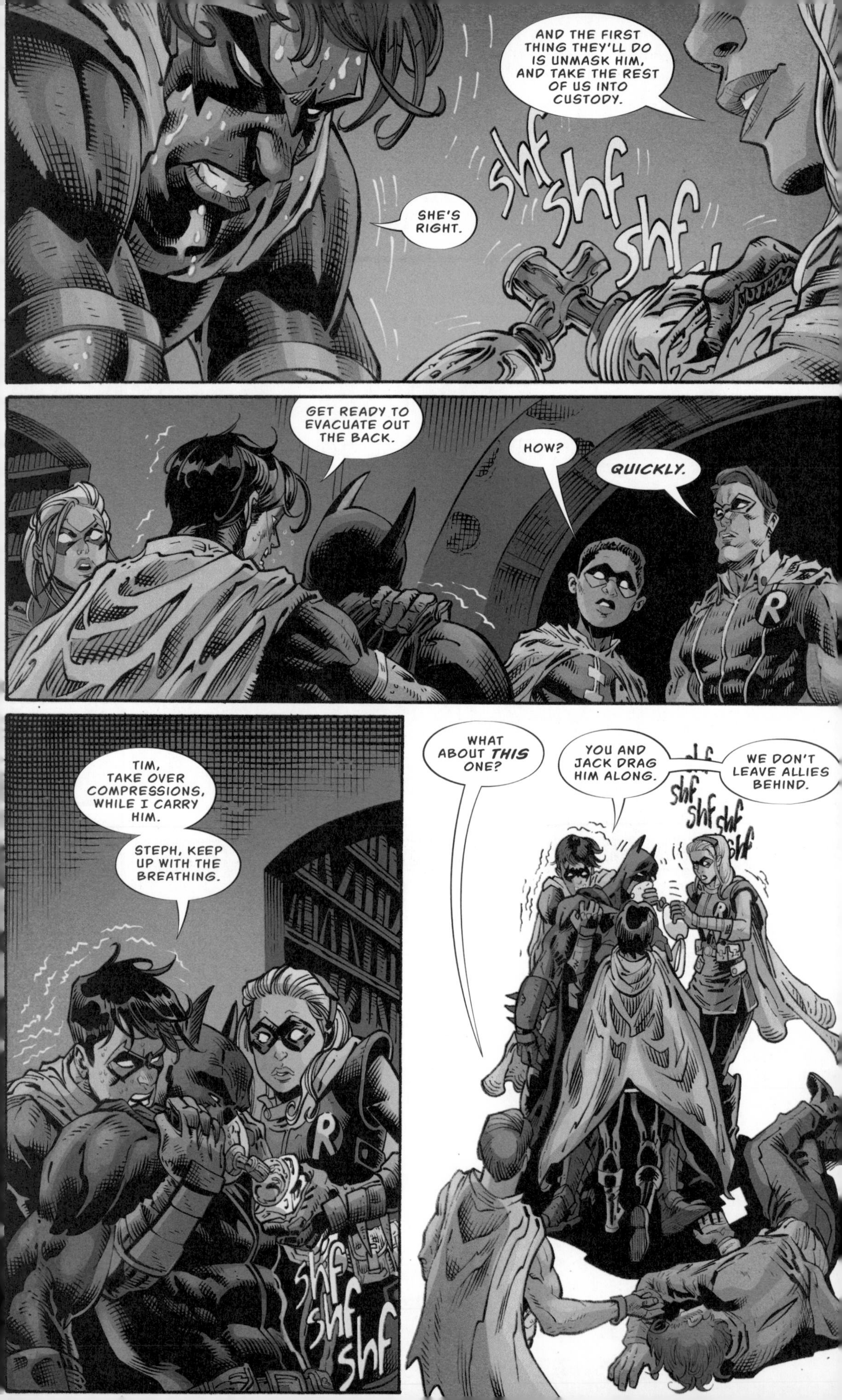
AND THE FIRST THING THEY'LL DO IS UNMASK HIM, AND TAKE THE REST OF US INTO CUSTODY.
SHE'S RIGHT.
shf shf shf
GET READY TO EVACUATE OUT THE BACK.
HOW?
QUICKLY.
TIM, TAKE OVER COMPRESSIONS, WHILE I CARRY HIM.
STEPH, KEEP UP WITH THE BREATHING.
shf shf shf
WHAT ABOUT THIS ONE?
YOU AND JACK DRAG HIM ALONG.
WE DON'T LEAVE ALLIES BEHIND.
shf shf shf shf

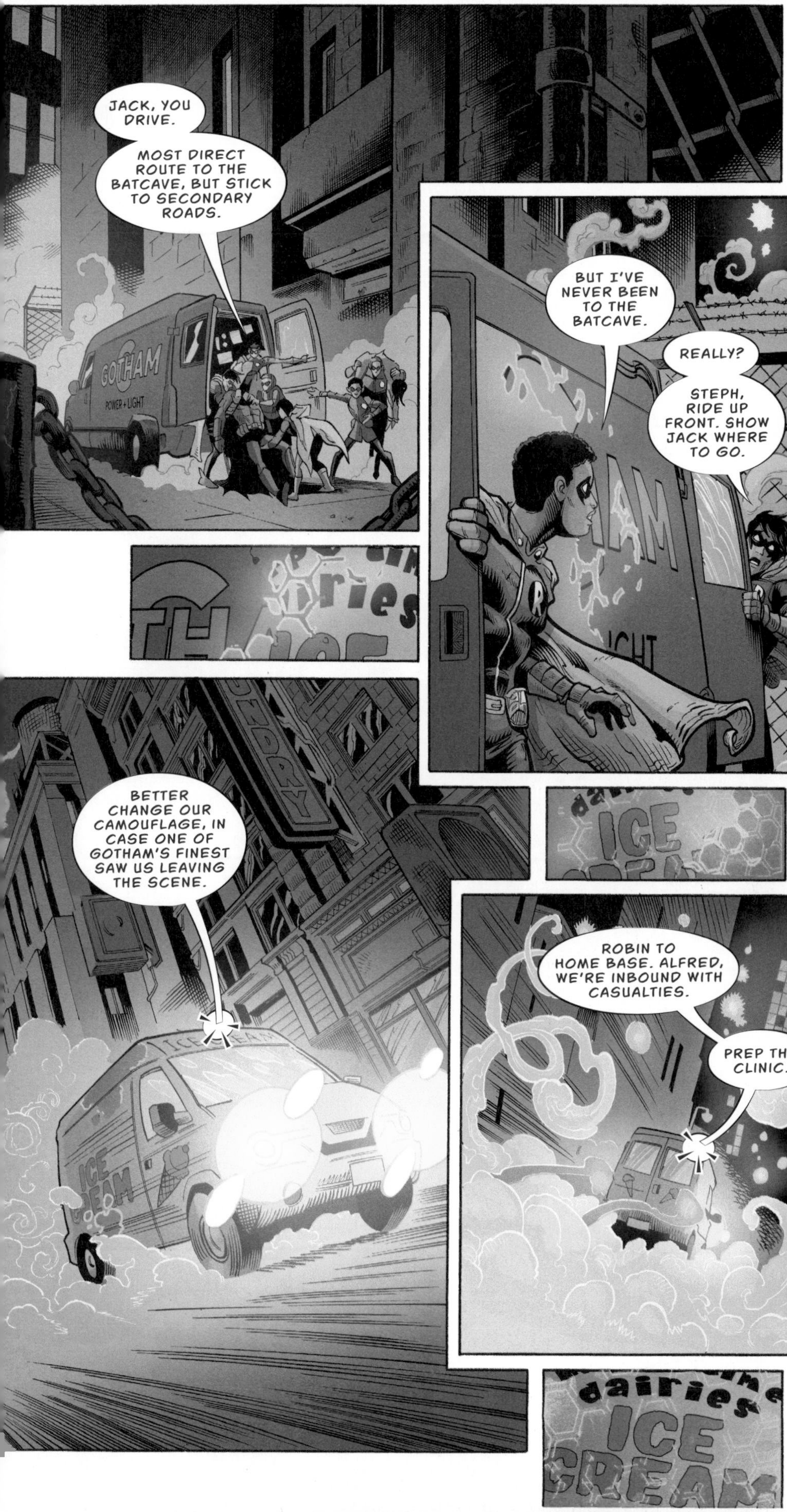
JACK, YOU DRIVE.
MOST DIRECT ROUTE TO THE BATCAVE, BUT STICK TO SECONDARY ROADS.
GOTHAM
POWER + LIGHT
BUT I'VE NEVER BEEN TO THE BATCAVE.
REALLY?
STEPH, RIDE UP FRONT. SHOW JACK WHERE TO GO.
BETTER CHANGE OUR CAMOUFLAGE, IN CASE ONE OF GOTHAM'S FINEST SAW US LEAVING THE SCENE.
ICE CREAM
ROBIN TO HOME BASE. ALFRED, WE'RE INBOUND WITH CASUALTIES.
PREP THE CLINIC.
dairies
ICE CREAM

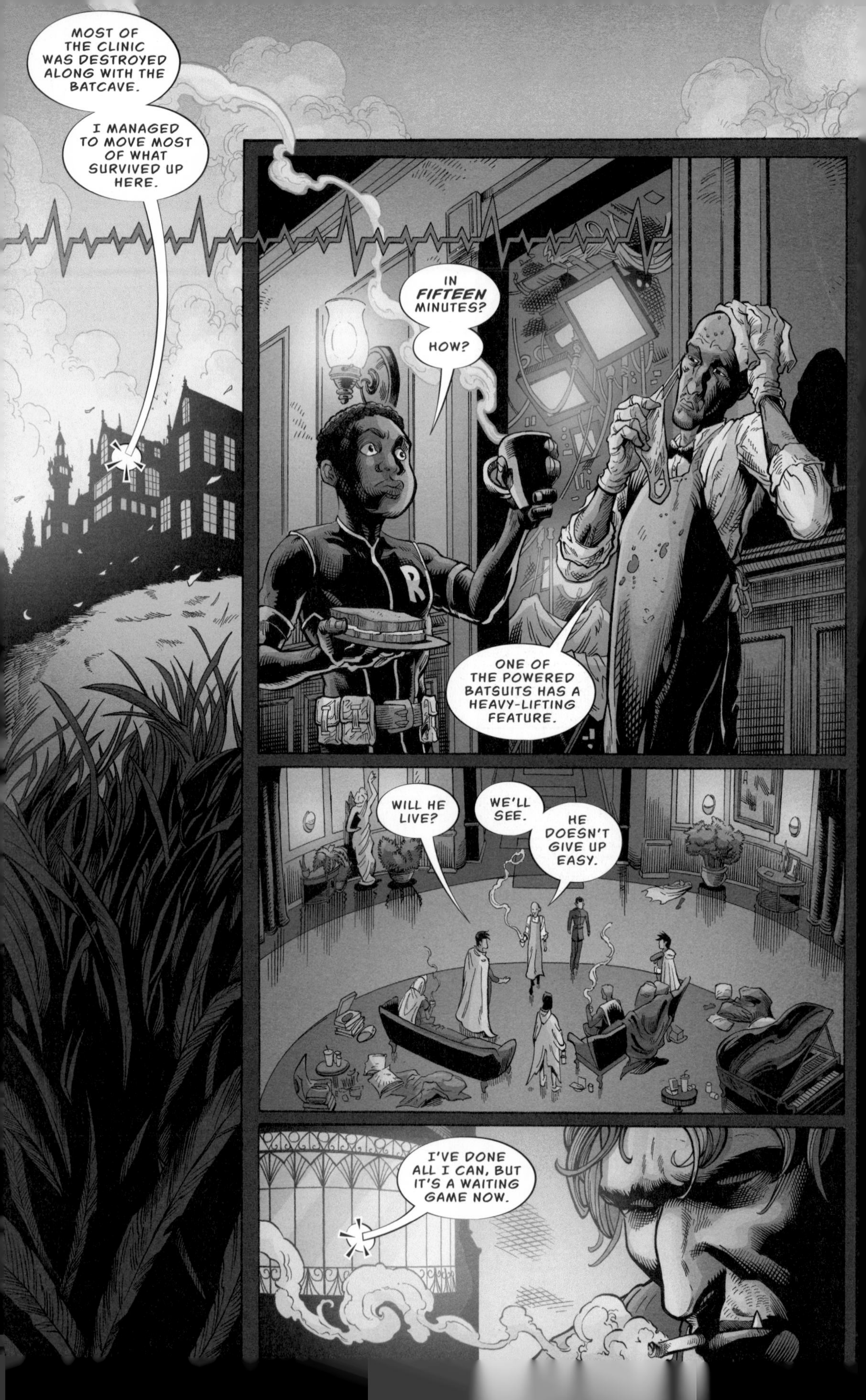
MOST OF THE CLINIC WAS DESTROYED ALONG WITH THE BATCAVE.
I MANAGED TO MOVE MOST OF WHAT SURVIVED UP HERE.
IN *FIFTEEN* MINUTES?
HOW?
ONE OF THE POWERED BATSUITS HAS A HEAVY-LIFTING FEATURE.
WILL HE LIVE?
WE'LL SEE.
HE DOESN'T GIVE UP EASY.
I'VE DONE ALL I CAN, BUT IT'S A WAITING GAME NOW.

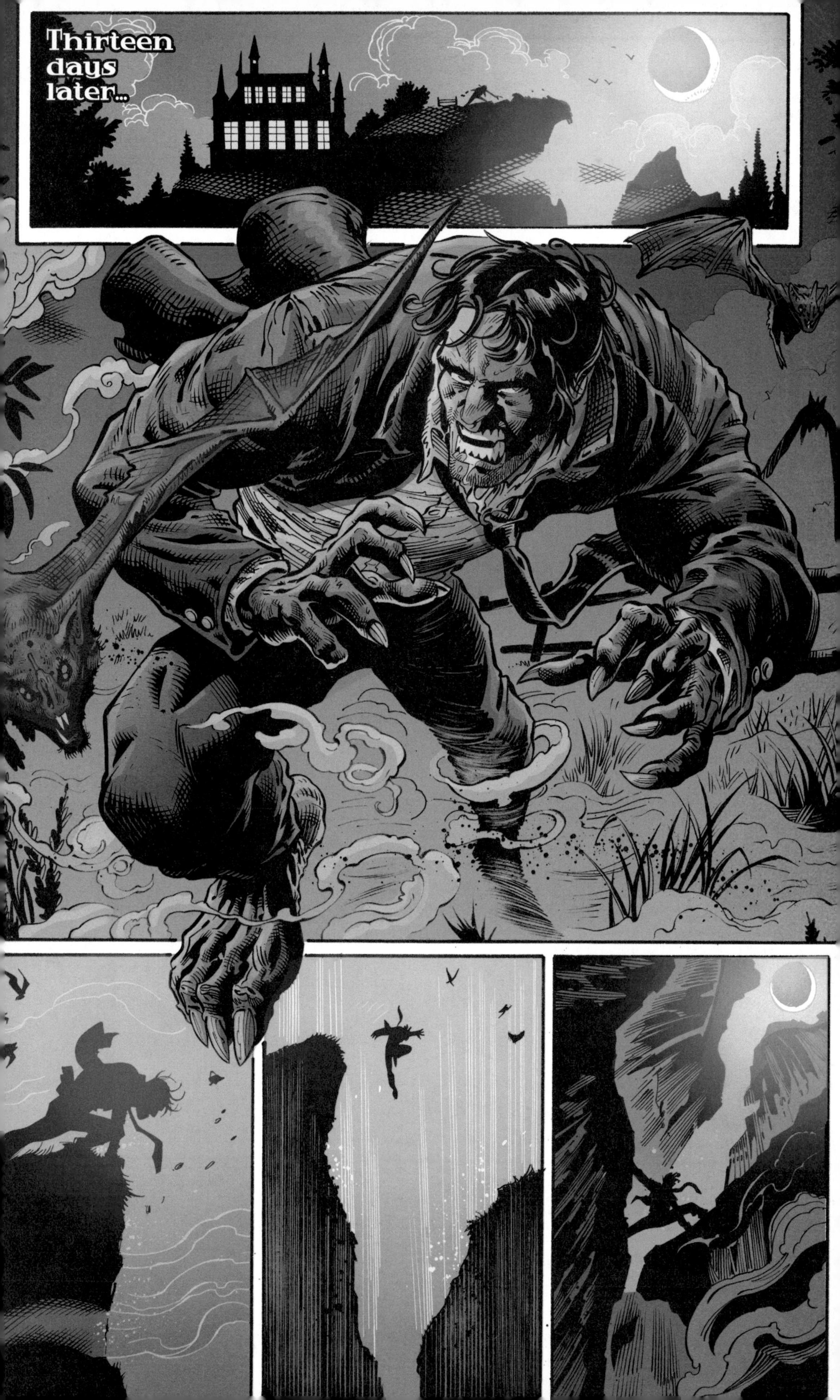
Thirteen days later...

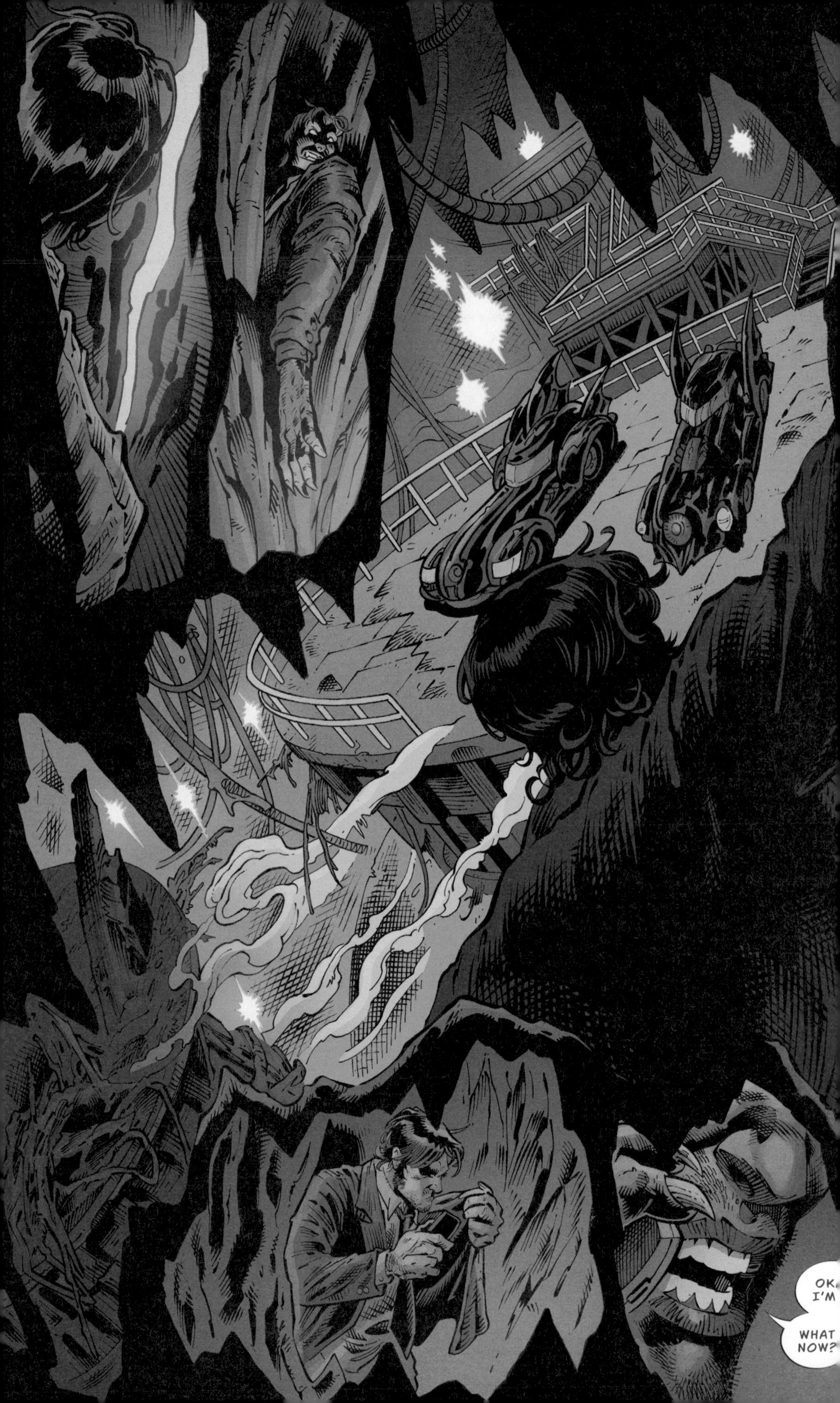

OK I'M
WHAT NOW?

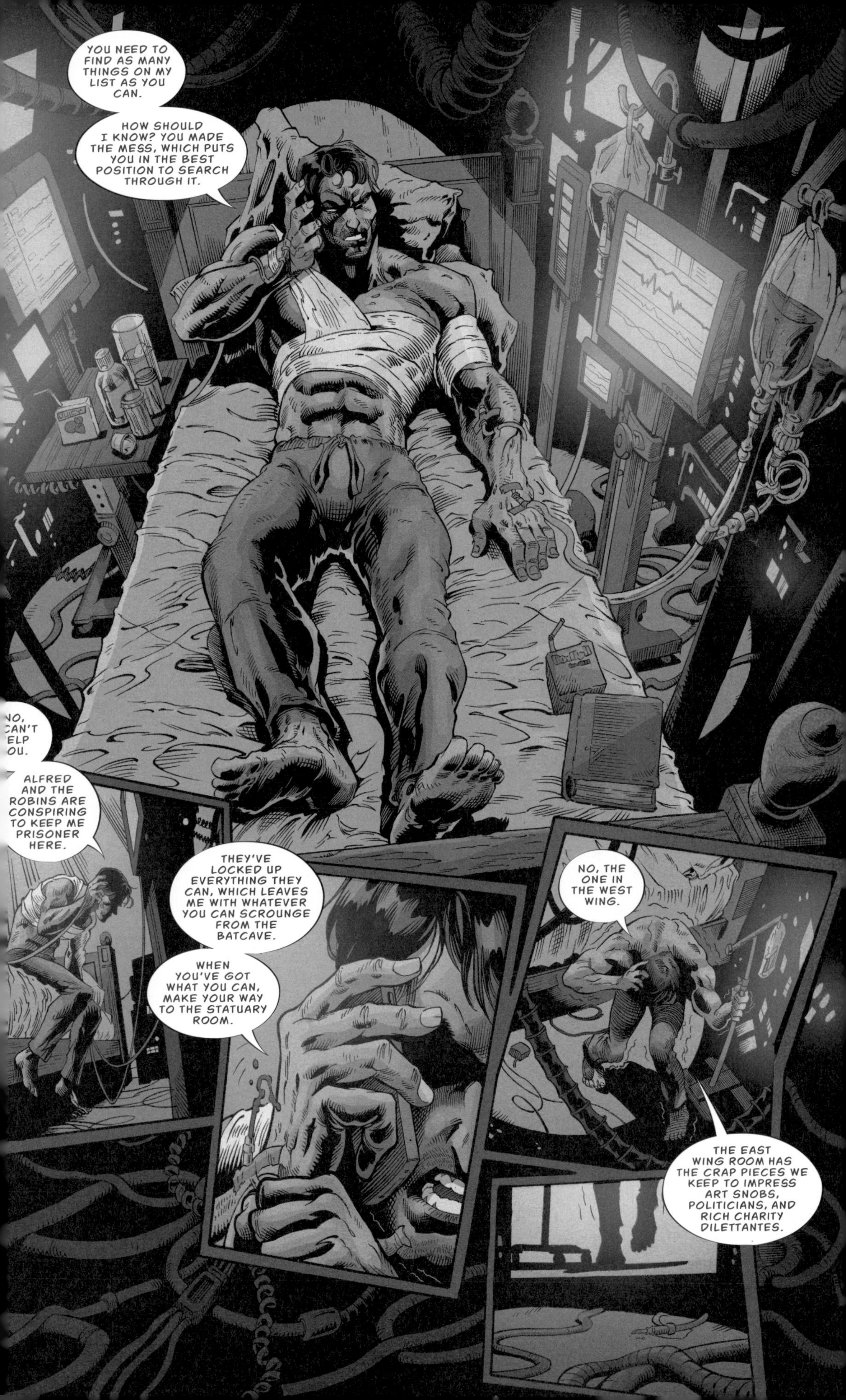
YOU NEED TO FIND AS MANY THINGS ON MY LIST AS YOU CAN.
HOW SHOULD I KNOW? YOU MADE THE MESS, WHICH PUTS YOU IN THE BEST POSITION TO SEARCH THROUGH IT.
NO, CAN'T ELP OU.
ALFRED AND THE ROBINS ARE CONSPIRING TO KEEP ME PRISONER HERE.
THEY'VE LOCKED UP EVERYTHING THEY CAN, WHICH LEAVES ME WITH WHATEVER YOU CAN SCROUNGE FROM THE BATCAVE.
WHEN YOU'VE GOT WHAT YOU CAN, MAKE YOUR WAY TO THE STATUARY ROOM.
NO, THE ONE IN THE WEST WING.
THE EAST WING ROOM HAS THE CRAP PIECES WE KEEP TO IMPRESS ART SNOBS, POLITICIANS, AND RICH CHARITY DILETTANTES.

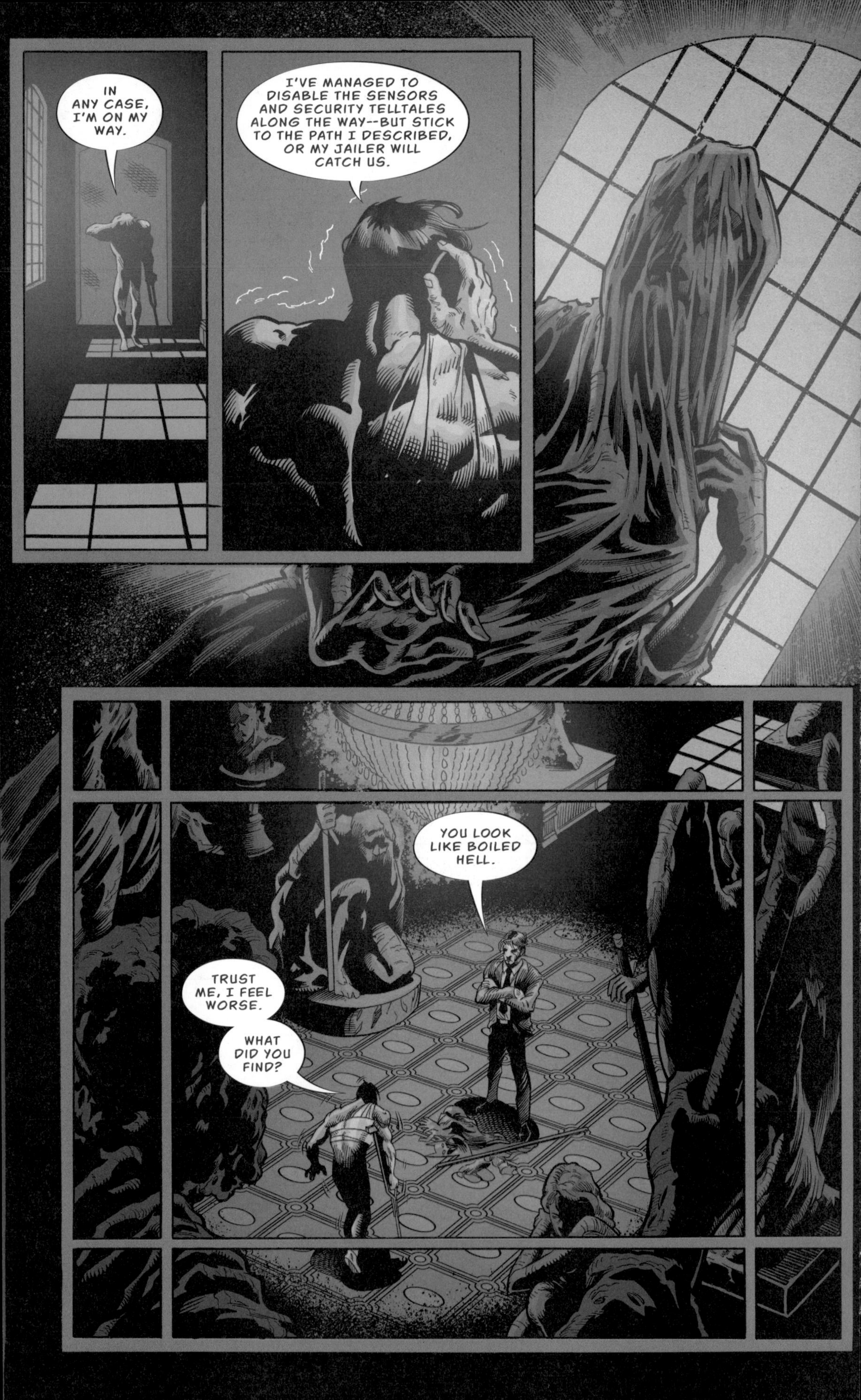
IN ANY CASE, I'M ON MY WAY.
I'VE MANAGED TO DISABLE THE SENSORS AND SECURITY TELLTALES ALONG THE WAY--BUT STICK TO THE PATH I DESCRIBED, OR MY JAILER WILL CATCH US.
YOU LOOK LIKE BOILED HELL.
TRUST ME, I FEEL WORSE.
WHAT DID YOU FIND?

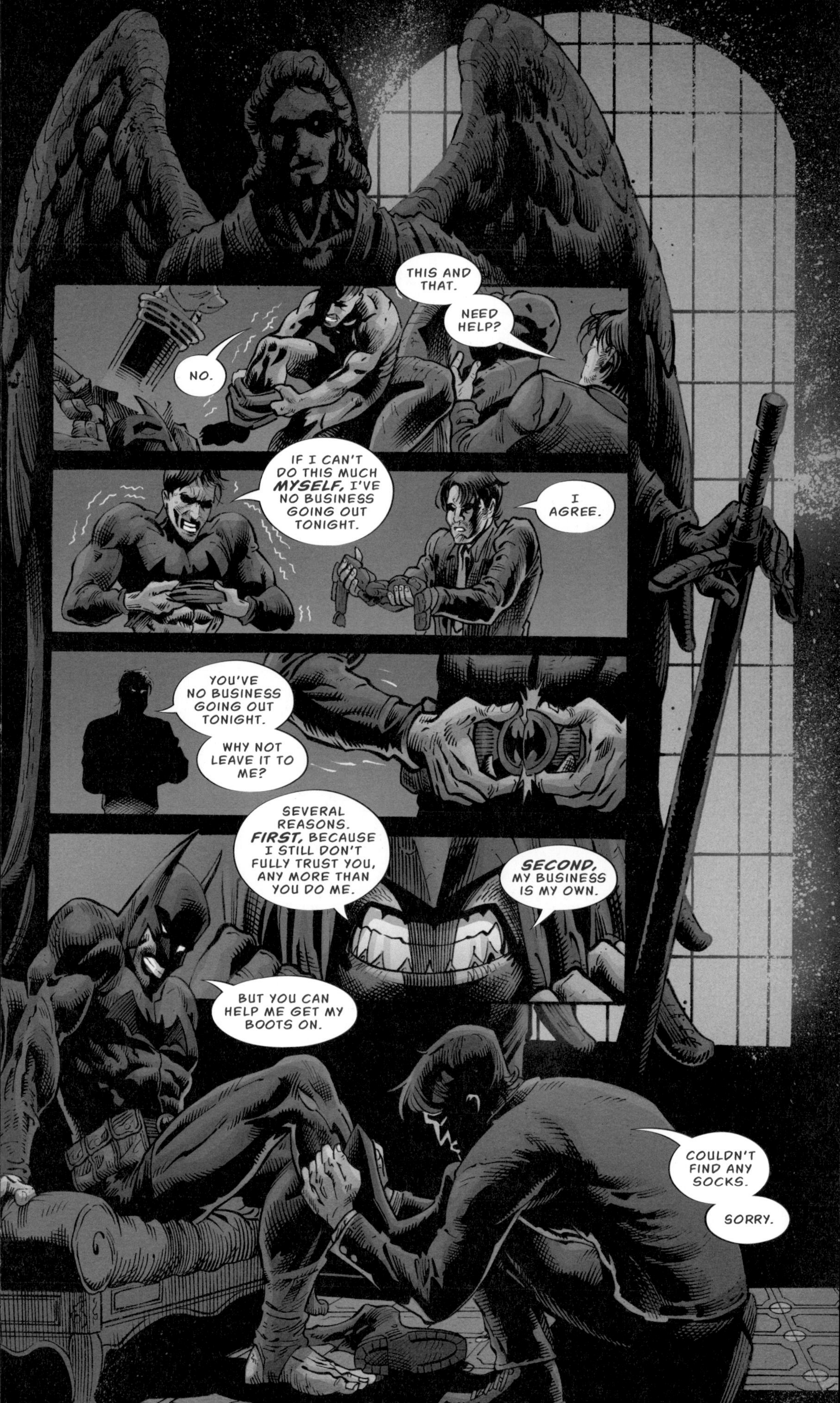
THIS AND THAT.
NEED HELP?
NO.
IF I CAN'T DO THIS MUCH *MYSELF,* I'VE NO BUSINESS GOING OUT TONIGHT.
I AGREE.
YOU'VE NO BUSINESS GOING OUT TONIGHT.
WHY NOT LEAVE IT TO ME?
SEVERAL REASONS. *FIRST,* BECAUSE I STILL DON'T FULLY TRUST YOU, ANY MORE THAN YOU DO ME.
SECOND, MY BUSINESS IS MY OWN.
BUT YOU CAN HELP ME GET MY BOOTS ON.
COULDN'T FIND ANY SOCKS.
SORRY.

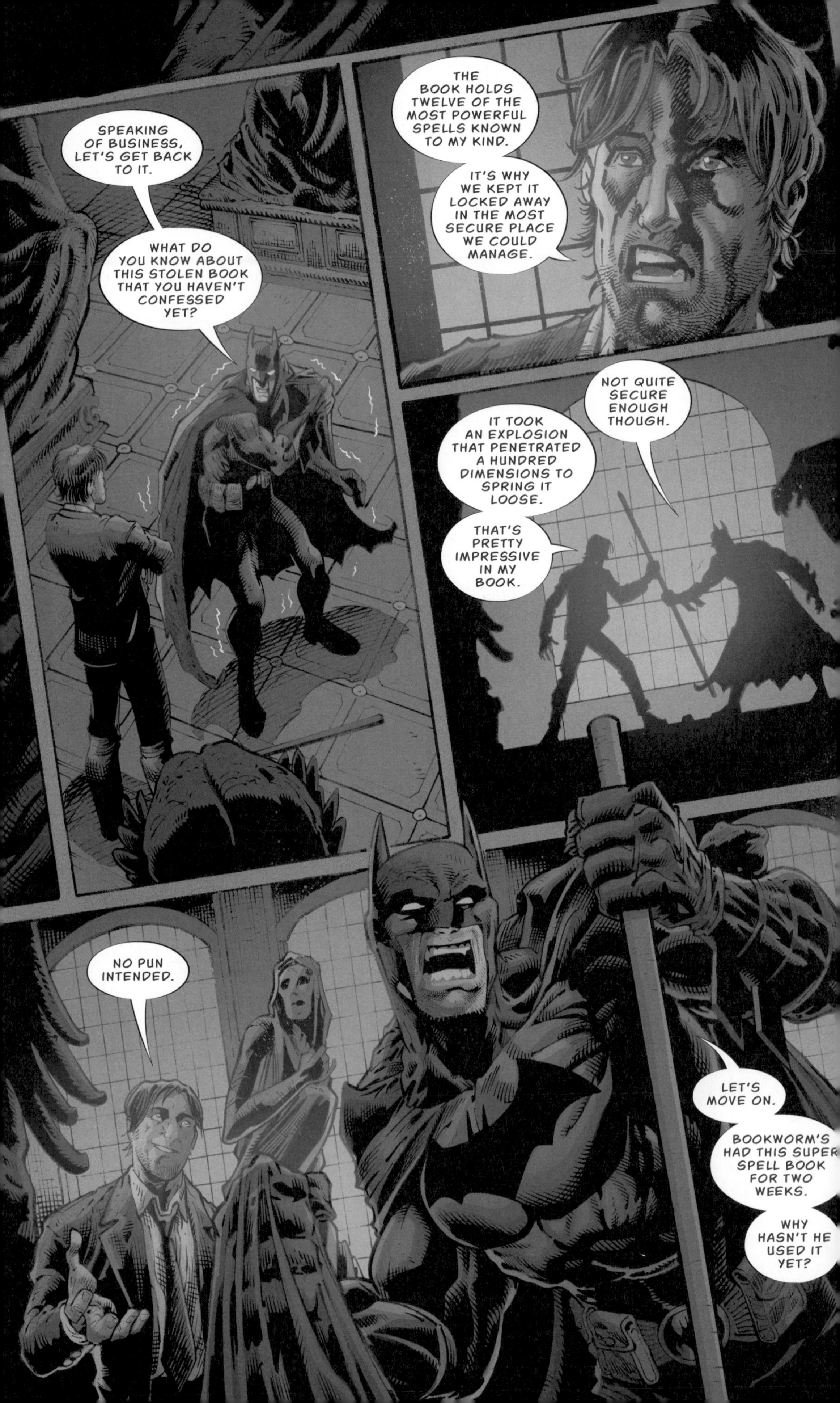
SPEAKING OF BUSINESS, LET'S GET BACK TO IT.
WHAT DO YOU KNOW ABOUT THIS STOLEN BOOK THAT YOU HAVEN'T CONFESSED YET?
THE BOOK HOLDS TWELVE OF THE MOST POWERFUL SPELLS KNOWN TO MY KIND.
IT'S WHY WE KEPT IT LOCKED AWAY IN THE MOST SECURE PLACE WE COULD MANAGE.
NOT QUITE SECURE ENOUGH THOUGH.
IT TOOK AN EXPLOSION THAT PENETRATED A HUNDRED DIMENSIONS TO SPRING IT LOOSE.
THAT'S PRETTY IMPRESSIVE IN MY BOOK.
NO PUN INTENDED.
LET'S MOVE ON.
BOOKWORM'S HAD THIS SUPER SPELL BOOK FOR TWO WEEKS.
WHY HASN'T HE USED IT YET?

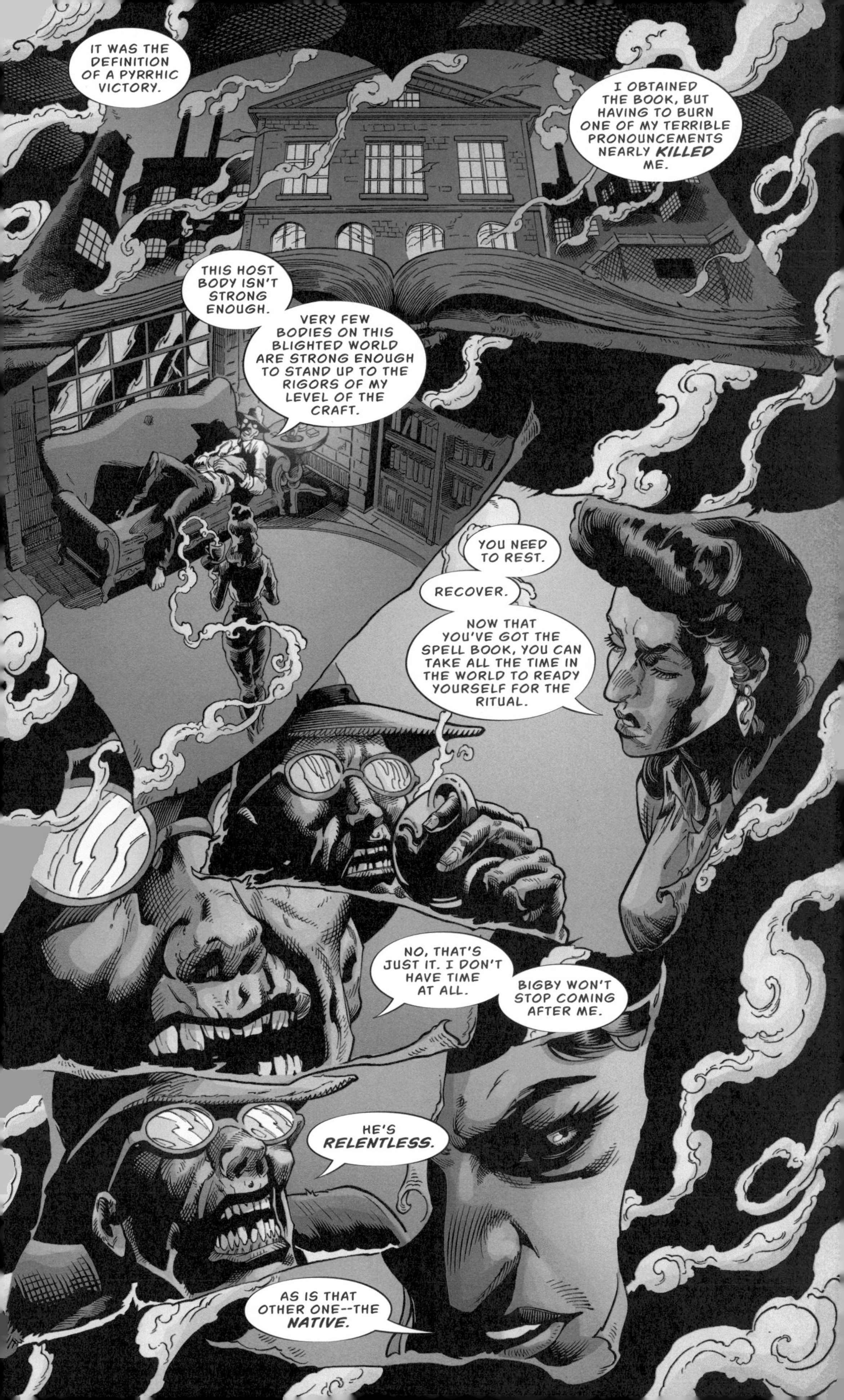
IT WAS THE DEFINITION OF A PYRRHIC VICTORY.
I OBTAINED THE BOOK, BUT HAVING TO BURN ONE OF MY TERRIBLE PRONOUNCEMENTS NEARLY **KILLED** ME.
THIS HOST BODY ISN'T STRONG ENOUGH.
VERY FEW BODIES ON THIS BLIGHTED WORLD ARE STRONG ENOUGH TO STAND UP TO THE RIGORS OF MY LEVEL OF THE CRAFT.
YOU NEED TO REST.
RECOVER.
NOW THAT YOU'VE GOT THE SPELL BOOK, YOU CAN TAKE ALL THE TIME IN THE WORLD TO READY YOURSELF FOR THE RITUAL.
NO, THAT'S JUST IT. I DON'T HAVE TIME AT ALL.
BIGBY WON'T STOP COMING AFTER ME.
HE'S ***RELENTLESS.***
AS IS THAT OTHER ONE--THE ***NATIVE.***

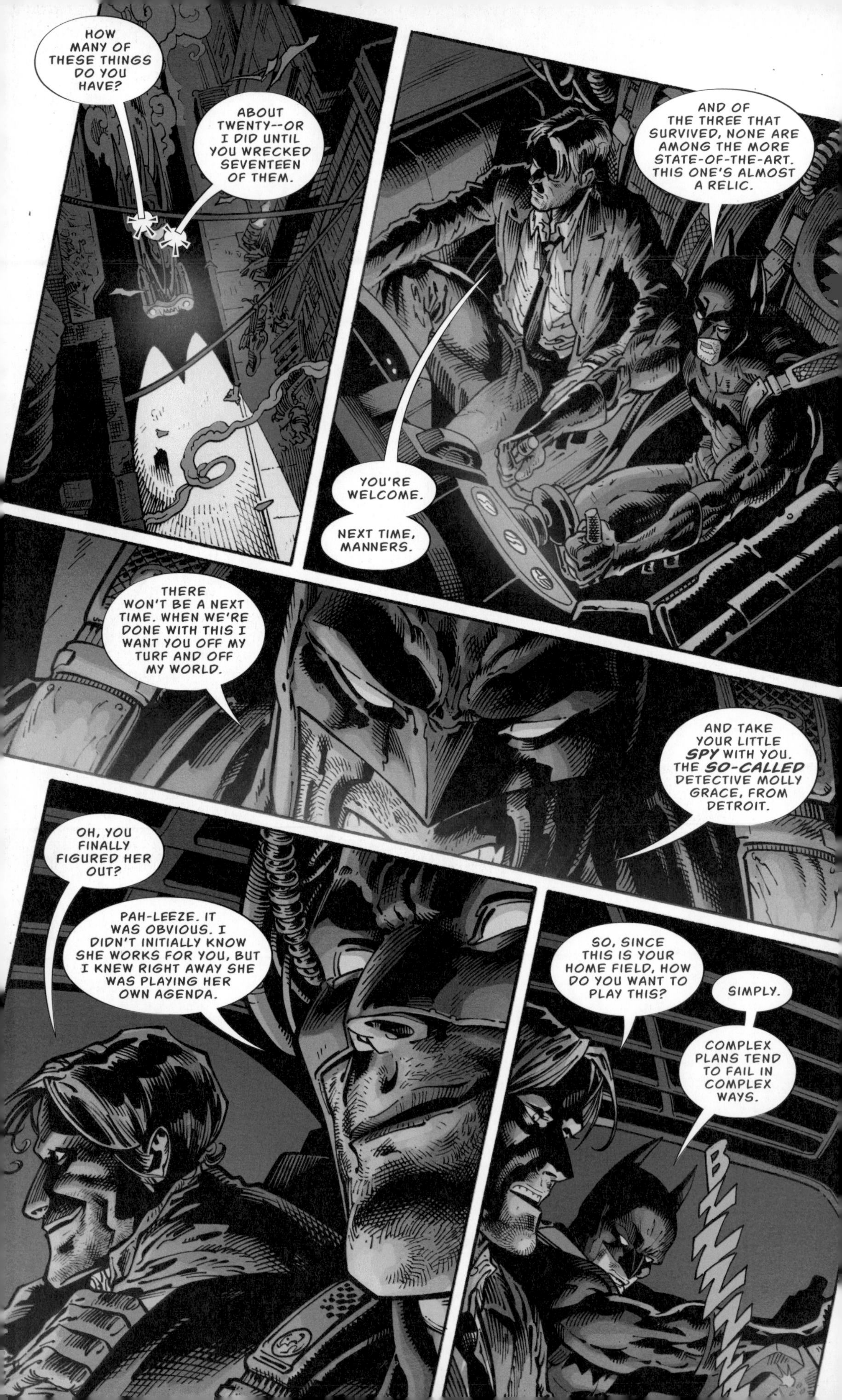
HOW MANY OF THESE THINGS DO YOU HAVE?
ABOUT TWENTY--OR I DID UNTIL YOU WRECKED SEVENTEEN OF THEM.
AND OF THE THREE THAT SURVIVED, NONE ARE AMONG THE MORE STATE-OF-THE-ART. THIS ONE'S ALMOST A RELIC.
YOU'RE WELCOME.
NEXT TIME, MANNERS.
THERE WON'T BE A NEXT TIME. WHEN WE'RE DONE WITH THIS I WANT YOU OFF MY TURF AND OFF MY WORLD.
AND TAKE YOUR LITTLE SPY WITH YOU. THE SO-CALLED DETECTIVE MOLLY GRACE, FROM DETROIT.
OH, YOU FINALLY FIGURED HER OUT?
PAH-LEEZE. IT WAS OBVIOUS. I DIDN'T INITIALLY KNOW SHE WORKS FOR YOU, BUT I KNEW RIGHT AWAY SHE WAS PLAYING HER OWN AGENDA.
SO, SINCE THIS IS YOUR HOME FIELD, HOW DO YOU WANT TO PLAY THIS?
SIMPLY.
COMPLEX PLANS TEND TO FAIL IN COMPLEX WAYS.
BHNNNN

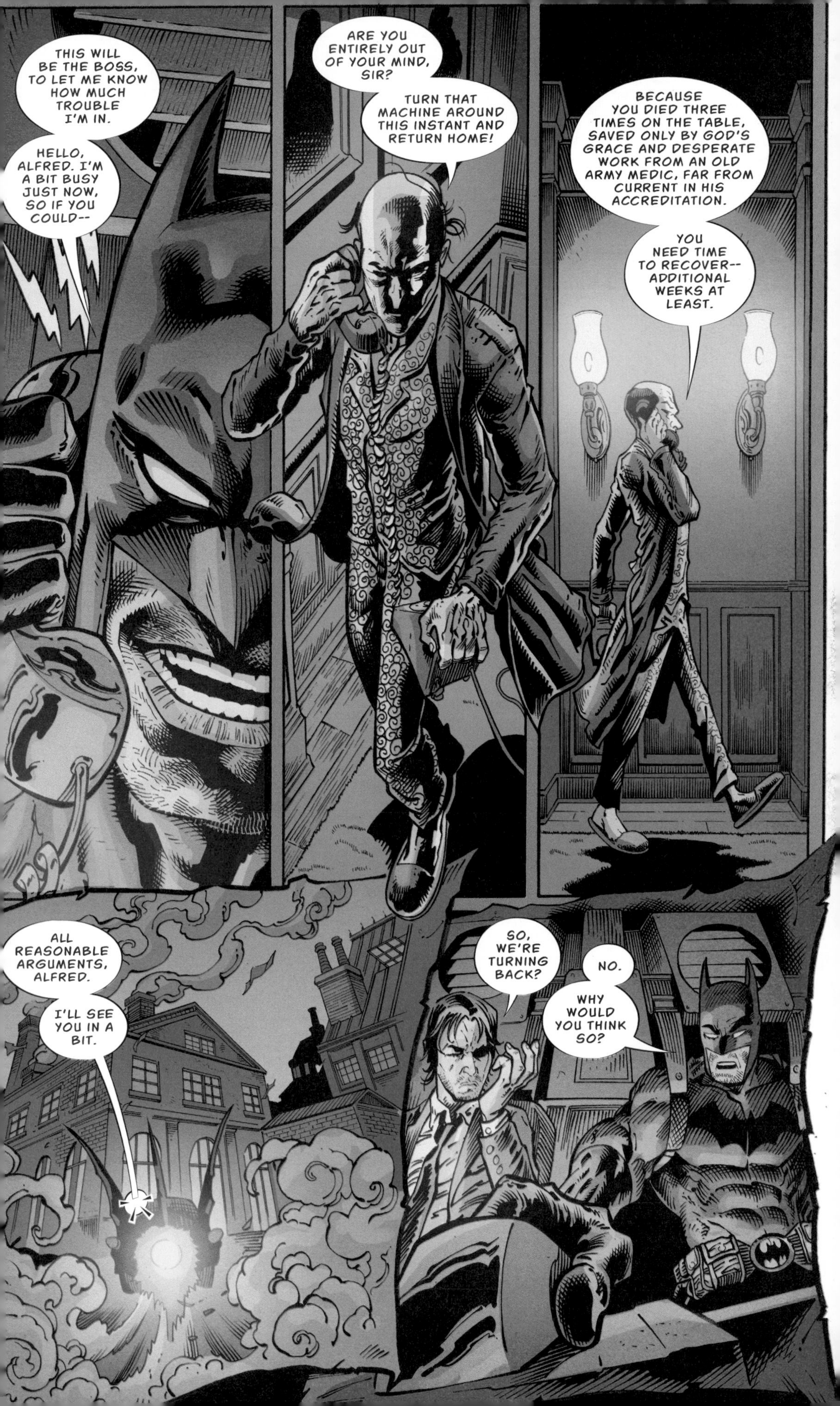
THIS WILL BE THE BOSS, TO LET ME KNOW HOW MUCH TROUBLE I'M IN.
HELLO, ALFRED. I'M A BIT BUSY JUST NOW, SO IF YOU COULD--
ARE YOU ENTIRELY OUT OF YOUR MIND, SIR?
TURN THAT MACHINE AROUND THIS INSTANT AND RETURN HOME!
BECAUSE YOU DIED THREE TIMES ON THE TABLE, SAVED ONLY BY GOD'S GRACE AND DESPERATE WORK FROM AN OLD ARMY MEDIC, FAR FROM CURRENT IN HIS ACCREDITATION.
YOU NEED TIME TO RECOVER-- ADDITIONAL WEEKS AT LEAST.
ALL REASONABLE ARGUMENTS, ALFRED.
I'LL SEE YOU IN A BIT.
SO, WE'RE TURNING BACK?
NO.
WHY WOULD YOU THINK SO?

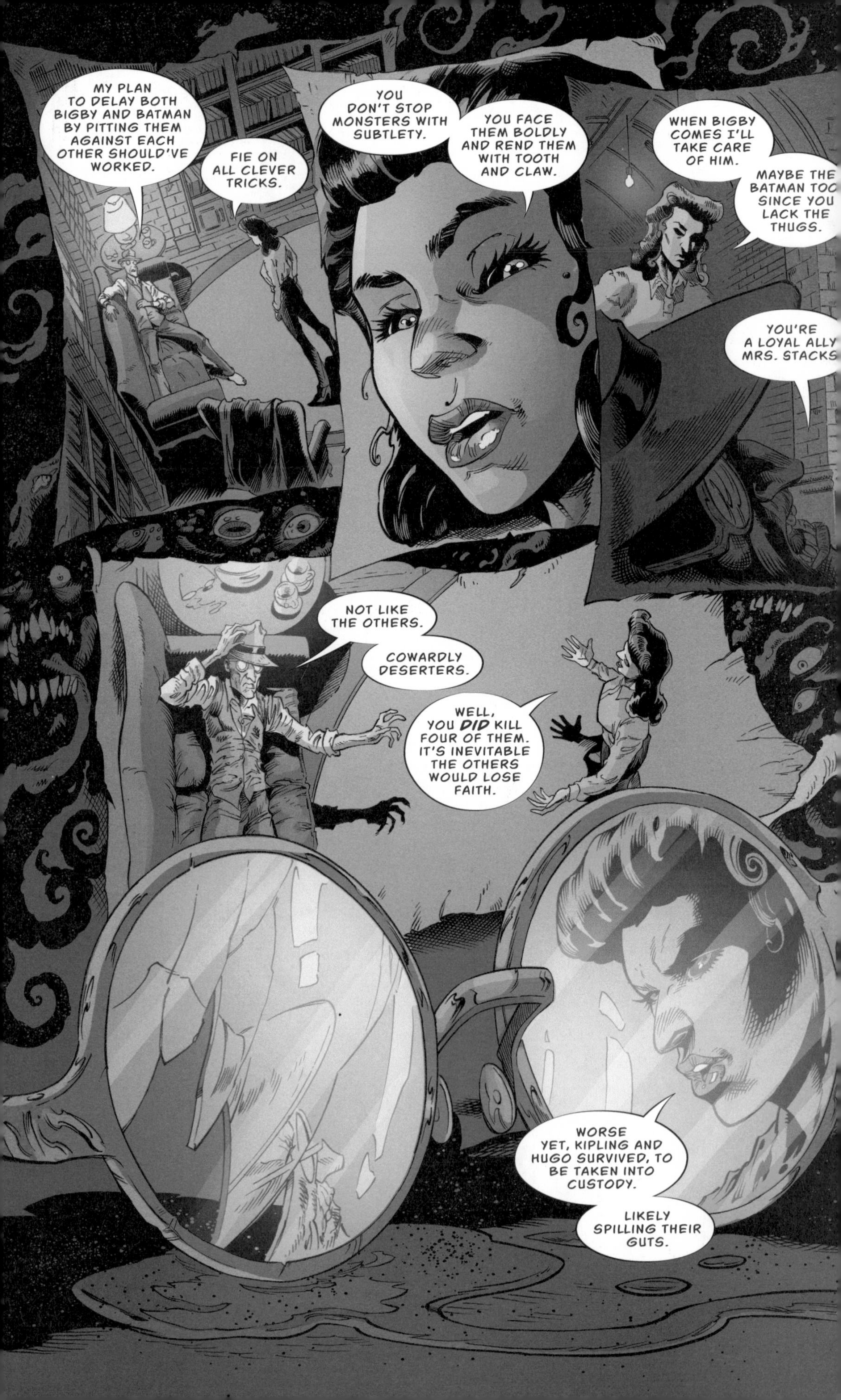

MY PLAN TO DELAY BOTH BIGBY AND BATMAN BY PITTING THEM AGAINST EACH OTHER SHOULD'VE WORKED.
FIE ON ALL CLEVER TRICKS.
YOU DON'T STOP MONSTERS WITH SUBTLETY.
YOU FACE THEM BOLDLY AND REND THEM WITH TOOTH AND CLAW.
WHEN BIGBY COMES I'LL TAKE CARE OF HIM.
MAYBE THE BATMAN TOO SINCE YOU LACK THE THUGS.
YOU'RE A LOYAL ALLY MRS. STACKS
NOT LIKE THE OTHERS.
COWARDLY DESERTERS.
WELL, YOU ***DID*** KILL FOUR OF THEM. IT'S INEVITABLE THE OTHERS WOULD LOSE FAITH.
WORSE YET, KIPLING AND HUGO SURVIVED, TO BE TAKEN INTO CUSTODY.
LIKELY SPILLING THEIR GUTS.

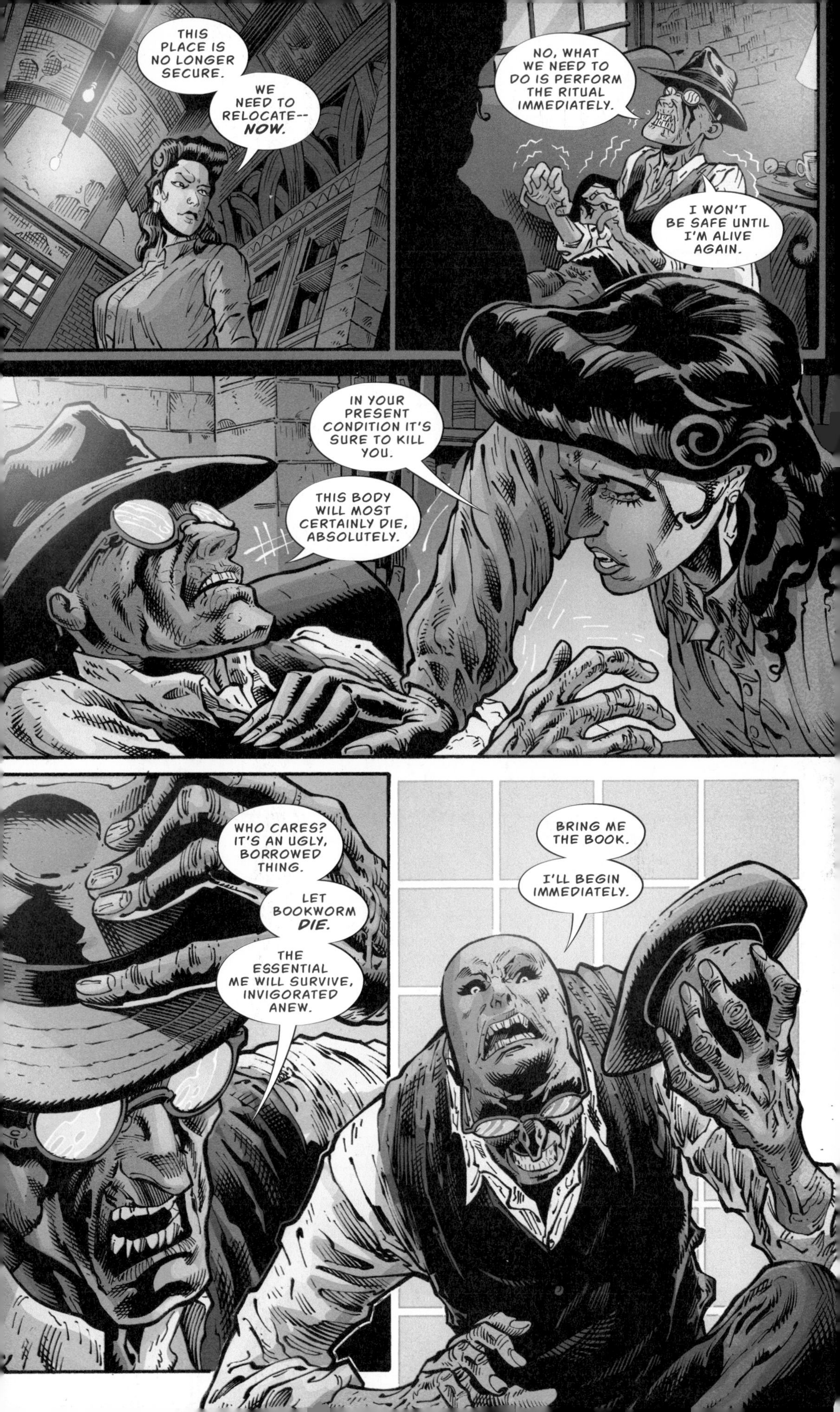

THIS PLACE IS NO LONGER SECURE.
WE NEED TO RELOCATE-- **NOW.**
NO, WHAT WE NEED TO DO IS PERFORM THE RITUAL IMMEDIATELY.
I WON'T BE SAFE UNTIL I'M ALIVE AGAIN.
IN YOUR PRESENT CONDITION IT'S SURE TO KILL YOU.
THIS BODY WILL MOST CERTAINLY DIE, ABSOLUTELY.
WHO CARES? IT'S AN UGLY, BORROWED THING.
LET BOOKWORM **DIE.**
THE ESSENTIAL ME WILL SURVIVE, INVIGORATED ANEW.
BRING ME THE BOOK.
I'LL BEGIN IMMEDIATELY.

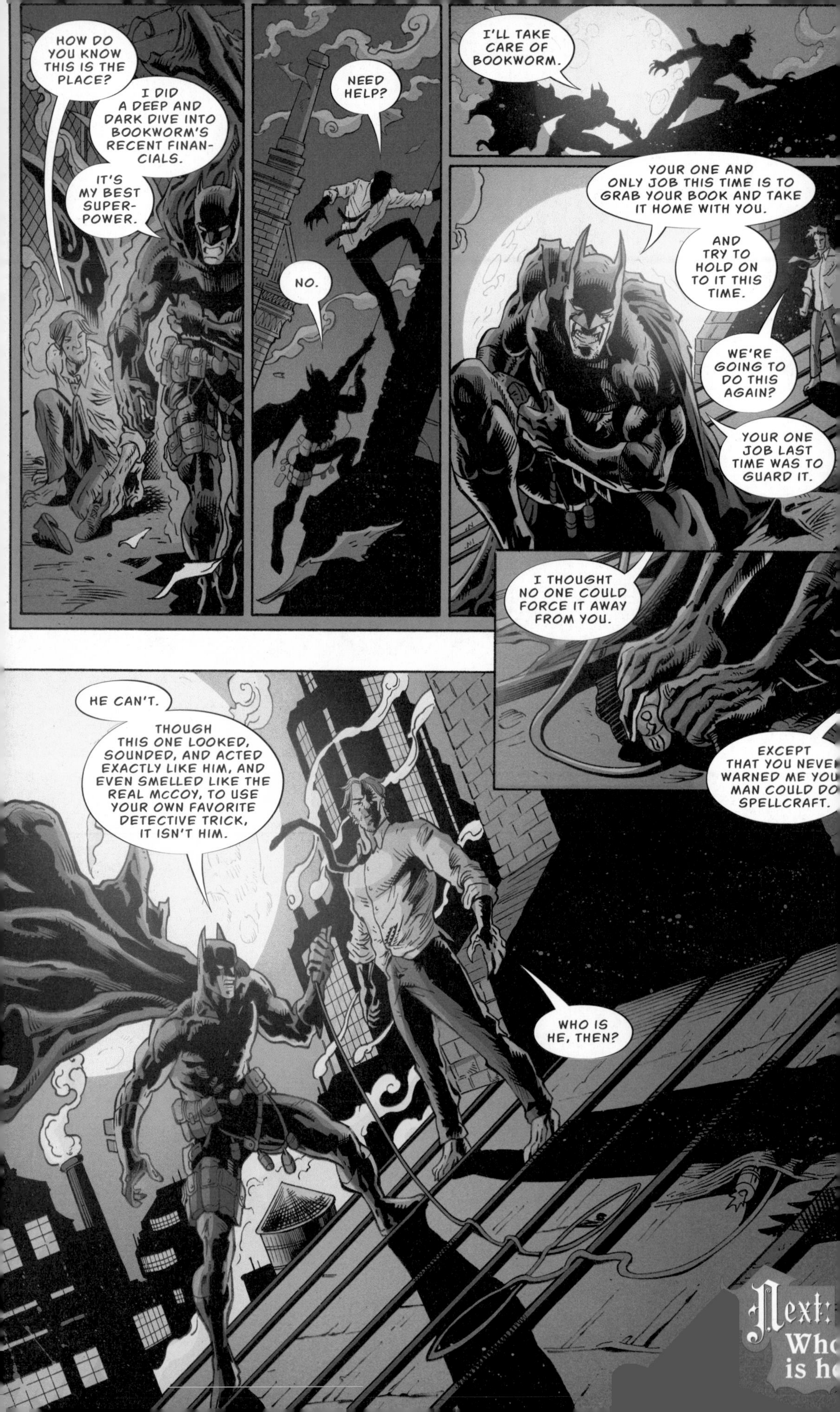

HOW DO YOU KNOW THIS IS THE PLACE?
I DID A DEEP AND DARK DIVE INTO BOOKWORM'S RECENT FINAN-CIALS.
IT'S MY BEST SUPER-POWER.
NEED HELP?
NO.
I'LL TAKE CARE OF BOOKWORM.
YOUR ONE AND ONLY JOB THIS TIME IS TO GRAB YOUR BOOK AND TAKE IT HOME WITH YOU.
AND TRY TO HOLD ON TO IT THIS TIME.
WE'RE GOING TO DO THIS AGAIN?
YOUR ONE JOB LAST TIME WAS TO GUARD IT.
I THOUGHT NO ONE COULD FORCE IT AWAY FROM YOU.
EXCEPT THAT YOU NEVE WARNED ME YOU MAN COULD DO SPELLCRAFT.
HE CAN'T.
THOUGH THIS ONE LOOKED, SOUNDED, AND ACTED EXACTLY LIKE HIM, AND EVEN SMELLED LIKE THE REAL McCOY, TO USE YOUR OWN FAVORITE DETECTIVE TRICK, IT ISN'T HIM.
WHO IS HE, THEN?
Next:

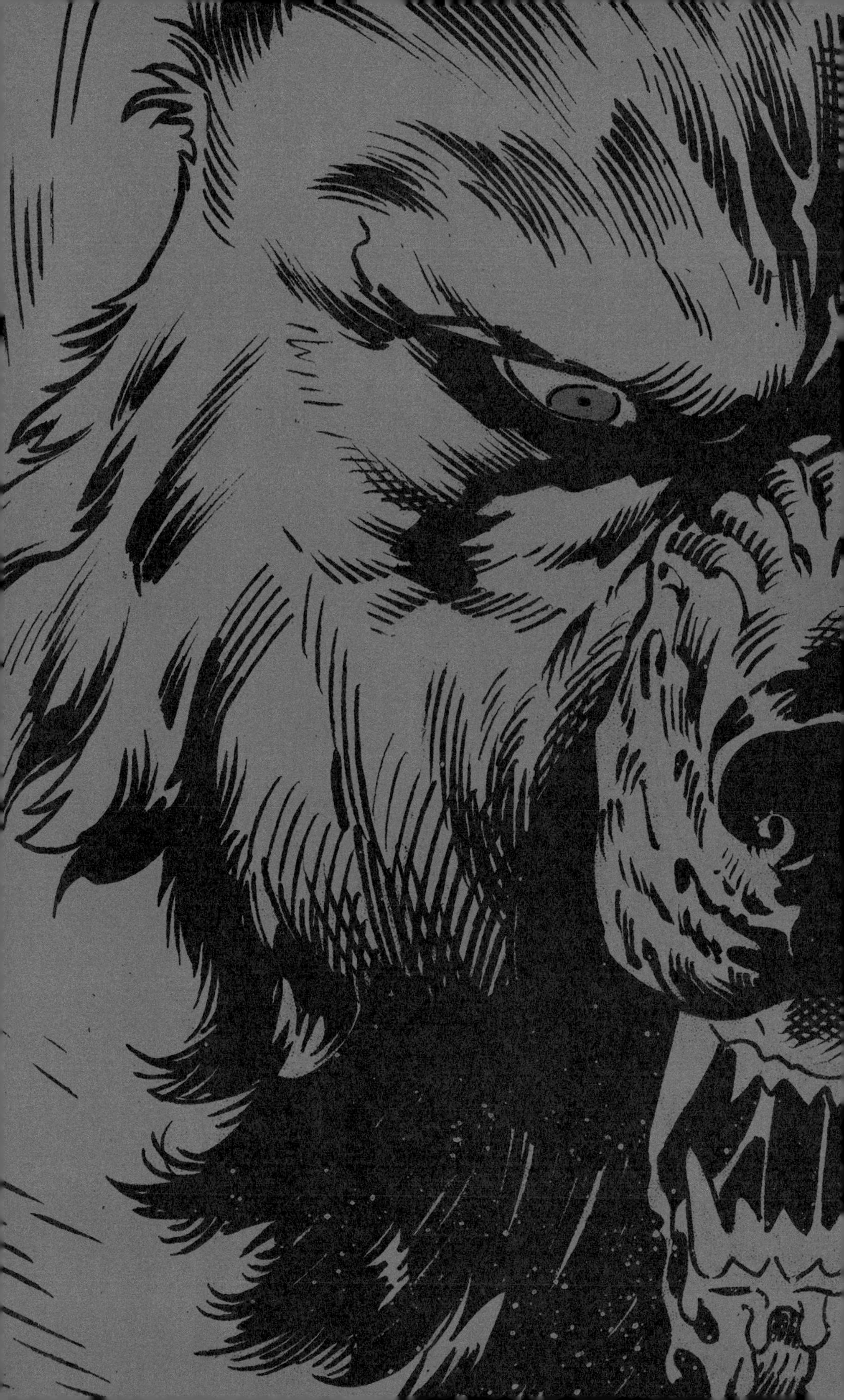

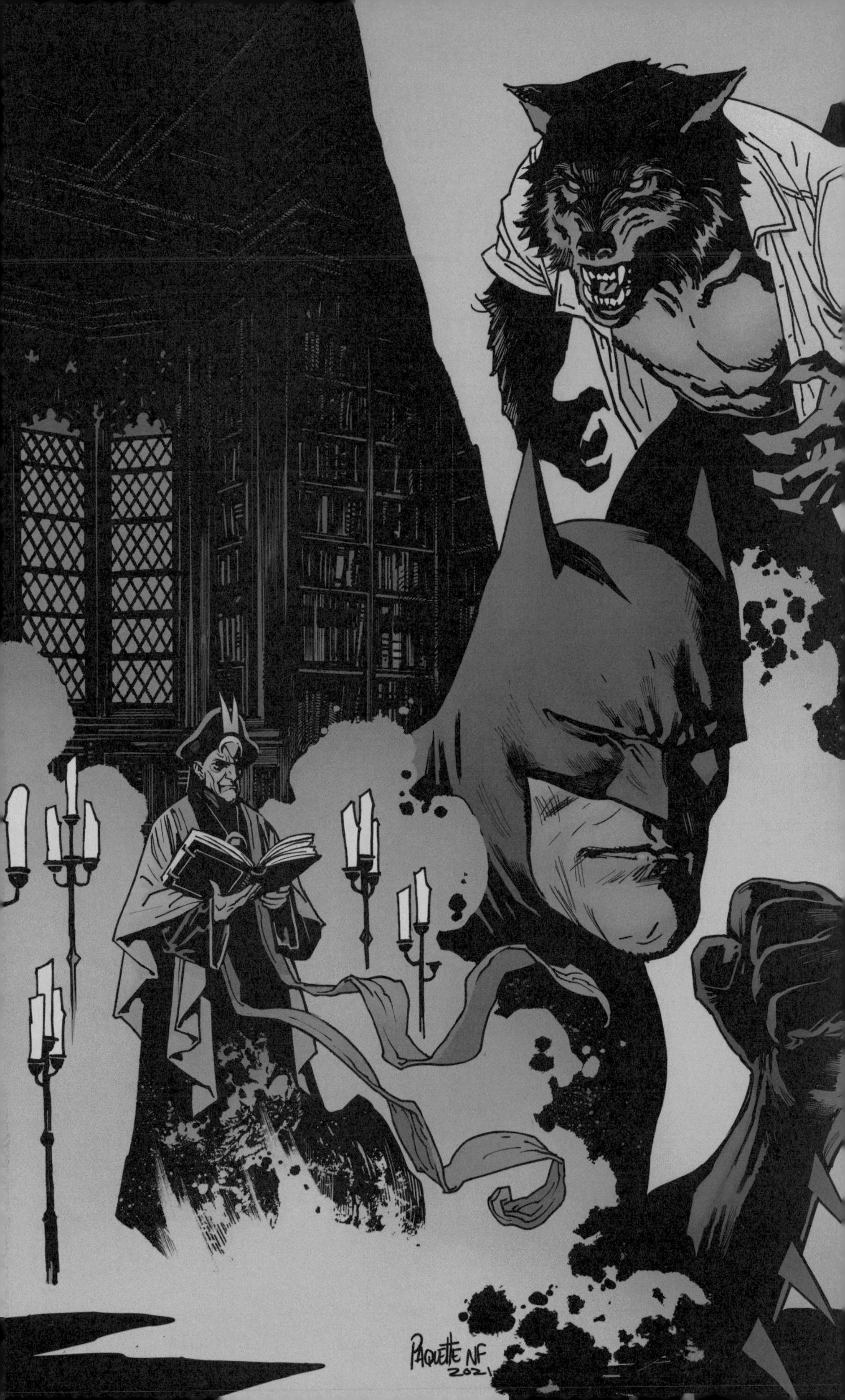
PAQUETTE NF
2021

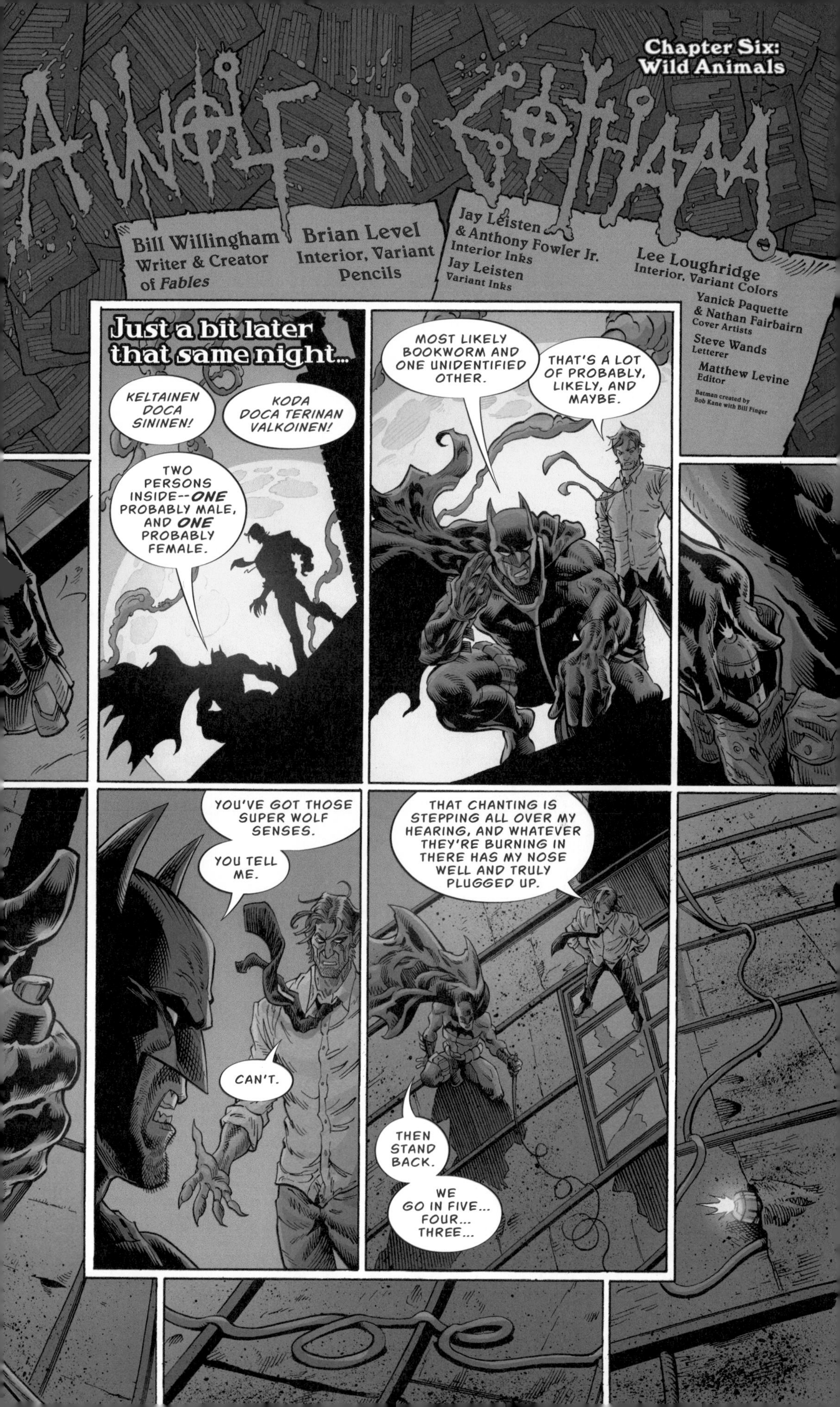

Chapter Six: Wild Animals
A Wolf in Gotham
Bill Willingham Writer & Creator of Fables
Brian Level Interior, Variant Pencils
Jay Leisten & Anthony Fowler Jr. Interior Inks
Jay Leisten Variant Inks
Lee Loughridge Interior, Variant Colors
Yanick Paquette & Nathan Fairbairn Cover Artists
Steve Wands Letterer
Matthew Levine Editor
Batman created by Bob Kane with Bill Finger
Just a bit later that same night...
KELTAINEN DOCA SININEN!
KODA DOCA TERINAN VALKOINEN!
TWO PERSONS INSIDE--ONE PROBABLY MALE, AND ONE PROBABLY FEMALE.
MOST LIKELY BOOKWORM AND ONE UNIDENTIFIED OTHER.
THAT'S A LOT OF PROBABLY, LIKELY, AND MAYBE.
YOU'VE GOT THOSE SUPER WOLF SENSES.
YOU TELL ME.
CAN'T.
THAT CHANTING IS STEPPING ALL OVER MY HEARING, AND WHATEVER THEY'RE BURNING IN THERE HAS MY NOSE WELL AND TRULY PLUGGED UP.
THEN STAND BACK.
WE GO IN FIVE... FOUR... THREE...

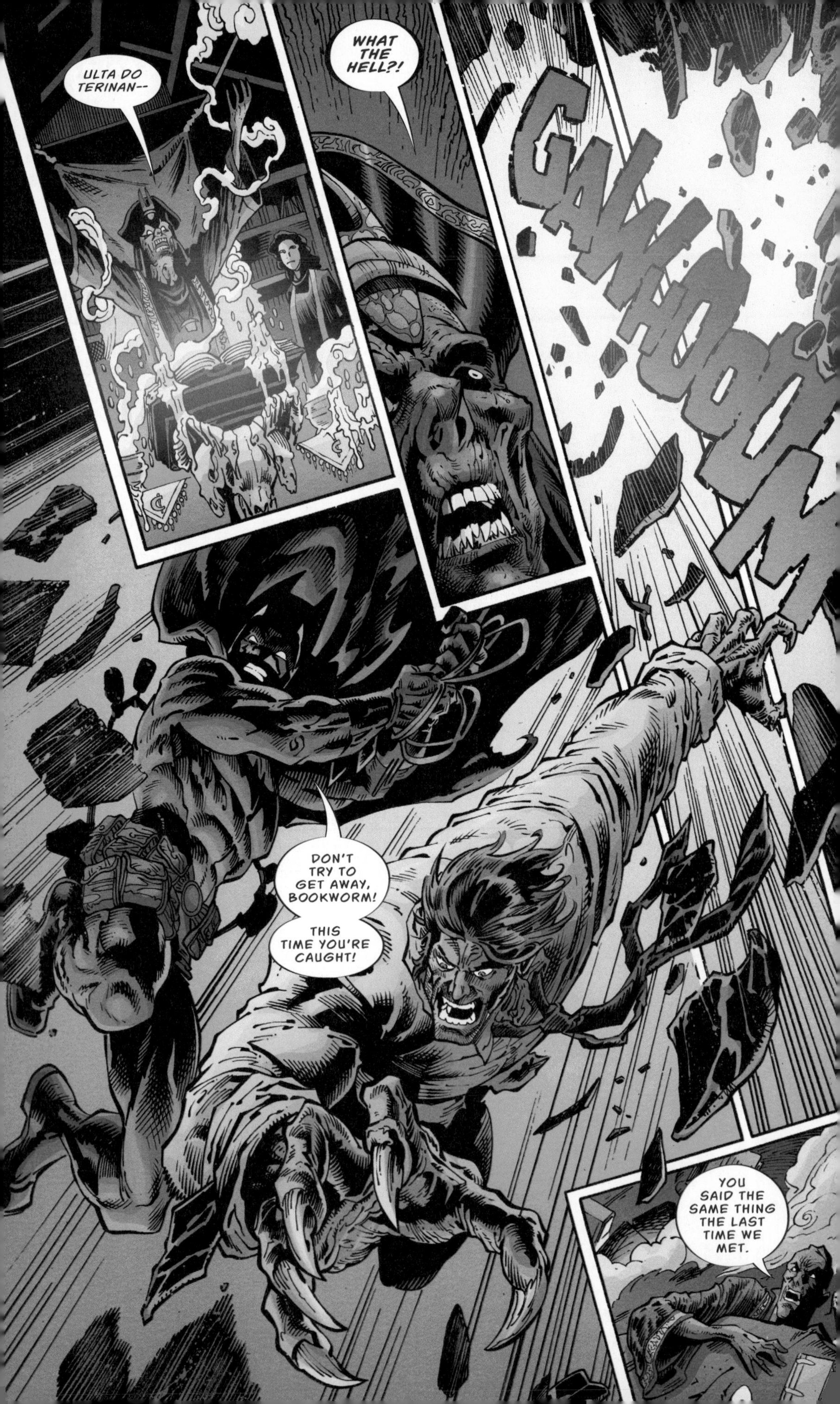
ULTA DO TERINAN--
WHAT THE HELL?!
GAWHOOM
DON'T TRY TO GET AWAY, BOOKWORM!
THIS TIME YOU'RE CAUGHT!
YOU SAID THE SAME THING THE LAST TIME WE MET.

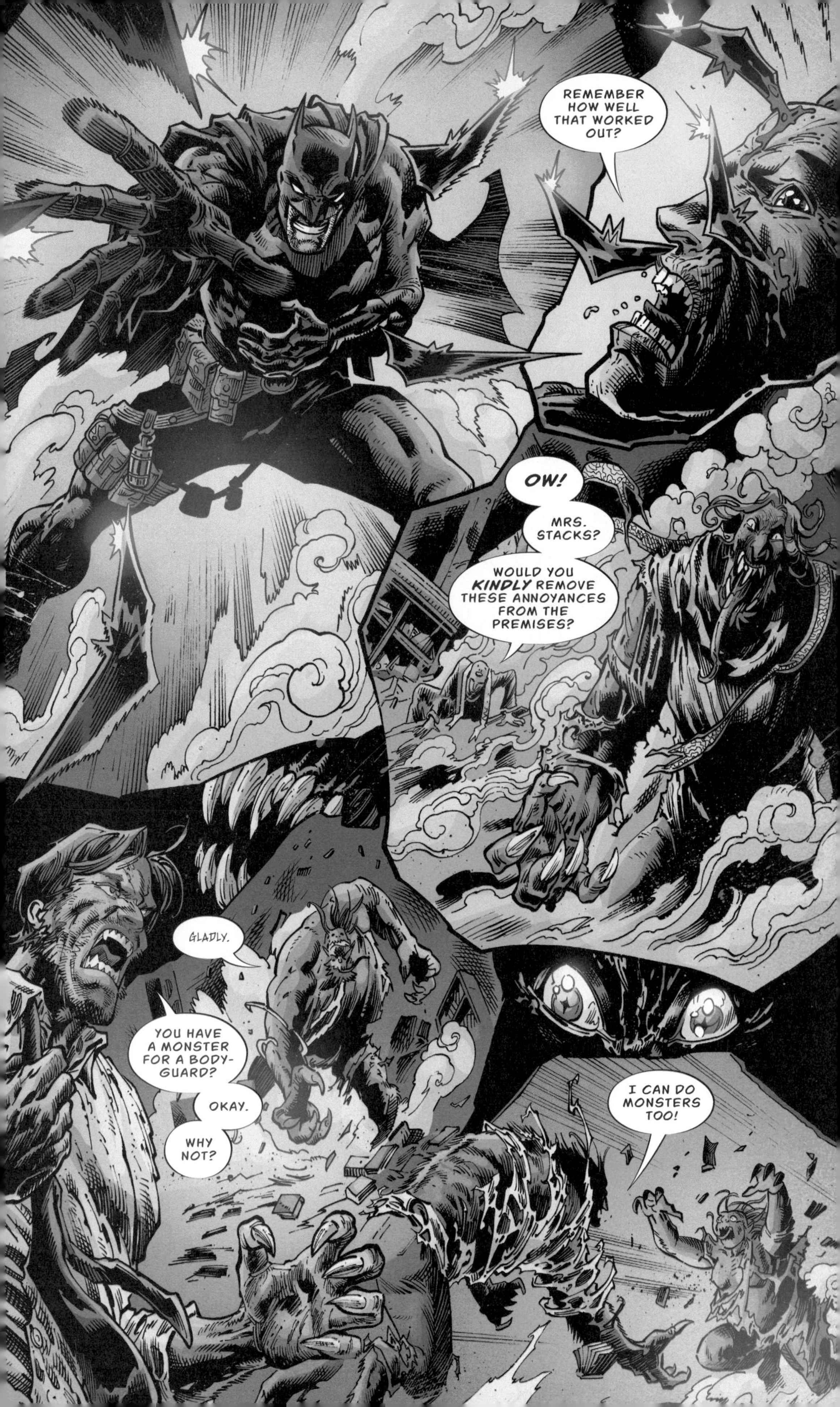
REMEMBER HOW WELL THAT WORKED OUT?
OW!
MRS. STACKS?
WOULD YOU KINDLY REMOVE THESE ANNOYANCES FROM THE PREMISES?
GLADLY.
YOU HAVE A MONSTER FOR A BODY-GUARD?
OKAY.
WHY NOT?
I CAN DO MONSTERS TOO!

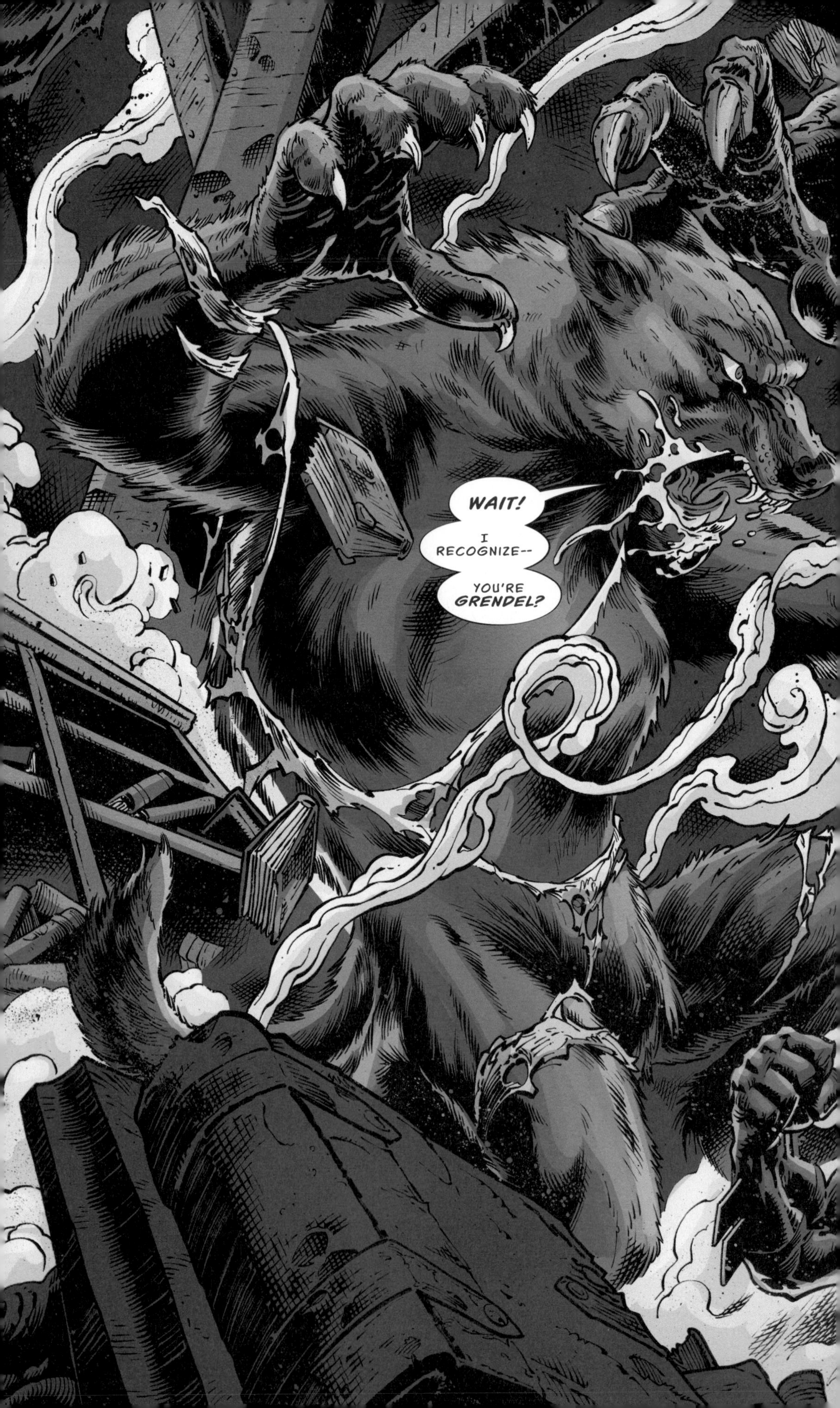
WAIT!
I RECOGNIZE--
YOU'RE GRENDEL?

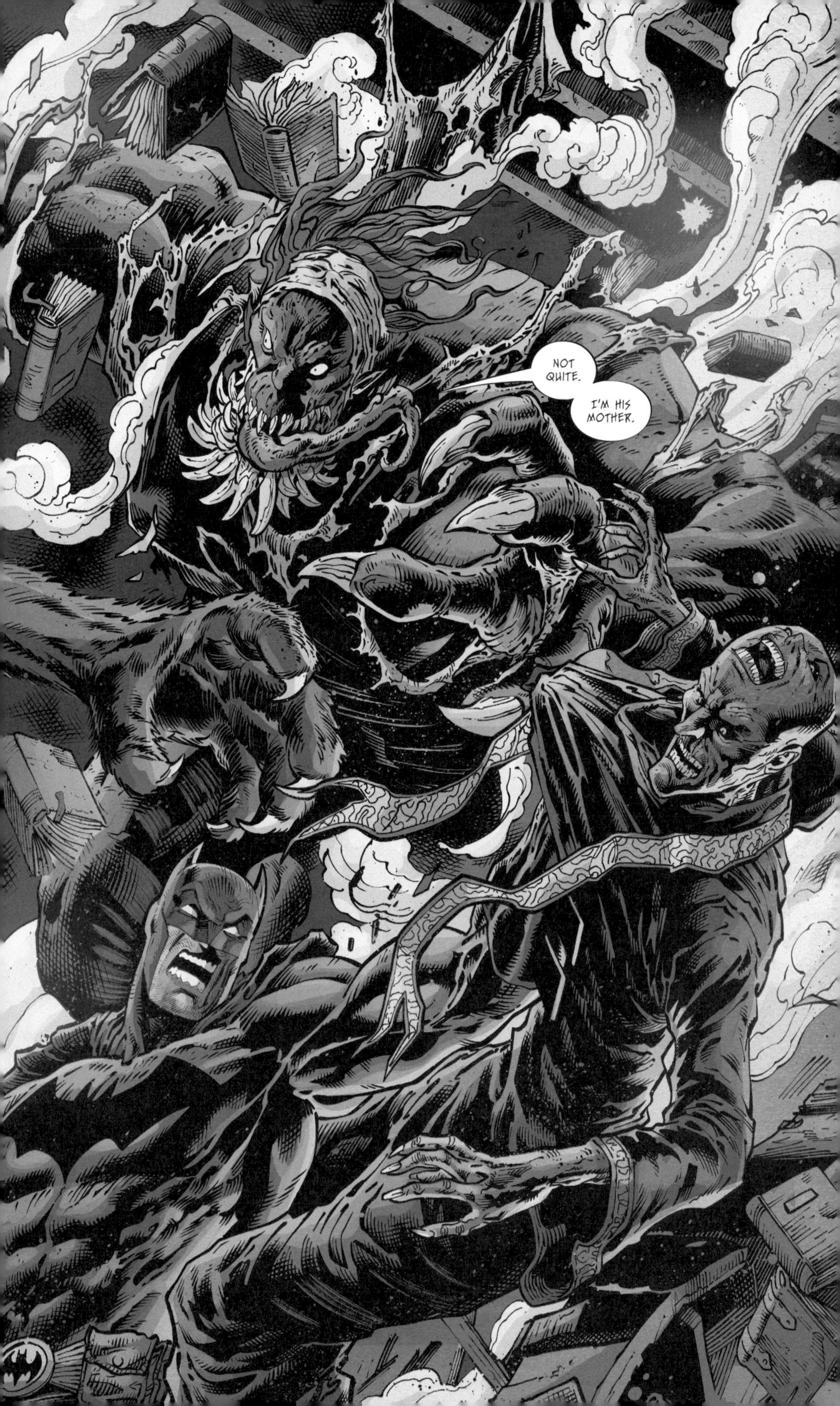
NOT QUITE.
I'M HIS MOTHER.

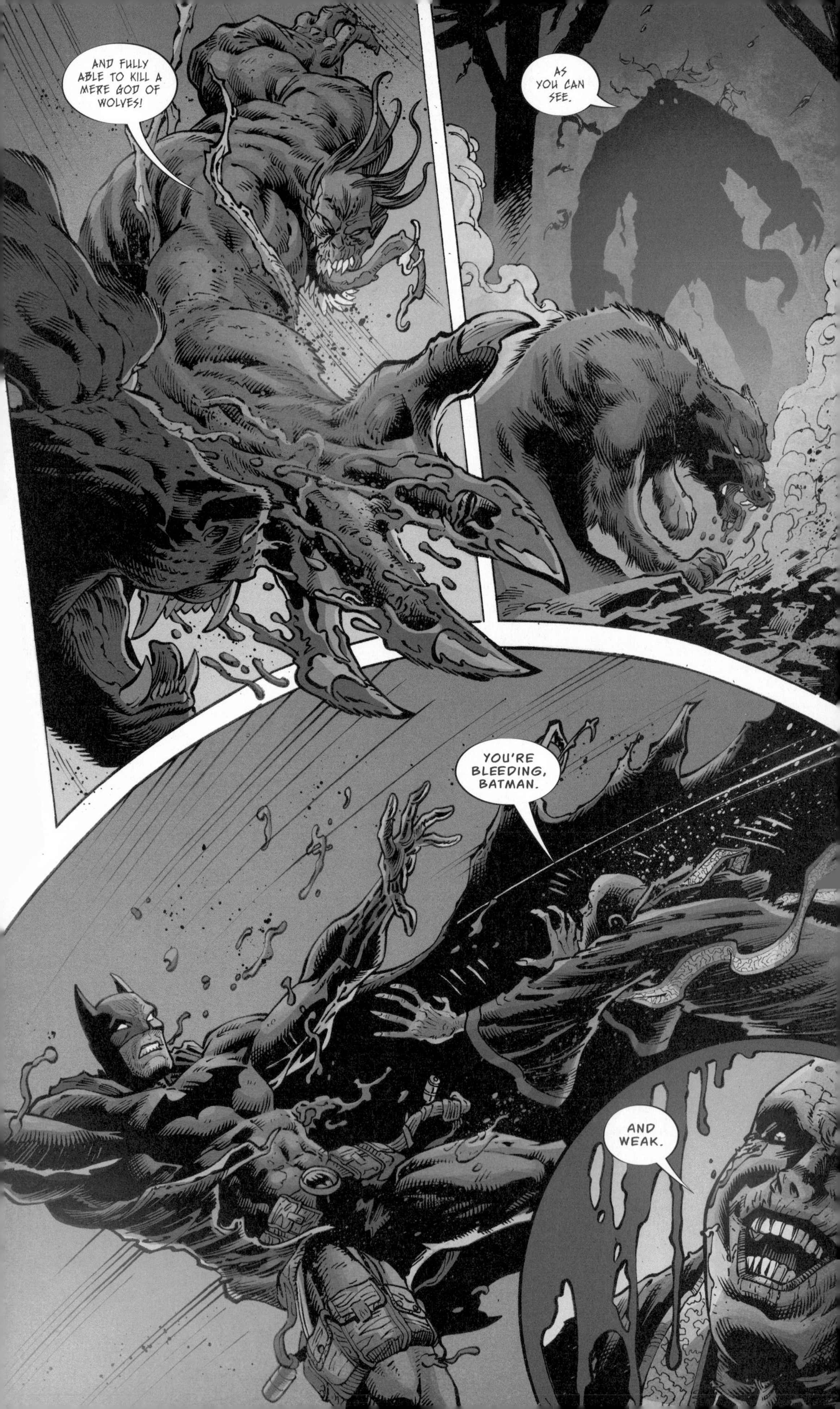
AND FULLY ABLE TO KILL A MERE GOD OF WOLVES!
AS YOU CAN SEE.
YOU'RE BLEEDING, BATMAN.
AND WEAK.

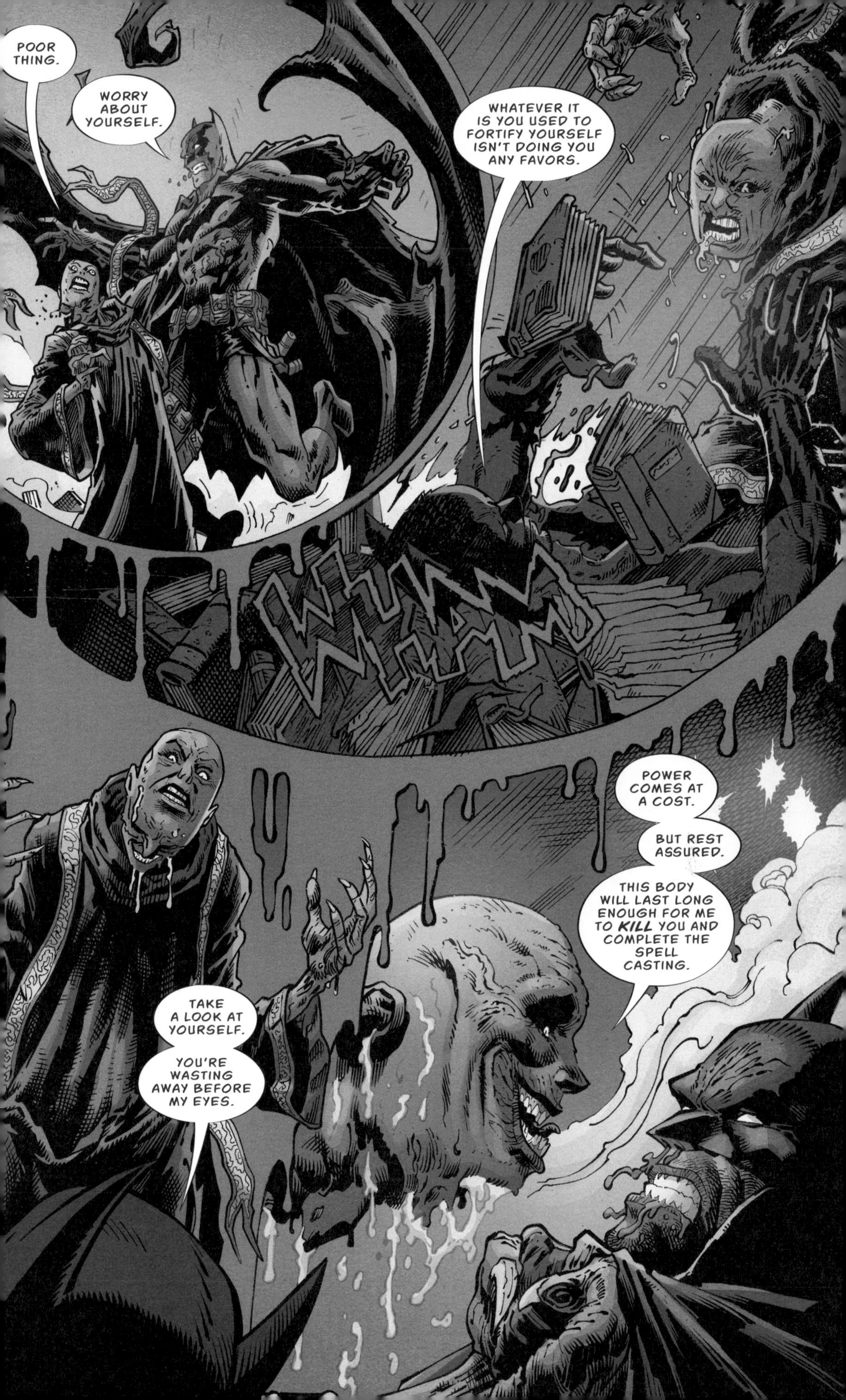
POOR THING.
WORRY ABOUT YOURSELF.
WHATEVER IT IS YOU USED TO FORTIFY YOURSELF ISN'T DOING YOU ANY FAVORS.
WHAM
WHAM
TAKE A LOOK AT YOURSELF.
YOU'RE WASTING AWAY BEFORE MY EYES.
POWER COMES AT A COST.
BUT REST ASSURED.
THIS BODY WILL LAST LONG ENOUGH FOR ME TO **KILL** YOU AND COMPLETE THE SPELL CASTING.

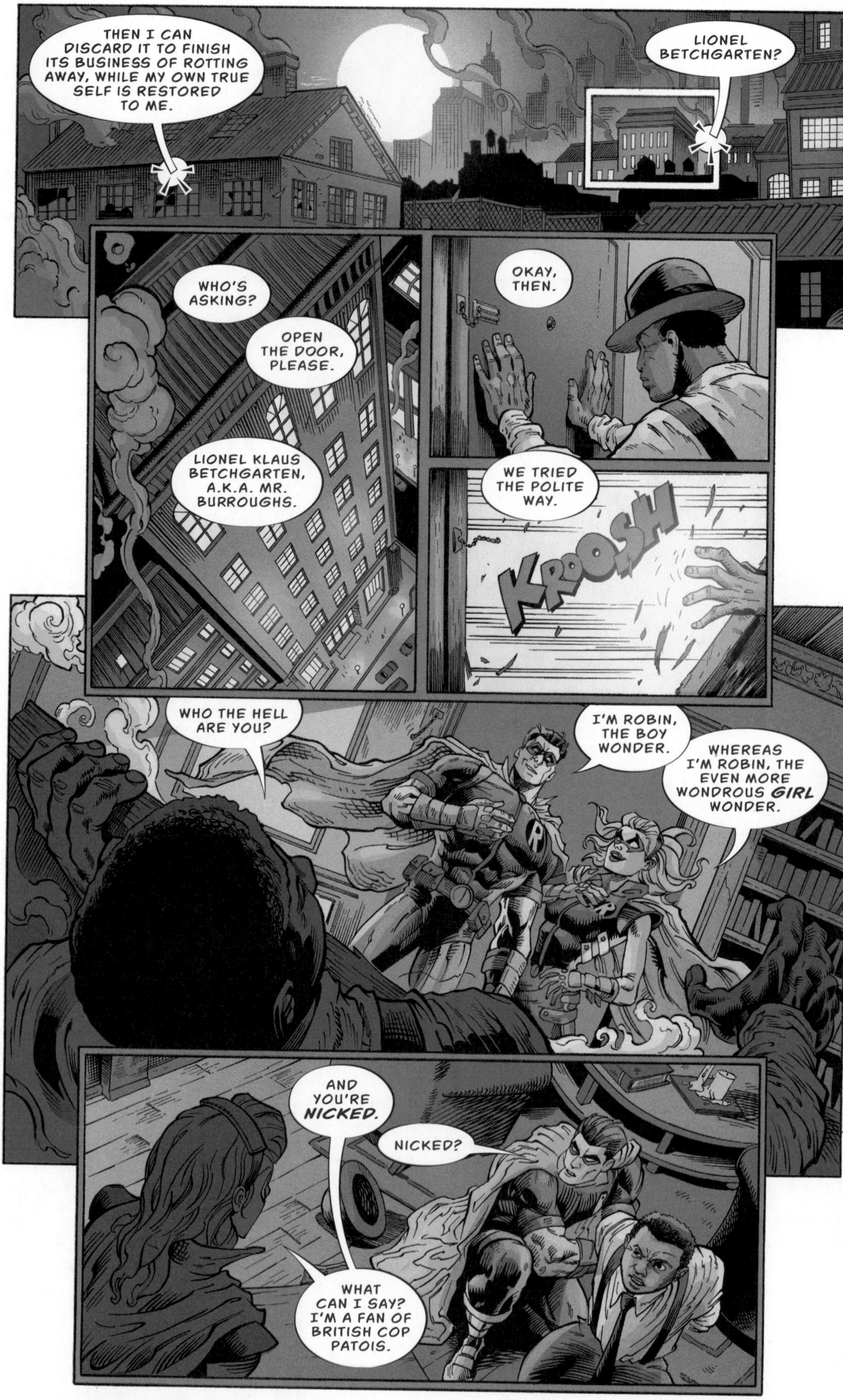
THEN I CAN DISCARD IT TO FINISH ITS BUSINESS OF ROTTING AWAY, WHILE MY OWN TRUE SELF IS RESTORED TO ME.
LIONEL BETCHGARTEN?
WHO'S ASKING?
OPEN THE DOOR, PLEASE.
LIONEL KLAUS BETCHGARTEN, A.K.A. MR. BURROUGHS.
OKAY, THEN.
WE TRIED THE POLITE WAY.
KROOSH
WHO THE HELL ARE YOU?
I'M ROBIN, THE BOY WONDER.
WHEREAS I'M ROBIN, THE EVEN MORE WONDROUS GIRL WONDER.
AND YOU'RE NICKED.
NICKED?
WHAT CAN I SAY? I'M A FAN OF BRITISH COP PATOIS.

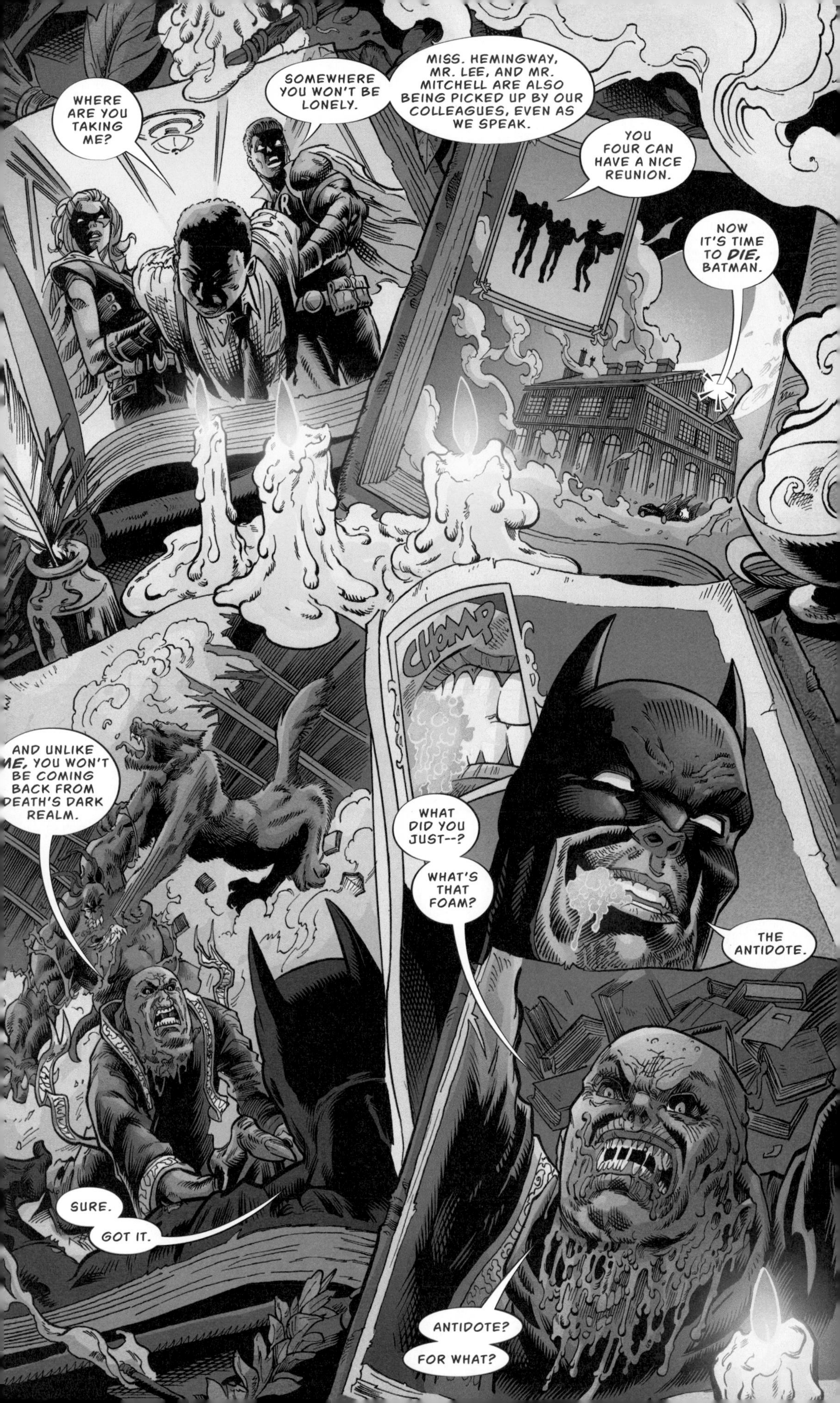

WHERE ARE YOU TAKING ME?
SOMEWHERE YOU WON'T BE LONELY.
MISS. HEMINGWAY, MR. LEE, AND MR. MITCHELL ARE ALSO BEING PICKED UP BY OUR COLLEAGUES, EVEN AS WE SPEAK.
YOU FOUR CAN HAVE A NICE REUNION.
NOW IT'S TIME TO *DIE,* BATMAN.
CHOMP
AND UNLIKE *ME,* YOU WON'T BE COMING BACK FROM DEATH'S DARK REALM.
WHAT DID YOU JUST--?
WHAT'S THAT FOAM?
THE ANTIDOTE.
SURE.
GOT IT.
ANTIDOTE?
FOR WHAT?

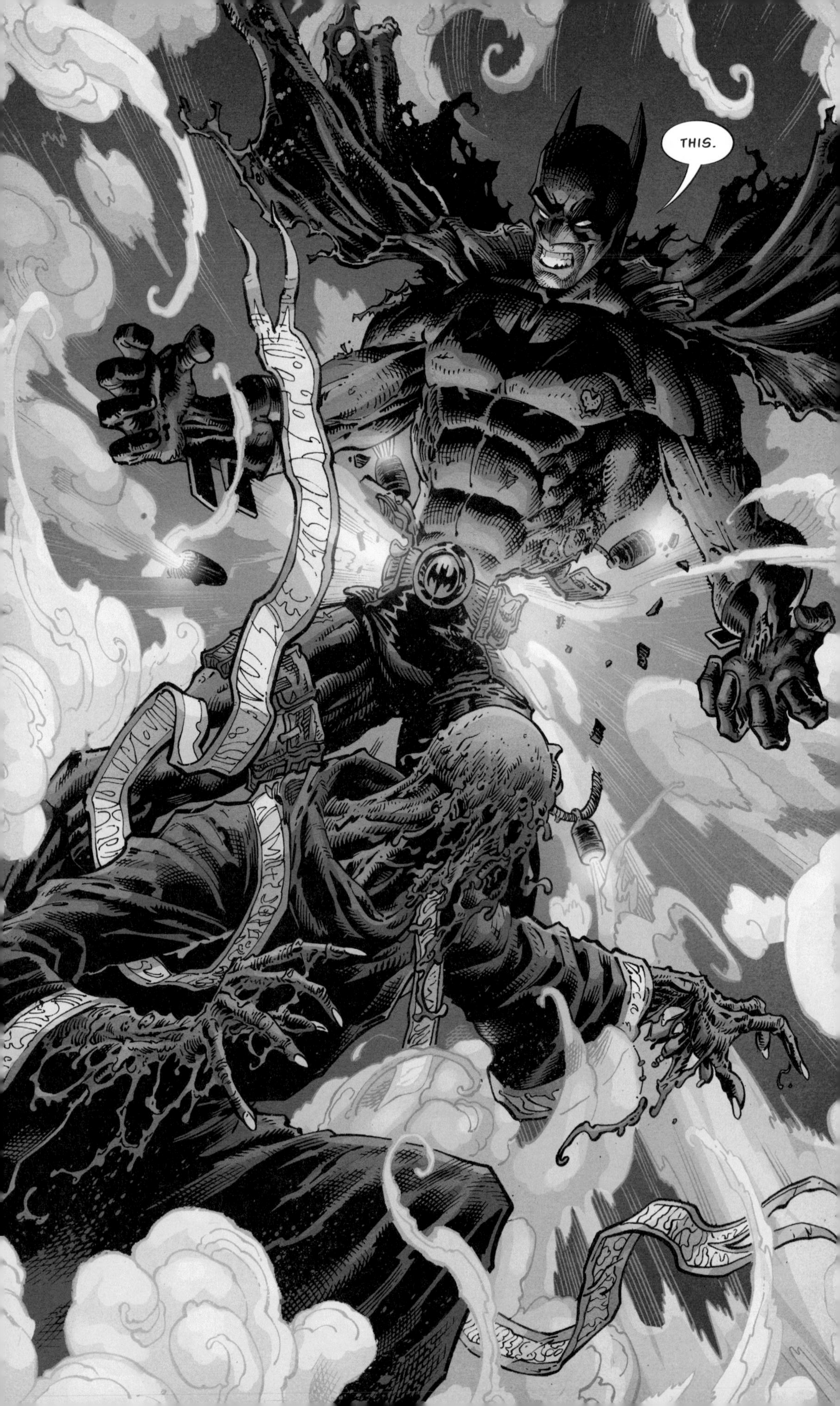
THIS.

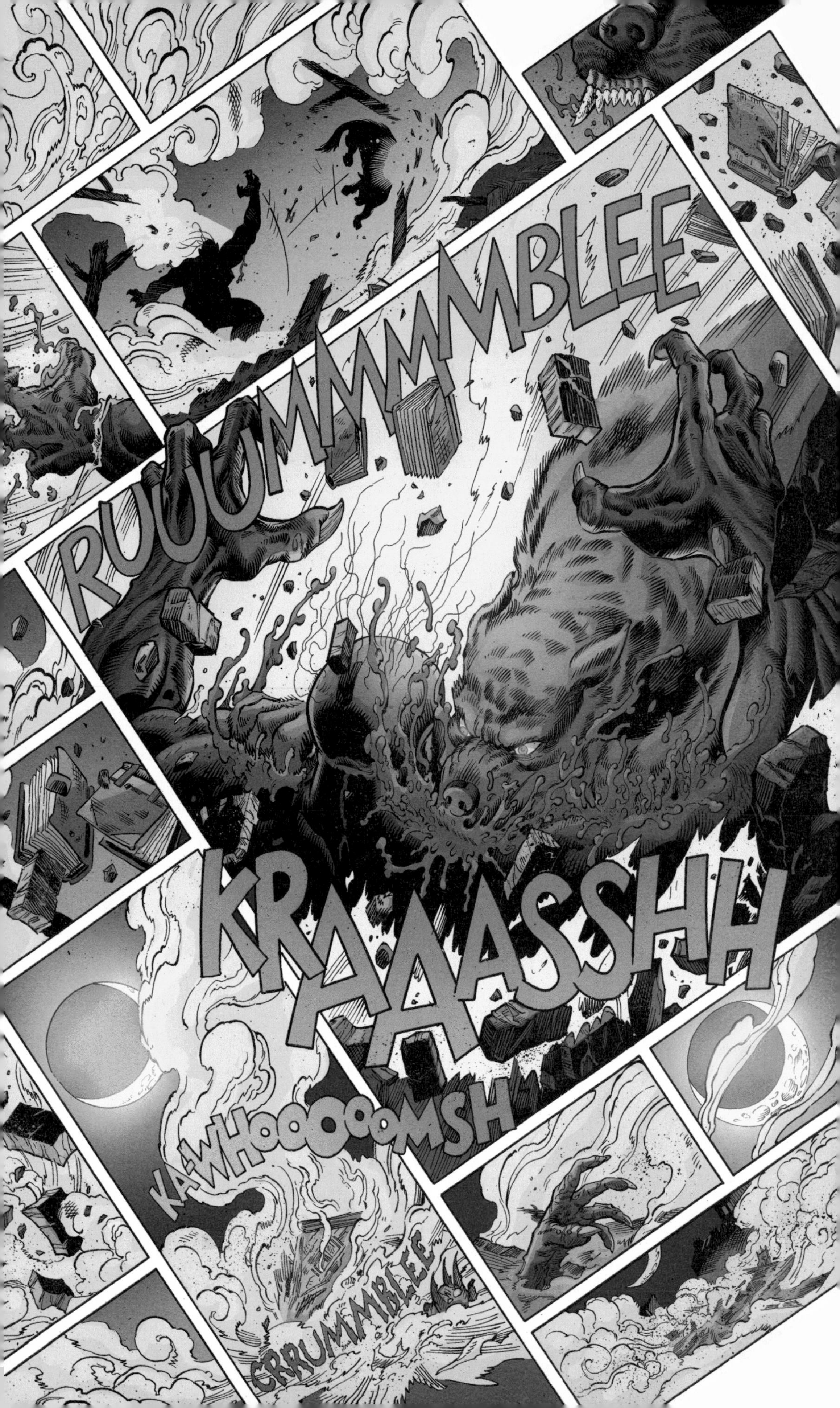
RUUUMMMMBLEE
KRAAASSHH
KA-WHOOOOOOMSH
CRRUMMBLEE

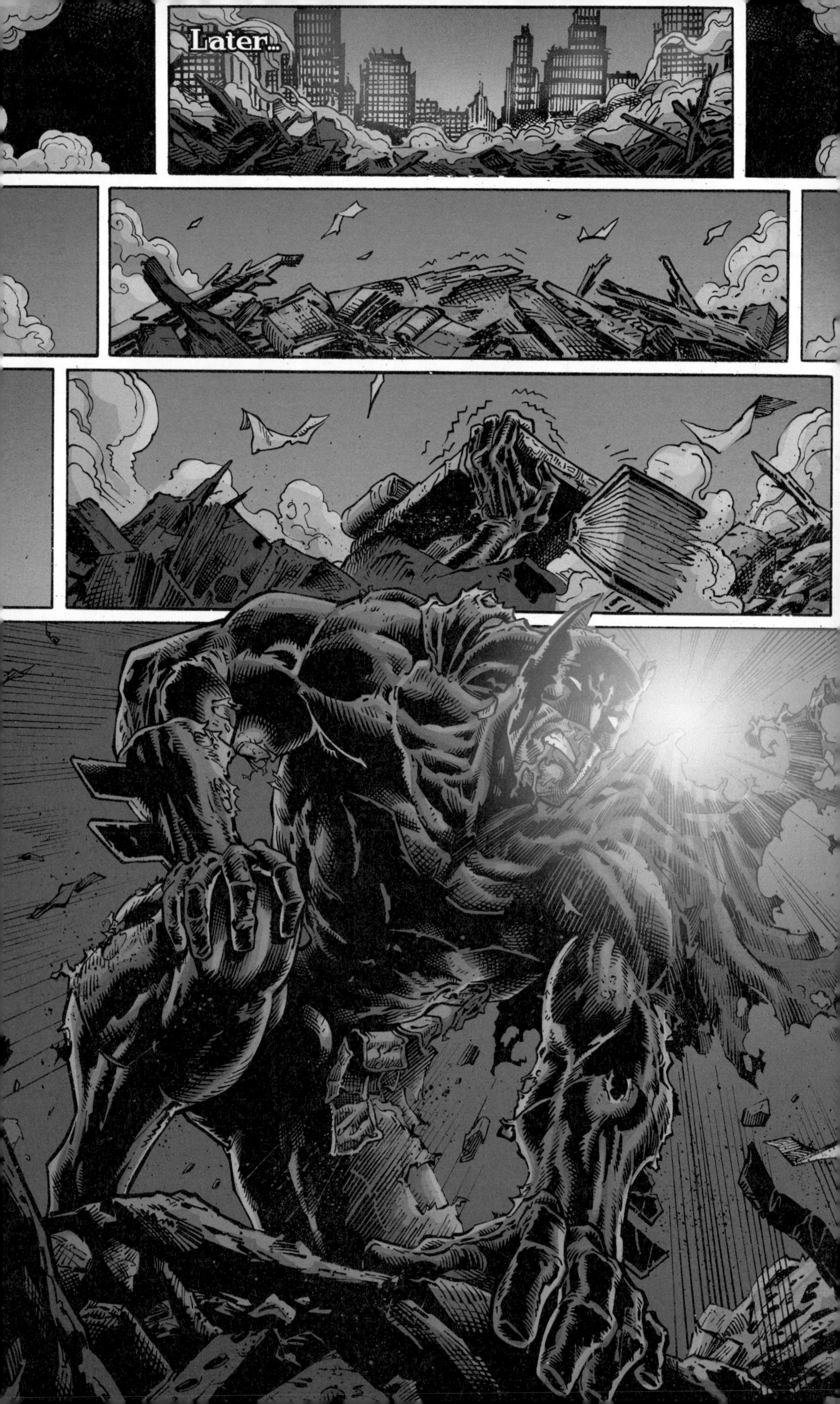
Later...

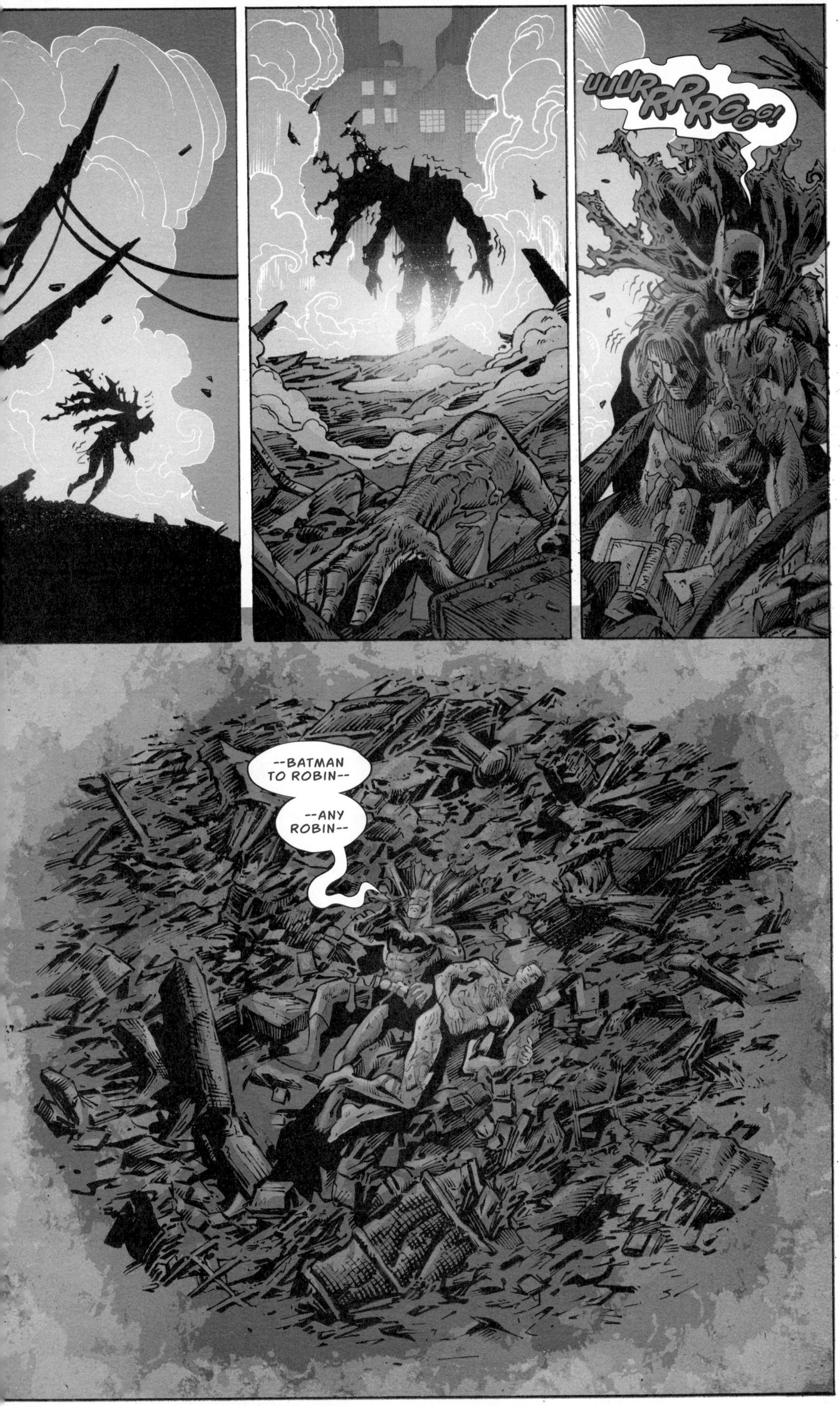
UUURRRRGGG!
--BATMAN TO ROBIN--
--ANY ROBIN--

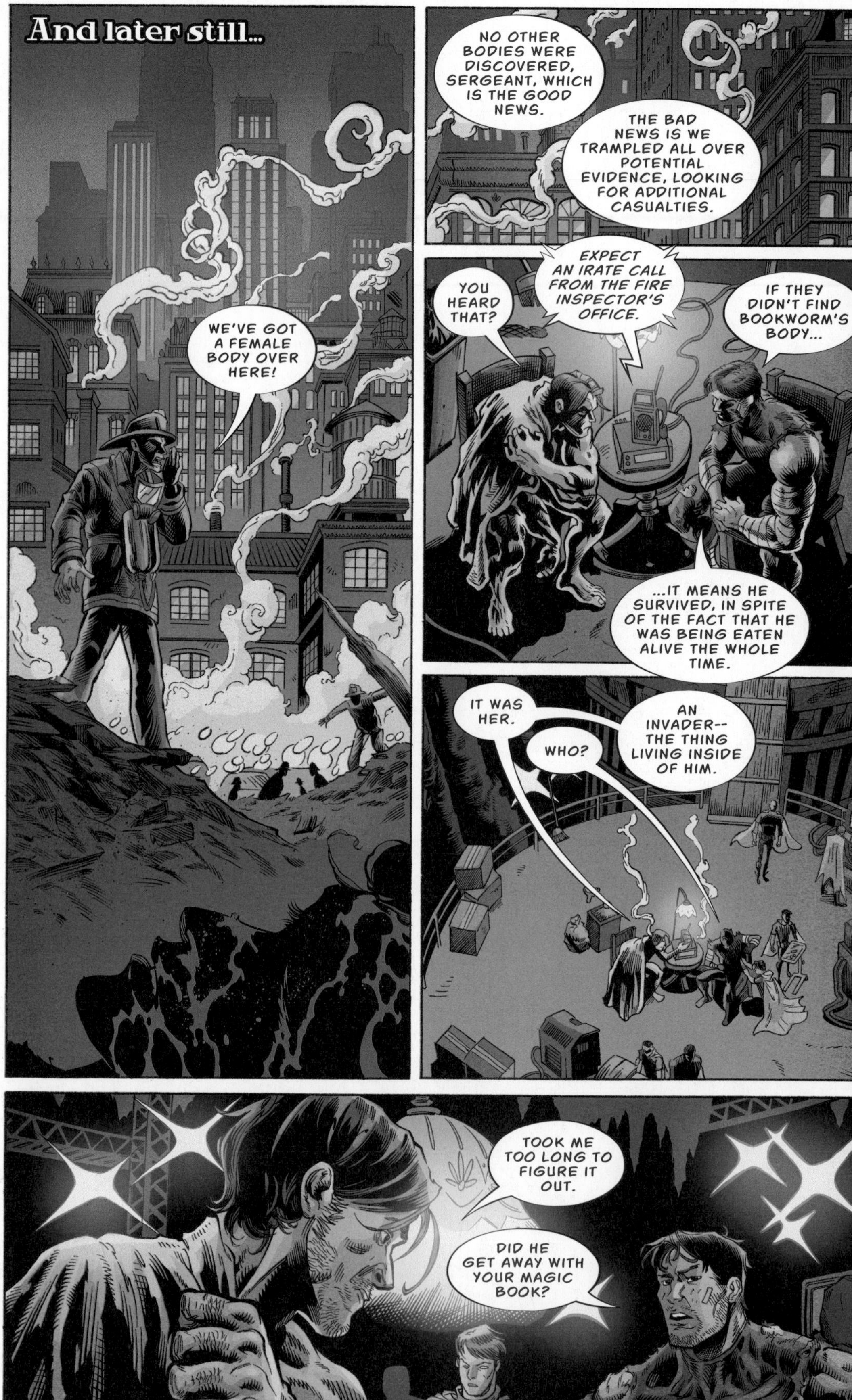

And later still...
WE'VE GOT A FEMALE BODY OVER HERE!
NO OTHER BODIES WERE DISCOVERED, SERGEANT, WHICH IS THE GOOD NEWS.
THE BAD NEWS IS WE TRAMPLED ALL OVER POTENTIAL EVIDENCE, LOOKING FOR ADDITIONAL CASUALTIES.
YOU HEARD THAT?
EXPECT AN IRATE CALL FROM THE FIRE INSPECTOR'S OFFICE.
IF THEY DIDN'T FIND BOOKWORM'S BODY...
...IT MEANS HE SURVIVED, IN SPITE OF THE FACT THAT HE WAS BEING EATEN ALIVE THE WHOLE TIME.
IT WAS HER.
WHO?
AN INVADER-- THE THING LIVING INSIDE OF HIM.
TOOK ME TOO LONG TO FIGURE IT OUT.
DID HE GET AWAY WITH YOUR MAGIC BOOK?

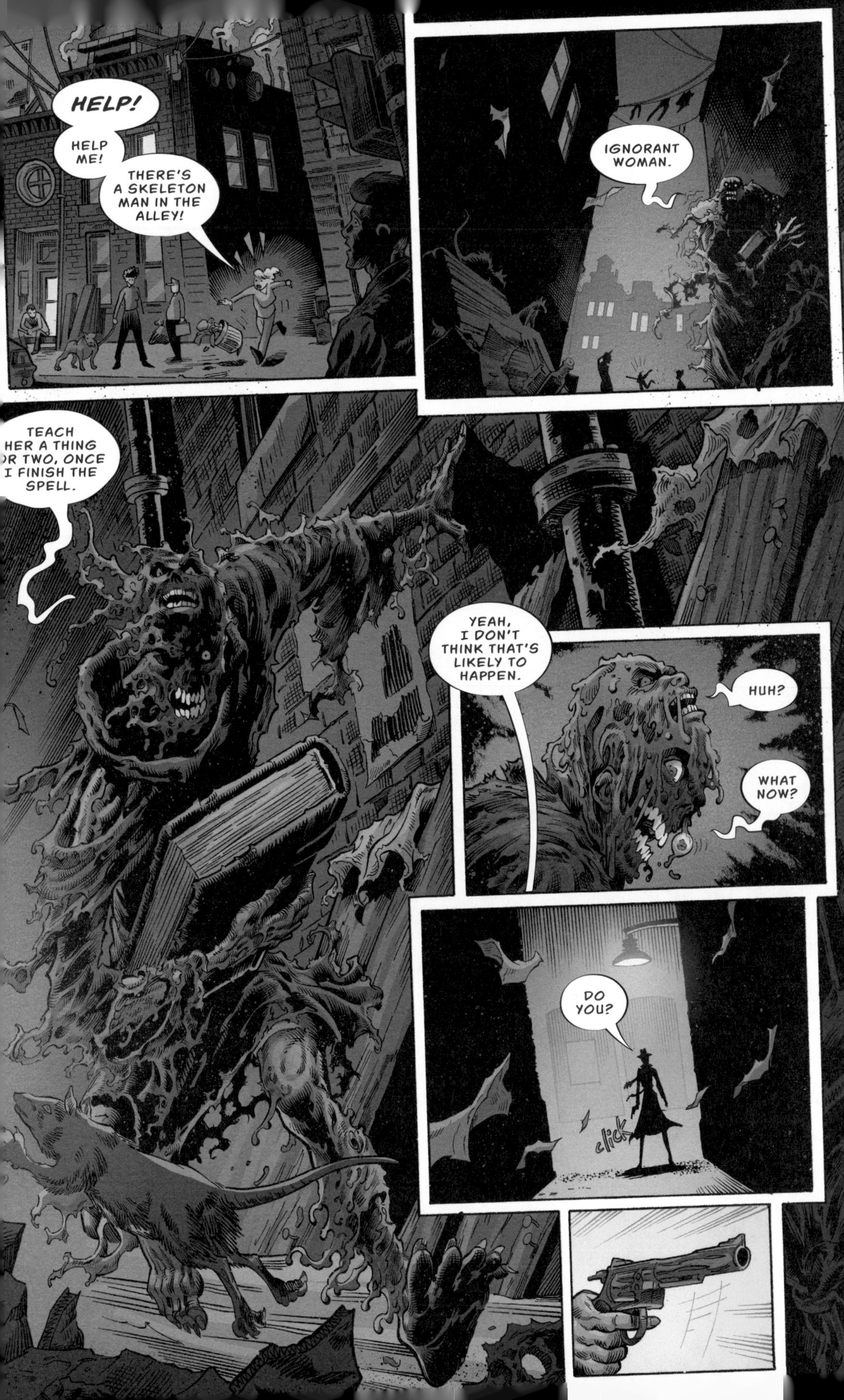
HELP!
HELP ME!
THERE'S A SKELETON MAN IN THE ALLEY!
IGNORANT WOMAN.
TEACH HER A THING OR TWO, ONCE I FINISH THE SPELL.
YEAH, I DON'T THINK THAT'S LIKELY TO HAPPEN.
HUH?
WHAT NOW?
DO YOU?
click

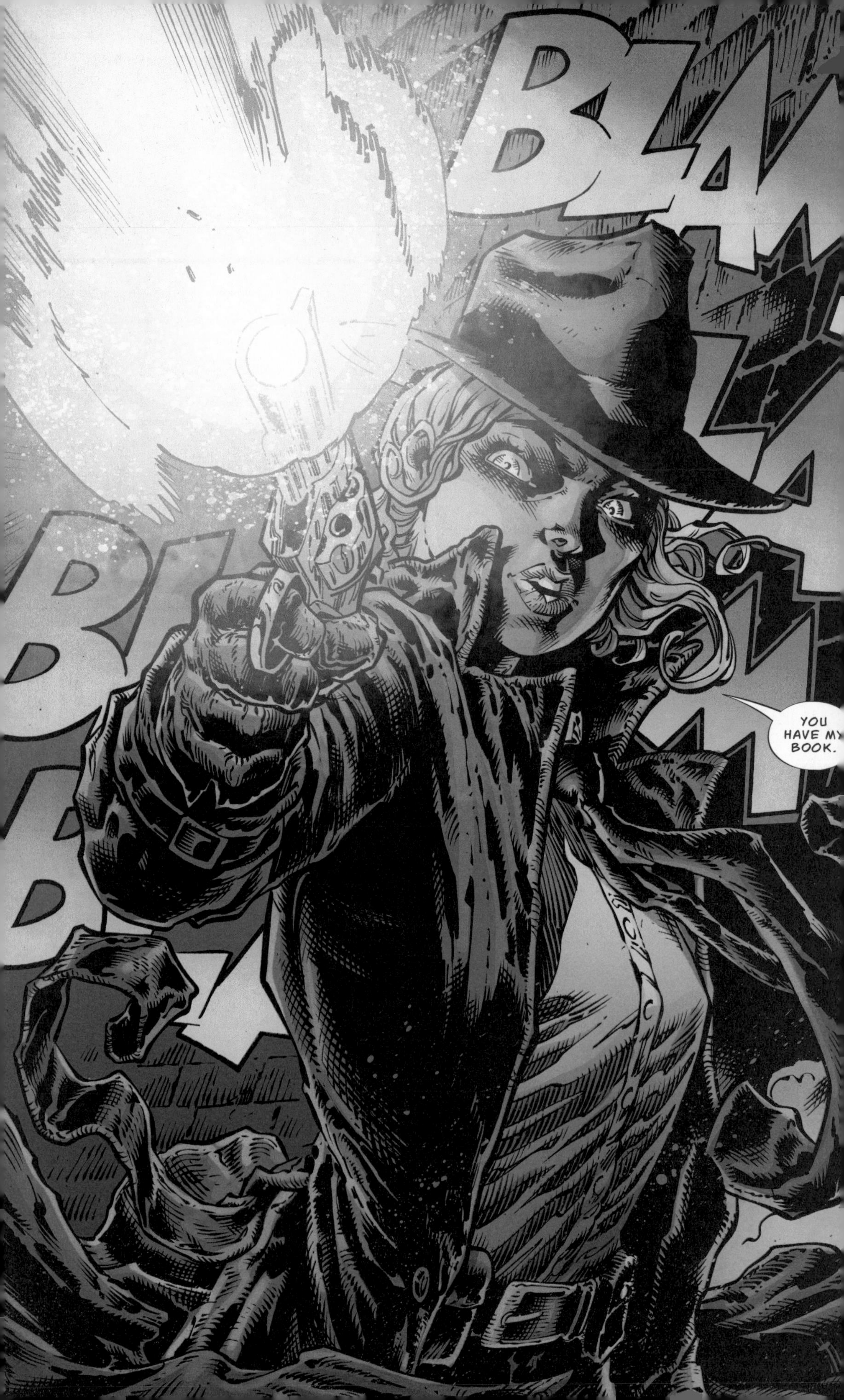
YOU HAVE MY BOOK.

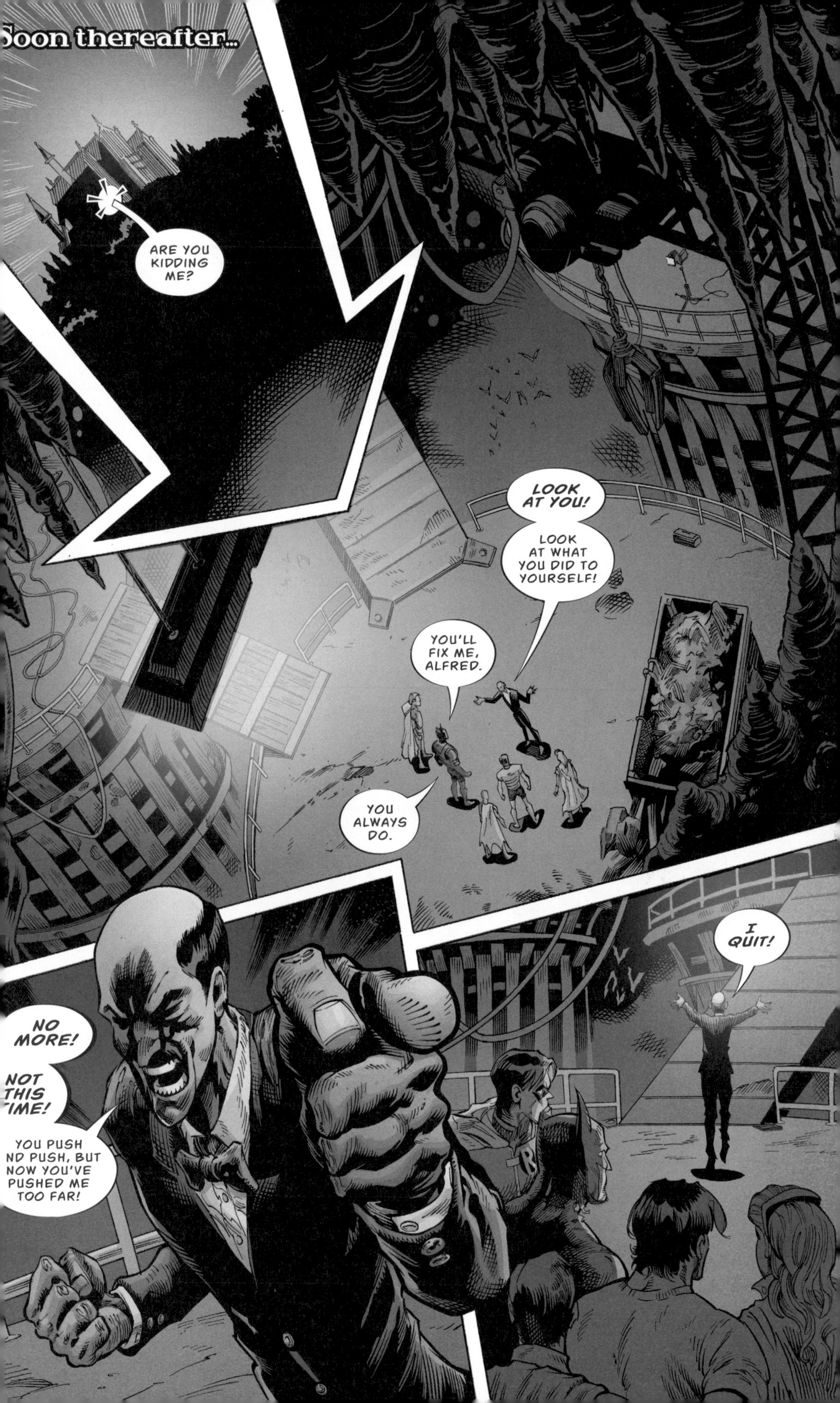

Soon thereafter...
ARE YOU KIDDING ME?
LOOK AT YOU!
LOOK AT WHAT YOU DID TO YOURSELF!
YOU'LL FIX ME, ALFRED.
YOU ALWAYS DO.
I QUIT!
NO MORE!
NOT THIS TIME!
YOU PUSH ND PUSH, BUT NOW YOU'VE PUSHED ME TOO FAR!

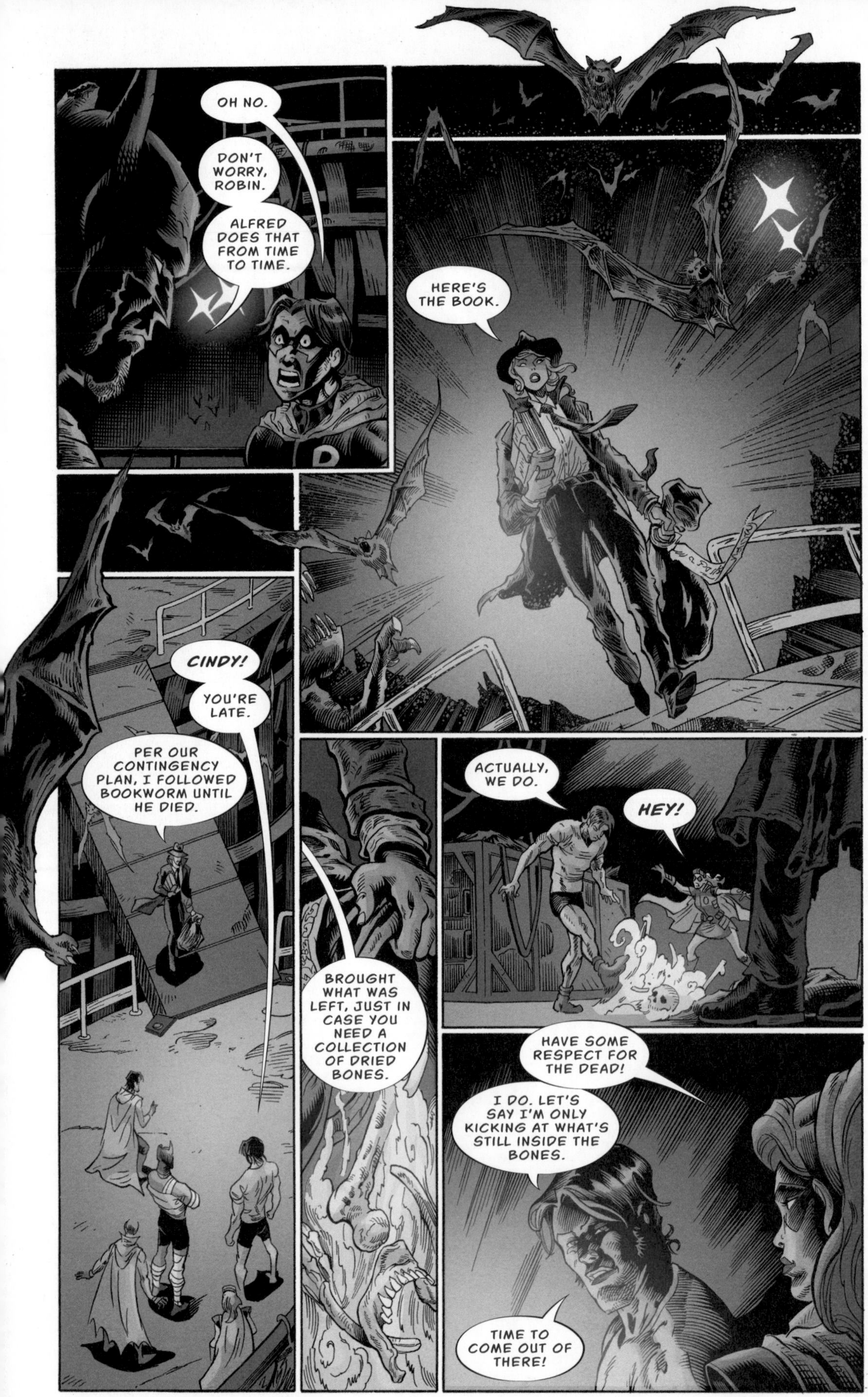
OH NO.
DON'T WORRY, ROBIN.
ALFRED DOES THAT FROM TIME TO TIME.
HERE'S THE BOOK.
CINDY!
YOU'RE LATE.
PER OUR CONTINGENCY PLAN, I FOLLOWED BOOKWORM UNTIL HE DIED.
BROUGHT WHAT WAS LEFT, JUST IN CASE YOU NEED A COLLECTION OF DRIED BONES.
ACTUALLY, WE DO.
HEY!
HAVE SOME RESPECT FOR THE DEAD!
I DO. LET'S SAY I'M ONLY KICKING AT WHAT'S STILL INSIDE THE BONES.
TIME TO COME OUT OF THERE!

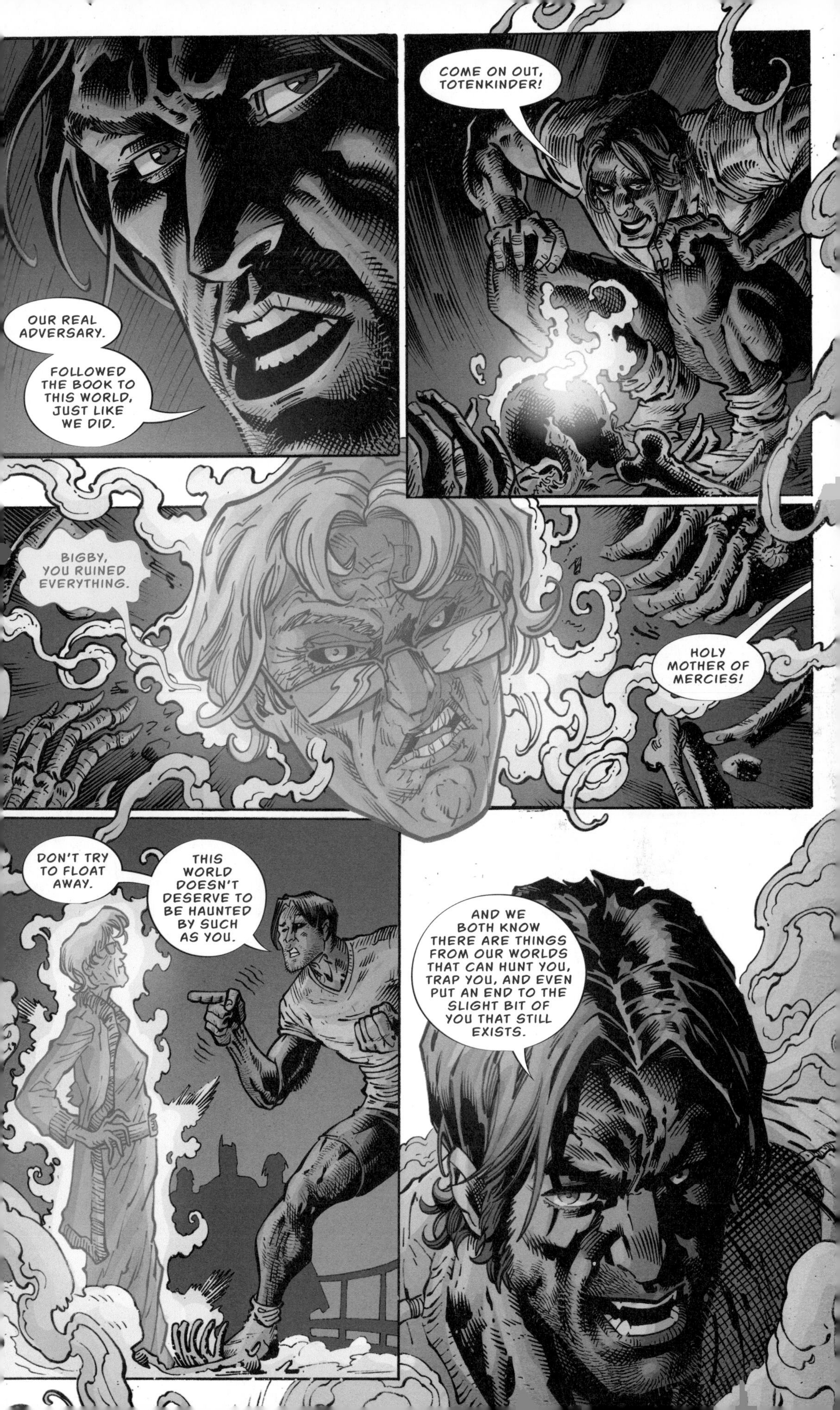
OUR REAL ADVERSARY.
FOLLOWED THE BOOK TO THIS WORLD, JUST LIKE WE DID.
COME ON OUT, TOTENKINDER!
BIGBY, YOU RUINED EVERYTHING.
HOLY MOTHER OF MERCIES!
DON'T TRY TO FLOAT AWAY.
THIS WORLD DOESN'T DESERVE TO BE HAUNTED BY SUCH AS YOU.
AND WE BOTH KNOW THERE ARE THINGS FROM OUR WORLDS THAT CAN HUNT YOU, TRAP YOU, AND EVEN PUT AN END TO THE SLIGHT BIT OF YOU THAT STILL EXISTS.

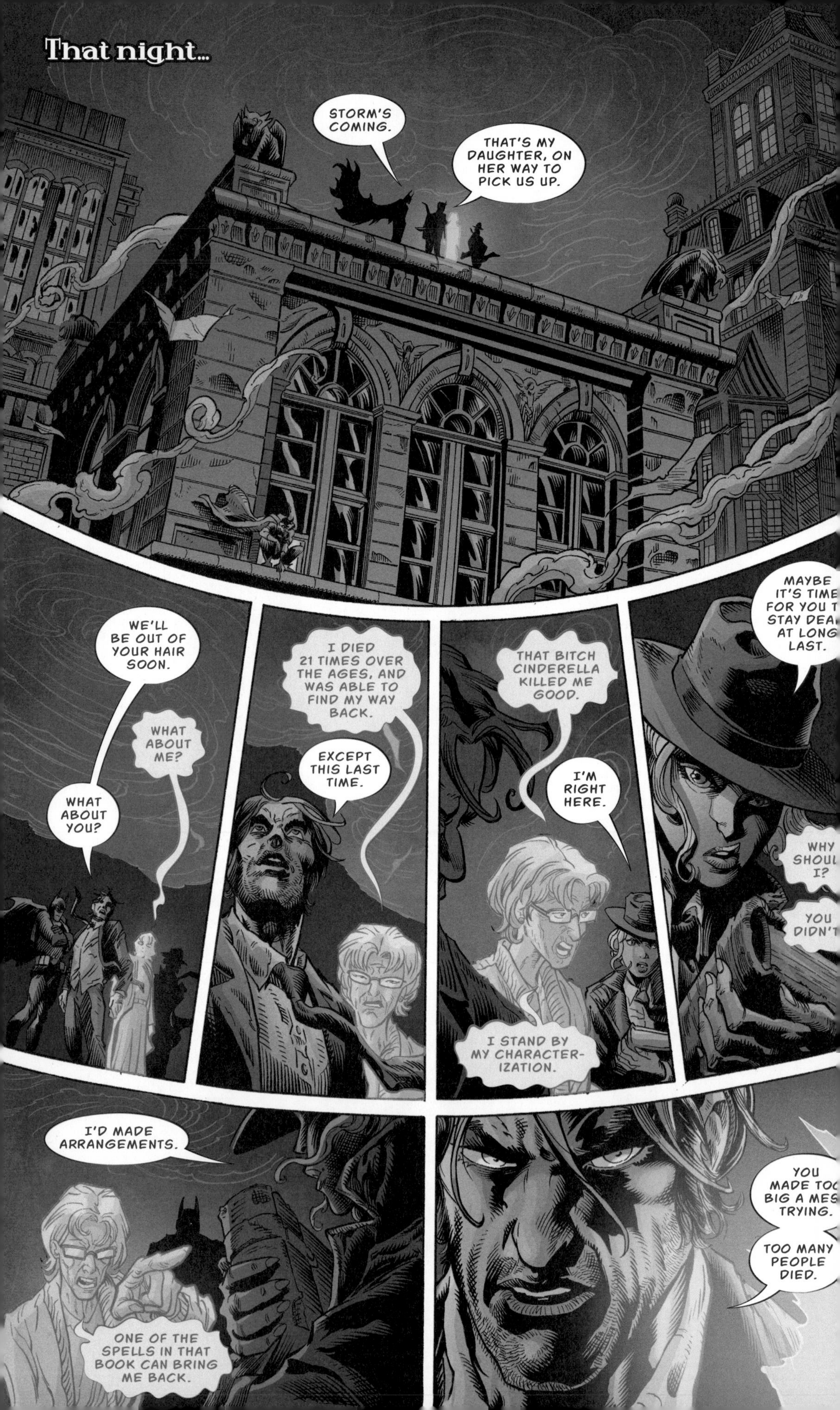
That night...
STORM'S COMING.
THAT'S MY DAUGHTER, ON HER WAY TO PICK US UP.
WE'LL BE OUT OF YOUR HAIR SOON.
WHAT ABOUT ME?
WHAT ABOUT YOU?
I DIED 21 TIMES OVER THE AGES, AND WAS ABLE TO FIND MY WAY BACK.
EXCEPT THIS LAST TIME.
THAT BITCH CINDERELLA KILLED ME GOOD.
I'M RIGHT HERE.
I STAND BY MY CHARACTER-IZATION.
MAYBE IT'S TIME FOR YOU T STAY DEA AT LONG LAST.
WHY SHOUL I?
YOU DIDN'T
I'D MADE ARRANGEMENTS.
ONE OF THE SPELLS IN THAT BOOK CAN BRING ME BACK.
YOU MADE TOO BIG A MES TRYING.
TOO MANY PEOPLE DIED.

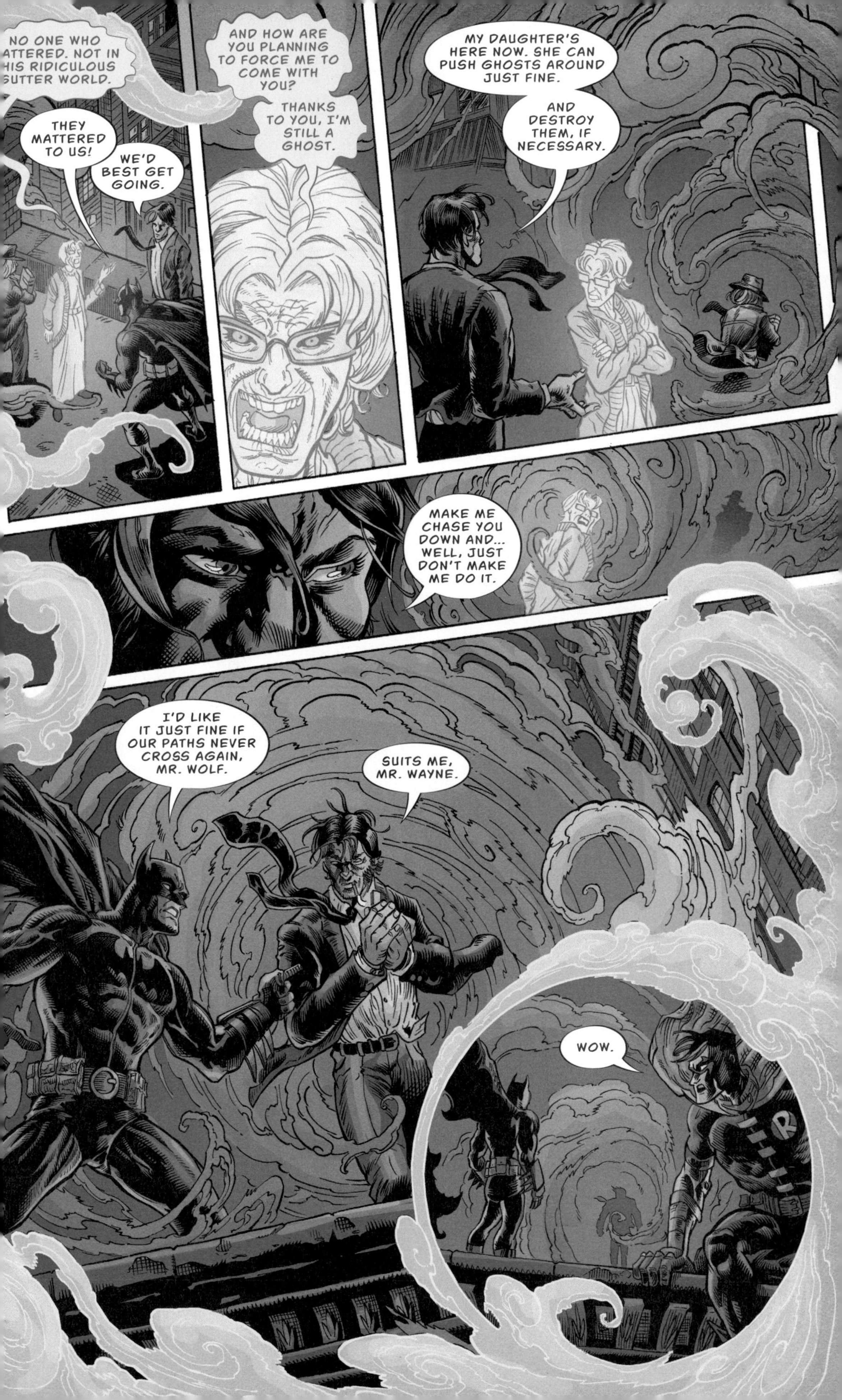
NO ONE WHO
ATTERED. NOT IN
HIS RIDICULOUS
GUTTER WORLD.
THEY MATTERED TO US!
WE'D BEST GET GOING.
AND HOW ARE YOU PLANNING TO FORCE ME TO COME WITH YOU?
THANKS TO YOU, I'M STILL A GHOST.
MY DAUGHTER'S HERE NOW. SHE CAN PUSH GHOSTS AROUND JUST FINE.
AND DESTROY THEM, IF NECESSARY.
MAKE ME CHASE YOU DOWN AND... WELL, JUST DON'T MAKE ME DO IT.
I'D LIKE IT JUST FINE IF OUR PATHS NEVER CROSS AGAIN, MR. WOLF.
SUITS ME, MR. WAYNE.
WOW.

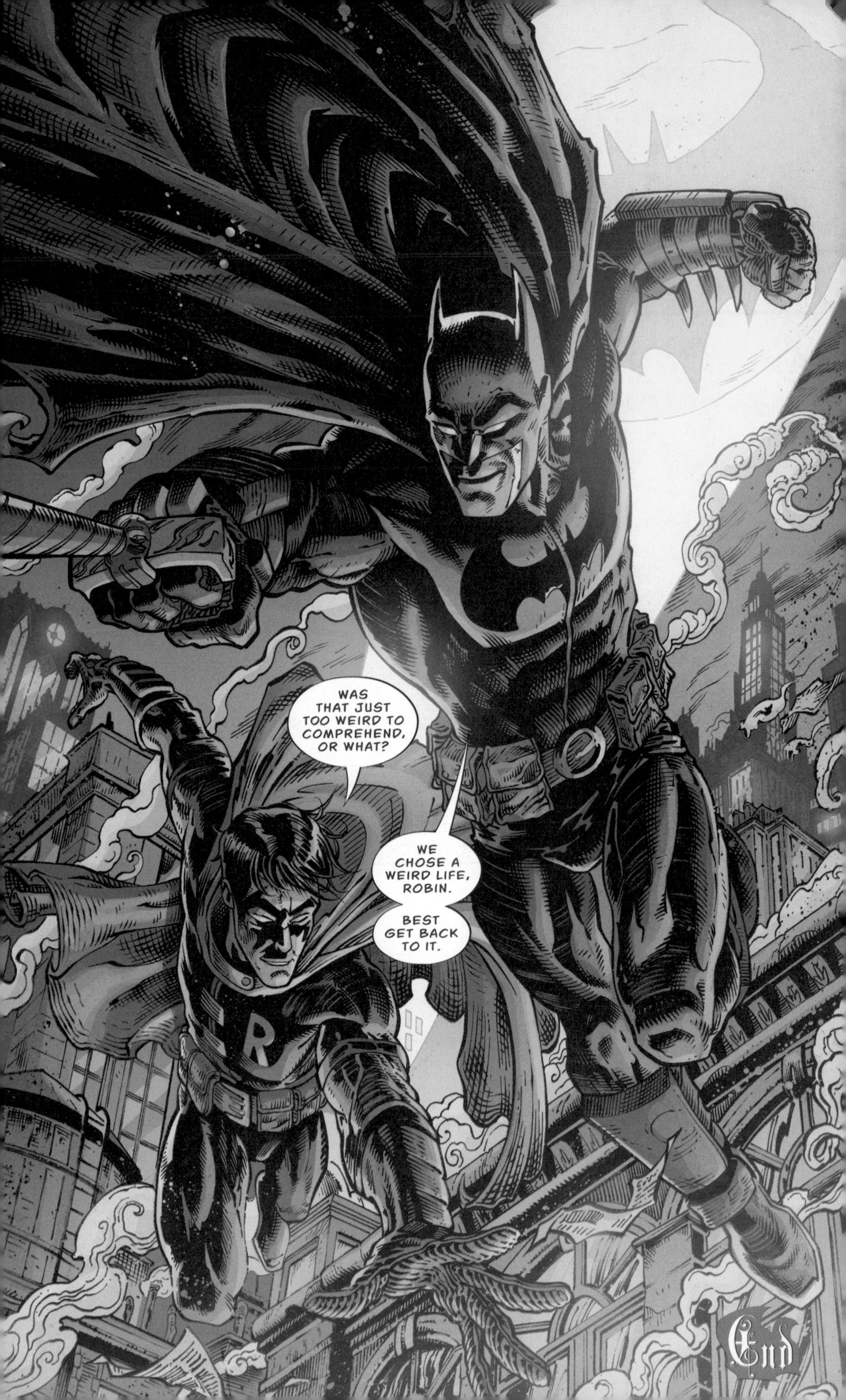
WAS THAT JUST TOO WEIRD TO COMPREHEND, OR WHAT?
WE CHOSE A WEIRD LIFE, ROBIN.
BEST GET BACK TO IT.
End

Batman vs. Bigby! A Wolf in Gotham **#1-6 Variant Covers by BRIAN LEVEL, JAY LEISTEN & LEE LOUGHRIDGE**

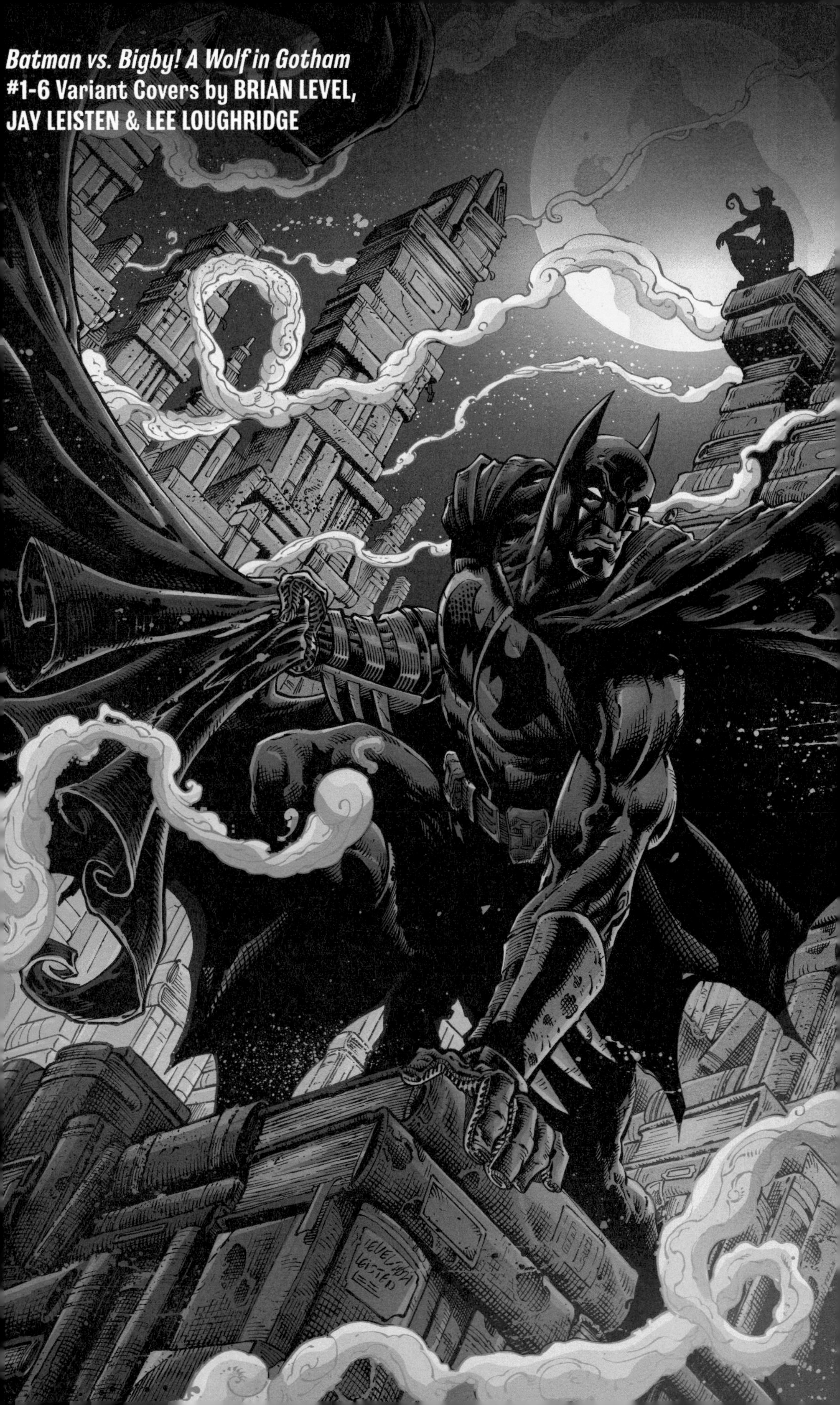

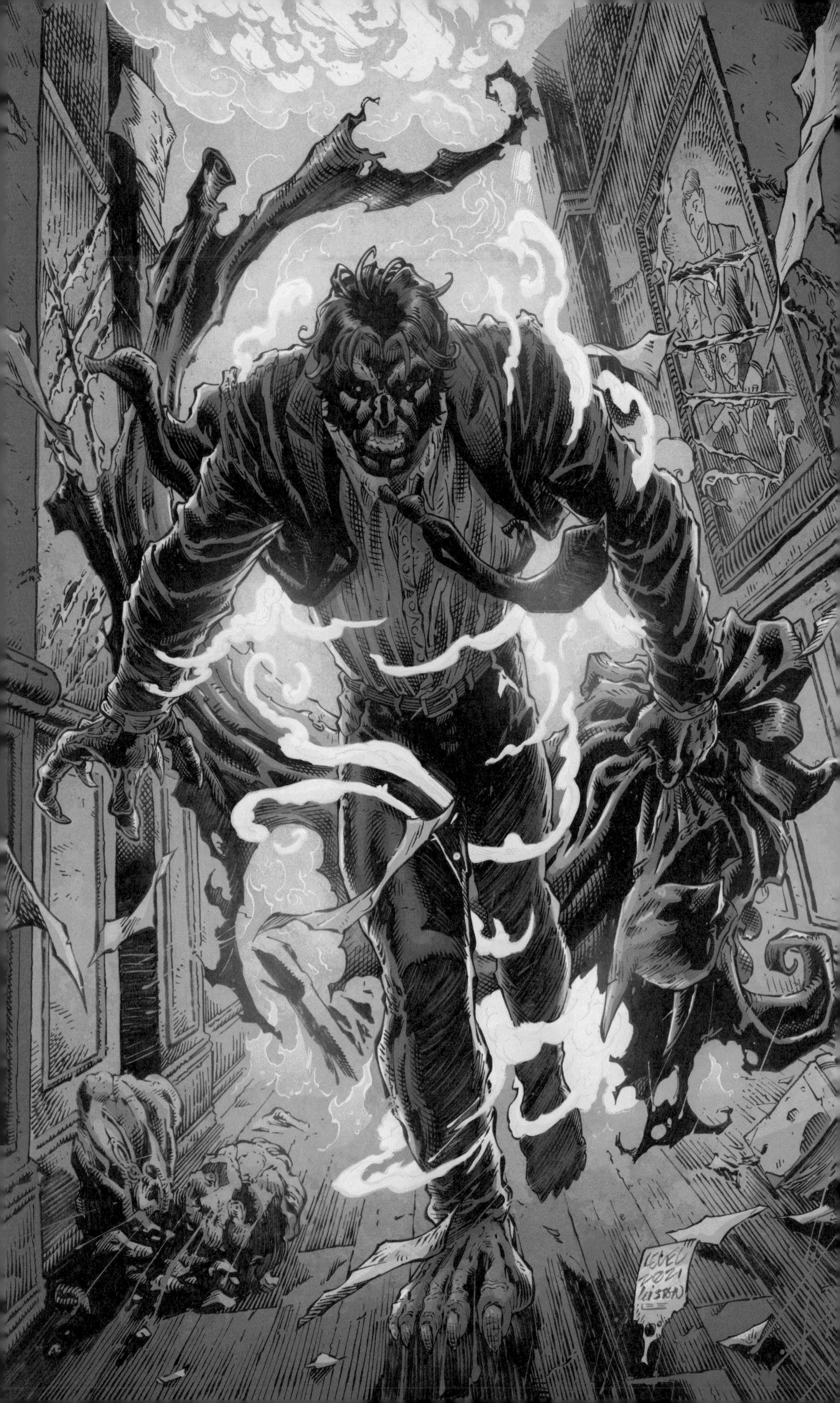

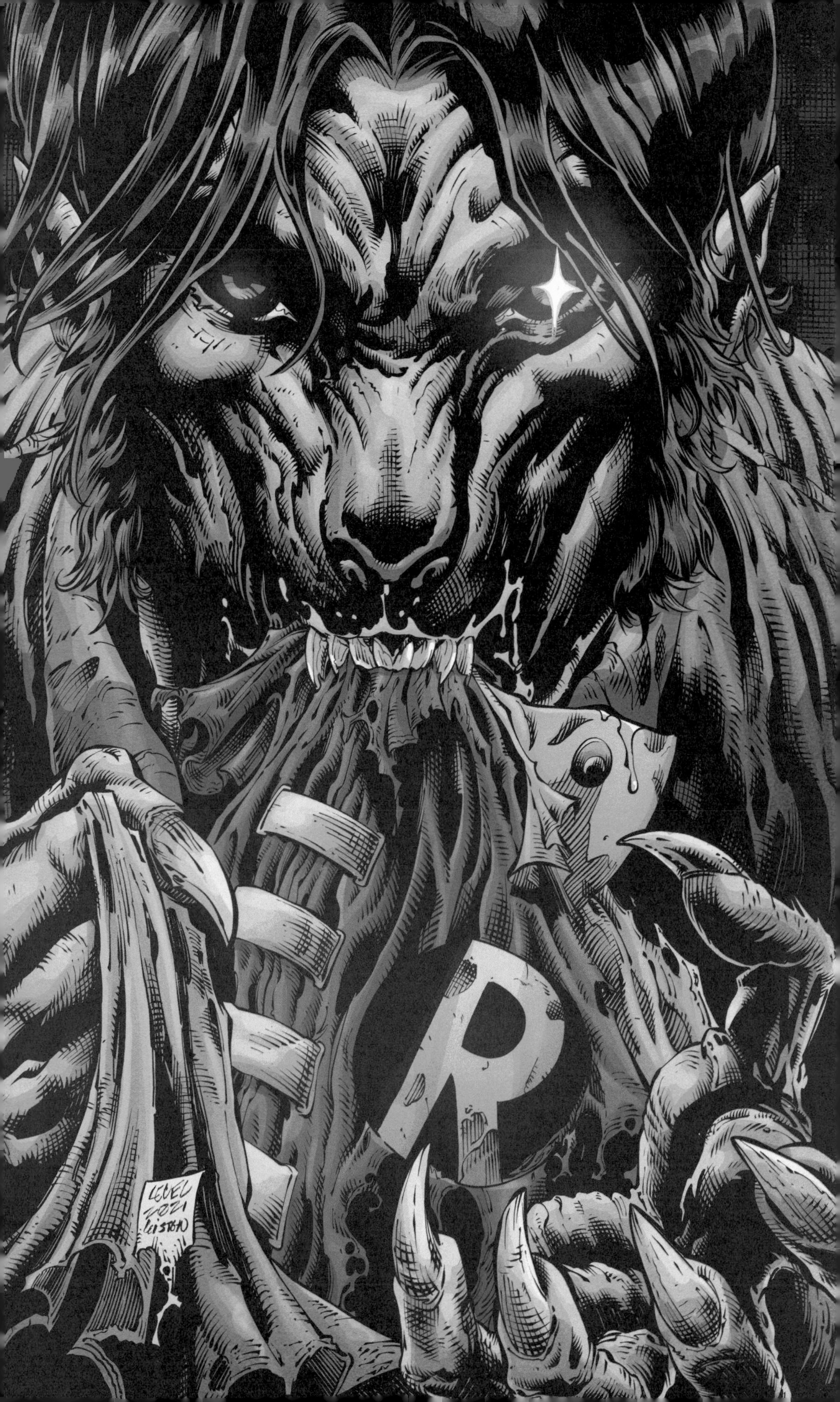

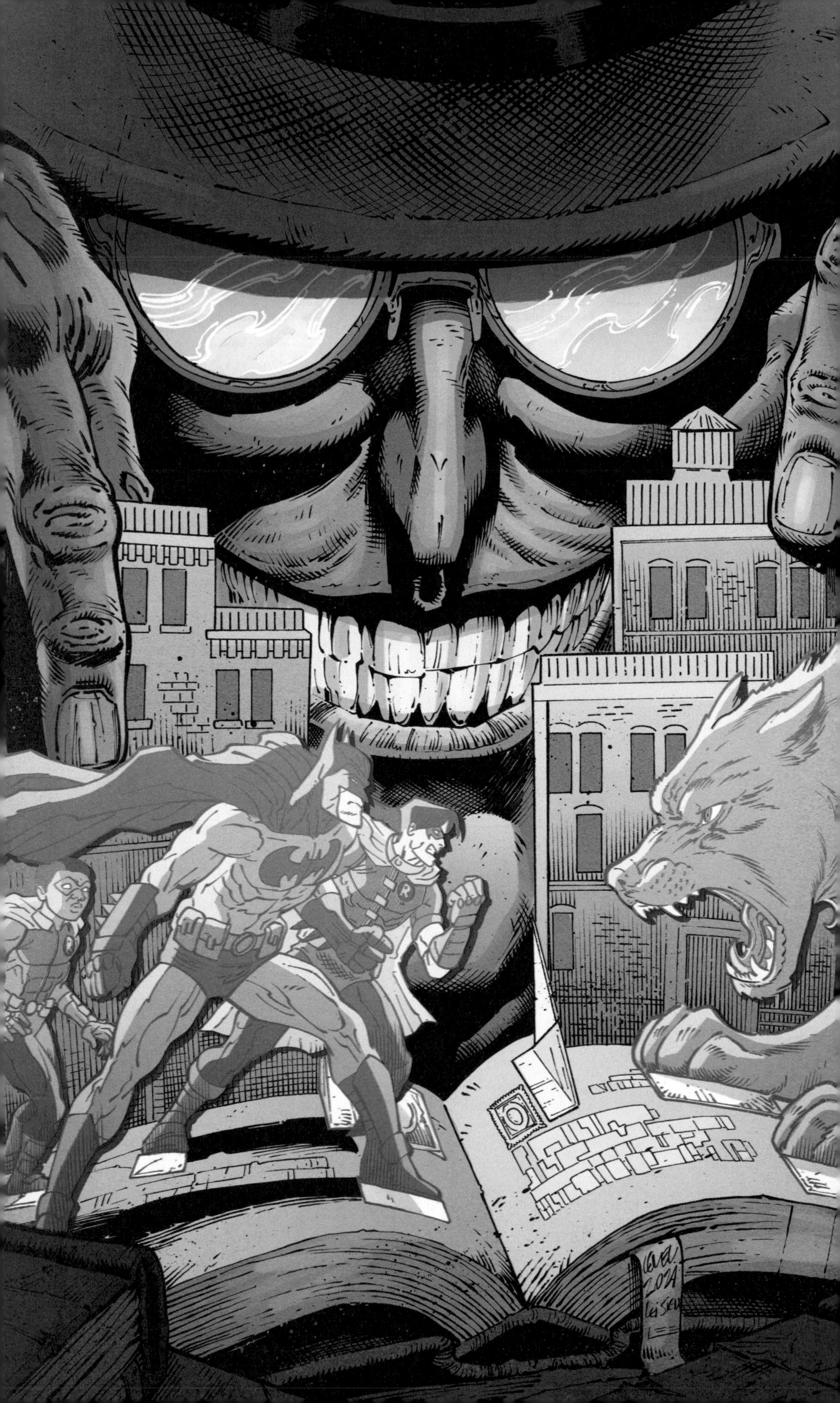

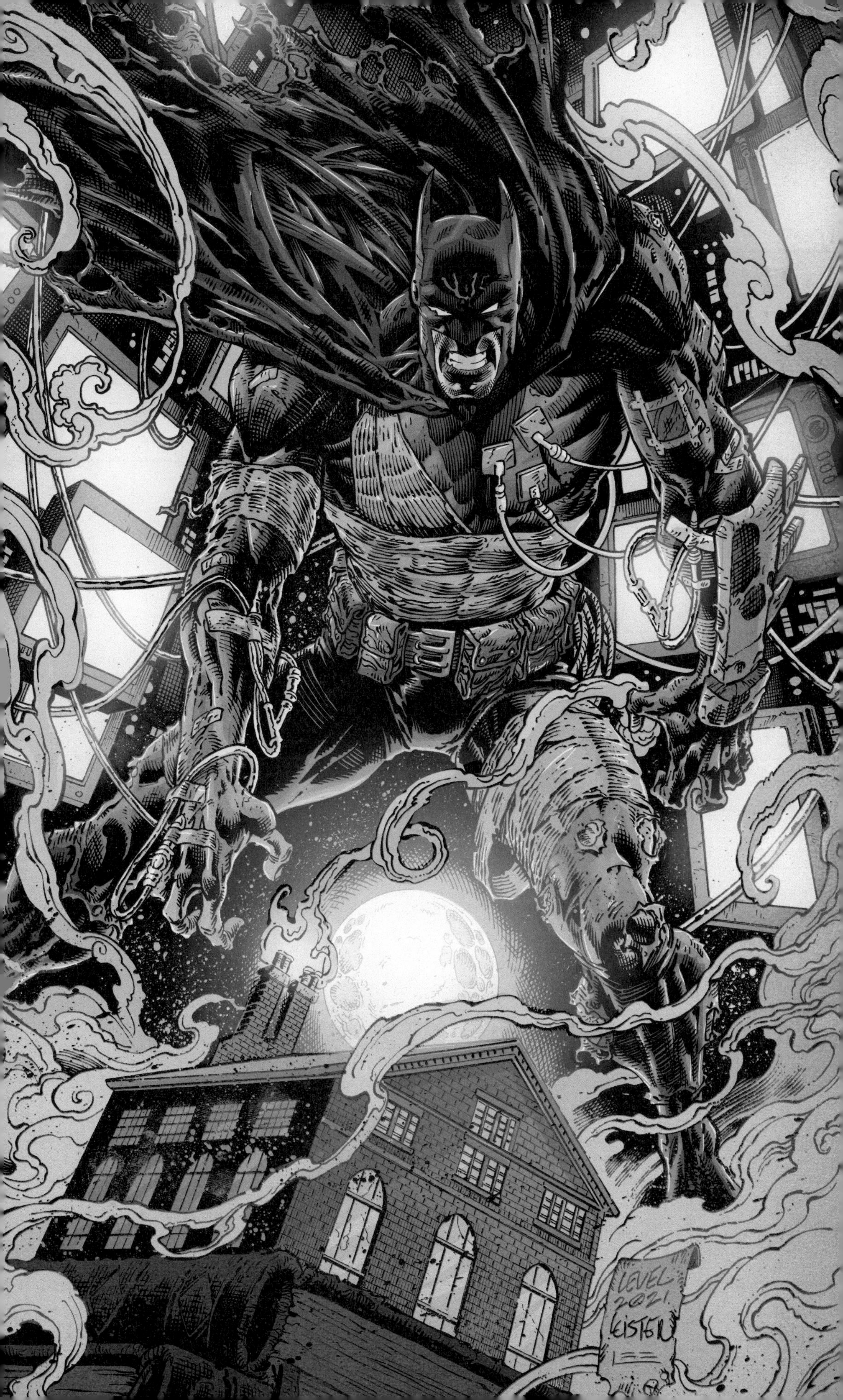
LEVEL
2021
LEISTEN

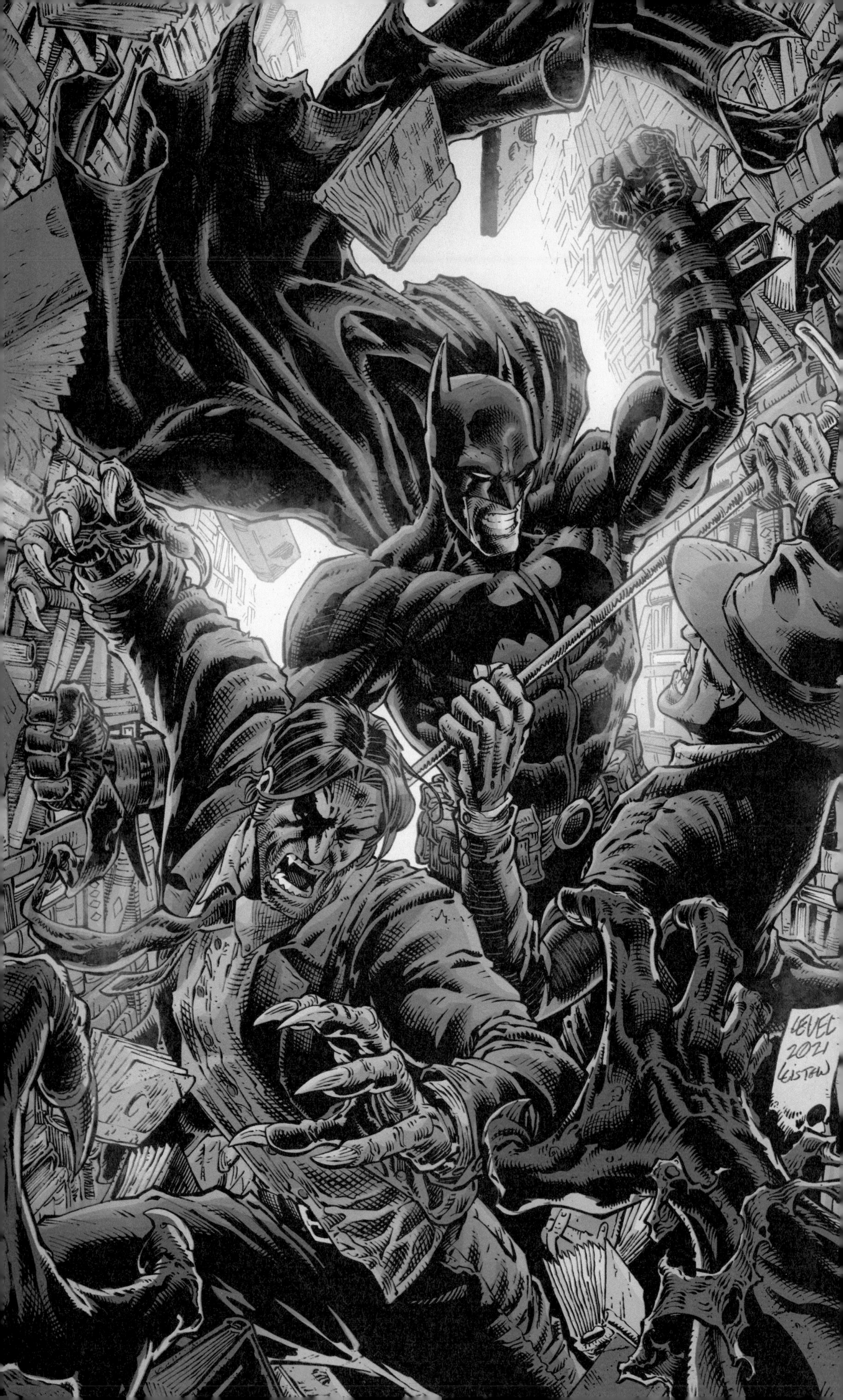